The Waverley Novels
and Their Critics

THE *WAVERLEY NOVELS*

AND THEIR CRITICS

BY

JAMES T. HILLHOUSE

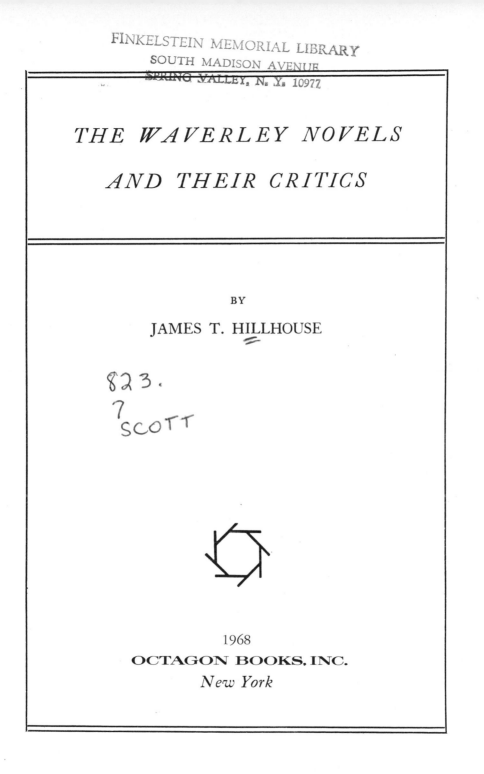

1968

OCTAGON BOOKS, INC.

New York

Reprinted 1968
by special arrangement with Mildred L. Hillhouse

OCTAGON BOOKS, INC.
175 FIFTH AVENUE
NEW YORK, N. Y. 10010

LIBRARY OF CONGRESS CATALOG CARD NUMBER: 68-22297

Printed in U.S.A. by
NOBLE OFFSET PRINTERS, INC.
NEW YORK 3, N. Y.

To M. L. H.

(WHO WOULD NOT APPEAR IN THE PREFACE)

This is indeed to be an author.—*Hazlitt (1824)*.

This transparent stream . . . becomes without warning the sea, the deep, the inscrutable, the universal ocean on which we put out with the greatest only.—*Virginia Woolf (1924)*.

PREFACE

Some years ago, having occasion to look up a few of the original reviews of the Waverley novels, I was greatly surprised to find in them so much adverse criticism. I had supposed that little or no fault was found with Sir Walter in his own time and that the standard list of his weaknesses now taken for granted by students of literature and easily found in any handbook, were the discoveries of our own highly trained, sophisticated technicians in the novel. But here they were, apparently recognized quite as plainly by Jeffrey and his fellow reviewers as by their successors of a century later. Perhaps the all-important charge of a lack of depth, which it was left for Carlyle to establish, should be excepted; but even that is now a century old.

This was the beginning of my interest in the subject. Before, I had had no special interest in the novels or in Sir Walter himself. But the reading and re-reading of the novels, of the various lives from Lockhart's to John Buchan's, of the journal and letters, has made me a partisan, as is probably evident enough in the following pages. I have not been able to rouse much enthusiasm over the more remote romances, *The Fair Maid of Perth,* for instance, but even so imperfect and inferior a novel as *The Pirate* (the one I happen to have read most recently) seems to me to bear about it the stigmata of great genius; and I would by no means retreat with certain critics into the absurd theory that "the man is greater than his work." I have not considered it my function, however, to express my own opinion on the novels here.

Once one has become something of a partisan, the modern indifference to Sir Walter, the slights and the condescensions, tend only to confirm one in his convictions. He refuses to be moved even by the legerdemain of Mr. Shaw, who (in his *Quintessence of Ibsenism*) makes a show of turning Jeanie Deans into an example of religious perversity and selfish conceit. My sentiments have not, however, determined me to believe that Scott is as widely read as ever, or that he will again be a popular idol.

The purpose of this book is to show what was thought about the novels, and why, during the various periods since 1814, and also to gauge their position with successive reading publics. It does not undertake to be a Waverley allusion book. But an attempt has been made to give a thorough sampling of different fields and to include the opinions of the most representative and important writers. So many people have commented on the Waverley novels that anything like a complete register would seem an impossible task, even if it were thought desirable. The criticism covered is also limited to English; the only Continental critics mentioned are a few whose works are generally translated and widely read in English, so that they have a direct bearing on British and American opinion. The danger, even with the best intentions, of misrepresenting or garbling the various critics cited in work of this sort is obvious; I only hope I have avoided it reasonably well.

Little has been done on this subject before. The most thorough study is a chapter on Scott's criticism of his own work in Margaret Ball's *Sir Walter Scott as a Critic of Literature*. There are also scattered, fragmentary bits of information in W. F. Gray's *Scott in Sunshine and Shadow* and John A. Patten's *Sir Walter Scott: A Character Study*. Even in Miss Ball's case, however, I have not felt that I was engaged in very serious repetition. My path has also crossed that of Mr. Frederic Blanchard in his *Fielding — The Novelist*. He has been concerned with many points which have interested me, though of course from the point of view of Fielding rather than Scott. I have been frequently indebted to his work for bibliographical hints.

I should express here my gratitude to my colleagues at the University of Minnesota, Mr. Douglas Bush (now at Harvard) and Mr. Joseph W. Beach, for their detailed criticism. Mr. Alan McKillop of the Rice Institute also made many suggestions of which I was glad to take advantage. I realize that I have made myself a burden to members of most departments of the University Library, although they have never in any way impressed the fact upon me. I am under obligation to the University of Minnesota for the publication of the book, and as for the University Press, I have never ceased to marvel at the infinite pains its editorial staff takes to make a book as nearly perfect in form as it can be.

J. T. H.

University of Minnesota
October 4, 1936

CONTENTS

PART I. 1814–1832

I. SCOTT'S FAME 3

II. SCOTT'S OWN CRITICISM OF THE NOVELS 15

III. REVIEWS IN THE EDINBURGH, THE QUARTERLY, AND
BLACKWOOD'S 40

IV. OTHER PERIODICALS 63

V. A GROUP OF RADICAL AND LIBERAL PERIODICALS . . 91

VI. LETTERS AND JOURNALS; NOVELISTS AND ESSAYISTS . . 107

VII. THE POETS OF THE PERIOD, ESPECIALLY COLERIDGE . . 142

PART II. 1832–1880

I. SCOTT'S CONTINUED POPULARITY 157

II. VICTORIAN CRITICAL PREJUDICES 188

III. THE THREE CHIEF ESTIMATES: CARLYLE, BAGEHOT, LESLIE
STEPHEN 214

PART III. SINCE 1880

I. FOREIGN INFLUENCES; THE READING PUBLIC . . . 231

II. DEPRECIATION AND DEFENSE 258

III. STYLE, PHILOSOPHY, AND CHARACTER 287

IV. SCOTT'S TREATMENT OF HISTORY 316

PART IV. RECAPITULATION

RECAPITULATION 331

INDEX 347

ERRATA

Page 32, note 25, line 12. For 'hedge hill' *read* 'hedge bill.'

Page 104, note 13. For '1833' *read* '1832.'

Page 260, line 17. For 'idealless' *read* 'idealess.'

Page 299, line 23. For 'In the matter' *read* 'As in the matter.'

Page 332, line 5. For 'to place' *read* 'a place.'

Part I · 1814—1832

CHAPTER I

SCOTT'S FAME

IN 1838, six years after Walter Scott's death, appeared Thomas Carlyle's essay on his genius, the most famous of all writings on Scott, affectionate and patriotic, but saddened by the devastating recollection that after all Sir Walter had no message, that he offered humanity no philosophy or idea. "Not profitable for doctrine, for reproof, for edification . . . the sick heart will find no healing here, the darkly struggling heart no guidance; the Heroic that is in all men no divine awakening voice." Thus Carlyle concluded that Scott, lacking such ballast, would founder and sink into oblivion, that his tremendous popularity had been a rash fierce blaze bound soon to dim, and that he, Thomas Carlyle, was in effect writing Sir Walter's epitaph and in the name of the reading public taking a sorrowful last leave of a man who, otherwise great, lacked a gospel. So the prophet of the Victorians dooms the "King of the Romantics," the leader of the great age that had just drawn to a close.[1]

What a prediction! From Carlyle's day to this critics and biographers have found it worth their while to descant on Scott's life and genius, and the public to buy his books. There are, it is true, many points to argue in the matter, but no one can deny the plain fact of the tremendous mass of Scott material that has accumulated in the last century or the publishers' profits that have accrued from the sale of his works. Of books and articles on Scott there has been no end; up to the very present there has always been an abundant current supply, and the steady stream

[1] Carlyle's essay appeared in the *Westminster Review* of January, 1838 (28:154). See also *Critical and Miscellaneous Essays,* Vol. IV (Scribner's, New York, 1899).

has on special occasions risen to a flood. The centenary of his birth, 1871, was the occasion of many hecatombs (as well as Leslie Stephen's essay, hardly a hecatomb); so was the publication of his journal in 1890, and of his letters in 1894.[2] His devotees have even remembered to mark the hundredth anniversary of individual novels — of *Waverley, The Heart of Midlothian,* and many others. And of lives of Scott there is also no end, despite the plain fact that his son-in-law, Lockhart, did the task once and for all, and that R. H. Hutton distilled from Lockhart the one necessary brief biography. Yet every few years another Scott enthusiast becomes sure that the world needs a new life of the great romancer, and finds a publisher who thinks such a life a profitable venture. We have lately seen another special revival. The year 1932, like 1871, was one of further critical and biographical celebrations.

It goes without saying, of course, that not all the discussion of Scott has been panegyric. He has had his detractors, some cool and aloof, some pleasantly condescending, and some frankly contemptuous. Yet, after all, they do write about Scott, and at length; at least they find it important, even necessary, to explain that he is now unimportant and is no longer read. Other prosperous writers have been tucked into their graves, have had their funeral sermons and their Carlyles, and have lain quiet and mouldered away into final nothingness, without one friendly voice to wish them back. But not Scott. His ghost still walks vigorously, and there are many powerful voices to assert that it is a ghost clad in very lively flesh and blood. And one may add that even detraction implies fame, especially when it raises up champions.

It is not to be denied that Scott's personality, quite apart from the quality of his books, has been of great service to him. He had all the qualities necessary for popularity. He was fond of all the social pleasures and made hosts of friends. He was a great

---

[2] The *Journal of Sir Walter Scott* (2 vols., Edinburgh, 1890), reprinted as one volume in 1891, to which references are made; *Familiar Letters of Sir Walter Scott* (2 vols., Boston, 1894).

raconteur, a wellspring of anecdote. He was infinitely generous, affable and kindly, and perfectly simple, straightforward, and unaffected; he never posed but always took himself and his works lightly — and this, we may be sure, was no pose. Indeed many have urged it against him as a proof of his triviality and his lack of serious respect for his art. His astounding success in itself increased his distinction, and the golden stream which was diverted to subsidize the lands and battlements of Abbotsford, whither tourists and enthusiasts flocked then as now, was put to a good use as far as the Scott legend itself was concerned. Abbotsford was in his own day, far more than it is now, an outward symbol and a visible sign of Scott's romantic genius.

There is nothing to mar the winning effect of his character; he seems the friendliest and kindest of our great writers whom we have known well, the one best able to appeal personally to the hearts of a broad public. There is nothing mean nor low to be alleged against him, nothing to break the general spell of his character. The only possible exception is his treatment of Constable and the Ballantynes, but this is vague and debatable ground, and is forgotten in the picture of his heroic struggle to retrieve his fortunes during his last few years. His treatment of his creditors, in fact, has been his crowning glory as a man.

Then in addition, Lockhart did for him what Boswell had done for Johnson; he preserved him as a living figure with all his graces intact — himself the hero of scores of vivid anecdotes. Lord Cockburn, the eminent Edinburgh jurist and long-time acquaintance of Scott, reveals as well as anyone the feeling that stirred the hearts of his generation when they thought of Walter Scott. He tries to describe the sense of almost national calamity that appalled the Scotch people when they learned of the financial disaster of 1826.[3] When Scott died, Cockburn wrote, "Scott is dead . . . Scotland never owed so much to one man." Again, as the volumes of Lockhart appeared, he read them at once and re-

[3] Henry Thomas, Lord Cockburn, *Memorials of His Time* (New York, 1856), pp. 266, 405, and its continuation, *Journal of Henry Cockburn* (2 vols., Edinburgh, 1874), I, 37, 134, 174–77; II, 251.

corded his impressions. He was dissatisfied, it is true, with much of the detail in the Lockhart. He thought many people had been given undue prominence because of some slight connection with Scott, and he declared after the first two volumes, "The two most extraordinary revelations to Edinburgh are, that John Irving had once a particle of literary taste and that there was once a time when Lady Scott was pretty and agreeable." He regretted too that Jeffrey's reviews should have been treated so calmly; for Lord Cockburn, Jeffrey was the greatest of British critics, and he thought the reviews in the *Edinburgh Review* "singularly just, and by far the most honorable testimonies that have ever been given to the genius of Scott."

But his great regret about the book was that it depreciated Scott's character! Such an opinion seems strange enough to those who think of Lockhart's *Life* as panegyric, but it did not strike Lord Cockburn so. He says that many blamed Lockhart for not idealizing Scott, and while he does not agree with them, it still seems to him that Lockhart includes much "useless and vulgar matter" and has thus given too worldly and mean a turn to Scott's character. He could have been true to life without producing such an effect, and Cockburn grieves to think that the biography may dispel the fascination of Scott's name for those who think only of his works and his fame. They will now see him as a tradesman concerned in profits, a man with many practical interests, and they will have it impressed upon them "how very narrow and shallow were all his public views." That is, for Lord Cockburn Scott was a hero with some small foibles which could hardly be mentioned without producing a false effect — a hero whose descents into the market place and whose fantastic Tory notions were trivial human errors to be glossed over and forgotten. And yet on the whole the portrait seemed to him to be true to life. No biography, he thought, gave a truer account: "it is Scott to the life," and in spite of the false impressions, "how much—how very much is there to admire and love." Thus he falls into a revery ("Dear Scott!"—) dictated by the deepest and tenderest of feelings.

As a result of all this, love of the man has fostered the love of his books — again and again one reads that it would be unkind to treat harshly the work of such a hero. Hence the regret of even his most severe critics; indeed Croce, one of the most disapproving of the lot, finds his kindly, charitable goodness his sole redeeming quality. On the whole, critics approaching the novels with their thoughts full of Lockhart have certainly been mindful of their fondness for Sir Walter himself, and have been either unwilling or unable to set the man himself aside, and consider the novels by themselves.

Of the tremendous popularity of the Waverley series when they were a novelty a century ago there is of course no doubt. Statistics of profits and of numbers of copies sold, as well as picturesque anecdotes by the score, testify to the avidity with which readers seized upon each new romance as it fell from the press. In fact, *Waverley* and its successors came to them like manna from heaven to starving travelers in a desert. The novel was in low repute, so far as it had any repute at all. The great novelists of the mid-eighteenth century were now classics; the once lively and vivacious Fanny Burney of *Evelina* had become the elderly and feeble Mme. D'Arblay of *The Wanderer,* and like her that ancient Scotch arbiter of letters, Mackenzie, "The Man of Feeling," was living on the triumphs of a bygone age. The only supporter of the tradition whom the critics could find it in their hearts to approach with real respect was Maria Edgeworth, and they knew well enough that she was not the peer of Fielding or Sterne. One there was, indeed, at least from 1811 on, worthy to be added to their company; but the clear and steady light of Jane Austen's genius attracted few eyes while the sudden and unexpected meteor of Scott himself was rushing across the heavens. She was reserved for a select few in her own generation, and did not live to read the first of the famous tributes to her powers.

The two great reviews, now well under way, condescended only in rare instances to recognize the existence of the novel. Jeffrey, who collected his contributions to the *Edinburgh* in

1844,[4] prefaced his reviews of novels with a reminiscence of the contempt in which the novel was held early in the century, a contempt that faded only when the sudden glory of *Waverley* burst upon them. To Jeffrey, Scott was the most remarkable product of the present age — there had been no influence equal to his since the days of Voltaire and Rousseau. He says that the Waverley novels "for many years together had occupied and delighted me more than anything else that ever came under my critical survey."

Another expression of the same sort — perhaps the most appealing to be found anywhere, and the one which mirrors most clearly the actual gratitude contemporaries felt for the novels — comes from Lord Cockburn. Looking back on the publication of *Waverley,* he says, "Except the first opening of the *Edinburgh Review* no work that has appeared in my time made such an instant and universal impression. It is curious to remember it; the unexpected newness of the thing, the profusion of original characters, the Scotch language, Scotch scenery, Scotch men and women, the simplicity of the writing and the graphic force of the descriptions, all struck us with an electric shock of delight. I wish I could again feel the sensations produced by the first year of these two Edinburgh works."[5]

Indeed Scott's admirers in his own day ranged from Goethe to humble Scotch shepherds. Goethe was conscious of faults in

[4] Francis, Lord Jeffrey, *Contributions to the Edinburgh Review* (4 vols., London, 1844), III, 426–96.

[5] See his *Memorials,* page 266. A less striking but still very vivid letter making much the same point came to Scott from his friend Morritt on July 14, 1814. He has just read the first volume of *Waverley* and says that if the rest is as good, it deserves a place among standard works and is far more important than its appearance as a mere novel indicates. "Your manner of narrating is so different from the slipshod, sauntering verbiage of common novels, and from the stiff, precise and prim sententiousness of some of our female novelists, that it cannot I think fail to strike anybody who knows what style is." He fears that it will not be appreciated, but "the strings you have touched of humor and pathos depending on natural character and real life have, with few exceptions indeed, been so seldom touched that they have all the charms of novelty to us, and therefore you must not wonder that we 'as strangers bid them welcome.'" Wilfred Partington, ed., *Private Letter Books of Sir Walter Scott* (London, 1930), p. 111.

detail, it is true, but he recognized in Scott a unique genius and admired the novels tremendously, seeing in their character portrayal the deepest insight into human character, achieved through constant observation and activity in the world. Goethe's praise of Scott, in fact, is as high as any Sir Walter has ever been given. It is hardly to be dismissed, as it is by Croce, on the ground that it is for his plotting, a field where Goethe himself was weak, that Scott was admired by the great German.[6] At the other extreme there is a letter of 1820 from a shepherd to Sir Walter, apologizing for his intrusion and his illiteracy (which is not great) and telling how much he had enjoyed the novels for their truth to the life and scenery that he himself had known. He remarks on the accuracy of the figures of speech and is especially curious as to how an educated man ever got the common dialect so perfectly.[7] Thus Scott had admirers from the highest to the humblest, who were drawn to him by the elements of deepest reality in his work and not merely by his obvious romantic novelty.

Or, as a highly dignified writer in the *United States Literary Gazette* [8] so beautifully puts it, in remarking on "the astonishing popularity of the Waverley novels," they "have worked their way in a few years from the lady's work table and the lounger's parlor window to a temporary fellowship at least with the dusty corpuses of the civilian and the ponderous polyglotts of the divine."

[6] See G. H. Needler, "Goethe and Scott," *Queen's Quarterly*, 31:38 (August, 1923). Carlyle speaks in his essay of the high range of Scott's admirers, and especially Goethe. The point seems to be established by Friedrich Gundolf, however, in his "Scott and Goethe," in H. J. C. Grierson, ed., *Sir Walter Scott Today* (London, 1932), that Goethe's opinions, especially those expressed to Eckermann, must be carefully discounted and interpreted. Goethe recognized a great genius in Scott, but he never thought of him as enthusiastically as he did of Byron, nor did he consider him as his own equal. "Their worlds did not touch"; Scott had no influence on him. Nor, one may add, is Goethe thought to have had any serious influence on Scott's mature work, except possibly in the case of Fenella, who was at once recognized as a reflection of Mignon. Louis Reynaud (*Le Romantisme*, 1926, pp. 177 ff.) sees the most pervasive influence of both Schiller and Goethe on the novels. But cf. Grierson, *Sir Walter Scott Today*, p. xi.

[7] See Partington, *Private Letter Books*, p. 321.

[8] *United States Literary Gazette*, 2:401 (September 1, 1825).

The attitude of the *Literary Gazette*,[9] a weekly routine review of new books, is also an index to Scott's great success. The *Gazette* did not review his books; it spoke of them humbly in terms of pure praise. Apropos of *The Pirate* it could declare the day for criticizing the Waverley novels past. Popularity had made both eulogy and cavils pointless.[10] Or the reviewer would sigh with relief at the chance to turn from his dull labors over other books to another one of the "Scotch or Scott's novels, as they are indifferently called."[11] He would then proceed at once to a long summary interspersed with copious quotation. As the *Gazette* boastfully informed its readers, it had its sheets of a new novel sent by post to London that the reviewer might hastily read them, prepare his account, and, sometimes trusting to delay by wind and tide, rush it into print and into the hands of the public a day or so before the boat from Scotland beat its way up the Thames and delivered its precious freight to the waiting binders. The *Gazette,* moreover, would prepare the way for a new novel; for *Kenilworth* by publishing well before its appearance articles on the history and present aspects of Kenilworth Castle, or for *Peverell of the Peak* (sic) by an account of the Peverell family and a description of the peculiar beauties of the Peak scenery.[12]

There is plenty of familiar evidence also of the rage for Scott in America. One letter from an American to Maria Edgeworth may serve to illustrate a popularity here which can be supported by scores of other testimonials. A Philadelphia publishing firm bought sheets of *Woodstock* to print from for £150, to be sent as fast as they were printed. Thus they could be reprinted and rushed into the market three weeks before the arrival of any copies of the English edition. The sheets of the last volume were forwarded on three different ships and were printed and bound within one day ("23½ hours") after their receipt, one hundred

[9] Not to be confused with the *United States Literary Gazette*, cited just above.
[10] *Literary Gazette,* December 22, 1821, p. 801.
[11] June 1, 8, 1822, pp. 335, 355.
[12] December 22, 1821, p. 801n.; October 28, December 30, 1820, pp. 689, 840; August 3, 1822, p. 487.

and eighty-five persons being employed. Of the first edition of
9,000 copies, nearly 8,000 were sold on the first day. A second
edition was prepared for, and immediate publication in New
York, Boston, and other cities expected.[13]

Across the channel, too, Scott's success seems to have been
fully as brilliant as at home. Maigron[14] tells of his overwhelming
influence on French writers, to whom his novels offered the most
important of models, and who found in him a warmth and life
which they missed in Racine, and in the tragedy and epic generally. Hugo, Dumas, Vigny, Balzac,[15] Stendhal (despite his reservations) loved him passionately, and saluted him religiously as a
master. For them, Maigron says, Scott's people had vivacity and

[13] See Partington, *Private Letter Books*, p. 300. This letter also makes a point
of the comparative cheapness of books in America. In England *Woodstock* sold
in three volumes for 31/6; in America in two volumes for $1.50, about one-
fifth. An editorial footnote to the review of *The Pirate* (reprinted from *Blackwood's*) in the Philadelphia *Port Folio* throws an interesting sidelight on the
results of these methods of publication. The Philadelphia edition of *The Pirate*,
having been reprinted from imperfect sheets, lacked the author's preface and had
a serious hiatus in the first volume. The publishers had secured a perfect copy
to print from, however, and were remedying these defects. Such occurrences
were doubtless typical of the system of hurried reprinting, piratical or otherwise, which constituted the publication of British books in America.

For an account of the piratical methods of Carey, the Philadelphia publisher,
see David A. Rendall, "Waverley in America," *Colophon*, 1:39 (July, 1935).
There is a good deal of information here concerning differences between the
English and American editions resulting from canceled pages. Mr. Rendall makes
the surprising mistake of interpreting the cancellation as proof that "Scott was
a meticulous workman, forever revising, correcting and polishing his novels until
the moment of publication, and ardent antiquarian that he was, intolerant of
the slightest error." As a matter of fact, revision in proof seems to have been
not only the last but also the first correction by Scott himself. He caught some
errors, but many escaped him.

[14] *Le Roman historique* (rev. ed., Paris, 1912). See especially pages 51–92,
passim. See also E. P. Dargan, "Scott and the French Romantics," *Publications of
the Modern Language Association*, 49:599 (June, 1934).

[15] Of all these, Balzac is doubtless the one whose praise would be most desired
today. Balzac's feelings toward Scott have been fully explored by R. H. Gordon
in "Scott and the Comédie Humaine," in Grierson, *Sir Walter Scott Today*.
The main point is that Balzac always, early and late, had the greatest reverence
and admiration for Scott, regarding him as a master and as a rival. Though he
did not approve all phases of Scott's work, he thought him one of the greatest
writers, possibly the greatest, of the age, "the Homer of the modern novel," far
above Byron, who had described only himself, and far above Cooper or Dumas.
Many of his ideas about subject and method he avowedly derived from Scott.

freshness, in fact the first of all virtues and the most essential of all gifts, and one then almost unknown (they were "rassasiés et dégoûtés des ternes et monotones grisailles des pseudo-classiques") — that is, life. Maigron quotes too the "vers epilep-tiques" of Cordellier:

Salut, Ivanhoe! débris de la Croisade
Honneur à toi! Salut, épopée! Iliade!

and also a satirical squib from *L'Abeille* of 1821 (before *Quentin Durward,* one should notice), which testifies to the strength of the popular vogue:

Du Walter Scott! du Walter Scott! Hâtez-vous, Messieurs, et vous surtout, Mesdames; c'est du merveilleux, c'est du nouveau; hâtez-vous! La première édition est épuisée, la seconde est retenue d'avance; la troisième disparaîtra, à peine sortie de la presse. Accourez, achetez; mauvais ou bon, qu'importe! Sir Walter Scott y a mis son nom,[16] cela suffit — et vivent l'Angleterre et les Anglais!

And when he died Sainte-Beuve wrote an article on his death (later included in the *Premiers Lundis*) declaring that while future generations might not value him as highly as had his own, he must always be recognized as a man of grand proportions, a great story-teller, and an immortal creator of human character.

One naturally approaches the contemporary criticism of Scott expecting panegyric, and of course panegyric lies on every side. The delight of his own generation in him was unbounded, and though Scott confessedly wrote for the reading public and not for the critics, there were plenty of critical writers who echoed the chorus of popular praise, and hailed the Great Unknown as another Shakespeare. But still there were murmurings. There were those who read coolly, who analyzed and glanced a second time at phrases and sentences, refusing to read as fast as the author had written or dictated. Indeed it is surprising to find how many of the faults that are charged against Sir Walter today

---

[16] Of course he had not, but this is another bit of evidence to show how transparent was the veil of his anonymity. According to Professor Dargan, Scott's name actually appeared on the title page of the translation of *The Heart of Mid-lothian,* published in December, 1818. *Op. cit.,* p. 601n.

and that we think are revealed to us because of our greater experience in the novel are merely echoes of remarks by the more critical readers in Scott's own time. That favorite rebuke that he had no message and no philosophical system was, to be sure, left to Carlyle and the earnest generations that followed, but the other weaknesses for which modern critics are likely to attack Scott were as apparent to many a century or more ago as they are now.

Take the matter of style, for instance. It is well known among us that Scott is wordy and diffuse, that he should have revised and boiled down, even though one does not demand from him Flaubert's agonizing researches for *le mot juste*. We point out his slipshod diction and his pompous eighteenth-century clichés, his "feathered denizens of the air," for instance. His disciple Stevenson and many others since have harped on such foibles as one of the irritating things about Sir Walter's books. Another source of irritation is his slowness in getting under way. He is apt to flounder about in a mass of introductory material, apparently getting his bearings and gradually deciding what he will do with his story, while the modern reader grows more and more impatient and often refuses to stay with him until he has mapped out his course and cast anchor. We all know not only the openings of Sir Walter's novels but the introductory paragraphs to his chapters.

These are not altogether to be explained as part of the style of another and more deliberate age which lacked the experience in technic of the giants of the later nineteenth century and the twentieth. They also offended and irritated the critics of his own time, who complain of them again and again. Jeffrey himself, whose love of the novels was as deep and heartfelt as one could wish, noted nevertheless that *Waverley* was "obviously very hastily and in many places unskillfully written" and pointed out that the description of Waverley's early life in England was "laborious and tardy." Croker in the *Quarterly* speaks of *Guy Mannering* as "this hasty and undigested work," and Hazlitt pauses in the midst of ecstatic praise in his great essay on Scott to

declare his astonishment at "the innumerable and incessant instances of bad and slovenly English in them [the novels], more,
we believe, than in any other works now printed" and finds it
patent that the author never reads his manuscript nor looks at
proof sheets. A reviewer in *Blackwood's* similarly qualifies high
praise of *The Bride of Lammermoor* and *A Legend of Montrose* with regret at "the careless and slovenly manner" of certain
passages.[17] Similar strictures crop out in many of their minor
brethren also. And so it is with the other familiar charges against
the novels. The heroines, it is said, are almost never thrilling,
but, like many of the phrases, conventional furniture. The
heroes likewise are lay figures. The chivalric upholstery of the
medieval novels is stagy and artificial. And so on. It is surprising
how open the eyes of Scott's contemporaries were to his weaknesses — all except that fatal lack of message, which Carlyle and
the Victorians were soon to shake their heads over.

Yet for readers of his own time these were mere specks in the
sun. They never thought of them as reasons for dismissing the
novels into a limbo of dull mediocrity. They might regret them,
but only to hurry on to the most ecstatic praise of great virtues.
For them the Waverley novels lent Scott a glory which dimmed
the light of every other great writer of his generation.

[17] Originally the carelessness noted was that of mere style, of diction, phrasing, etc. As time went on, careful readers began to notice, or at least to make
more of, the slips in factual detail that sprang from too rapid writing. An especially amusing instance, the preposterous comparative ages of Cedric and his
father, is analyzed in the *Atlantic Monthly* for January, 1892 (69:140). This had,
as a matter of fact, been noticed when the novel was new. See the *Literary
Gazette,* July 29, 1820, p. 490.

CHAPTER II

SCOTT'S OWN CRITICISM OF THE NOVELS

MANY MODERN critics of Scott have declared his own comments on his novels to be among the best criticisms of them in his own time. His candor and cool detachment, his serene, unruffled good nature and ever-ready humor, his refusal to take his work with passionate, deadly seriousness and to consider himself as a prophet or high priest of Romance, in short his utter lack of vanity, all superimposed on his own peculiar understanding of his great store of historic materials and his genius in handling it, did conspire together to make him the best qualified critic of his own romances, however strange that may seem. Whatever he writes is interesting not merely as showing the author's own feeling about his books but as really crystal-clear analysis of their purposes and values. The engaging frankness and humorous good nature which pervade his remarks on his own work and which especially lend them authority and conviction may be illustrated in his choice of a motto for the general preface to the collected edition of 1829–1832, the "Magnum Opus." He lights upon Richard II's rueful complaint at his deposition,

>   . . . And must I ravel out
> My weaved-up follies? . . .

and, going on to speak of his early and merely tentative interest in novel-writing, declares, "those who complain, not unreasonably, of the profusion of the Tales which have followed *Waverley,* may bless their stars at the narrow escape they have made by the commencement of the inundation which had so nearly taken place in the first year of the century, being postponed for fifteen years later." One of the best exhibitions of his humorous fancy occurs in the preface to the *Tales of the Crusaders* in the good-natured comments on the imposture *Walladmor* and the possibility of grinding out Waverley novels by steam power. Having declared *The Betrothed* heavy enough to break down anything, but *The Talisman* a novel that goes trippingly off, he admits that *Walladmor* had seemed to be the creation of Douster-swivel with the aid of a steam engine, but that in general such methods could be applied only to the commonplace parts, "such as the love-speeches of the hero, the description of the heroine's person, the moral observation of all sorts, and the distribution of happiness at the conclusion of the piece." How many writers would thus make sport of their recognized weaknesses? Of course there are those who see in all this only an escape from responsi-bility and the artistic conscience. Yet surely there are other points of view equally profitable and salutary. Never does this humor fail him, whether he is discussing history, pointing out his own lapses, or defending himself from critical attack.[1]

The three classical instances of his comment on his own works are his review of *Tales of My Landlord* in the *Quarterly* in 1817, his preface to *Nigel,* and remarks on his imitators in his journal in 1826. But many other allusions, chiefly in his prefaces to the novels, but also in his letters and journal, amplify and round out the various impressions created in the three most famous in-stances. The prefaces are especially fruitful. Their chief purpose is the exposition of historical sources and description of the originals of his characters, but continually one finds in them new light on his critical points of view.

[1] Alan D. McKillop in an acute and closely packed centenary lecture deliv-ered at the Rice Institute (*Rice Institute Pamphlet,* April, 1933) points out that Scott's habit of humorous self-depreciation — his real humility combined with "the easy manners of the eighteenth century gentleman," the amateur — while very refreshing, perhaps goes too far; the pure romanticists have gained ground at the expense of those who had "a shrewd and humorous realism." Cf. also R. S. Rait, "Walter Scott and Thomas McCrie," in Grierson, *Sir Walter Scott Today.*

Aside from his comments on his aims and method of work, and his attitude toward his public and the critics, the subject that has most interested writers on Scott is his defense of himself against the storm he raised among his own countrymen by his portraits of the Covenanters in *Old Mortality*.

This was the chief subject and real reason for his own review of *Old Mortality* and *The Black Dwarf* in the *Quarterly* in 1817. *Old Mortality* for the first and only time in his career had embroiled him with Scotchmen, many of whom had taken umbrage at what they considered a frivolous and unsympathetic portrayal of the old Covenanters. They had, indeed, found a loud mouthpiece in a divine named McCrie, who attacked the novel in a series of articles in the *Edinburgh Christian Instructor*. Scott records in his journal [2] that he despised and at first refused to read them, but finally was driven not only to read them but to write what was virtually a reply. Here was a kind of criticism which above all others Scott would wish to avoid. He clearly wished, moreover, to explain and justify his own method with history and to support the truth and accuracy of the impressions of the Scottish past that he was establishing here and in the earlier novels. The information about the novels (especially the originals of the characters) and the background of minute local information almost give away the authorship of the essay.[3]

[2] See page 818. He also wrote to Lady Louisa Stuart on January 31, 1817, "I really think there is nothing in the book that is not fair and legitimate subject of raillery; and I own I have my suspicions of that very susceptible devotion which so readily takes offense: such men should not read books of amusement; but do they suppose because they are virtuous and choose to be thought outrageously so, 'there shall be no cakes and ale.' — Ay, by our lady, and ginger shall be hot in the mouth too." And he declares that he is not going to read McCrie's attacks or pay them any attention. See H. J. C. Grierson, ed., *Letters of Sir Walter Scott* (9 vols., incomplete, London, 1932–35), IV, 381.

[3] The authorship of the essay has been thoroughly established. Scott later (1827) spoke of it as being by Erskine, who wrote it from materials Sir Walter had furnished him with, and there is one passage at least, a comparison with Shakespeare, which is not according to Scott's practice. The whole manuscript is, however, in Scott's hand. See the *Times Literary Supplement*, November 8, 1918, p. 529. Scott was quite capable of enjoying the humor of imitating his ecstatic reviewers and letting such a passage stand. He occasionally allows Jedediah Cleishbotham to speak in terms which Walter Scott *in propria persona* never **used.**

It was with the national and historical aspects of his novels, indeed, that he was most concerned. Against attacks on his superstitious material he defended himself strongly; the English especially, he insisted, were unable to realize how deeply traditional superstition was ingrained in Scottish character. He also wanted it clearly understood that his use of superstition was not Gothic; in his journal entry for February 3, 1826, he insisted, "My object is not to excite fear of supernatural things in my reader, but to show the effects of such fear upon the agents in the story." He pointed out too that a great number of the characters in the novels were drawn from actual originals, which he described in detail, and in addition he discussed the various qualities of Scottish character which the novel and its predecessors had illuminated.

On *The Black Dwarf* he wasted little time, but he does defend it against charges of improbability by citing the facts and the historical characters on which it was founded.[4] His interest in *Old Mortality* is obviously deeper. After summarizing the story and pointing out a passage borrowed from Defoe, he goes on to his defense of his Covenanters. He insists that in all important facts and impressions the author is true to history and supports the contention with a deluge of anecdotal information. He submits with sly humor that in small points the author is not so trustworthy; for instance, he makes Dalzell wear boots — a circumstance which was historically untrue. With much stronger emphasis, he defends the author as a historian not only of events

[4] In a number of letters written when the two novels were fresh from the press he delivers the same judgment; to Lady Louisa Stuart on November 14, 1816 (in a letter quoted at length in the next note); to John Murray on December 16 (*The Black Dwarf* was not very original and was lame and impotent in its conclusion, but *Old Mortality* was "both true and powerful"); to Joseph Train on December 21 (*Old Mortality* seems to be by the same hand as *Waverley*, etc., and "displays the same knowledge of Scottish manners and scenery and the same carelessness as to arrangement which characterize these curious narratives." The first tale is "below par" but the second "exceedingly good indeed"); and to Miss Clephane, December 16 ("The first is hurried and I think flat, but the second opens new ground and possesses great power of humor and pathos"). Lady Louisa was of course the only one of these correspondents who was supposed to know of his authorship. See Grierson, *Letters*, IV, 292, 318, 323, 331.

but of manners and minute incidents; and, praising him as "the intimate of the living and the dead," asserts that he has gone to Nature for his people and has not forced Nature to comply with his plot as a first interest. His characters are as lively as Shakespeare's, and must be his intimates, for especially in his dialogue he catches the true sentiment of the Scotch peasant in characteristic diction. He carefully defends the accuracy of well-known historical characters, especially Claverhouse, and then apropos of the Covenanters proceeds to discuss the propriety of ridicule in connection with any religious subject. He gives a historical sketch of these sectaries, emphasizing "the atrocities or absurdities of a people whose ignorance and fanaticism were rendered frantic by persecution."[5] The whole concludes with a humorous reference to the rumor that Thomas Scott, the brother in Canada, was the author of the novels.

Scott's anxiety to avoid any charges of a light and unsympathetic treatment of the Covenanters is revealed by his return to the subject the next year in Jedediah Cleishbotham's address to the reader in *The Heart of Midlothian,* where as Jedediah he

[5] In his letter to Lady Louisa Stuart of November 14, 1816, Scott reveals not only the way his novels grew under his hand but the nature of his inspiration as a dramatic historian — an inspiration more carefully explained in the *Quarterly* article. He tells her that he had intended to write "four tales of the manners of Scotland in her different provinces." "But as no man that wrote so much ever knew so little what he intended to do when he began to write or executed less of the little which he had premeditated, I totally altered my plans before I had completed my first volume." He had given himself too narrow limits, and "could not lounge easily within so small a circle." "So I quarrelled with my story, and bungled up a conclusion as a boarding school Miss finishes a task which she had commenced with great glee and accuracy. In the next tale I have succeeded better, at least I think so: . . . there are noble subjects for narrative during that period, full of the strongest light and shadow, all human passions stirred up and stimulated by the most powerful motives, and the contending parties as distinctly contrasted in manners and in modes of thinking as in political principles. I am complete master of the whole history of these strange times, both of persecutors and persecuted, so I trust I have come decently off, for as Falstaff very reasonably asks, is not the *truth* the *truth?*" A reflection of this from the reader's point of view came from the Duke of Buccleuch, who wrote Scott on December 19, 1816, that he liked *The Black Dwarf* but thought *Old Mortality* "not only very amusing but highly interesting, as it throws a light on a particular part of history not generally well understood." Partington, *Private Letter Books,* p. 287.

speaks of the author's "warm, yea partial interest in the deeds and sentiments of our forefathers," and continues,

He whom his adversaries describe as a perjured prelatist is desirous that his predecessors should be held moderate in their power and just in their execution of its privileges, when truly the unimpassioned peruser of the Annals of those times shall deem them sanguinary, violent, and tyrannical. Again, the representatives of the suffering nonconformists desire that their ancestors, the Cameronians, shall be represented not simply as honest enthusiasts, oppressed for conscience-sake, but persons of fine breeding and valiant heroes. Truly, the historian cannot gratify these predilections. He must needs describe the Cavaliers as proud and high-spirited, cruel, remorseless, and vindictive; the suffering party as honorably tenacious of their opinions under persecution; their own tempers being, however, sullen, fierce, and rude; their opinions absurd and extravagant and their whole course of conduct that of persons whom hellebore would better have suited than prosecutions unto death for high treason. Natheless, while such and so preposterous were the opinions on either side, there were, it cannot be doubted, men of virtue and worth on both, to entitle either party to claim merit from its martyrs.

And to support further the impartiality of the author, Jedediah volunteers the information that one of his ancestors was a Quaker and oppressed by both sides, "even to the extenuation of his purse and the incarceration of his person."[6]

This defense of *Old Mortality*, though interesting by itself, is really only one illustration of Scott's primary concern with history, of his conception of himself as a kind of historian and the novels as a kind of dramatized history. Indeed, there is plenty of direct evidence in his own comment to show how consistently the germ or nuclear idea and inspiration of the novels was a historical and social one; invariably Scott thought of a given novel as illustrating some trait of national character, describing some

[6] Scott's impartiality as a historian is defended by most of his sympathetic modern critics. The most important case after the Covenanters' is Queen Mary's. Concerning her he wrote Lady Louisa Stuart on December 14, 1820, "I do not design any scandel [sic] about Queen Bess whom I admire much altho like an old *true-blue* I have malice against her on Queen Mary's account . . . But I think I shall be very fair . . ." Grierson, *Letters*, VI, 311.

phase of civilization, or painting the portrait of some great historic figure — Mary Stuart, Elizabeth, or Louis XI. His conception of himself as a historian and his dependence on history appear too in his letters when he turns to the more historical romance of *Ivanhoe* and its successors. He wrote John Ballantyne on August 2, 1819, of *Ivanhoe:* "I think you will make a good thing of it for the subject is quite new. I am not afraid of working myself out — not that I should not soon do so were I to depend on my own limited invention, but the range of the past and the present is at my disposal and that is inexhaustible." A little later, when he was working on *Kenilworth,* he wrote Constable, September 10, 1820, asking for data on Cumnor Hall. "I wish you would have it copied out for me, and should like indeed to know anything that occurs to you about the village of Cumnor, its situation, etc. I like to be as minutely local as I can." And when he came to write *Quentin Durward* during 1823, his letters were full of requests for sources or for details of information, showing clearly the difficulties he had created for himself when he undertook to be "minutely local" about Plessis-le-Tours and other places off his native heath. He was now chained to books, and obviously felt it a great handicap.[7] Indeed, as has already been said, the greater part of the prefaces is devoted to the historical bases of the novels, the originals of the characters, or the sources of the incidents. A mere exciting story of love and adventure tricked out in costume and upholstery was not what he aimed at. As a matter of fact, both he and his critics were concerned at the way he left the story to fend for itself while he enjoyed himself as a historian.[8]

This comes out countless times. Take for instance the oft-quoted passages on his imitators in his journal for 1826. On October 17 he writes that he has been reading with pleasure Harrison Ainsworth and Horace Smith, and that he seems to have

[7] See Grierson, *Letters,* V, 445; VI, 265–66; VII, *passim.*

[8] It is worth noting that Goethe thought the foundation of Scott's success lay in the glorious richness of the materials of British history. The Germans, he said, had a dull and chaotic history to draw upon for similar works. See G. H. Needler, *op. cit.*

trained up a hundred fighters who do about as well in the field
as he himself. Indeed, he adds, if he published anonymously he
would fare no better with the public than they; so he will continue to use his *nom de guerre* and take advantage of "the prejudice in favor of the original patentee." The next day, however,
his critical judgment had become somewhat clarified. The reading of these imitators, he says, helps him to see his own errors.
Besides, he sees that he has the great advantage over them of
"doing it more natural." They have to cram for their books,
while he can draw on a seasoned and well-stored memory. Then,
too, they drag in too much history, although he himself sins that
way at times. He is conscious that he has considered his plots too
lightly — merely as strings by which to pull up a succession of
scenes [9] — but he repents and will try to amend. "I must not," he
adjures himself, "let the background eclipse the principal figures — the frame overpower the picture." Another fault of his
followers which calls into play his usual candor is their "stealing"
from their sources, which they do too openly. He notes in Horace
Smith whole pages from Defoe, whereas when he himself steals
he is at great pains to conceal it. Yet after all he must cast about
for some way of escape from his followers, who are bound at last
to run the historical novel into the ground.[10] But alas, the one
way of novelty that occurs to him is "to depend for success on the
interest of a well-contrived story" and that, "woe's me," he can
never manage to do, "for the ideas rise as I write." Still he deter-
mines to think up something and steal a march on them all.

[9] He had expressed this same idea by means of the same figure in the review
of *Old Mortality* in 1817.

[10] The search for novelty and the desire to escape imitators went hand in
hand. *Ivanhoe* was of course the first departure from the path of the Scotch
novels, and fear of imitators was an evident motive. He wrote to Lady Louisa
Stuart in January, 1820, "I am glad you found anything to entertain you in
Ivanhoe. Novelty is what this giddy-paced time demands imperiously, and I
certainly studied as much as I could to get out of the old beaten track, leaving
those who like to keep the road, which I have rutted pretty well." See Grierson,
Letters, VI, 116. Three years later his language about imitators is a little stronger.
He wrote Morritt on January 11, 1823, that he hoped to do well with *Quentin
Durward,* "where the vulgar dogs of imitators have no sense to follow me." *Ibid.,*
VII, 308.

Here, clearly, is the clue to Scott's own approach to his novels —the plot "a string by which to draw up a succession of scenes," with the danger of "the background eclipsing the principal figures, the frame overpowering the picture," and, for method, "the ideas rising as I write." He was always the historian, the patriotic nationalist. He seized upon some dramatic contrast of characters or parties and ignored narrative technic in his eagerness to bring to life his historic or nationally typical characters and to set them moving against a vivid scenic background. His mention of Maria Edgeworth[11] as a source of inspiration, his desire to do for Scotland what she had done for Ireland, is an indication of this, as also of the realistic quality of his romance. He wrote in the 1829 preface to *Waverley*, which had been a trial balloon to determine whether he should turn novelist or not, that it was "put together with so little care that I cannot boast of having sketched any distinct plan of the work," but that Waverley's wanderings, managed with so little care, gave him a chance to introduce scenery and manners and to depend for success on reality of matter rather than skill. He sinned thus elsewhere, he says, but never so much as here. He had even written to his friend Morritt at the time of publication (July 28, 1814) that he had purposely let the first volume flag, "to avoid the ordinary error of novel writers, whose first volume is usually their best";[12] but, he went on, "it may really boast to be a tolerably faithful portrait of Scottish man-

[11] He even wrote to her through James Ballantyne expressing a sense of debt for inspiration. See J. G. Lockhart, *Memoirs of Sir Walter Scott* (10 vols., Edinburgh, 1882), IV, 405.

[12] Scott was not always as unconscious of technic as some of his later critics would make him. Replying to James Ballantyne, who had objected to his introducing certain material in dialogue, he explains that he has to get it in for plot, and while flat enough in dialogue, it would be still worse expressed by the author himself. He adds "I mention this only to show that when I am dull there is a design." Grierson, *Letters*, IV, 2. He makes the same point with great spirit in the frequently quoted "Black Hussar" letter, where he violently rejects the proffered criticism of certain publishers' readers, saying he had never heard of such impudence and that he knew when he was writing badly as well as the next person. Professor Grierson compares the version of this letter which he found with the startlingly different one published by Lockhart, as well as the politic and judicious revision which James passed on to the offending critics. *Ibid.*, p. 276.

ners, and has been recognized as such in Edinburgh." In *The Antiquary,* too, he was fearful of a lack of interest, rating it below *Waverley* and *Guy Mannering;* still, he said, "there is some salvation about it, for if a man will paint from nature, he will be likely to amuse those who are daily looking at it."[13] It was always the matter, social and historical, that absorbed him.[14]

Sir Walter's modesty and his open and frank determination to suit the public obscure the fact that he felt strongly the power and dignity that might belong to the true historical novelist or romancer. In his article "Metrical Romances" in the *Edinburgh Review* in 1806 [15] he had declared that the romances taught us what our ancestors were, and history what they did; and that if we had to give up one or the other a choice would be difficult. In the famous review of *Old Mortality,* again, his most serious and systematic defense of his position, he maintained that an author who could recall "faithfully and strikingly" a bygone age produced "a composition in every point of view dignified and improved; and . . . leaving the light and frivolous associates with whom a careless observer would be disposed to ally him, takes his seat on the bench of the historians of his time and country." And a decade later, in reviewing Hoffmann's novels,[16] he had claimed for the historical novel if nobly done a place by the epic. He was not the person, however, to be continually asserting such a view, and remarks of this color are rare. Indeed, as far as the moral effect of novels in general was concerned, he had declared — in the early twenties when at the height of his fame (in his life of Fielding) — that while novels might "sometimes instruct the youthful mind by real pictures of life and sometimes awaken their better feelings and sympathies by strains of generous sentiment and tales of fictitious woe, beyond this point they are a

[13] Lockhart, V, 142.

[14] In his essay on the life of Kemble (1826) he specifically defends historical fiction as furnishing many readers with all their historical knowledge; they would never look at regular histories, and therefore the fiction serves a real purpose for them. *Quarterly Review,* 34:196 (June, 1826).

[15] *Edinburgh Review,* 7:387 (January, 1806).

[16] *Foreign Quarterly Review,* 1:60 (July, 1827).

mere elegance, a luxury contrived for the amusement of polished life."

Yet the historical impetus, the outlook of the historian writing to bring history to life for the reading public, is everywhere apparent. *Guy Mannering,* for instance, began as the tale of an individual frustrated in his attempts at good by the intervention of a malevolent character, and successful at the end only after a fearful struggle (as Scott says, like one of the tales of La Motte-Fouqué which he read later); but this plan was soon abandoned, and left traces of itself only in the first few chapters. The book developed into one of the most characteristically Scotch novels of the whole list, and Scott came to think of it as the second of a series of three depicting Scotch life in the second half of the eighteenth century. The prefaces to *Waverley* and *Guy Mannering* make it obvious, however, that such a conception of a series did not occur to him until he came to *The Antiquary*. But in the original preface to *The Antiquary* he said that he had emphasized here and in *Guy Mannering* characters of the peasantry, who had preserved their traditional quality and expressed themselves with less restraint than higher social orders. "I agree with my friend Wordsworth that they seldom fail to express [their feelings] in the strongest and most powerful language. . . . The antique force and simplicity of their language, often tinctured with the Oriental eloquence of Scripture, in the mouths of those of an elevated understanding, give pathos to their grief and dignity to their resentment." And, he adds, "I have been more solicitous to describe manners minutely, than to arrange in any case an artificial and combined narrative, and have but to regret that I felt myself unable to unite these two requisites of a good Novel." Surely he here betrays a higher aim than that of contriving "a mere elegance, a luxury for the amusement of polished life." Jeanie and David Deans in *The Heart of Midlothian* are certainly the center of that novel, and were created to show forth what Scott thought the finest traits of Scotch peasant character and to serve as an *amende* to the feelings wounded by *Old Mortality*.

Again in *The Monastery* he undertook to show the opposition in the Reformation of "a strong Catholic and an ardent Protestant," and in *Kenilworth* Elizabeth was the nucleus of the book, he says, as Queen Mary had been in *The Abbot*. So too in *The Pirate* he had been primarily concerned with the condition of society or state of civilization in the northern islands, and had tried to reconstruct it from a few hints and clues he had picked up on his voyage of 1814. In planning *Nigel,* as he wrote to Constable on September 30, 1821, the character of James I was the originating idea. "The next will be a tale I think of the days of *Gentle King Jemmy,* our Scottish Solomon — it is a pity that rare mixture of sense and nonsense, pedantry and childishness, wit and folly, should remain uncelebrated. He is attempted in the novel called Forman [by Abel Moysey] but not with a strong hand."[17] In *Nigel* he had wished to do over with George Heriot, a humble Scotch character, what he had done with Jeanie Deans, that is to present a hero in whom were substituted "worth of character, goodness of heart and rectitude of principle" for "high birth, romantic sensibility or any of the usual accomplishments of those who strut through the pages of this sort of composition." Much the same feeling comes out in the preface to *The Two Drovers,* one of the finest, if not the finest, of the shorter tales, where he again appeals to the sympathies through a humble Scotch hero. He laughs over the literary Highlanders who throng the pages of hack novels as thick "as at a Caledonian ball," and says he won't go back to the days of clans and claymores. "Have at you, gentle reader, with a tale of *Two Drovers*. An oyster may be crossed in love, says the gentle Tilburina, and a drover may be touched on a point of honor, says the Chronicler of the Canongate." His first idea of *Quentin Durward* is revealed in letters to his friend Daniel Terry, the actor, and to Morritt; "my idea is, *entre nous,* a Scotch archer in the French king's guard, *tempore* Louis XI, the most picturesque of all times."[18] Thus, time and again, does he make clear the historical and social nature of the

[17] Grierson, *Letters,* VII, 16.
[18] *Ibid.,* VII, 281, 308, November 10, 1822, and January 11, 1823.

ideas at the heart of his novels, and impress upon his readers his quality as a historian.

As a matter of fact, in the 1831 preface to *Peveril,* in the course of a defense of himself against charges of anachronism, he sketches the whole process of composition of one of his novels as he himself conceived it.

A poor fellow like myself, weary with ransacking his own barren and bounded imagination, looks out for some general subject in the huge and boundless field of history, which holds forth examples of every kind — lights on some personage, or some combination of circumstances, or some striking trait of manners, which he thinks may be advantageously used as a basis of fictitious narrative — bedizens it with such coloring as his skill suggests — ornaments it with such romantic circumstances as may heighten the general effect — invests it with such shades of character as will best contrast it with each other — and thinks, perhaps, he has done some service to the public, if he can present to them a lively fictitious picture, for which the original anecdote or circumstance which he made free to press into his service only furnished a slight sketch.

As a matter of fact, charges of historical inaccuracy in delineation of Scotch character were the only ones he was much concerned in refuting. The best illustration of this is the discussion of the Cameronians in the *Quarterly* and in the preface to *The Heart of Midlothian.* But in a preface to the third edition of *Waverley* he adduces many instances from actual life to refute charges against his portraits of the Highland character, and he takes pains to defend the realistic Scotch portraits in *St. Ronan's Well,* by declaring in answer to English critics, who he says pursued the book "with hue and cry," that they were perfectly recognizable to Scotch readers.[19] Again in the case of Norna, in *The Pirate,* he says frankly that she was a failure, but he is loath to accept the critical verdict against her, especially the charge that she was a mere imitation of Meg Merrilies. Still, true to his practical principles, he adds that doubtless if she had been suc-

[19] Lockhart (VII, 206) comes to Scott's defense with his own experience of riffraff seen at watering places both British and foreign. A later reader might add also Thackeray's sketches of similar types, especially in *The Newcomes.*

cessful she would not have had to be defended or explained. So too Scott refused to accept the general decision that Caleb Balderstone, in *The Bride of Lammermoor,* was a caricature, though he did admit that "he might have sprinkled rather too much parsley over his chicken."[20] On the other hand, once at any rate he takes such a charge lightly. Remarking in his 1831 preface to *Kenilworth* on the fact that the historian Robertson had attacked the portrait of Elizabeth as revealing Scotch prejudices, he simply says, "What so liberal a historian avows, a poor romance-writer dares not disown." And charges of mere anachronism of circumstance, which he regarded as within the special license of a romancer, he refused to worry about unduly. In the final preface to *Peveril* he says directly about general charges of anachronism, deviation from historical fact, and so forth, that the author of romances does have a right to indulgence; and in reply to "Mr. Mills, the author of the *History of Chivalry and the Crusades*," who had taken offence at Scott's creation of a female relative of Richard I, he says that the gentleman "was not, it may be presumed, aware that romantic fiction naturally includes the power of such invention, which is indeed one of the requisites of the art."[21] *Anne of Geierstein* was the only novel where he seemed to think he had really sinned in anachronism. He admits in his preface of 1831 that at the time of writing he had not had access to a suitable library, and proceeds not only to recount errors detected by Francis Palgrave but to add others to the list himself.

Perhaps the most striking characteristic of Scott's remarks on his novels is their practical nature, his calm acceptance of the public as a judge of his work and his analysis of the reasons for failure. The critics, as individuals, apart from the public voice, he was usually quite willing to disregard or to differ from; but the judgment of the public was final, and he accepted it readily,

[20] Lockhart, VI, 88.

[21] Scott wrote Mills (whom he calls Milne) an interesting letter in which he patiently explained to that scholar the difference between the use of actual sources and the literary device of inventing fictional sources for fictional material. Grierson, *Letters*, IX, 271.

with no repining. Certainly one would have to go far to find so engagingly frank a statement by an author of his own weaknesses and failings. About his calm dismissal of certain characters, episodes, or devices in the novels there was not the slightest trace of false modesty, nor on the other hand the morbid and unhappy sense of failure and futility that chronically oppressed Thackeray. In his view there had simply been a mistake, a bit of bad judgment, which he was able in most cases to analyze and explain.

The classic expression of his feeling about his own work and his relation with critics and public is of course in the preface to *Nigel,* written in 1822. In characteristically candid, straightforward utterance, he declares, "I care not who knows it, I write for general amusement, and though I will never aim at popularity by what I think unworthy means, I will not, on the other hand, be pertinacious in the defence of my own errors against the voice of the public." He proceeds, from a slightly different angle, to consider the faults urged against his work — the same, it may be noted, that he himself cited in the *Quarterly.* He admits that the plot is not admirable, that he cannot write to a careful plan ("all the quirks and quiddities that I might have devised for my reader's amusement would lie rotting in my gizzard") and implies that it is enough, and all that should be expected, if he has written a few good, unlabored scenes that do their duty with his readers. As for the "hasty huddling up" at the end, which he is told he ought to avoid for the sake of his reputation, he merely declares, "Let fame follow those who have a substantial shape," and denies that all the ingenuity of Adolphus, who had just demonstrated the authorship of Scott, can prove his identity.

Other charges of haste and carelessness he passes over lightly. He is told that respect for the public should induce him to take more pains with his story, but declares that he cannot waste time with the critics and thinks the public takes little account of an author himself, but only of his books. Besides, he insists that his best work and that too which has been praised as the most finished has been his fastest, that it is a case of striking while the iron is hot, that even when he has laid out an orderly plan for a book, its characters and incidents grow under his hand. "My regular mansion turns out a Gothic anomaly." Then too, when he strikes a good character, "a Bailie Jarvie or Dalgetty," he has to cut loose or he becomes "prosy, flat, and dull."[22]

Nor does he disdain to take notice of the charges of commercialism, which by now flew thick and fast. The laborer, he reminds his critics, is worthy of his hire; "as for my own emolument, it is won by my toil," and he may do with it as he will. He admits that an author should not write merely for gain, and believes that no work so written ever did succeed. Yet he calls it mere cant to insist that one should not think of his honorarium, and declares that even without money he should probably write as long as he pleased the public, for he has "felt as strongly as most folks the love of composition" and is not hypocrite enough to pretend to disdain the things money gives. The concurrent charge that he was running himself out in rapid commercial production he also faces calmly and serenely. He merely says that probably he will exhaust himself and that when he does the public will desert him and he will stop.

Yet he does not fear for the future or posterity. He does not believe that future generations will necessarily forget him or that "present favor necessarily infers future condemnation." The best authors, too, have been the most voluminous, and he hopes that some of his work will live; "it has often happened that those who have been best received in their own time have also continued to be acceptable to posterity" — again an engagingly characteristic point of view. Here is to be found the coolness and detachment toward his own work of which much has been made; but with it is a feeling of calm assurance that the best of his writing had the elements of permanence and that future generations would not forget his name entirely. This, to be sure, is not over-

---

[22] Writing to Maria Edgeworth through James Ballantyne in 1814, he had said that Rose in *Waverley* was less finished than he had intended to make her, but the humorous characters grew on him to the prejudice "of those of a more elevated and sentimental kind." Lockhart, IV, 405.

weening ambition, but it is not on the other hand the utter carelessness of fame and thought only for profit that too many critics have ascribed to him. Also important to notice is the definite crystallization of these charges against his work, not only by 1822 but even as early as January, 1817, when they were clear enough to draw answers or frank admissions from him in his review in the *Quarterly*. That is, such charges began to be made at once, from 1814 on, and were all of them oft-repeated old stories in the early twenties.

The remarks in the preface to *Nigel* are restated and supplemented in the 1831 preface to *Peveril*, where in reference to charges that he should have cut short his career as novelist with *Nigel*, he declares again that he did not care for mere fame, that he would have had to discover new tricks, and was too old a dog. He says again that he had decided to stop writing as soon as he learned from his public that his books were no longer wanted, and such a signal had not yet been given. Then too, he adds, no man recognizes or is willing to recognize his own failing powers.

Indeed, most of the ideas in the preface to *Nigel* are to be found reiterated elsewhere in prefaces, letters, or the journal. His belief that he himself must write fast, and that rapidity did not account for failure is to be found in his remark about *The Monastery,* his most important failure, that though not very interesting "it was written with as much care as the others, that is, with no care at all; and,

'If it is na weil bobbit, we'll bobb it again.' "[23]

Peveril he himself did not much care for. It was written under difficulties and done too slowly. As he told Morritt, the fourth volume "I wrote [under Ballantyne's prodding for more strength and spirit] in 14 days as much too fast as the others were too slow." Indeed, he tired of it "most damnably."[24] And here too one may cite his famous remark that the most admirable quality of his work was "a hurried frankness of composition which

[23] Lockhart, VI, 212.
[24] Grierson, *Letters*, VII, 308, January 11, 1823.

pleases soldiers, sailors, and young people of bold and active disposition."[25]

And of his relations with the public, and his feelings about posterity, he had written as early as 1808 to Miss Seward, "Let me please my own generation and let those who come after us judge of their taste and my performances as they please; the anticipation of their neglect or censure will affect me very little."[26] In the dark days of 1827 one finds him saying that he is "constitutionally indifferent to the censure or praise of the world," and that he has never given himself up to self-conceit and cares little if he loses his reputation; at least he has had the crown in his day.[27] Yet the next year he writes, as he is working on *Anne of Geierstein,* that he cannot bring himself to believe in the danger of not satisfying the public, though it is harder to satisfy himself.[28] One can have little doubt that in general Scott's attitude toward the public was a friendly, kindly, and respectful one. It had amply rewarded him to be sure, but still he seems to have believed in its tact and intuition and to have considered its judgments sound — far more reliable, in fact, than the critics'.

Yet in times of despondency and discouragement in his last years, struggling under the appalling millstone of his debts, he speaks with a contempt of the public worthy of the pure idealist.

[25] *Journal,* 212–13. Regarding his "hurried frankness," he could make such an astounding statement as that in a letter to David Laing, to whom he was sending some manuscript verses, "The enclosed is a *prima cura.* I never wrote anything over clean as it is called." Grierson, *Letters,* VIII, 407. Cf. also V, 477. He counted of course on the Ballantynes to check his own copy, as they continually did, while he himself read proof, and on occasion could take umbrage over so small a matter as a printer's error of *Paques deux* for *Paques Dieu,* the oath of Louis XI. See Grierson, *Letters,* VII, 346, March, 1823. But one cannot generalize from such a letter as that he wrote Lockhart about an article on Pepys for the *Quarterly.* The copy, he says, is totally uncorrected and must be very inaccurate, hence he must see the proofs. "Perhaps I have made it too long or introduced too many extracts — if so use the pruning knife, hedge hill or axe ad libitum. You know I do not care a curse about what I write or what becomes of it." This letter was written to Lockhart. Moreover its date, January 16, 1826, in the midst of the financial crisis, explains the depression of the last sentence. See Grierson, *Letters,* IX, 367.

[26] *Letters* (1894 edition), I, 125.

[27] *Journal,* pp. 495–96.

[28] *Ibid.,* p. 639.

He says for instance of his last two novels, those which "smelled of the apoplexy," "I am ashamed, for the first time in my life, of the two novels, but since the pensive public have taken them, there is no more to be said, but to eat my pudding and to hold my tongue."[29] There is also such a remark as, "I thank God I can write ill enough for the current taste, and will undertake to throw as much pepper into the pottage as will make them of the right leaven for the taste of this generation,"[30] and the equally pungent confession, "I have very little respect for that dear *publicum* whom I am doomed to amuse like Goody Trash in *Bartholomew Fair* with rattles and gingerbread; and I should deal very uncandidly with those who may read my confessions were I to say I knew a public worth caring for or capable of distinguishing the nicer beauties of composition. They weigh good and evil qualities by the pound. Get a good name and you may write trash. Get a bad one and you may write like Homer, without pleasing a single reader. I am, perhaps, *l'enfant gâté de succès*, but I am brought to the stake, and must perforce stand the course."[31] But such outbursts are easily to be explained by the clouds under which Scott was living. This had never been his habit of thought; rather he had believed cheerfully that it was for the writer to do his best, to submit to the public judgment as to the laws of nature, and "to stand the shuttlecock's fate."

Indeed all through his own remarks on the novels this practical and thoroughly realistic view is never really lost. He always from *Waverley* on took the public verdict as the real one, to be accepted as a matter of course, and then in the case of a failure proceeded to find the reasons for it. These remarks, however, taken together and not garbled, have nothing of the tone of the hack novelist — Scott wrote for money and was pleased by finan-

[29] *Ibid.*, p. 887, in a letter to Lockhart from Naples. He had earlier (page 875) confided to his journal, on learning of a satisfactory sale of these two novels, "And yet I think it is the public that are mad for passing those two volumes, but I will not be the first to cry them down in the market, for I have others in hand, which, judged with equal favour, will make fortunes of themselves."

[30] See Alexander Allardyce, ed., *Letters from and to Charles Kirkpatrick Sharpe, Esq.* (2 vols., Edinburgh, 1888), I, 352.

[31] *Journal*, p. 690.

cial success and applause, but as he himself says he also wrote *con amore*. He shows clearly (note his remarks on his imitators for instance) that he realized the great and distinguishing value of his immense stores of historical knowledge; he believed that his best work might well live for posterity; he had theories and general principles which mingle with and modify the tone of what might otherwise be merely the good-natured confidences of a hack writer. Indeed, it is less than a half truth, it is a sensational piece of superficiality, to say that Scott wrote for Abbotsford, as though he were no better than a climbing brewer or merchant.

Scott's first really disappointing novel was *The Monastery,* and his prefaces to it and its successor, *The Abbot,* reveal very well his attitude toward his work. The White Lady and Sir Piercie Shafton were the two great flaws. As he says, the one was denounced as unnatural, the other as impossible. Moreover, there was little to atone for them; "the incidents were inartificially huddled together," no part of the story was really interesting, and the catastrophe was motivated by external historical events about which the reader knew little. He admits that real life does not pursue a course of regular consistency amid an economical group of characters and that the older picaresque novels like *Gil Blas* and *Roderick Random* seem to take account of this fact, but that more than this is expected of the novelist, *vide Tom Jones.* Yet, he concludes, the book was not a total failure, judging from sales — "literary reputation is [seldom] gained by a single effort, and still more rarely is it lost by a solitary miscarriage."

The preface to *The Abbot* continues this theme. The sales of *The Monastery* had not been bad; in such matters there must be "leisure for the tide to ebb and flow." He declares that he had never valued abstract literary reputation greatly nor considered the novelist "high in the ranks of literature," and he emphasizes the "sincerity and candor" with which he had spoken on this subject, though in an imaginary character, in the preface to *Nigel.* Still, he had wished to try again and restore the reputation lost in *The Monastery.* He reasserts his belief that the most popu-

lar authors had been the most prolific. Despite occasional failures
they had succeeded, and the public realized only at their death
what they had accomplished. There is a general assumption, he
says, as Voltaire's case shows, that an author must decline, that
his successive works must gradually sink; thus there is a public
prejudice which an author can hope to overcome only "by patience and exertion." And the writer, if fearful, may retire, seeking to save what he already has; but in the long run he will stand
higher if "he keeps his ground and stands the shuttlecock's fate."
Thus, in *The Abbot* he returned to the attack, taking courage
from his incognito, and proceeded to write a sequel, omitting the
various unsuccessful elements of *The Monastery*. Here too, he
realized that he was taking a chance. He knew, he says, that it
was easy to capture the public by advertising a tale about a
popular figure like Alfred or Elizabeth, and that this satisfied the
bookseller, though it had serious repercussions for the author if
he failed to live up to his promise. Still, he felt that a story about
Mary Stuart should be within his powers and ought to win back
the public easily.

In other instances too Scott showed the utmost willingness to
recognize defects in this novel or that. *St. Ronan's Well,* he wrote
in the 1832 preface, had not had its just due from the English,[32]
but he admitted that it was not the best subject for him; his way
of life had brought him little into such a setting, and "the con-
sequence perhaps was that the characters wanted that force and
precision which can only be given by a writer familiarly acquainted with his subject." He had indeed earlier expressed dissatisfaction with *St. Ronan's Well*. While revising it for a new
edition he wrote that he thought the language "rather good,"
but that "the fashionable portraits are not the true thing. I am

[32] Of *Nigel* he had written to James Ballantyne that it "deserves a better
reception from the public, and like the Antiquary will one day get it." See
Grierson, *Letters,* VII, 278, November 8, 1822. The letters contain several other
interesting brief assertions of confidence in this or that novel. He expected
great things of *The Heart of Midlothian. Ibid.,* V, 13, 50, November 10, 1817,
and January 14, 1818. And just as he expected a great recovery from *The Monastery* in *The Abbot,* he hoped that *Quentin Durward* would win back ground
lost in *Peveril. Ibid.,* VII, *passim,* early 1823.

too much out of the way to see and remark the ridiculous in society. The story is terribly contorted and unnatural, and the catastrophe is melancholy,[33] which should always be avoided."[34] And of *The Betrothed,* which is perhaps the weakest of the whole series, he explains that in his ignorance of the period and setting he was "as thickly wrapped as an Egyptian in his fog," while many of his contemporaries were as well informed "as if they had been inhabitants of the favored land of Goshen." Hence his avoidance of the real subject in *The Betrothed,* which he compares to *Hamlet* with Hamlet omitted. Hence too his attempt in *The Talisman* to avoid settings and characters that might challenge comparisons with the better informed Orientalists among his colleagues.[35] When he came to *Count Robert* and *Castle Dangerous* the case was different. Lockhart tells the distressing story of Sir Walter's tortured labors over these novels, but Sir Walter himself speaking as Jedediah Cleishbotham merely says that the manuscripts, though cast aside for some time as in a condition not fit for the press, still contained passages to show that "severe indisposition had been unable to extinguish altogether the brilliancy of that fancy which the world had been pleased to acknowledge in the creations of *Old Mortality, The Bride of Lammermoor,* and others of those narratives." The preface ends with a plea for indulgence and consideration.[36]

[33] He wrote Lady Louisa Stuart of *The Abbot* that "the mournful termination is certainly an objection to the general reader and may hurt its popularity"; and to Mrs. Hughes, who was not in the secret of his authorship, concerning *Kenilworth,* "I could have wished the author had chosen a more heroical death for his fair victim." While working on *Quentin Durward* he was humorously concerned over the death of Louis XI, who actually died in great torment, and told Ballantyne, "I will perhaps employ the next three volumes in killing him my own way." Grierson, *Letters,* VI, 311, 384; VII, 344.

[34] *Journal,* p. 231.

[35] Final preface to *The Talisman.*

[36] There is an interesting criticism, though private, in a letter to Morritt on *Rob Roy:* "I trust you have read Rob by this time. I did not much write him *con amore,* and I think he smells of the cramp as the Bishop of Grenadas sermon did of the Apoplexy. Above all I had too much flax on my distaff and as it did not consist with my patience or my plan to make a fourth volume I was obliged at last to draw a rough, coarse, and hasty thread." This is a reference of course to one of his worst cases of "huddled up" plots. See Grierson, *Letters,* V, 50, January 14, 1818. The letters continually remind one how often Scott wrote

Equally frank are the explanations of various other details in the history of the novels. The whole story of the *Waverley* manuscript, the lesson of *Queenhoo Hall*, the language of which was addressed too often to antiquarians to suit the general public, the presentation of *Waverley* as an anonymous speculation, the continuance of anonymity without solid reason but merely as a whim, all these serve still further to illuminate both the character of the author and the books themselves.

Especially significant is the search for new fields, the desire for variety. In his final preface to *Ivanhoe* he admits that he forsook the Scotch matter for fear of exhausting his material, boring his readers, and getting the name of a mannerist. And, he adds, the experiment was so successful that he had never hesitated since to venture outside Scotland whenever he wished. In the same way in *St. Ronan's Well* he chose a domestic subject for its novelty and out of fear that he might exhaust his regular field. Again, in the *Tales of the Crusaders* the choice of subject was not to his own taste but was made on the advice of friends, once more for the sake of novelty. Here too he felt as he had in *The Abbot;* the subject was a good one, but the interest while easy to excite was harder to satisfy.[37] Or the search for novelty may even reveal itself in a conception of character in an unusual, startling light, as in the case of Conachar[38] in *The Fair Maid of Perth*, where he decided to show the tragedy of "the brave coward or cowardly brave man" instead of the more obvious comedy, despite his pre-

while suffering from attacks of the "cramp," really gallstones. From *Rob Roy* on, he continually fears that this or that may smell of the cramp or the apoplexy, and there is frequent reference to the heroic remedies of his physicians, especially in the way of laudanum and calomel. Under the nervous strain of financial difficulty after 1825 the condition was terrifically aggravated. Early in 1826 there were days when he could neither write nor spell, and from then on the "apoplexy" progressed in good earnest.

[37] See the prefaces to these novels in the collected edition.

[38] Very few modern critics seem especially familiar with *The Fair Maid of Perth* and the character of Conachar. Balzac declared that no one but Scott would have risked him and that he himself wished to do such a character on a grander scale. See R. H. Gordon, *op. cit*. E. A. Baker in Volume VI of his *History of the Novel* (London, 1935) offers such characters as Conachar, Clara Mowbray, and Redgauntlet as proof that Scott's psychology was becoming deeper and more complicated in his later novels.

monitions that James Ballantyne would not approve so unortho-
dox a treatment.[39] "But what can one do? I am hard up as far as
imagination is concerned, yet the world calls for novelty." In
this case the search for novelty resulted in a highly original character, called by Senior "perfectly tragic," more complicated psy-
chologically than usual, and indeed worked out with the deepest
feeling as a kind of expiation of his earlier harshness toward his
black sheep brother Daniel.[40] But in general the effects of the
search for novelty were not so happy. Ideally, Sir Walter should
have stuck to the Scotch ground; despite their success, the *Ivanhoe's* never rose to the level of the *Old Mortality's*. This is clear
enough now; it was clear to good critics in his own day; but the
very nature of his genius called for continuous activity, and that
seemed both to him and his advisers to imply the novelty of new
characters and new settings.[41]

[39] Scott's deference to the prudent judgment of James Ballantyne and Constable
has frequently been held against him. That he continually had suggestions, from
Ballantyne especially, the letters make perfectly clear. Sometimes he accepted,
sometimes refused them; occasionally, as in the most important case, the story
of Clara Mowbray in *St. Ronan's Well*, he yielded after a fight. In regard to a
bit of unfavorable criticism by "J. B." he wrote him, on November 11, 1824,
that he thought he could find a remedy, "but I greatly doubt your recipe," and
perhaps Constable was right in suggesting a season of fallow. He assured
Ballantyne, however, that he valued frank and candid criticism highly and that
he thought his opinion, though fastidious in some trifling matters, was always
authoritative on general effects. See Grierson, *Letters*, VIII, 416. Writing to
Constable about the somewhat discouraging sale of *Quentin Durward*, he asked,
"Has it diminished your general confidence in this sort of literature?" and
promised not to be vexed or angry at a candid reply. *Ibid.*, VIII, 76. He wisely
accepted Ballantyne's suggestion of the title *Redgauntlet* instead of his own
notion of "Herries," but he merely laughed at Constable's palpably commercial
idea of calling *The Monastery* "The Nunnery." *Ibid.*, VIII, 203; VI, 145. Yet he
would not yield to Ballantyne's fear of encroaching on what seemed to be
Mrs. Radcliffe's field. *Ibid.*, IX, 403. In the case of *St. Ronan's Well* he did
finally agree to tone down the dangerous story of Clara Mowbray's secret love
affair, but he wrote, "you would never have quarrelled with it, had the thing
happened to a girl in gingham; the silk petticoat can make little difference."
For both his original and revised versions, see the *Athenaeum*, February 4, 1893,
pp. 154–55. Cf. also Lockhart, VII, 208–09. His action here is quite like Hardy's
bowdlerizing of Eustacia Vye for the magazine public. Other instances of Ballantyne's advice are noted elsewhere.

[40] *Journal*, p. 492, and Lockhart, IX, 222.

[41] Still another good illustration of the search for novelty, also against the
advice of "J. B.," comes as Scott is working on *The Highland Widow*. He

After all, where could one go for a more just and lucid statement of the excellences and defects of Scott's method than to these comments of his own? And where will one get better clues to the personal qualities that strengthened so greatly his hold on his public? His dictum that readers thought little of an author, but only of his books, surely did not hold in his case — the man and the books were too much one.

thinks the tale in his "bettermost manner," "but J. B. roars for chivalry. He does not quite understand that everything may be overdone in this world, or sufficiently estimate the necessity of novelty. The Highlanders have been off the field now for some time." *Journal*, p. 222, July, 1826.

Of course the motive in the search for novelty was the maintenance of public interest. Yet in one case at any rate Scott was pleasing himself and gratifying a wish for change and variety. He dropped his work on *The Monastery* and took up *Ivanhoe*. He wrote Lady Louisa Stuart on August 23, 1819 (Grierson, *Letters*, V, 474) that he was doing this and that *Ivanhoe* "is a great amusement to me." He was also playing with the idea of having the two novels published by different houses and in different formats for a highly characteristic reason: "I am rather curious to know if I can be detected in both instances." See also Lockhart, VI, 188, February, 1820. As Lockhart and Sir Walter were walking together, "He talked without reserve of the novel of the *Monastery*, of which he had the first volume with him; and mentioned, what he had probably forgotten when he wrote the Introduction of 1830, that a good deal of that volume had been composed before he concluded *Ivanhoe*. 'It was a relief,' he said, 'to interlay the scenery most familiar to me with the strange world for which I had to draw so much on imagination.'"

CHAPTER III

REVIEWS IN THE EDINBURGH, THE QUARTERLY, AND BLACKWOOD'S

AMONG SCOTT'S contemporaries his most important reviewer, book by book, was doubtless Jeffrey, whose love for
the romances has already been noted. The magisterial pages of
the *Edinburgh* were deemed above the trivialities of the novel,
but in 1814 when *Waverley* suddenly delighted the world, the
Edinburgh and Jeffrey at last found a novel worthy not only of
attention but of high praise. The book was declared, in spite of
certain patent defects in style and management, to be the work
of genius and fit to "take its place rather with the most popular
of our modern poems, than with the rubbish of provincial romances."[1]

Its greatest excellence, the editor maintained, lay in the Scottish minor characters, and the impressions of Scotch life which
they establish. Jeffrey recognizes too the historical import of the
novel; its object of presenting "a faithful and animated picture
of the manners and state of society that prevailed . . . in the
earlier part of last century," and its success in reproducing the
contrasts in Scotch character which the world had forgotten until
"the '45" itself had brought them out so startlingly — "the wild
but brilliant picture of the devoted valour, incorruptible fidelity,
patriarchal brotherhood, and savage habits, of the Celtic Clans,
on the one hand — and the dark, intractable, and domineering
bigotry of the Covenanters on the other."

Here at the very beginning, then, in Jeffrey one finds a judg-

[1] Jeffrey's reviews of the novels are all to be found in his *Contributions to the Edinburgh Review*.

ment that has been confirmed by the most sure-footed and well-poised of the later critics — a just and clear recognition of the author's true sources of distinction — while at the same time the novelty and brilliance of the new work failed to blind him to defects that in the course of time have come to be emphasized more and more. For some time Jeffrey took note of all Scott's novels, reviewing them separately or in groups after a lapse of two or three years.

In his second article, in 1817, on *Tales of My Landlord,* he came out still more nobly in praise of the "Great Unknown," to him actually unknown of course only by courtesy. He declared that there was no name to which these novels would not add luster and pointed out their good sense, good nature, powerful fancy, and vigorous intellect, in unusual conjunction with a deep human sympathy. He found here creative power recalling Shakespeare. Also, there are phrases of an odd sound in modern ears, which have heard so often that Scott is slow and ponderous —"narrative kept constantly full of life, variety, and colour; and so interspersed with glowing descriptions and lively allusions and flying traits of sagacity and pathos, as not only to keep our attention continually awake, but to afford a pleasing exercise to most of our other faculties." Yet this was the effect the novels made on their original readers; plenty of reviewers echo it.

Jeffrey's moral point of view is equally foreign in some respects to modern ones. He declares that the author's most remarkable, and perhaps his most delightful talent is that of representing "kindness of heart in union with lightness of spirits and great simplicity of character, and of blending (like Burns) the expression of warm and generous and exalted affections with scenes and persons that are in themselves both lowly and ludicrous." It is very honorable in the author too that his dominant interest is in the Moral — in the amiableness of his characters. Thus he has no misanthropy, no sarcasm, satire, or bitterness or fierceness of resentment, but is all indulgence, and relenting — quite unlike the intolerant "Laureates and Lakers," whose weaknesses become fully apparent when they are compared with the author of

Waverley. What modern novelist could hope to appeal to a critic of Jeffrey's position on such a basis?

Jeffrey makes here another point, however, which the modern friendly critic of Scott delights to emphasize; that, though in politics a Tory ("and, we are afraid, something of a latitudinarian both in morals and religion") he should have succeeded so surprisingly with the lower classes, showing them as human beings with subtle and complicated motives. He is still of the opinion that the great distinction of the novels lies first in the delineation of homely Scotch characters, who come out on the page as complete human beings — Dandie Dinmont, he says, is the best rustic portrait ever exhibited to the public — and next "in the delineation of the grand and gloomy aspects of nature, and of the dark and fierce passions of the heart." Above all he sees the author as national and Scottish, another point that in the light of its emphasis in later criticism is highly important.

But here too as in *Waverley* certain faults cannot be denied. The greatest Jeffrey finds to be the "virtuous young ladies," who are unnecessarily tame and mawkish. Nor does he approve of Pleydell, "a harsh caricature," or Dirk Hatteraick, nor very much of Meg Merrilies, who seems to him too fantastic, too "poetical," too far from the solid realities of common life that he consistently admires as the greatest of all values in the novels. He considers that the author is often betrayed into "forced and vulgar exaggerations" and that he succumbs to the temptation to overwork his most striking and highly colored characters, and to hold them too long on the stage. In *The Antiquary* he thinks the title character himself the great blemish on the work, and, like most later critics, finds him especially wearisome at the opening, that is, of course, while Sir Walter is getting his bearings. He also refuses more than qualified approval to Edie Ochiltree, whom many have thought one of Scott's most inspired characters; like Meg Merrilies he is too "poetical." But, "the family of the fisherman is an exquisite group throughout; and at the scene of the funeral, in the highest degree striking and pathetic."

On *The Black Dwarf* Jeffrey wastes little time, but goes on soon to *Old Mortality*. On the more purely artistic side Jeffrey is not especially enthusiastic; too many of the characters, though excellent, seem to parallel more or less closely those of *Waverley*. His interest really is in the historical aspect of the novel. What he appreciates above all else is Scott's historical sense of the currents of common life. The public life of this period, the later seventeenth century, he says, was very black; it was a time of corrupt and despotic government. Yet the novel shows how private life runs on much the same as ever, how "few men, in short, are historic characters." The true end of history, he goes on, is to reveal the state of the common man, and it is the great merit of the novel that it does so. As for the charges brought by the Presbyterians against the book, Jeffrey is definitely on the author's side, defending the Biblical language and profanity on dramatic grounds and truth to life, and insisting that a fair balance is maintained between the hostile factions. Though the author shows the ridiculous side of the sectaries, he also invests them with fine virtues; nor does he palliate the faults of the royalists; their bloodthirsty persecution and cruelty, their resort to torture, make the blood boil.

The next year *Rob Roy* is favored with a separate review. Jeffrey declares it not so good as the earlier novels, but still, better than anything else of the sort. He now makes the point that it is "not in his story that this author's strength lies," and implies that he thinks no better of the heroes than the heroines. Diana Vernon, a heroine whom most critics treat more kindly than Scott's other young ladies, he says is "extremely elegant and fascinating" but at the same time absolutely impossible, a conclusion that few will doubt. Again it is the common characters that catch his eye, especially Nicol Jarvie and Andrew Fairservice. The first, he says, is "an inimitable picture of an acute, sagacious, upright and kind man, thoroughly low bred and beset with all sorts of vulgarities," and "both he and Andrew are rich mines of the true Scottish language."

Two years later he reviews *Ivanhoe* and the collected novels. Again, comparison with Shakespeare: there has been "no such prodigy of fertility" since Shakespeare; "the novels render conceivable to this later age the miracles of the Mighty Dramatist." Though he would not put the novelist on a level with Shakespeare for his qualities of original genius — no author is fit for that honor — he has enough of the same qualities, Jeffrey maintains, so that for the first time in two hundred years such a comparison can be made without being ridiculous. And again also criticism that is as acceptable today as when it was written: *The Heart of Midlothian* is comparatively languid; the Porteous mob is heavy, and George Staunton extravagant and unpleasing, the catastrophe improbable and startling, and the Saddletrees and David Deans tedious by the end of the story (there has always been a wide divergence of opinion on the merits of David Deans), hardly acceptable substitutes for the generous and kind rustics so typical of the author. Yet on the other hand the trial and the scenes with Argyle are greatly to be admired, and Jeanie is the boast of the book, perhaps the greatest of all the author's exploits. She is, he says, "in the highest degree both pathetic and sublime; and yet she never says or does any one thing that the daughter of a Scotch cowfeeder might not be supposed to say . . . she is never sentimental, nor refined nor elegant," and though she shines in difficult situations, she seems to act merely with a natural good sense quite characteristic of many in her station. *The Bride of Lammermoor* too has greatness to save it from its weaknesses. The absurdly exaggerated poverty of the hero and the characters of Caleb and Sir William Ashton are weak points, but Ailsie is exquisite, the witches as a group even surpass those in *Macbeth,* and the whole has the tone of "deep pathos and genuine tragic interest." For the character of Dalgetty in *Montrose* too he has the highest praise, including comparisons with Shakespeare, though with the reservation that there is too much of Dalgetty, whereas Shakespeare never exhausts his Pistols or Falstaffs — praise which Sir Walter quotes with pride in his final preface to *Montrose*.

In the case of *Ivanhoe* especially Jeffrey catches the point and arrives at conclusions that have been echoed frequently ever since. Though doubtless the most broadly popular of all the novels, *Ivanhoe* has never had the support of the critics. The author, Jeffrey says, has been reduced to the vulgar staple of armed knights, jolly friars, serfs and fools, though he has at times given these theatrical creatures the illusion of humanity.[2] Moreover, he believes that the brilliance of *Ivanhoe* is allied more properly to that of the earlier poems than to the realities of prose, which he says he prefers "whether in meter or out of it." He admits that when he comes upon such characters he cannot follow their drift; "we soon feel not only that [they] are contrary to our experience, but that they are actually impossible." It is the situations, he says, not the characters, that hold our interest, and declares that after watching the pageant for a time we turn again to "our Waverleys and Antiquaries and Old Mortalities."[3]

Jeffrey's disappointment with *Ivanhoe* did not abate at the appearance of the novels that followed. He considered *The Monastery* and *The Abbot* the least meritorious of the whole series so far, and condemned the White Lady, the alabaster cavern, and Sir Piercie Shafton as very bad. *Kenilworth* he called a "flight of another wing" and thought it rose almost to the level of *Ivanhoe*, though it was still of an inferior type in that its effect was secured

[2] Compare the remarks of an obscure writer in the *United States Literary Gazette*, 2:401 (September 1, 1825). In reviewing the *Tales of the Crusaders* he speaks of the unconvincing qualities of characters of another age as constructed by a novelist. Macbeth he says is a human being of any age and in any costume, but the characters here are of very doubtful probability, even if one is not antiquarian enough to check them up.

[3] In a footnote (*op. cit.*, iii, 481) Jeffrey speaks with delight of the quotations from "Old Plays" at the heads of chapters, and says he takes it for granted that they are original — as of course they are for the most part. Scott wrote Constable an amusing letter on this subject: "It is odd to say but nevertheless it is quite certain that I do not know whether some of the things are original or not, and I wish you would devise some way of stating this in the title. The author of *Waverley* finding it inconvenient to toss over books for a motto generally made one without much scrupling whether it was positively and absolutely his own or botched up out of pieces and fragments of poetry floating in his memory. But this would have an awkward effect if he was supposed to found merit on them as original." See Grierson, *Letters*, VII, 104, March 23, 1822. For a contemporary investigation of the incidental poetry quoted in the novels, see the *Retrospective Review*, 2d series, 1:16 (1827).

by brilliant scenes and situations. Elizabeth, however, he thought a great success, and he was surprised to discover that "upholstery and millinery could be made so engaging" and could so heighten the effect of Amy herself. But Leicester seemed weak and he found altogether too much of Michael Lambourne, Varney, Foster, and Alasco — all of whom he thought savored far too strongly of the "demoniacal character" and the atmosphere of the Newgate Calendar. And of Amy's death he declared that it was too sickening and pitiful to be endured. Here of course Jeffrey showed a distaste for the sensational crime and romanticized low life which was soon to become a vogue in fiction, pouring money into the pockets of Harrison Ainsworth, Bulwer, Dickens, and many others.

For *The Pirate* he could say still less. It was full of minor blemishes, but suffered a greater blot in the deeply inconsistent character of Cleveland; in fact the author seemed to have changed his design in the course of the work. Most of the other characters he dismisses as failures or inferior instances of earlier types. Yet he can praise the book as showing in general the pliability and vigor of the author's genius. *The Fortunes of Nigel* pleased him better. Though the characters were not varied or the story interesting, being merely a series of sketches, weak and incoherent, the book was valuable as a sketch of the manners of the period, though not of its real life. It was based, Jeffrey thought, too much on the rather fantastical pictures in the Stuart plays, which reveal superficial extravagances and peculiarities rather than the common realities of life. The only real individuals were King James and Richard Moniplies. But after all (like *The Pirate*) it bore the impression of Scott's genius and demonstrated his ease and force, his brilliancy and spirit.

Scott continued to produce romances for another decade, but Jeffrey reviewed no more of them. His favorite of the lot was *Waverley*. He was attracted almost exclusively by the realistic Scotch character and was thrilled by the Scottish nationalism of the earlier works. It is not difficult to guess that with Scott's lapse from this field into the theatricality of *Ivanhoe* and *Kenilworth*

Jeffrey's interest ebbed, until, after *Nigel,* he found it better to leave the later novels alone. Certainly, taking his comments on *Ivanhoe* into account, one may guess at his judgment of *Woodstock* or *Count Robert of Paris.* Here again his attitude is in line with that of the main body of later critics, for it has become a mere critical commonplace to prefer the earlier novels with their Scotch matter to the later ones. But among contemporary reviewers, Jeffrey saw the truth more clearly and sharply than anyone else except Hazlitt, and illustrated it more consistently and with more acutely chosen and specific details.

The *Quarterly,* like the *Edinburgh,* noticed all the Waverley novels for many years. The first three, *Waverley, Guy Mannering,* and *The Antiquary,* were reviewed as they came out by Croker in papers that add little glory to him or the periodical. Lukewarm and cautious, they show little understanding or appreciation of the newly revealed genius which Jeffrey had rushed to meet with open arms, but take refuge only too often in pointing out the faults and weaknesses which it required no great critical acumen to recognize. Of these reviews, Lockhart said,[4] having just praised Jeffrey's *Edinburgh* essays, they "will bear the test of ultimate opinion as badly as any critical pieces which our time has produced. They are written in a captious, cavilling strain of quibble which shows as complete blindness to the essential interest of the narrative as the critic betrays on the subject of the Scottish dialogue which forms its liveliest ornament." And when some of the later novels were entrusted to Nassau Senior (according to Lockhart, "a critic second to few") Lockhart fancied that Gifford was convinced that he had made a grievous mistake in the matter of the first three reviews.[5]

[4] Lockhart, IV, 404.

[5] See Lockhart, VI, 423. For a modern expression of the same nature see Professor Seccombe's essay on *Guy Mannering* in the *Times Literary Supplement,* January 21, 1915, where he cites Andrew Lang on the subject. Poole's *Index* ascribes these reviews to Gifford himself, and Lockhart's second comment might be taken to imply Gifford's authorship, but Croker's biographers definitely claim the doubtful honor for him. See L. J. Jennings, ed., *The Croker Papers* (3 vols., London, 1884), I, 93; also Walter Graham, *Tory Criticism in the Quarterly Review* (New York, 1921), pp. 50, 51.

Of the first three novels Croker [6] put *Waverley* far and away at the head, with *Guy Mannering* well beneath it, and *The Antiquary* winging a middle flight between. His review of *Waverley* is typical of the old-fashioned, formal, ponderous essay. It opens with a résumé of the history of the novel form, which is traced from the older, and according to Croker, original type, where "heroes all generosity and ladies all chastity, exalted above the vulgarities of society and nature, maintain through eternal folios their visionary virtues, without the stain of any moral frailty or the degradation of any human necessities." A second stage he finds to be revealed in the characters of Gil Blas and Tom Jones, who stand as type specimens of the human race. The present age has gone, Croker says, beyond this generic description to show us "men of a peculiar nation, profession, or temper, or, to go a step further — *individuals.*" The older type he finds comparable to the pictures of Raphael, Correggio, or Murillo; the new can aspire only to the level of Teniers or Gerard Dow. Yet, he hastens to add, though they are not sublime, he likes the modern type and would not have Miss Edgeworth or the author of *Waverley* undervalued. They are "less comprehensive and less sublime — but not less entertaining or less useful. . . . We do not believe that any man or woman was ever improved in morals or manners by the reading of *Tom Jones* or *Peregrine Pickle,* though we are confident that many have profited by the *Tales of Fashionable Life* and the *Cottagers of Glenburnie.*"

How far Croker missed fire, not only in his estimate of Scott but of Miss Edgeworth, one sees in his contention that *Waverley,* called a Scotch *Castle Rackrent,* is, though similar in matter, actually on a higher level and "may be safely placed far above the amusing vulgarity of *Castle Rackrent,* and by the side of *Ennui* or *The Absentee,* the best undoubtedly of Miss Edgeworth's compositions." Miss Edgeworth, it may be seen, had her full meed of praise in her own time, though Jane Austen did not.

[6] Croker's reviews in the *Quarterly* appeared as follows: *Waverley,* 11:354 (July, 1814); *Guy Mannering,* 12:501 (January, 1815); *The Antiquary,* 15:125 (April, 1816).

The bulk of Croker's long review is given over to very full quotations, chiefly, it must be allowed, to illustrate the Scotch quality of the novel. In concluding his analysis he declares, "Waverley . . . is far from being its hero, and in truth the interest and merit of the work is derived, not from any of the ordinary qualities of a novel, but from the truth of its facts and the accuracy of its delineations." If this may perhaps be taken in Croker's favor, what is to be said of his final dictum? "We confess that we have, speaking generally, a great objection to what may be called historical romance, in which real and fictitious personages and actual and fabulous events are mixed together to the utter confusion of the reader and the unsettling of all accurate recollections of past transactions, and we cannot but wish that the ingenious and intelligent author of *Waverley* had rather employed himself in recording *historically* the character and transactions of his countrymen *Sixty Years Since,* than in writing a work which, though it may be, in its facts, almost true, and in its delineations perfectly accurate, will yet in sixty years *hence* be regarded, or rather probably, *disregarded* as a *mere* romance, and the gratuitous invention of a facetious fancy."

Croker's strictures on the style and organization of *Guy Mannering* have already been noticed. Indeed, he was unable to find much good to say of it in other respects. Its inferiority to *Waverley* was, he thought, due chiefly to its less spirited setting and characters, and he was offended by what seemed to his jaundiced taste the vulgar slang and dialect of the realistic characters. It is notable that he failed to appreciate Dandiē Dinmont as did Jeffrey. He disliked too the use of astrology in a story of the late eighteenth century (with prophecies even coming true!) and he found Pleydell a terrible bore. Yet he has to confess after all his growling that he has read the book with interest and amusement. *The Antiquary* pleased him better. Here, as in *Guy Mannering,* he objected to the supernatural and considered the story itself neither novel nor probable. In other respects, however, he found *The Antiquary* successful, its great merit being that its characters were *men*. He also quoted long passages to illustrate various high qualities: the author's power of fine description in the scene where Sir Arthur and Miss Wardour are caught by the tide, his skill in dialect, and his reality in dealing with human character. In spite of adverse criticism in detail, the review is practically all in terms of high praise. On the other hand, taking the novels as a sequence designed to present society in three successive periods, he thought them a failure, since, he said, the author had established no real and sharp distinctions between epochs. This criticism is hardly valid; Scott is obviously presenting these novels in historical sequence, but that he wished to illustrate any sharp social changes that had taken place during the later eighteenth century is not at all clear. Indeed his own prefaces in the collected edition show that the genesis of the first two novels in his own mind had nothing to do with any such scheme, though the possibility of it did become apparent to him when he came to *The Antiquary*.[7] Altogether these reviews, distinctly inferior in their acumen, are of far less interest than Jeffrey's, as perhaps one might expect.

The next *Quarterly* review, in the issue of January, 1817, was Scott's own essay on *Old Mortality*, which has already been described. Hereafter the *Quarterly* was silent on the novels until 1821, when it published a long review by Nassau Senior [8]

[7] Interesting light is thrown on the feeling in 1810 toward the period of 1750 — "Sixty Years Since"— by a letter of that date from James Ballantyne to Scott, when the original fragment of *Waverley* had just been submitted to him. He felt that there was too much antiquity in the character of Waverley. Really 1750, he said, was a modern period, with Johnson writing and Garrick acting and "our fathers alive and merry," and nothing altered, beyond the cut of a coat. Lockhart, III, 300.

[8] Senior (1790–1864) was primarily a political economist of the school of Malthus and Riccardo. He was regarded as being more liberal and having more common, practical sense than many of his colleagues in the dismal science, though at present some of his arguments seem rather startling. At any rate he became very eminent and was the chief expert in the government report leading to the Poor Law of 1834. He was widely acquainted among literary people and was interested in literature. He wrote the review of *Vanity Fair* for the *Edinburgh* as also its review of *Uncle Tom's Cabin*, which in the 1850's was treated with the utmost reverence. See the *Dictionary of National Biography*.

of the intervening novels from *Rob Roy* to *Kenilworth,* and then separate articles by the same writer on *The Pirate* and *The Fortunes of Nigel.* The first essay seems originally to have had a preamble of some eight pages on the general nature of the novels, which was cut by the editor but reprinted by Senior when he collected his literary essays in 1864. In this deleted opening Senior commented on the firmly fixed popularity of the novels, called them "the most striking literary phenomena of the age," and cited the attractions to which various critics had ascribed their popularity — the descriptions, the characters, the pathos and humor, the pure morality. Senior himself ascribes it to the successful union of "the most irreconcilable forms and the most opposite materials. . . . tragedy and the romance, comedy and the novel" — a contention which he elaborates in great detail and with academic profundity, but which apparently failed to impress the editor, though it was true enough and had in its essentials been remarked upon before — by Jeffrey, for instance.

He then proceeds to examine the series of novels under review. Though a professed admirer of the author, of whom he speaks in terms of high reverence always, he emphasizes the weakness of the plots, the slow and tiresome openings, the insipid heroes and the tiresome bores. In analyzing the characters his judgment seems to be excellent, and his exaltation of *The Heart of Midlothian* and *The Bride of Lammermoor* above the others of the group would be acceptable to the later critic. It is notable, on the other hand, that he does not seem to realize clearly that Scott was working in a different *genre* when he wrote *Ivanhoe* and the other romances. Senior admits that a second reading of *Ivanhoe* shook his original faith in the book, and his remarks on *Kenilworth* show that he felt the melodramatic and stagy qualities of this type; but he nowhere strikes the nail on the head as Jeffrey had when he pointed out with damaging clarity what Scott had done in deserting his own Scotland for the meretricious appeals of a false antiquity. It is perhaps worth noting that Senior is fairly liberal in the matter of Scott's juggling with history. He speaks for instance of the "pleasing anachronism" of Shakespeare in *Kenilworth* and is in general tolerant of such rearrangements, though he does, with some propriety indeed, object to wide deviations from fact when such well-known characters as Leicester are involved.

Senior's reviews of *The Pirate* and *Nigel* are distinctly less favorable in tone, especially the latter; in both he again attacks the weakness of plot construction, the disappointing heroes and the insufferable bores. Though he finds many details in description and character to praise in *The Pirate,* he calls it inferior to most of the other novels, and is especially severe on the character of Cleveland, which changes with what seems to him a shifting of the writer's whole plan of the novel. Of *Nigel* he says at the end, "In dramatic power and in delineation of character it is equal to anything our author has written" — surely praise that is little justified — but goes on to declare that the "obscurity and improbability of the fable, the uninterestingness of all the actors, excepting the King, and the harassing, or degrading or painful nature of the scenes through which we follow the hero" place it beneath the other novels. Here Senior betrays a preoccupation with moral purity and propriety which was to wax into its full glory a generation later. Indeed he assumes a thoroughly Victorian air of superiority when in objecting to the Alsatian scenes of debauchery, he declares that their only artistic merit can be one of resemblance (one thinks of the modern photographic novelists) which he himself cannot judge; such scenes "excite neither our sympathy nor our curiosity."

Senior reprinted in his collection of 1864 [9] another group review written in 1829 for the *London Review,* a journal which according to Lockhart [10] had a life of only two or three issues. While maintaining his high regard for Sir Walter, still the greatest man of the age, Senior clearly feels the falling off of the last period. For *Peveril of the Peak, Quentin Durward, St. Ronan's Well, Woodstock,* and *The Fair Maid of Perth* he has

[9] *Essays on Fiction* (London, 1864). Note the review by Henry James below, page 172. Senior's *Quarterly* reviews appeared as follows: *Rob Roy,* etc., 26:109 (October, 1821); *The Pirate,* 26:454 (January, 1822); *Nigel,* 27:337 (July, 1822).
[10] Lockhart, VII, 118.

at best lukewarm praise. *Redgauntlet,* however, excites his enthusiasm. It recalls to him the time "when the genius of the author of *Waverley* broke [upon us] with the full force of surprise" and he details at length the appeal of the natural scenery in the story, while still remarking that in Scott, as in Shakespeare, "the principal merit . . . is always the variety and individuality of his characters." Strangely, he rates *The Talisman* high, on the somewhat strained theory that as Scott recedes into the more and more remote past his imagination supplies with increased power the lack of actual historical material. Yet it does not rank with *Ivanhoe,* "the first working of the feudal mine, while the ore was rich and abundant and the laborer toiled with all the spirit and diligence of a discoverer." "The *Tales of the Crusaders* show that the bonanza is over; that either the vein has become poorer, or the miner more careless." For the tales in the first *Chronicles of the Canongate,* except *The Surgeon's Daughter,* he has the highest praise. *The Highland Widow* shows unwonted mastery of plot, and his favorite, Chrystal Croftangry (really an introductory sketch), is a masterpiece of simplicity and quietness, without any dependence on plot or powerful situation, thus illustrating Scott's ability to do without them.

After Senior's reviews of 1821 and 1822, the *Quarterly* noticed Scott's novels twice; in a review by Lockhart of his *Lives of the Novelists* in September, 1826, and in an essay on "Historical Romance," in March, 1827. In the first essay, which is largely an elaborate consideration of the history of the novel form and its relation to drama, there are several interesting allusions to Scott's novels. Speaking of the great increase in the reading public, Lockhart points out that each of Scott's novels had stimulated the sale of the historical sources on which it was based, especially Comines in the case of *Quentin Durward,* and old Scotch tracts and memoirs in the case of *Waverley* and *Old Mortality.* He adds moreover that "novel readers, who remain in our time exclusively novel readers, would have been in the immense majority of cases readers of exactly nothing at all had they lived a hundred years ago."

Of Scott's own qualities as a novelist, Lockhart declares that though he lacks Fielding's power of plotting and his wit, "he much more than atones for such deficiencies by the display of a far wider combination of excellences than is to be found in any one novelist besides. He has widened the whole field to an extent of which none that went before him ever dreamed; embellished it by many original graces as exquisite at least as any that their hands had introduced; and ennobled it by the splendors of a poetical imagination more powerful and more exalted by far than had ever in former days exerted its energies elsewhere than in the highest of the strictly poetical forms — epic and tragic." He has excelled not only other British novelists, but even "the two greatest foreign masters, Cervantes and Le Sage, in the copiousness of his creations." And all this he has done without sacrifice of his "firm healthiness of feeling . . . and masculine purity of mental vigour." Scott's unparalleled vogue, he says, has had both good and evil effects. It has stimulated the production not only of the other best novels of the time, *Anastasius* and the books of John Galt, but also the deluge of imitations, where his formula is employed, but his real powers are missed — his humor and pathos, his wide knowledge, his easy style, his grasp of character and fertility of invention. In such a general summary as this, one gets an impression of the power Scott had over his contemporaries, and the place he held in the literary hierarchy after a dozen years of novel writing, though to be sure his eminence had been as great for many years. The critics could not miss the falling off in the novels he was now writing, but when they drew back and observed the whole world of his creation it was as astounding as ever.

In the *Quarterly's* final essay, the same tone continues. Entitled "Historical Romance" and headed as a review of Scott's novels from *Peveril* to *Woodstock,* two novels by Horace Smith, and Schiller's *Wallenstein,* it avoids the usual catalogue and is in reality an analysis of Scott's power, with Schiller's drama and Smith's novels used as noble and ignoble objects of comparison. It is clear to the author that Scott's power lies in his historical quality, and he cites the modern and more realistic *St. Ronan's Well* as negative proof of his thesis. In *Waverley*, he says, Scott reveals the full depth and scope of his power; "we feel at once that we are in the power and at the will of a master." He has a whole world of characters, all "the legitimate progeny of his own creative genius," shaped and perfected from their originals in the crucible of his poetic mind. Still, the inferiority of his later work is apparent, consisting "in a certain boldness of plot, incident, and character"; there is no longer the exuberant outpouring of the first ones, chiefly because the materials of action are exhaustible. *Redgauntlet,* though it shows "the hand of a superior artist," is still "an inferior kind of *Waverley.*" The writer analyzes ingeniously the frequently mooted point of Scott's diffuseness; one finds in him a diction "diffuse, not from weakness, but the facility resulting from much practice in composition" — "a perfect mastery over the instrument of language" — "the excess of what he has to communicate makes him diffuse." The writer also lays stress on the theory that Scott does well not to go too far in trying to differentiate character by the manner of speech rather than the matter, which is after all the real essential. He even feels that absorption in manner is proof of an inferior genius, of a Ben Jonson in comparison with a Shakespeare. After this general theorizing the author devotes most of his essay to a very elaborate comparison of *Quentin Durward* with *Wallenstein,* an attempt to lend dignity to the historical novel by placing it on an equal footing with historical drama; and finally to a dismemberment and total maceration of Horace Smith's *Brambletye House* and *Tor Hill,* as samples of historical novels embodying Scott's formula but totally lacking his genius and spirit.

Of the three chief literary periodicals of the time, *Blackwood's* has much less of significance and interest to offer on the subject of the Waverley novels than either the *Edinburgh,* with Jeffrey's penetrating and sympathetic analyses, or the *Quarterly,* which if less original and just, had the benefit of Scott's own review and the carefully written essays of Nassau Senior, somewhat heavy and over-elaborate, but still replete wih interesting clues to critical points of view of the period. *Blackwood's,* which did not enter the field until 1817, missed the first novels, but reviewed *The Heart of Midlothian* in 1818 and a half dozen more during the next five years, thereafter noticing only the tales in the *Chronicles of the Canongate.* It is certainly not without significance that all these three journals should have kept up a steady stream of reviews until the same time in the early twenties and then have stopped suddenly after *The Fortunes of Nigel.* Scott's prestige certainly did not decline, for in later general essays and casual allusions he is referred to with even greater veneration than at first, but it seems clear enough that his later novels were in general disappointing to the admirers of his earlier work. At any rate none of these three leading periodicals was enough interested in the novels after *The Fortunes of Nigel* to review them consistently. The *Chronicles of the Canongate* are the only later stories that the critics welcomed as cordially as the earlier work; these shorter tales, it seemed to them, were illuminated by the same flashes of genius that had dazzled them ten years earlier. Here, of course, as in most other points the contemporary reviewers are at one with later critical judgment, which finds, especially in *The Two Drovers,* writing which is unparalleled in any of the full-length novels of the same period.

The reviews in *Blackwood's* are in general of a routine nature and quality. Except for a highly eulogistic essay on Scott's dramatic qualities in 1826, there are no general essays on a broad basis, but merely perfunctory, individual analyses, cut according to pattern. Moreover, they frequently fly wide of the mark, so far in fact as to seem on occasion palpably absurd.

Nowhere is this truer than in the very first, the review of *The Heart of Midlothian.*[11] This novel of course represents most glaringly the defects of Scott's work, but at the same time it reveals the best of his genius, a fact that the finest critics of the period, like Jeffrey and Hazlitt, were quick to see. The *Blackwood's* reviewer, however, did not see with the eyes of Jeffrey

[11] *Blackwood's,* 3:567 (August, 1818).

or Hazlitt, chiefly, it would seem, because of notions about "vulgarity" of subject. He admits that the novel is appealing because its historical events are still remembered and have a strong sentimental interest, and because the details are really accurate in all important points. Jeanie Deans, too, is in a way very interesting, as is also the portrait of her father, and he cannot deny that her character is always in keeping and is of a most inspiring moral quality. Still he feels that there is too much of the Deans family in the book, too much "of the concerns of a cowfeeder and his daughter." In fact he deprecates the tendency in recent literature to concern itself "not only with low but with vulgar life"; thus has the muse "soiled her petticoats, if not dimmed her beauty." The same "classical" tendency reveals itself in his judgment of Madge Wildfire, of whom he can merely report that there is too much of her also, that insanity is disgusting and should be shown sparingly. Of the dialogue in general he says that at certain points of high feeling it is excellent, but in others there is too much vulgarity, which is allowed to creep into the talk even of the Duke of Argyle, a vulgarity of the sort to which people of his breeding could not conceivably descend. The homely similes too, while doubtless true to life, are too vulgar and too frequent, and the critic urges the author to write more slowly and carefully and to avoid "writing himself down." The only specific points in the review which the modern reader can approve are his dislike of some of the tiresome minor characters, and the declaration that the last volume is *de trop* and was probably written at the behest of the publisher to fill up space and justify an exorbitant price.

This failure to appreciate and understand *The Heart of Midlothian* is more damaging than the rhapsodies of overpraise with which he greeted the later novels, especially those of more remote periods.[12] Evidently the *Blackwood's* reviewer (or reviewers per-

---

[12] Later reviews in *Blackwood's* appeared as follows: *Lammermoor* and *Montrose*, 5:340 (June, 1918); *Ivanhoe*, 6:262 (December, 1819); *The Monastery*, 6:692 (March, 1820); *Kenilworth*, 8:435 (January, 1821); *The Pirate*, 10:712 (December, 1821); *Nigel*, 11:734, 747 (June, 1822); *Chronicles of the Canongate*, 22:556 (November, 1827).

haps) was dazzled by the brilliant theatricalities of *Ivanhoe* and its successors, which he valued much more highly than the earlier portraits of homely Scotch character. Certainly his selection of details for praise is not highly creditable. In the review of *The Bride of Lammermoor* and *Montrose*, for instance, after the almost inescapable remark that parts are done in "a careless and slovenly manner," he emphasizes as the great glories of *The Bride* the character of Lucy Ashton, the best of all Scott's heroines, and the comic elements, especially the character of Caleb Balderstone! Over *Ivanhoe* he goes into raptures. He thinks that the new method in dealing with a remote period may smell too strongly of antiquarian research, but declares that the novel equals the best of its predecessors. Rebecca he finds the crowning glory of the book, and the tournament a magnificent climax. The scene between Rebecca and Front de Boeuf at the siege of the castle he quotes entire, and can imagine nothing "finer than the mixture of northern and oriental sublimities, in the high-wrought passions of the persons of this scene."

The Monastery inspires him to declare that "the two most remarkable men of the present day are unquestionably the Duke of Wellington and the author of *Waverley*," but he goes on to express his high admiration for the White Lady of Avenel — a chief source of irritation to most critics — though he doubts her proper place in the novel. Over *Kenilworth* too he rhapsodizes. He misses, it is true, "the poetry of the heart communing with nature," but is overwhelmed by the splendid pictures of pomp and chivalry, the character of Elizabeth, "both as feminine and royal," the highly dramatic scenes, the most impressive of which he finds to be Tressilian's denunciation of Varney, and the wonderful description of manners, surpassing even that of *Ivanhoe*. Yet after all this, the review ends with the hint that Scott's desire to dazzle and please his public "operates as a drag on the ascending power of genius and prevents the search after intellectual beauty and poetical feeling from being carried as far as it might be."

The reviews of *The Pirate* and *Nigel* seem especially ill-judged. *The Pirate* he cannot praise too highly. Norna is incomparably superior to Meg Merrilies, and the pirates too stir his enthusiasm; "nothing can be better than these sea characters." He writes similarly of the characters in general, of the description, which is "of the most bewitching excellence and beauty," and the poetry — "our language possesses few things more exquisite than the solemn antique music . . . of the Rheimkennar." Here the validity of the historical novel is the main point. The critic approves *The Pirate* especially because it has a fictional hero who does not have to be distorted, like Leicester in *Kenilworth,* to fit the plot. Altogether he finds Scott the greatest of British historians; in after years "the best and truest lights" will be found in him. "Cervantes, not Mariana, is the true historian of Spain." *Nigel* the reviewer places in the category of *Ivanhoe* and *Kenilworth,* but thinks it of even superior quality: "it will give more delight in the perusal to discerning readers." The power of the separate scenes, independent of plot and suspense, which is slight, proves surely Scott's greatness as a novelist. The tone of the book he says is "as fresh and lively as the transactions of last week," and he admires greatly the character of James, who he thinks is really more deserving of respect than he would at first seem to be. The only serious defect in the book he takes to be the want of tragic feeling, which he is not sure after all is a real defect, for it pleases especially, he thinks, "females . . . who like to suffer," and is a taste much less popular than formerly. At the present, he continues, there is "more scope for fancy character and knowledge of the world," and the reader is now "more awake to beauty in the shifting forms of a creative imagination."[13] On the whole, one doubts whether Christopher North and his associates could have taken much pride in this series of reviews. It is easy to forgive a critic for waxing enthusiastic over novelties like *Ivanhoe* and *Kenilworth,* but even in Scott's own age there were plenty of reviewers whose

[13] Later in the same issue an "Occasional Contributor" describes graphically his pleasure in reading *Nigel* at breakneck speed in one sitting.

discrimination was such that the best opinion a century later would be little disposed to revise their main judgments.

Except for the essay in 1826 [14] on Scott's dramatic powers, which contains the most extravagant praise (including comparison with Demosthenes as well as Homer and Shakespeare), and describes Sir Walter as "the most original, vigorous, fertile and essentially dramatic genius of the age," the only other contemporary article on Scott in *Blackwood's* is the one on the *Chronicles of the Canongate* in 1827. This review is devoted chiefly to *The Highland Widow,* the other tales being dismissed in a paragraph each. Of *The Two Drovers* it is said that, though in a lower key, it is absorbing, and the catastrophe is terrible. *The Highland Widow* is praised in particular for its opening. What could be better for the opening of a tale of pity and terror, the critic asks, than the contrast between the young girl and the "withered beldam." "With how few simple, sweeping, and grand touches is the scenery brought before the imagination!" — and the few figures, how finely contrasted and combined! Elspat watching her son Hamish in his drugged sleep is presented "in a few paragraphs given with a fearful force, we verily believe, beyond the reach of any other living writer." And of the combat in which Hamish refuses to surrender, "the poetry and philosophy of this terrible scene are equal to anything in the whole range of dramatic composition." The reader, the critic continues, gets the impression of an irresistible, sweeping Fate, and feels "a grand unity in the ruling passion of the tale." Furthermore, in defense of the poetical tone of peasant speech in the story, he insists that Highland peasants "under the power of passion do often speak poetry."

This superlative praise, which rings much truer than that of the preceding reviews, is enforced and supported by a long preface from the pen of Christopher North himself, a spirited celebration and defense of Scott's genius. In characteristic vein he apologizes for *Blackwood's* lack of attention to Scott during the preceding years; Sir Walter's works, he says, are universally

[14] *Blackwood's,* 19:152 (February, 1826).

known, and other reviews brightened their pages with extracts for their own good, a device Maga need not resort to. He then proceeds enthusiastically to proclaim Sir Walter's greatness. He disposes summarily, according to his custom, of various stock criticisms of the novels, denouncing as an ass the critic who complains of ill-constructed plots (when stories in real life are ill-constructed) or who hints that Sir Walter employs an assistant, or denies greatness to a novelist whose bases are in history. He is contemptuous of the idea that Scott will not be read a hundred years hence — "The passions that play their parts in the grand fictions of this writer are primary and permanent, and such as have at all times been chief actors on the theatre of the world. Therefore they shall never be hissed off." When men tire of humanity they will tire of Scott and at the same time of Shakespeare. "To be sure, there are changes of fashion apparently so wide and so deep that they seem for a while to shake even the very foundations on which the works of the most transcendant genius are laid. But it is only our eyes that are dazzled or confused — the pillars remain firm and the roof of the building is still 'by its own weight immovable and steadfast.' " More specifically he praises Scott for his national quality, his incarnation of Scotch life and spirit, and for the strength and renewed life he has given Scotland, taking a fling by the way at the cockney critics who refuse to value him highly. And again we find that linking of Scott's name with Shakespeare's and Homer's, which was to recur times without number during the next century — "the Novels and Romances and Tales of Scott, the whole glorious heap taken together, comprehend a fuller, we do not say finer, portraiture of the peculiar character of many different Peoples, under more varieties of aspect than even those Epics [Homer's] and those Tragedies [Shakespeare's]," though he does add that there is much in these two that lies beyond Scott's power.

This same vein comes out again in Christopher North's essay "An Hour's Talk about Poetry." [15] After running through all the

---

[15] See John Wilson ("Christopher North"), *Recreations of Christopher North* (2 vols., Edinburgh, 1857), I, 179.

contemporary poets, he concludes, as he began, that the age, though it had produced much fine poetry, had not produced one fine poem. In speaking of Scott and his national materials, he calls to mind the veneration of the whole people for Sir Walter. Scotland, he says, had forgotten her whole history, "till Sir Walter burnished it all up till it glowed again . . . and the past became the present." We now know our own people of all ranks and all periods, represented in thousands of his characters. He is not Shakespeare, but he has conceived and created "as many characters, real living flesh and blood human beings, naturally, truly and consistently, as Shakespeare." It had been thought that he and Burns between them had exhausted the Scotch matter in their poems, but then came the novels, "fresh floods of light pouring all over Scotland," and other scenes too. Until he came, the people of the past were buried in their tombs, but he has resurrected them, and clad their dry bones again with flesh and blood. Has he written a great poem? "We do not care one straw whether he has or not; for he has done this — he has exhibited human life in a greater variety of forms and lights, all definite and distinct, than any other man whose name has reached our ears; and therefore without fear or trembling we tell the world to its face, that he is, out of all sight, the greatest genius of the age, not forgetting Goethe, the Devil and Dr. Faustus." And so Christopher North goes on to a contemptuous reduction of Byron to a disciple of Wordsworth, all for the greater glory of Scott. "What? Scott a greater genius than Byron! Yes — beyond compare." This is not all of it exactly reasonable criticism, but it has its points, and is besides eloquent testimony to Scott's supreme position in his own age. Such enthusiasm, however, is a little hard to reconcile with the rather malicious words from the same source on little personal foibles of Sir Walter, which drew a remonstrance from Lockhart.[16]

[16] See John Wilson, *Noctes Ambrosianae* (4 vols., Edinburgh, 1856), III, 89, and Andrew Lang, *Life and Letters of J. G. Lockhart* (2 vols., London, 1897), II, 109.

CHAPTER IV

OTHER PERIODICALS

THE REVIEWS in the *Edinburgh,* the *Quarterly,* and *Blackwood's* are in a way the most important contemporary notices of the novels because of the fame of the periodicals themselves, but there were of course many others in less famous periodicals. The *London Magazine,* Colburn's *New Monthly,* the *Monthly Review,* and the *Anti-Jacobin Review* all paid a good deal of attention to the novels. Hazlitt contributed two reviews to the *London Magazine* and an essay to the *New Monthly,* and thus lent distinction to both magazines. The *New Monthly* reviews are interesting in so far as they reveal a consistent tone and point of view of their own, and those in the *Anti-Jacobin* furnish an excellent illustration of political bias and conventional morality in literary criticism; otherwise the writing in these four may be dismissed as perfunctory and unoriginal.

The articles in the *New Monthly,*[1] obviously all of them by one hand and running from 1822 to 1825, are significant chiefly as revealing a full recognition of Scott's falling off after 1820 and the inferiority of the romances to the Scotch novels. Here of course they stand in sharp contrast with the *Blackwood's* series, which, after the scornful remarks on *The Heart of Midlothian,* rise in a steady crescendo of praise. The predominant tone is one of regret, even distress, that so great a writer should become mechanical and conventional, and that he should forsake the

[1] Formerly a political organ. When Campbell was made editor in 1821, it became one of the chief literary periodicals.

fine field of realistic Scotch character for the theatrical glitter of
medieval chivalry and a bogus antiquity. The first review,[2] of
The Pirate, in general damns with faint praise. The critic declares that though *The Pirate* is fairly good it is clear that the
author "will never equal his first works." He refuses to join the
chorus of "boundless exultation" and "tremendous eulogies" in
spite of his great admiration for the author. It seems to him
obvious that the later novels are being written for the bookseller;
their stuff is the same but it has become standardized and has
lost its freshness and freedom. He foresees too that the peculiar
charms of the novels are liable to exhaustion, especially in their
appeals to the beauties of nature and in their use of the supernatural.

The most important of these reviews is the one on *The
Fortunes of Nigel,* which the critic has read with "mingled admiration and regret." It opens with a discussion of Scott's style
which must appeal to the modern reader. Scott's famous statement in his preface that his most successful work had been his
most rapid, the critic refuses to take as a sufficient defense of "the
quantity of dull and commonplace matter which is retained in
his volumes." He wishes the author would "give us more of his
best . . . with a smaller portion of alloy." There is no reason
why "the noble pictures of external nature, the fresh and breathing characters, the high tragic scenes, which of late he has
scattered sparingly through his works, should not be presented
within a smaller space. . . . He is not bound down by his
story to a certain quantity of dullness." Posterity will not select,
as they will lines from a poet. Many a passage "worthy of immortality, will, we are afraid, be weighed down by the inferiority of
the matter with which it is encircled." The critic wonders if
Fielding, for instance, would have survived if he had merely left
fine passages so embedded. These cogent remarks have been
sustained by the verdict of time, and their point tacitly allowed
by those modern devotees of Scott who admit his dull stretches,

[2] The reviews in the *New Monthly* ("Colburn's") appeared as follows: *The
Pirate,* 4:188 (1822); *Nigel,* 5:77 (1822); *Peveril,* 7:273 (1823); *Quentin Durward,*
8:82 (1823); *Redgauntlet,* 11:93 (1824); *Tales of the Crusaders,* 14:27 (1825).

but urge us to endure them for the sake of the oases that are bound to come sooner or later. Forecasting the fate of the various novels, the critic prophesies that *The Bride of Lammermoor* has the best chance with posterity; it is the "most complete," and is "almost as single and harmonious as a tragedy of Sophocles." As for *Nigel,* the work under review, he finds fine passages, but they are far between and "the intervals are singularly dreary." The general management of the book is bad and the main characters of the story poor. Nevertheless he likes the pictures of London life and the delineation of King James, the best figure in the novel. The review closes with a melancholy wish that the book were only better, and that the author would stop writing for the market and proceed in less of a hurry; like other popular authors, he is "grown as periodical as the Editor of a Magazine."

The next novels reviewed fare still worse. For *Peveril of the Peak* there is not even faint praise, but utter damnation. The critic admits that it shows more of an attempt at art and form, but declares that it has no good stuff in it — better careless masses with brilliant spots than well-planned stories with no flesh and blood upon their bones. In his review of *Quentin Durward* he reverts again to the matter of haste, and the fixed regularity with which the novels were appearing. As for Sir Walter Scott's being the author, he doubts Scott's time for the work amid so many known activities, unless — and the inferiority of the later ones suggests it — he merely directs the process of manufacture. *Quentin Durward,* it is true, is artistically much better than its predecessors; the author "has broken new ground and seems invigorated by the freshness of his subject." But this does not make up for other lapses — the frequent anachronism and more especially the lowering of moral interest. "The infamous Louis XI," his satellites, and the cruel and mercenary archers — what is their effect as compared with that of Jeanie Deans? This may spring, he thinks, from the author's perverse Toryism and fondness for "decorating despotism"; certainly it is a bad and misleading influence!

In *Redgauntlet,* too, the critic bears down hard on the moral side. He finds here an interest too exclusively in mere external pictures, too little in moral effects, the unfortunate result probably of the author's Toryism. Besides, he deplores the occasional "vulgarity" of style in such passages as "since Mother Eve ate the pippin without paring." The final review is of the *Tales of the Crusaders*. In these the descent is found to continue; the later tales had kept some of the earlier splendors, though somewhat faded, but these show a distinct fall. The critic recognizes clearly enough the weakness of these novels. The remote age of the crusades is "too vast and too visionary" for such a process. He has little faith in stories so concocted, and slight respect for their melodramatic wonders. As he quite pertinently remarks, "An Arabian tale is no doubt a good thing, and a true Scotch novel is still better; but the elements of the two cannot well be harmoniously blended."

Viewed across the gap of a century the ideas of this critic seem remarkably sound and penetrating, although doubtless readers of a later age are only faintly disturbed by the danger of moral contamination from Scott's Tory predilections or by the evil example of Louis XI. For some reason or other, possibly the same as Jeffrey's, these reviews came to an end in 1825, but it is to be doubted if the critic would have altered the tendency of his comments had he continued. He observed clearly the gradual decline of Scott's genius, and doubtless would have had little to offer on the last group of novels except still severer strictures.

It is perhaps worth noting that *Colburn's* published a half dozen years later, in 1831,[3] a criticism of Scott in quite another vein, a panegyric typical of those enthusiasts who then and ever since have run to the defense of their hero against any sort of unfavorable criticism, a defense that Sir Walter has really never needed. This particular writer praises Scott at every conceivable point, even making it a virtue that he freely rewrote for publication old ballads which he had collected. He attacks indignantly the contemporary critics who, as he says, lagged behind the

[3] *Colburn's*, 31:72 (1831).

public as the novels appeared, praising only when it was safe or when they had to. All unfavorable remarks he labels captious and querulous, maintaining that what the myopic critic sees as a huddled plot, weak narrative, a "poisoning of the pure fountains of historic truth," is in reality merely the result of Scott's true delineation of character, a point of view that is somewhat reminiscent of Christopher North's. Above all does he resent the attacks on Scott's old Cameronians, who he says reveal especially Scott's fidelity to and understanding of Scotch character. The writer dissents, however, from the critical judgment already well established that the novels were much greater than the romantic poems that had preceded them. In declaring the end of *Marmion* finer than anything in the novels, he would have found very few to support him in his own time or since.

The articles in the *London Magazine* [4] except for Hazlitt's reviews of *The Pirate* and *Peveril* and an excellent general essay in the first issue are not of great interest. There are reviews of *Ivanhoe, The Monastery, The Abbot, Kenilworth, Redgauntlet, Tales of the Crusaders, Woodstock,* and *Chronicles of the Canongate,* and a review of the first volumes of the new edition of the novels which began to appear in 1829. The tone is in general unfavorable, even bitter and condemnatory, and each essay

[4] In addition to the reviews mentioned there is one by De Quincey of *Walladmor,* the German imitation of Scott. For an account of John Scott, the ill-fated first editor of the *London Magazine,* see a paper by Jacob Zeitlin in the *Journal of English and Germanic Philology,* 20:328 (July, 1921). Mr. Zeitlin thinks that almost certainly the general essay of January, 1820, and the reviews of *The Monastery* and *The Abbot* were by John Scott. He also quotes from an attack on *Blackwood's* (*London Magazine,* May, 1820) in which John Scott speaks slightingly of Hunt, Shelley, and Byron, and then breaks out, "The author of the Scotch Novels appears among these perverters as if charged to restore to literature its health and grace, to place it again on its fair footing in society, legitimately associated with good manners, common sense and sound principle . . . The vivacity, keenness, intelligence and easy elegance of Sir Walter's mind, as manifested in his poems and other avowed publications, become sublimated into genius of a high standard in the merits of the novels; but the kind is not altered, the *degree* only is increased." John Scott's authorship of the essay of January, 1820, is further supported by an allusion of Hazlitt's in his essay on Scott in *The Spirit of the Age:* "We believe the late Mr. John Scott went to his death-bed with some degree of satisfaction, inasmuch as he had penned the most elaborate panegyric on the *Scotch Novels* that had as yet appeared!"

reiterates the stock objections and complaints about the later novels.[5]

The first general article, however, is written with the greatest pains and consideration and is imbued with an enthusiasm equal to Hazlitt's. Without declaring the Great Unknown the greatest writer of the present, the critic asserts, "There is no living author whom we would so much wish to be." He emphasizes Scott's healthy morality as being encouraging to human nature and destructive of "the noxious and the dangerous," and praises his characters as drawn from the very fountain-head of nature. In character drawing he is, like Shakespeare, transparent, and though unequal to Shakespeare or several others in imagination, yet no modern writer has equaled him in catching Nature's reflections and casting them back to his readers. "The power and sagacity of his perception" will give him permanence, and his quality is proved by such characters as Nicol Jarvie, whom the ordinary writer would never have seen nor understood.

The writer sees, moreover, majesty and grandeur — true national quality — in Scott's characters, and a practically universal variety. All through the essay he repeats his belief that the Waverley novels are unique and never can be paralleled; it is impossible, he thinks, that such a combination of gifts can again occur — sooner even another Milton — and his opinion that no other country than Scotland offers the novelist such a striking combination of vivid qualities to portray, makes him even surer of his thesis. He finds important the aspects of religion and piety revealed in such characters as Mause Headrigg and David and Jeanie Deans, but admires even more Scott's presentation of the mysterious and superstitious element in the Scotch character, and he calls on the Scotch to show due gratitude to one who has caught their traditional character before it disappeared.

[5] They appeared as follows: "The Author of the Scotch Novels," 1:11 (January, 1820); reviews in the order named: 1:79, 565 (January and May, 1820); 2:427 (October, 1820); 3:188 (February, 1821); 10:69 (July, 1824); 12:593 (August, 1825); 15:173 (June, 1826); 18:409 (November, 1827); and 23:610 (June, 1829). Hazlitt's reviews, which are discussed later (Chapter VI), appeared in January, 1822, and February, 1823 (5:80 and 7:205).

These ideas, all of which anticipate the best modern criticism of Scott, are overcast with a distinctly moral preoccupation which somewhat disfigures the essay. There is frequent insistence on Scott's goodness, excellent moral effect, and so on; and Mrs. Brunton, a popular and highly virtuous novelist of the time, is called to testify to Sir Walter's excellent influence.

The individual reviews are worth little attention except as they indicate still further the growing dissatisfaction with the novels. Except for the one of *Kenilworth,* the first one, of *Ivanhoe,* is the most friendly of the series, but is, at most, lukewarm, finding little to praise except Rebecca and Isaac and the description of their status in society. Quite justly, the reviewer declares that the memorable characters are much fewer than in earlier novels. *The Monastery,* at least by comparison with the other novels, is damned outright, the best compliment the critic can make being implied in the remark, "Cette pièce est mauvaise, mais c'est toujours le mauvais de Voltaire." The review of *The Abbot* begins "Failure the second!" and goes on to declare it the worst so far produced. The critic asserts that it has only one striking character, Queen Mary, and that the author should have stopped with *Ivanhoe,* where he had created in Rebecca an incomparable heroine rivaled only by Clarissa Harlowe! *Kenilworth* pleased the critic much better. His only important objection is to the anachronistic use of such famous figures as Raleigh, Shakespeare, Spenser, and Sidney; otherwise his comments are highly favorable. He finds here a dramatic power beyond anything in the earlier novels, and praises the representation of the common life of the period and the character of Michael Lambourne. He admires the use of the cabala in the plot, gives specimens of a style to be found in no other author, and designates the character of Elizabeth and the description of the festivities at Kenilworth as the finest parts of the novel. Altogether, "Here he has manfully recovered himself and shines out . . . the brightest object in the living galaxy of British genius."

The last three reviews are entirely hostile; they are not merely

unfavorable analyses of the individual novels, but actually constitute a damnation of Scott's methods in general. The reviewer
of *Redgauntlet* allows that the dialogue is "spirited and force-
ful," but otherwise he is almost, if not quite, contemptuous.
He compares Scott with Byron, finding in both an extraordinary
facility of composition combined with great difficulty in inventing characters. He deplores the habit of writing enormously
upon any or no subject, grinding out novels at high speed to the
detriment of his composition. He declares that the irrelevancy
and irregularity of the plots becomes insufferably tedious, and
even maintains that Scott's greatest defect is his poverty of
character invention, holding up the characters in *Redgauntlet*
to scorn as "mere blotches," vague and undifferentiated. In
Redgauntlet too he finds many instances of "childishness of
fancy," and naïve attempts at sensation — a design to frighten his
readers as children rather than to excite them as men.

The *Tales of the Crusaders* is treated with outright contempt;
indeed, the review is disagreeable to the point of seeming sour
and peevish. The reading public is likened to dogs waiting im-
patiently for food, and getting nothing but tough gristle from
their master. The metaphor then shifts to the cask that is
running dry and being adulterated with inferior wine. Occasionally it seems as good as ever, but in a moment "runs foul and
vapid" again. The reviewer had hoped the author's bores were
done with, but he finds them here worse than ever. He is equally
disdainful of the romantic incidents of the stories, the stock
romantic characters — dwarfs, hermits, etc. — and the tiresome
descriptions of clothing and furniture, all of which he says have
been lifted out of antiquarians like Strutt or Grose. *Ivanhoe*,
he remarks by the way, is built up out of Chapter I of Henry's
history. He wishes "the Unknown gentleman would condescend
to be less childish and absurd than he has on various occasions
chosen to show himself, not only here but through the whole
nearly of his romances." He wonders how long the author will
keep on — obviously he writes solely for money, and cares nothing for reputation; and suggests that he might try to write

history, or if he must go on with novels, turn to the religious sort. "Being a Scotchman he might talk metaphysics at least as well as *Tremaine* . . . Canting is as easy as lying."

In much the same vein, though not quite so bitter, the review of *Woodstock* is merely a development of the theme that Sir Walter has become a "duffer" or revamper in the novel trade. In the opinion of the critic, "*Woodstock* smacks strongly of age, or of an invention which lacks a season of fallow; it is prosy to the last degree, feeble in story, barren of incident, and its characters either remind us of something better that we have had before, or are melancholy and tedious failures." The only mitigation of such remarks is the rather grudging statement, frequently to be found in such context, that a bad novel by Scott is more readable than a tolerably good one by any other author. Evidently such strictures were relative, not absolute, and Sir Walter was being measured by yardsticks he himself had furnished in the past. In *The Two Drovers,* however, the *London Magazine* found work of which it could speak with enthusiasm. In the character of Robin Oig, the scenes, the tale itself, the author of *Waverley* was again on his own ground and again showed himself unrivaled. This, indeed, is another bit of testimony to the clear recognition by contemporary critics of what really distinguished these novels.

The review of the early volumes of the collected edition, the "Magnum Opus," contains little new material. There is the usual high praise for the early Scotch novels, in this case especially *Waverley* and *The Heart of Midlothian,* and the usual relegation of the romances to a second place. Indeed, *Ivanhoe* and its successors in spite of their brilliance are gathered together in the general condemnation, "Instead of comedy and tragedy of the highest order, it is only melo-drame." Here, the critic points out, the author works from books and not from his own observation. As for Scott's information to the reader about historical sources and his methods of work, the critic does not like it; it seems to him simply an uncovering of machinery. He does not enjoy the "exposition which Sir Walter makes of the progress of his mind during his literary career . . . in the talking of self."

The *Anti-Jacobin Review* survived long enough to review some of the earlier novels — *Waverley, Guy Mannering, The Antiquary, Rob Roy,* and *The Heart of Midlothian.*[6] Its comments are by no means striking and are interesting now chiefly for their complacency toward a writer who seemed to have Tory leanings, but also for their moral preoccupation and an occasional passage of panegyric. It compliments the author on his delicate handling of the politics of '45 so as to give no offense; it endorses the "sound principles" and "sentiments which convey a very favorable idea of the author's intellectual powers and moral faculties" and so "afford a rational employment for a leisure hour"; and it assures the reader that such novels do no harm — their author is no German mystic and no revealer of vice to youth, since depravity appears only to an edifying end. It finds many flaws and weaknesses in detail, but still realizes that a third genius in the novel has now come to the assistance of the only two worthy practitioners, Mrs. West and Miss Edgeworth (who has talent, but might be either pagan or Christian). It draws favorable comparisons with Cervantes and Le Sage, finds that a certain scene (the meeting of Rob Roy and Nicol Jarvie in prison) "is scarcely to be equalled in the whole compass of English literature," and in the review of *The Heart of Midlothian,* after recalling how "*Waverley* dazzled us by the brilliancy, astonished us by the magnitude, and surprised us by the novelty of the characters and conceptions of uncultivated men and . . . by the picturesque scenery" of the background, discovers still after four years, "all the audacity, the probability, the savage grandeur and romantic delicacy of character and scenery."

The *Monthly Review,* which was much more a routine register of new books than the other periodicals, noticed all of Scott's

---

[6] They appeared as follows: *Waverley,* 47:217 (September, 1814); *Guy Mannering,* 48:544 (June, 1815); *The Antiquary,* 50:625 (July, 1816); *Rob Roy,* 53:417 (January, 1818); *The Heart of Midlothian,* 55:212 (November, 1818).

novels as they appeared, from *Waverley* to the *Tales of the Cru-saders* in 1825, but thereafter only *Anne of Geierstein* in 1829.[7] This series, though fuller than the others, is the least interesting and important because of its perfunctory nature. The reviews all follow pretty closely the hack procedure of extended summary and citation of representative passages, and reveal a minimum of analysis and detailed criticism. What there is, is generally lumped at the beginning or at the end, though the summary of the story halts occasionally for a brief comment. On the whole the effect is distinctly pallid and negative. Though less outspoken and independent than the better magazines, the *Monthly Review* nevertheless indicates like them the course that critical opinion on the novels was running. The first reviews are distinctly ami-able and friendly, though one looks in vain for anything approaching enthusiasm or recognition of new greatness. Of *Waverley* it is remarked quite calmly that it seems to be a new type and, equally calmly, that the characters, both major and minor, are carefully discriminated and are probably drawn in many cases from originals. It is also pointed out that the local materials are drawn largely from a volume of letters published in 1754,[8] a new method in novel-writing. The following reviews are of much the same order. Easily the most laudatory is that of *Guy Mannering,* where the writer goes so far as to speak of "consummate observation" of all ranks of life, and to praise Meg Merrilies as "wildly sublime." Such enthusiasm, however, is nowhere else to be met with; the critic usually maintains his composure and refuses to venture beyond the bounds of caution. In several instances, as in the reviews of *Old Mortality* and *Rob Roy,* there is practically nothing but summary and citation, yet altogether, as far as the critic is willing to commit himself, his judgment in these first reviews seems to be good, and he selects

---

[7] All Scott's novels from *Waverley* to *Woodstock* (1814–26) were reviewed as follows: 75:275; 77:85; 82:38, 383; 87:356; 89:387; 91:89, 404; 93:67; 94:146; 97:69; 98:169; 100:187; 101:187; 103:61; 105:198; 107:160; 110:73; and *Anne of Geierstein,* 119:288 (1829).

[8] This is of course absurd. Scott's sources, especially in Scotch matters, were tremendously wide and various.

for praise points and qualities that have appealed to the best of the later critics.

Not so much can be said for some of those that follow. In his review of *The Heart of Midlothian* he points out the author's special excellences, which seem to him to be his interest in subjects other than love (the usual staple of novelists), his easy credibility, his true picture of all grades of national life, and his excellent use of dialect. Yet he fails to appreciate the excellences of the book, being apparently blinded by its numerous and all too obvious defects, which lead him to rank it far below its predecessors. He makes the same error in reviewing *The Bride of Lammermoor* and *Montrose,* which it seems to him sink still lower, the candles burning low and the festivities flagging. One need not expect high praise for *Montrose,* or for the character of Caleb in *The Bride,* but an utter condemnation of the old women as a feeble imitation of Shakespeare, and the cool allowance that the later tragic scenes show "very considerable ability," and that the tale is better in conception than in execution — these judgments do not stand in the critic's favor. One may note that several years later in the review of *Quentin Durward, The Bride* is praised as the most "poetical" of the novels, and is called a perfect epic.

The reviews of the historical romances that began in 1820 with *Ivanhoe* contain, some of them, more important and more justifiable dicta. *Ivanhoe* the critic rejects as inferior to the earlier type, chiefly because of its "glaring" departure from authentic history; its chief attractions aside from its descriptions and its pictures of manners, which he admires, belong, he thinks, "to the province of history rather than of romance." Like most other critics then and now this writer felt the flatness and lack of energy in Scott's ladies; he speaks to the point when he says, "In Rebecca and Rowena love is the most quiescent, the best regulated and the most sedate sentiment imaginable." *Kenilworth* he found a more successful example of the type, largely because it was not thrown so far back in time as *Ivanhoe;* indeed he rated it as excellent in almost every way. The remarks on the other historical romances, however, seem erratic, chiefly on the side of too high praise. *The Abbot,* admittedly one of the weakest of the novels, brings out the judgment that its author was a complete master of the awful and terrific, and *The Pirate* and the *Tales of the Crusaders* and *Anne of Geierstein* seem to be praised beyond their deserts in comparison with some of their worthier brethren. *Anne of Geierstein,* for instance, is said to belong with the best of the whole list; all the special marks of genius one had found in Scott's earlier works — his antiquarian lore, his descriptive power, his art of making things live — still show in these pages. His failures the critic avers have been due always to an unwise choice of time or scene. Certain other novels, *The Fortunes of Nigel, Peveril,* and *St. Ronan's Well* fare much worse; in fact beyond praising individual scenes in *Nigel* and the character of Fenella in *Peveril* the critic finds nothing good to report. *St. Ronan's Well* he condemns, as have most other critics; not, however, for the obvious reason that the subject was out of Scott's proper field, but rather on the ground of weakness in plot and lack of novelty in character.

With a few deviations, these reviews taken together follow the general tendency of contemporary criticism. The earlier novels fare the best, as usual, except for *The Heart of Midlothian* and *The Bride of Lammermoor,* and after 1820 there is an increasing amount of dissatisfaction and fault-finding, with the usual insistence on careless and rapid composition, repetition in situation and character, and inarticulate plotting. And, as with the other magazines, most of the novels of the last five or six years are unnoticed. As has been said before, there is too little space accorded to actual discussion in these reviews to make them comparable with the more elaborate and carefully considered essays in the best periodicals. In many of them the critic seems merely to have gone in for all praise or all blame, often without much judgment. At any rate Scott's novels are hardly to be handled so; even in the poorer ones there are signs of genius to be recognized, just as the best ones also display characteristic flaws.

The *Critical Review,* like the *Monthly Review* a survival

from the eighteenth century and a routine register of new books, lived only long enough to comment on the early novels; it died in 1817. Its reviews of *Waverley, Guy Mannering,* and *Old Mortality* are valuable and interesting only as they emphasize certain obstinate prejudices. The review of *Waverley* begins with the flat statement: "This romance, lavishly extolled by the Scotch reviewers, is attributed to the pen of Walter Scott. Why a poet of established fame should dwindle into a scribbler of novels, we cannot tell. At all events, we are not among his flatterers, and candidly affirm, we neither like the work nor the subject; but the name of Walter Scott claims attention." After the usual summary and series of quotations, the review ends with the declaration that *Waverley* might have appealed to English as well as Scotch readers had the author made it less national and "divested [it] of its endless Scotch idioms, Gaelic allusions, scraps of Latin; . . . yet, the main incidents are merely the rebellion of 1745, treated novel wise." To this critic the appearance of *Waverley* was no sign in the heavens, it was merely a futile rehash of the history of 1745.

In the two succeeding reviews the contempt is moderated, but both are at best perfunctory in their praise of a few scattered points. *Guy Mannering* is called "creditable" and said to "revive the animated portraits of Fielding, Smollett, Richardson" though too often written in language intelligible only to the Scotch; writers like Lady Morgan and the Edgeworths, who clearly have the same aim, write in a more acceptable style. The character of Meg Merrilies alone stirs the reviewer to anything like enthusiasm; in her he admits that there are touches of grandeur and sublimity. Yet there still remains the irritating barrier of the Scotch language, and there is also the immorality and impiety of the book; "it advocates duelling, encourages a taste for peeping into futurity — a taste by far too prevalent; and it is not over nice on religious subjects." *Old Mortality* is not so good as either *Guy Mannering* or *The Antiquary;* here again is the objection to the Scotch dialect; indeed, the author, emboldened by his growing fame, seems to grow careless in all respects about his writing. — Altogether, then, the author of *Waverley* was a scribbler of novels who might rise to the level of Lady Morgan and Miss Edgeworth if he could only escape his nationalism and make himself understandable to the English![9]

To this English group may be added the most important American literary periodicals of the period, the *Port Folio* of Philadelphia and the *North American Review,* both of which contain a good deal of material on the Waverley novels.

The *Port Folio* (1801–1827) was the longest lived and the most successful American magazine to be established before the advent of the *North American* in 1815.[10] Now, however, in the period of the Scott novels, it is gradually declining. It seems rather dependent for its opinions on its English brethren, not only reflecting them in its own comments, but even reprinting entire essays. It is also marked by a strong moral and religious preoccupation. It obviously feels in duty bound to justify the reading and writing of novels at all, and is careful to let its readers know exactly where it draws the line. The impression given is clearly that it was catering to a much more strait-laced public than that served by comparable English reviews and magazines.

It would be difficult to find more ecstatic praise of Scott than that in the *Port Folio;* after *Waverley*[11] it greeted the novels with open arms and its tone in casual allusions to Scott himself is always reverent and affectionate. It published extended and rapturous reviews of *Guy Mannering, Ivanhoe,* and *Kenilworth,* and reprinted *Blackwood's* equally rapturous review of *The*

[9] See the *Critical Review* as follows: *Waverley,* 5th series, 1:288, *Guy Mannering,* 1:600, and *Old Mortality,* 4:614 (1814–16).

[10] See F. L. Mott, *A History of American Magazines, 1741–1850* (New York, 1930), 178 ff., 223 ff.

[11] Its review of *Waverley* was prefaced by an editorial note doubting Scott's authorship on various grounds, including the quality of the work. The review itself has very little point, being devoted largely to excursions suggested to the reviewer's mind, such as the propriety of calling Mackenzie the Scottish Addison. The reviewer likes Fergus and Flora, however, and recognizes that the Scotch characters form the best part of the book; but his highest praise is that the author has been able to imitate Maria Edgeworth successfully. The reviews that follow are in an utterly different tone.

Pirate,[12] but gave a wail of hurt disappointment at *The Monastery,* was only mildly pleased with *The Abbot,* and announced briefly its dissatisfaction with *Redgauntlet.*[13]

The delight expressed in the four favorable reviews, including the one from *Blackwood's,* could hardly be exaggerated. *Guy Mannering* is said to be compact of unalloyed imagination and to possess "boundless variety of incident and character." It is "full of life and action," and the reader sees in the characters real people, recognizable and close to Nature, and yet always original. Meg Merrilies was as awful to the reviewer as a figure in Salvator Rosa, and his only real objections are to the character of Dominie Sampson as somewhat caricatured, and to the fulfillment of the prophecies, which he feared might have "a mischievous tendency in weak minds." This was a thought which, as it happened, had worried one or two English critics.

Over *Ivanhoe* the critic was even more ecstatic, declaring that he had been thrown into such a state of excitement that he was unfit to review it, just awakening as he was from a dream of beauty and wonder in the days of Richard I and returning to prosaic life. He has enough detachment left, however, to express his surprise at Scott's new departure in dipping so far back into history and to give warning that the necessary use of much antiquarian matter makes unusual demands on the reader. About *Kenilworth* he is not quite so lyric, though his praise is of the very highest. He begins with a general defense of the historical novel as encouraging the study of history and declares that these novels do not misrepresent history but are true to actuality; they show an "alliance between fancy and fact," and the result of the book may very well be added readers for "the invaluable pages of Hume." And though *Kenilworth* may not

[12] As also the *Critical Review's* notice of *The Black Dwarf* and *Old Mortality,* perfunctory and colorless, and a brief summary of the *Monthly Review's* account of *St. Ronan's Well* as a failure.

[13] Reviews in the *Port Folio* appeared as follows: *Waverley,* 3d series, 5:326 (1815); *Guy Mannering,* 5th series, 2:159 (1816); *Tales of My Landlord,* 4:400 (1817); *Ivanhoe,* 9:300 (1820); *The Monastery,* 9:337 (1820); *The Abbot,* 10:370 (1820); *Kenilworth,* 11:161 (1821); *The Pirate,* 13:73 (1822); *St. Ronan's Well,* 17:336 (1824); *Redgauntlet,* 18:197 (1824).

rise to the heights of *Ivanhoe,* it has "breathless interest" and reveals "complete dominion over his characters." Some of the dialogue, it is true, is "rather tedious because . . . carried on by persons who are vile and vulgar to a disgusting degree"; yet there is here the author's "wonted eloquence"; and "the style is generally in that free, bold, and striking manner which has captivated all classes of readers; the old and the young; the gloomy, the grave and the gay."

These three reviews are long, with a great deal of summary and quotation. To *The Monastery,* on the other hand, the *Port Folio* devoted only two pages, although the critic's disappointment is so expressed as to seem an even greater compliment to Scott than the review of *Ivanhoe.* He even wonders if the book is not a forgery; the whole business of the supernatural and the character of Sir Piercie Shafton he finds utterly disgusting and unworthy of Scott, "for to him these works are now very generally attributed." The Waverley novels, he protests, "are to our age what the writings of Homer and Shakespeare were to theirs . . . such works supersede and obliterate almost all former creations of the same species."

The Abbot was recognized as a partial recovery, but the critic was unable to speak in his earlier vein. It was "another delightful creation" and was well sustained on a middle level, but there was nothing in it to compare with the great passages of the early novels; and, though Queen Mary was beautifully presented, all the other characters were distinctly inferior. He thinks too that the union of fiction and history may have its disadvantages; one must have a happy ending, in spite of the fact that with historical characters it may not be convincing. Besides, he does not approve a sequel, with romantic youth degenerating into staid middle age. He takes an opportunity also to deplore the comparison with Shakespeare. Such simple characters, formed from a few qualities and fitting so neatly into their rôles cannot bear comparison with the reality and universality of Shakespeare's creations. Clearly the critic, though still friendly, is disposed to find fault; his early ardor has burned itself out. And when, a little later,

Redgauntlet appeared, he dismisses it briefly as showing a great falling off of the author's powers, though he extracts one long passage from the character of Peter Peebles to show how even here the author's genius may flash out. Thus the *Port Folio's* reviews follow the typical arc, rising from 1814 to 1820 and thereafter falling rapidly away.

These reviews set the dominant tone for the *Port Folio* in its dealings with Scott. Occasional briefer comments rarely fall below this level of praise. The coolest and most temperate is a criticism of *Ivanhoe* in a special department called "Adversaria," where the writer indicates various weaknesses in plot and language, though, he adds, "when a basket of fine strawberries are generally ripe, I will not quarrel about a few green ones." He even says that Scott's popularity is greater than he deserves; Scott is never really great either in prose or in verse, though he is "certainly a clever, entertaining, interesting and often instructive novelist." This is indeed faint praise, at least by comparison. Still another comment on *Ivanhoe* appeared two years later, but this time in more reverent tones. A few "slight blemishes" in plot and character are pointed out, but at the end there is "unfeigned praise of the extensive research, the playful vivacity, the busy and stirring incidents, the humorous dialogue and the picturesque delineations."[14]

When Scott received his baronetcy, the *Port Folio* expressed the greatest admiration both of his character and his works, and especially for his moral effect. His pictures of human life and character, it maintained, "outstrip all rivalry but that of the great dramatic bard."[15] It seized too on Adolphus' *Letters to Heber*[16] with the utmost delight. The book was said to be by no means what one might expect — a trite, obvious work to prove something already perfectly well known; there were to be found in it "high intellectual excitement," and "a lesson of judicious and elegant criticism," but its great service was to bring

[14] *Port Folio*, 10:95 (1820); 13:493 (1822).
[15] *Ibid.*, 9:509 (1820).
[16] *Ibid.*, 13:136 (1822).

all of Scott's excellences into a focus of dazzling intensity. The reverence of the *Port Folio* for Scott may also be gauged by its attitude toward Cooper, who might be expected to have the advantage of patriotic bias, but the reviews of *The Spy* and *The Pioneers* [17] are barely lukewarm, and the highest point of approbation seems to be reached in characterizing the Spy himself as "the Edie Ochiltree of these volumes." On Mrs. Radcliffe too, who seemed, well after the passing of her vogue in England, to be an important figure in America, the critic cast a cold and disapproving eye.[18] Miss Edgeworth was the only novelist the *Port Folio* writers approached at all as they did Scott, and that almost entirely because she was edifying.

Really more interesting than the direct comments on Scott are the numerous discussions of novel-reading in the *Port Folio*. It is clear that the editors felt the need of justifying the novel itself as a department of literature, a feeling quite pervasive in England too, though the purely moral and religious pressure against the novel evidently affected the *Port Folio* more strongly than it did similar British journals. Indeed, taking them all together, these general essays do not harmonize at all with the spirit of the reviews of Scott. They must certainly have been written to placate or mollify a strongly evangelical body of subscribers, to whom the novel was one of the snares of Satan.

The first remarks on the subject serve as a preface to the review of *Guy Mannering*, where the essayist declares the taste for romances a natural one and insists that it is of great general educative value to the young, especially to develop taste and manners and to mold the imagination. Yet, he says, it is of service to the finest minds also. It is a source of inspiration to poets, and it lightens and gives variety to graver reading and helps to maintain what is only too easily lost, "habitual gayety and liveliness of thought."

[17] *Ibid.*, 13:90 (1822); 15:230 (1823).
[18] Yet when she came to die, the *Port Folio* (16:137, 1823) published a eulogy of her artistic qualities which, though cold and formal, must have satisfied her most ardent admirers.

These remarks are serious and earnest enough, but subsequent
ones are much more so; for the most part those that follow bear
much more strongly the evangelical imprint. A lengthy survey
of the history of the novel [19] (in which Scott does not figure)
leads up to a disquisition on Miss Edgeworth, who is declared
to be excellent for her morality and philosophy, though she
lacked the saving grace of religion. "The best way of serving the
cause of morality would have been never to have lost sight of its
only legitimate source." Yet she is superior to all her contemporaries; Mrs. Radcliffe, for instance, "an extraordinary female,"
exhibits an "ignorance nearly equal to her imagination, and
that is saying a great deal," but she is nevertheless "irresistibly
and dangerously delightful." Another article of 1820 [20] makes a
point of artistic quality in the novel; that is, it must be dramatic,
not didactic. Besides, the author says, one should not insist on
the ascetic point of view of a St. Simeon Stylites; all pleasure
should not be cut out of life. But such exhortation, revelation
enough by itself of the state of public taste, makes up only a
small part of the article. Much more notable are the demands
that the novel must not merely do no moral harm, it must not
hurt "natural or revealed religion." And novelists would do well,
considering the dire examples of Voltaire and Rousseau, to
avoid philosophical speculation. The real tendency of the writer
comes out strongly too in comments on women novelists, who
are remarkable, he says, for the fineness, delicacy, and sensibility
with which they portray everyday, domestic life; though men are
superior in the *Tom Jones* or *Roderick Random* type, naturally
enough, since women could never know the society described in
such novels. But this is good; otherwise "we should have the sex
deprived of that vestal purity which constitutes its chief ornament, and which gives us a foretaste upon earth of celestial
enjoyment." Let woman keep out of this arena, "in which to
win the highest prize of victory is scarcely glory."

Later in this year [21] the same pen (one would guess) comes

[19] *Ibid.*, 9:266 (1820).
[20] *Ibid.*, 10:221 (1820).
[21] *Ibid.*, 10:509 (1820).

to the defense of Scott. Replying to an open letter to Scott reprimanding him for not "making the interests of morality and religion any part of his plan," the critic contends that this is mere negative censure. Scott should not be attacked unless he has actually undermined morality and religion. This nothing can excuse; in fact, literary art and skill make subversive novels all the worse, all the more dangerous. But if Scott's stories are merely entertaining, not positively harmful, he should not be attacked.

Such tempered moderation as this disappears from later pronouncements on the subject; indeed, they grow increasingly strict and puritanical. The *Port Folio* reprints, one must suppose with approbation, an article from the *Christian Observer*[22] on novel-reading, with Scott's *Pirate* as a chief example. Here fiction is divided into three levels, the vicious, the indifferent, and the good, with the Waverley series in the limbo of the second. The *Observer* regrets that Scott's novels have been allowed in many Christian homes where novels in general are forbidden; merely trifling books are too widely read, and their bulk is altogether too great. Scott, it is admitted, has no bad intentions — though one might take exception to a few "offensive oaths and profane exclamations," and in *The Pirate* there is too much "irreverence for the words and sentiments of the sacred Scriptures." Yet on the whole Scott is more decorous than even Richardson. He has great genius and it is a pity that he should waste it in triviality. The very real evils of novel-reading are clearly shown by the fact that thorough novel-readers find the Waverley series tame, not voluptuous enough.

A little later [23] there appeared the last of these articles, it

[22] 14:236 (1822). Macaulay's father was editor of the *Christian Observer*. Macaulay's sister speaks of the great amount of novel-reading in the family, and says that her father did not approve of it, although he allowed it. He published in the *Observer* an anonymous contribution defending novels and especially those of Fielding and Smollett. This article, which terrifically scandalized many of his subscribers, came, he discovered later, from the pen of his young son, Thomas Babington. See G. O. Trevelyan, *Life and Letters of Lord Macaulay* (2 vols., London, 1876), I, 60–61.

[23] 16:461 (1823).

would seem, a downright statement of the evils of novels as a class, with assertions that the style and language were generally bad, as were also the morals and the effects upon the mind, which they relaxed and enervated. Against this background of prejudice toward the novel the enthusiastic reviews of Scott in the *Port Folio* take on the appearance of missionary work; the critic seems an eager apostle of liberal culture trying to persuade subscribers that they could read Sir Walter, at least, without danger to their immortal souls.

The *North American Review* was as enthusiastic in its devotion to Scott as was the *Port Folio*. There is, however, a noticeable difference in tone between them. The *North American* is distinctly more ponderous, more magisterial; contributors seem impressed, or possibly oppressed, with the dignity and responsibility of their position. It is perhaps for this reason that, though they are always mindful of morality and the dangers of "vulgarity" (i.e., realism) they seem much less anxious to conciliate pious readers and feel free to write with complete independence. Their high seriousness shows itself in an unwillingness to review a book by itself; the solid part of a review is generally an elaborate philosophical discussion in which the author's whole production is reviewed and his fundamental relations with art, morality, or religion are minutely analyzed and judged. It is quite evident that the *North American* aspired to be in America what the *Edinburgh* and the *Quarterly* were in England. It is in these ponderous introductions, however, that the most significant comment on Scott is to be found.

Indeed, the *North American* reviewed only three of the novels as they appeared, and all of these were early ones — *Guy Mannering, Old Mortality* (and *The Black Dwarf*), and *Rob Roy*. There was also a review in 1831 of the earlier novels of the collected edition as pirated in Boston, but aside from the usual philosophical preliminaries, the writer devoted himself to comments on Scott's new prefaces and notes.[24]

[24] *North American Review*, 1:403 (September, 1815), W. Tudor; 5:257 (July, 1817), J. G. Palfrey; 7:149 (July, 1818), E. T. Channing; and 32:386 (April, 1831), W.

The first of these, of *Guy Mannering*, is the weakest, a typical routine review consisting of a page and a half of discussion, two of summary, and thirty of extracts. The author seems interested chiefly in propriety and dignity. He thinks the new novel equal to *Waverley*, except that its character range runs lower (he has in mind Meg Merrilies, Dominie Sampson, Dirk Hatteraick, and Dandie Dinmont), a fact which he says debars the novel from permanent literature; the higher characters should have been more carefully developed. He is also irritated at the vulgarity and carelessness of the language — the Scotch dialect, the smugglers' and gypsies' cant and Dirk's low Dutch, and even more by such coinages as *appetising* (from the French *appetisant*) and such a plural as *neatnesses* — "an instance of the modern fashion of making all substantives plural, which only adds to the hissing sound of the language without any increase of force . . . absolutely barbarous."

The two other reviews, however, rise to higher levels than the first. The review of *The Black Dwarf* and *Old Mortality* dismisses Scott's weaknesses as due to carelessness and recklessness, although like other serious critics the writer has moral qualms about the introduction of "the marvellous" into a modern story and what he thinks comes close to vulgarity in language. But of these points he thinks little in comparison with the spirit and eloquence of the work. The very carelessness, he says, is that of an accomplished person of great power. He is especially impressed by the author's ability to bring to life the strange society he describes; the ordinary novelist could not possibly do it. In short, his art in all its phases shows the very greatest power. *The Black Dwarf* itself is disposed of quite rightly as a comparative failure showing scattered sparks of genius, especially in the psychological involutions of the dwarf's character. *Old Mortality* the reviewer recognizes as superior; in fact he sets it above *Guy Mannering*. Yet like many other Americans he trips on the subject of morals — he cannot bring himself

B. O. Peabody. The record of authorship of articles in the *North American* (vols. 1–125, 1815–77) has been preserved and published in an analytical index.

to approve of certain characters whose morals in real life would be objectionable, and who would furnish poor models of conduct to impressionable readers. Yet, in discussing Scott's authorship, which he (like Tudor in the review of *Guy Mannering*) thinks certain, he loads Sir Walter with the highest praise, and declares, "He holds the tenure of his immortality most firmly by his novels."

The review of *Rob Roy* is still more definitely in terms of panegyric, first of all on the novels taken together. The author's use of history, his wide experience and knowledge, his depiction of nature, his depth of feeling, are all dilated on. One may call them novels, it is said, but they are actually "views of the real world, given by a man who observes it widely, justly, and feelingly, and passes by nothing however low and shrinks from nothing however terrible, which God has placed here as a part of his system." [25] Turning to *Rob Roy* itself, the reviewer indicates certain characteristic weaknesses, especially in various points of plot construction, and admits at the end that the book might have been better. Still, he says, it shows the author "not yet exhausted . . . he has not yet forsaken invention and become an artisan." The usual long summary of the novel, moreover, is interspersed with highly favorable comment, especially on the description of scene and on the characters of Diana Vernon, Nicol Jarvie, and, with reservations, of Rob Roy himself.

It is in more general comment rather than in the discussion of these novels that the attitude of the *North American Review* comes out best. In considering a single novel, notice of certain weaknesses was unavoidable, but in a broad survey and especially in comparison with other novelists, Scott's supremacy was equally beyond question.

As they looked back over the earlier history of the novel, these reviewers found no one to place beside Scott. This fact they frequently implied, and occasionally developed in detail. W. B.

---

[25] One needs to read very little of the later depreciatory comment on Scott to see how modern realism has modified the idea of Scott's "passing by" and "shrinking" from nothing.

O. Peabody in his review of the collected novels expresses in stronger terms than any of the rest the *North American's* reverence for Scott, a reverence felt for no other novelist. Peabody waves aside as superficial carpings all the common objections to the Waverley novels in matters of plot, heroes, and stock characters. Any diminution of interest in the later novels, he insists, is due merely to the fading of novelty. Even Scott's style, which had caused many objections, is praised for its simple clarity, especially when held up beside that of Coleridge and other "children of the mist." And there is a section too on the fine qualities of Scott's personal character, especially his lack of jealousy and his serene consciousness of strength, which the novels, with a breadth of scope and freedom impossible in the poems, reveal perfectly.

Peabody declares that all earlier novelists are inferior. Fielding, whom he ranks even below Maria Edgeworth both "in talent and in moral taste," he considers narrow and parochial; indeed to posterity Fielding is bound to seem vastly inferior to Scott. Smollett barely deserves mention, but Richardson stands the closest, though he, like Fielding, is too local, too much absorbed in external details. Of current writers, Peabody is even more scornful. He expatiates on Scott's moral purity and then brings in "the brazen impudence" of Bulwer and tosses aside all the newer novelists, with their lunatic asylums and Newgates, as low, mechanical, and sensational; the author of *Cyril Thornton* (Thomas Hamilton) is the only younger writer he is willing to mention in the same breath with Scott. Maria Edgeworth is really the only other novelist of whom these reviewers speak with any comparable respect. In fact, she is glorified by Edward Everett [26] as having a power over common life hardly inferior to Scott's, though of course in "the higher and more splendid qualities" she cannot stand the comparison. The attitude toward Cooper, the most important of the American novelists, is also enlightening. Like the *Port Folio,* the *North American* was ap-

[26] "Miss Edgeworth," *North American Review,* 17:383 (October, 1823).

parently unmoved by patriotic impulse. Indeed, the reviewer of
a group of Cooper's novels [27] regrets that Cooper has always to
be read in comparison with Scott, and wishes that he might be
read by himself for the pleasure to be obtained from his American scenes. Yet the critics themselves cannot avoid the comparison; the reviewer of Cooper's *Red Rover* [28] stops to exclaim
over the blazing up of Scott's genius in *The Talisman* after
several disappointing ventures.

They also make the point of Scott's supremacy by emphasizing
his importance as an innovator and his great services to the novel
as a literary form. Bryant, in reviewing *Redwood,*[29] a new
American novel by C. M. Sedgwick, remarks with the utmost
emphasis that twenty years ago no one would have believed
possible the wonderful improvement in the novel that the author
of *Waverley* has since brought about, and Jared Sparks, the
historian, reviewing a batch of American novels in the next
issue [30] remarks on their superiority and ascribes it to the influence of Scott especially, and also of Maria Edgeworth. It is
because of them, he says, that "the graver part of the community"
has taken restrictions off novel-reading.[31]

Again, W. H. Prescott,[32] the most eminent of these critics,
declares that Scott has done far more than anyone else for the
novel since the beginning of its renaissance in the early
eighteenth century. He is to be compared only with Shakespeare,
over whom he even has certain notable advantages in the free-

---

[27] W. H. Gardiner, *North American Review,* 23:150 (July, 1826).

[28] G. Mellen, *ibid.,* 27:139 (July, 1828).

[29] *Ibid.,* 20:245 (April, 1825).   [30] *Ibid.,* 21:78 (July, 1825).

[31] Sparks develops some strange notions to explain the success of the historical
novel. He thinks it is easier to write because it is based on actual fact, and the
scenery is that of real places. Hence there is less demand on the author's
imagination. He also thinks it more dramatic than the older forms; the author
holds himself aloof and makes his characters more real and independent. The
national quality and local color, he decides, is for the most part a drawback, since
people are much more attracted to the unknown. It would be hard to imagine
a series of critical remarks on the subject that time has shown to be more
consistently wrong. He ends, however, with the statement that Scott has many
high qualities that cannot be imitated, but regrets his carelessness in composition and his use of obsolete and foreign terms.

[32] "Novel Writing," *North American Review,* 25:183 (July, 1827).

dom of form the novel gives him, with the consequent possibility of wider illustration, as well as the "superior opulence of his literary acquirements" and the resultant "greater variety of information."[33] Indeed, he has given "a healthful character" to fiction and raised it to new levels. What would one not give for something comparable to *Old Mortality* about ancient Rome? There are echoes of this in Peabody's review of the collected novels, when he declares that they are prose poems, and that the historical romance is the finest form of the novel, one requiring a hand of "easy and gigantic strength."[34] He says too that the great test of the novels is a second reading, and that they not only stand it, they require it.

The *North American* reviewers, like those of the *Port Folio* and many in England, were concerned of course with the status of the novels as history and their effect on the study of history. Peabody, for instance, insists that historical fiction does not undermine the work of the historian, and that as far as distortion is concerned the novelist is the less liable to error since his characters represent classes and not individuals — an ingenious, if doubtful argument, which shows at any rate a desire to make out as good a case as possible.

The reviewer of *Old Mortality* takes an even more surprising stand. After a defense of the novel in general, in which he asserts that its low reputation comes from no inherent defects, but from its having fallen sometimes into bad hands, he goes on to doubt the efficacy of making the novel too serious and informative, although he cannot help approving such tendencies and recognizing that ideally they are desirable. "It is not to be disguised," he says, "that the mass of novel-readers are readers only for amusement. There is danger of driving them away by so grave a

[33] Prescott had earlier compared Scott and Shakespeare in "French and English Tragedy," *North American Review*, 16:124 (January, 1823). He says here that they are alike in their national and romantic spirit, and that, while Scott cannot meet Shakespeare in the matter of philosophy, he surpasses him in his "wordly, good-natured shrewdness," shown in such characters as Pleydell and Edie Ochiltree. He is inferior, too, in the supernatural, but has done all that can be done with local superstition.

[34] Note the strength of this theory among the Victorians. See page 188 ff.

pretension. Their moral nutriment, to be received, must be all insinuated. They must be taught and amended, while they imagine they are only entertained." This writer, however, seems to be the only one who had such misgivings; in general it was felt that the "improving" qualities brought into the novel by Scott and Miss Edgeworth were most fortunate. Still it is worth noting that this reviewer does predict, in a way, what has happened in the modern novel, which in its most ambitious forms has become highly exclusive, making no attempt at all to reach any considerable number of the reading public.

It is clear too that these early reviewers, in the *North American* as elsewhere, are in the habit of undertaking the defense of the novel as a respectable form, thanks most of all to Scott, and that they are almost sure to argue for its value as a moral agent. Yet many of them wish it definitely understood that at the same time they consider a plainly didactic method inartistic. For instance, W. H. Prescott in his article on "Novel Writing," defending the lack of absolute poetic justice in Scott, deplores the didacticism of Miss Edgeworth as leading to the violation of probability. It would be possible to collect a good many such instances. Yet, from a modern point of view, these critics all seem very strong for the didactic, and their aesthetic scruples have a rather tentative and perfunctory ring.

Altogether, these passages from the early years of the *North American,* like those from the *Port Folio,* reflect an esteem for Scott in America not to be surpassed even in Edinburgh. And perhaps the most important aspect of this esteem is the way in which it broke down, in all but the most rigid circles, the moral and pietistic barriers against the novel in a prevailingly evangelical society. The Waverley novels, if one is to believe these critics, practically by themselves opened pious, middle-class households to the novel. Scott was not only thrilling, he was pure, he was inspiring, he inculcated the noblest ideals, and, if he did not preach and instruct, he did not at least say anything subversive of natural or revealed religion. Not even Richardson — "the saintly Samuel" — was as suitable to the family reading circle as he.

CHAPTER V

A GROUP OF RADICAL AND
LIBERAL PERIODICALS

THE UTILITARIAN *Westminster Review* appeared first in
1824, just at the time when the better magazines were beginning to neglect Scott, but it reviewed in a consistently hostile
tone *Redgauntlet, Woodstock,* and *Anne of Geierstein,* as well as
the German imitation, *Walladmor.*[1] The burden of the complaint is always the carelessness and thinness of this later work,
and the sorry comparison it makes with the novels written ten
years earlier. The review of *Redgauntlet* opens with sarcasms at
the exclamations of wonder over Scott's fecundity. The critic is
surprised that he does not write even more, in view of the thinness of his current novels, wherein genius fails to keep even
pace with the pen, and the result is of "the stamp and order
of the Minerva Press." The most to be said for *Redgauntlet* is
that it is not so poor as its immediate predecessors, and in the
analysis that follows we learn that Scott succeeds in demonstrating objections to three ways of telling a story — the letter, the
diary, and narrative — all of which he uses badly. One incident
(the challenge at the coronation) is labeled ridiculous, another
(Darsie's danger from the tide) is said to be "infinitely inferior
to that of the same nature in *Reginald Dalton* [by Lockhart]
from which the idea is manifestly borrowed," and even the descriptions, which critics in their blackest moments conceded to
be excellent, are denounced as "singularly weak and ineffective."

[1] As follows: *Redgauntlet,* 2:179 (July, 1824); *Woodstock,* 5:399 (April, 1826);
Anne of Geierstein, 11:211 (July, 1829); *Walladmor,* 3:273 (January, 1825).

This critic is willing to praise only *The Tale of Wandering Willie* (to which, however, he denies originality) and some few character sketches, especially Peter Peebles; to arrive at these, he says, one must toil through many barren stretches.

The same aggressively hostile spirit, more extreme here than anywhere else, is just as apparent in the criticisms that follow. As cutting as any are the remarks on *Walladmor,* the German imitation foisted on the book trade as written by Scott himself. The critic allows it all of Scott's merits, as well as one he will never achieve — it is in only two volumes. The review of *Woodstock* runs to fifty-eight pages of utter damnation, the reviewer's justification for so long an essay on a book he thought worthless apparently being his belief that a thorough exposition of Scott's decline and fall was badly needed. Sir Walter is told that he should have stuck to Scotch history; his first essays in English history, though faulty, had succeeded. His antique language, whether of Richard I or Charles I, is said to be always the same, and in addition is marked by "violent endeavor after quaintness," phrases cribbed from Shakespeare, and a style overfigurative, alliterative, and "poetical," affected and improper for prose romance. *Woodstock* is condemned throughout the regular category of reviewers' points. The dialogue is anachronistic and diffuse; the story "unhappy in its conception and barren in great and agitating events," and as usual full of melodramatic machinery to catch the devotee of the Minerva Press; and the plotting highly improbable and unmotivated. The usual pedantic bore is worse than ever, and the hero as inconsequential as usual. The character of the old cavalier on the contrary reminds one of Scott's earlier and greater days, and actually belongs in the gallery of fine portraits in the early novels. Finally the historical accuracy and the fundamental truth of the book are denied. The critic cites historical sources to show that Scott's portraits of Charles II and Cromwell are false, as are also those of the anti-royalists and Independents. The review rises to the sarcastic climax, "Such is an HISTORICAL romance by the author of *Waverley!*"

Though the review of *Anne of Geierstein* three years later is distinctly unfavorable, the tone is more reasonable and sympathetic. The only question about a new Scott novel, the critic says, is whether it is as good as his others, and this one is disappointing. Scott's chief appeal has always been made through fine individual characters like Nicol Jarvie, Dalgetty, and Claverhouse. *Anne of Geierstein* depends much more than usual on the attempt to recreate a whole age, or on general historical background, which is much less attractive to the average reader. Certain elements of the story are objectionable, notably the "diabolism" of the meetings of the Vehmgericht ("we are too old for these fantastic horrors"); the book is too much a "romance of pulleys and ropes," and the Philipsons are poor characters. On the other hand the historical subject matter is good, and the pictures of the Swiss peasantry and the Duke of Burgundy excellent. In spite of the fact that the critic finds the original sources clearer and more interesting than the novel, he concludes that altogether the book is worthy of praise. It is easy, he says, to select passages for either praise or blame, but after all no one but Scott could so have described Swiss scenery or the court and character of the "bon roi René" of Provence.

The hostile tone of these reviews is no doubt justified in part by the actual falling off of the later novels, and the fact that a comparison with the first ones is always implied, but the extreme animosity of all but the review of *Anne of Geierstein* is obviously traceable to political motives. The *Westminster* was of course a radical organ, bound to be anti-Tory and hence anti-Scott as soon as a political issue was raised. Hence the climactic strictures on the political bias of *Woodstock*. This is merely a general tendency of the age, and in Scott criticism finds its most important expression in the angry diatribes of Hazlitt. And as far as Scott himself was concerned, one needs only to recall the early differences with Jeffrey and the whole story of the founding of the *Quarterly*, which was to serve as a proper Tory counterbalance to the misguided Whiggery of the *Edinburgh*. It is quite possible that the more lenient attitude of the last essay was due to the growing sympathy with Scott in the misfortunes of his last years. It cannot be said that the very late novels like *Anne of Geierstein* are better than *Woodstock,* yet *Anne* is much more kindly reviewed. Sir Walter's gallant struggle made it dangerous, indeed almost indecent, to treat him roughly. There is little reason to think that *Anne of Geierstein,* had it come a few years earlier, would have been treated any more tenderly than *Redgauntlet* or *Woodstock.*

Strong support for such a belief is offered by a review of *Tales of a Grandfather.*[2] Here was a book involving definite political and historical ideas, such as the *Westminster* was bound to testify against. Yet the reviewer praises wholeheartedly where he can, and in politics dissents only after careful apology. These tales are declared to be a classic as great as anything Sir Walter has ever written, though so modest in form that the public may not realize it. Of the style not enough can be said; there is purity, exactness, finish, "strength which hides itself under ease and urbanity," condensed philosophy, "living truth and descriptive power," "Homeric simplicity and grace"; in fact, it is much superior to that of his earlier work. But, the critic continues, "veneration for the author must not be allowed to induce blindness toward the defects of the politician," since "whatever is written by Sir Walter Scott is read by everybody who has leisure to open a book." There follows an exposition of the liberal point of view, in which Sir Walter is set down as a Tory, though an enlightened one, and a man who if he has not helped the world to progress, has at least hindered retrogression in his own party. This article would seem to indicate fairly the growing sympathy and tenderness for an aging and distressed hero, of whose work the critics had a few short years before shown signs of tiring, to put it mildly.[3]

[2] *Westminster Review,* 10:257 (April, 1829).

[3] The young John Stuart Mill was at this time writing for the *Westminster,* but was apparently the author of none of these reviews. He did, however, write an article in the *Edinburgh* in 1824 (*aetatis suae* 18!), where Scott is condemned as useless — an article he later dismissed as a boyish exercise; and also a review of the *Life of Napoleon,* which he demolished as history, though he granted

In other liberal or radical and anti-Tory organs, like the *Examiner* and the *Athenaeum,* the same political antagonism and irritation is quite apparent, coming out not only in articles on Scott, but in casual remarks, like one in a review of Hazlitt's *Napoleon* (1828) to the effect that Scott was the slave of opinions and of the associations of his environment,[4] and is also tempered in the later twenties by sympathy and reverence for the hard-pressed author. The other general tendencies appear too, all leading as usual to the conclusion that the first novels were the best, that the finest thing in them was the depiction of Scottish national life and character, and that the defection to pure romance, produced at the rate of several long novels a year, was a fatal error.

That dangerously democratic publication, the *Examiner,* could be friendly enough to Scott.[5] For instance, its review of

it attractive as fiction, which he said made it especially dangerous. Compare similar remarks in the review of *Tales of a Grandfather.* G. L. Nesbitt in *Benthamite Reviewing* (New York, 1934), pp. 105 ff., comments on the reviews of Scott in the *Westminster.* Mr. Nesbitt is probably justified in speaking of these reviews as the most unfavorable ones Scott received, "thoroughly scathing." Still, there had been others that had used the word "failure," and it is certainly not accurate to say that Scott's novels were favorably reviewed as a matter of course, or that careful examination of them was to be found only in the *Westminster* or the *New Monthly.* There had been innumerable careful examinations of them ever since 1814.

[4] An article in the *Christian Spectator* for February, 1825 (7:80) represents the anti-Tory animus combined with a pious, evangelical point of view. The subject is "Imitation Waverley Novels," but most of the space is given up to an analysis of Scott's own novels, and the argument is finally summed up as follows: "Our opinion of the Waverley Novels, then, is briefly this. Looking at them as works of taste, as a monument of genius, as a manual of human nature, we give them all the praise they claim. Looking at them as historical representations, while we admire their impressiveness, we condemn their partiality [i.e., in medievalism, Toryism, and the alleged anti-Puritanism of *Old Mortality*] and send the reader to correct his conceptions by the less vivid but more accurate delineations of history. Looking at them in their moral and religious tendency, we deprecate their influence [i.e., Scott made no positive effort to stimulate "holier feelings," and Fergus, Rob Roy, and Ravenswood are bad influences]. Such is the master."

[5] Reviews appeared in the *Examiner* as follows: *Kenilworth,* March 11, 1821; *The Pirate,* December 30, 1821; *Nigel,* June 2, 1822; *Redgauntlet,* July 11, 1824; *Tales of the Crusaders,* July 3, 1825; *Chronicles of the Canongate,* November 4, 1827; *Fair Maid of Perth,* June 1, 1828; *Anne of Geierstein,* June 14, 1829. The *Examiner,* June 27, 1825, had reprinted from the *Scotsman* a much more favor-

Kenilworth is almost uniformly favorable, and indeed gives evidence of no political irritation. Elizabeth is a splendid character, though the other main historical characters are not so interesting, and it is only to be regretted that Sir Walter Raleigh alone represents the famous group of brilliant Elizabethans of whom Sir Philip Sidney at least might have been revived. The scenes at Cumnor Place and the inn, and all the imaginary characters are excellent, but the heroine, Amy, cannot be considered the equal of Flora MacIvor or Jeanie Deans.

The review of *The Pirate* is damning, not only on artistic but also on political grounds. The writer admits Scott's excellence in description, in vivifying the bare outlines of traditional matter, and in illustrating habits and manners, "which is his highest qualification," but finds this novel in comparison with his earlier ones as barren as the Orkneys where it is set. Moreover, the satire on agricultural reformers is objectionable, besides being anachronistic, and clearly illustrates Scott's conservatism; he would "keep mankind eternally in the same state." His use of superstition, especially of omens which are fulfilled — and in a story as late as 1723 — is very dangerous morally, and is merely an item in his general tendency to color all old customs and habits of thought, including superstitions and the very errors of medievalism, to make them attractive. *The Fortunes of Nigel*, like *Kenilworth*, apparently did not arouse a political animus, but did stir the critic to declare that it was a mere abortion, and that Scott knew he was taking liberties with his public, as his quotation of the old line "Story? Lord bless you. I have none to tell, Sir," very well showed. In spite of good descriptive passages and many good scenes, the critic finds it obvious that a novel once in six months would be better than one every three. The same strain recurs in the review of *Redgauntlet,* where Scott is accused of absolutely snoring and is told that he ought to lie fallow for two or three years. The story itself

able review of the *Tales of the Crusaders* than its own, which appeared a week later. Note also, October 9, 1825, "Bad English in the Scotch Novels," a long list of instances.

is not only badly managed, with its successive use of letters, parallel journals, and a kind of nondescript appendix, but its very matter is stale — Jacobite stories are threadbare, the Stuarts furnish a miserable nucleus for a romantic tale of high adventure, and the Pretender, "a poor drunkard," is conjured up for no dignified purpose.

The *Tales of the Crusaders,* as usual, suffer as badly. The reviewer says that compared with the best they "exhibit a pretty decent tumble," though they are no worse than the worst. He goes on to argue that Scott's forte lies in costume and manners rather than in character, and in classes rather than in individuals. *The Talisman,* though better than the hackneyed *Betrothed,* is as wild as Ariosto, and has only one good character, Richard. The heroes and heroines, as ever, are entirely negative. He finally bursts out with the declaration that "even the vulgar begin to yawn at melodrama. and processions, turbans and helmets, caftans and coat-armor" and serves notice that he will read no more such novels unless he has a reasonable hope of finding more characters like Bradwardine, Nicol Jarvie, Jeanie Deans, Dandie Dinmont, and Rebecca, who "give Nature and substance to so much dress, decoration and scene-painting." He also attacks the "flat humor" of the introduction, which indicates that the author is about to publish a life of Napoleon. He hopes this is not so; "few writers are less fitted to deal with facts which resemble fiction than such as have been long employed in endeavoring to make fiction resemble fact."

The succeeding reviews are, as has been already pointed out, distinctly milder. The *Chronicles of the Canongate* the reviewer estimates as an average sample of Scott's genius. He approves most highly of *The Two Drovers,* although the central figure, another Rob Roy, is possibly too extravagantly romantic. Better than the stories themselves he likes the introductory links of the narrator, a point where he agrees with certain other critics. Yet on the whole, he continues, Scott's supremacy lies in the romantic; in dealing with real life he is sometimes weak. The edge of this criticism, however, he softens with a concession that is continually urged by modern critics, that one must expect to find "comparative insipidity and flatness as an occasional set-off in a writer so unpremeditated and spontaneous as Sir Walter Scott." These same points are re-echoed in the review of *The Fair Maid of Perth*. This novel is again coolly evaluated as average Scott, and the critic seems to find it objectionable that the romanticist should entertain by idealizing, that he should falter in approaching actualities and cast a glamor over material that in real life would be far from brilliant. The same tolerance, and one might add indifference, marks a review of *Anne of Geierstein*. The reviewer asserts that Scott cannot write a thoroughly bad book, but obviously he can find nothing good to say of the work he is discussing — it suffers from the weight of too much history, the author has been careless of morality in the political and social sympathies he has expressed, some of the romance is "Radcliffe redivive," and the love as always, except in *Lammermoor* and *Rob Roy*, is insipid. The general trend of the *Examiner's* criticisms seems clear enough. It is practically that of the *Westminster*. There are vigorous attacks on the novels before Scott's bankruptcy, and leniency toward those after it. The most perceptible difference is perhaps that the pendulum of the *Westminster* swung much wider. As at first it was more violent, so later it was more lenient, and more positively friendly.

The *Athenaeum,* another periodical initiated in the late twenties, shows a surprisingly active interest in Scott during his last four years, publishing frequent reviews as well as a number of general essays. These are in general more elaborate and carefully considered than the *Examiner* articles, but the characteristic tone is the same, in fact very much like that noticed in the *Westminster*. Considering that the series rises to a climax with two highly laudatory notices of *Count Robert* and *Castle Dangerous,* in regard to which most reviewers seemed to think complete silence the most charitable policy, one may mark the *Athenaeum* critics as the most friendly of Scott's later reviewers.

The first important notice of Scott appeared as the ninth essay in a series, "Sketches of Contemporary Authors," by the youthful editor, Frederick Denison Maurice.[6] His *Tales of a Grandfather* had, however,[7] been called one of the best children's books ever written, perfect of its kind, and the reviewer had shown understanding by pointing out that it was really suitable to children, yet at the same time did not treat them as "pretty dears" or "amusing idiots." Maurice's essay reveals not only the attitudes already spoken of but also a point of view that the Victorians were to insist on shortly, that Scott lacked philosophy and depth. Considering Maurice's later career, and his importance as a representative Victorian, this is hardly surprising. The earnest seekers for instruction were beginning to show themselves.

Maurice begins by praising Scott superlatively as an observer. He had always taken things in perfectly, had noted every fine shade and detail not only in the expression of character but in the background and the natural scenery of his settings. He was always interested in his materials and never bored by them. Hence if description alone were necessary he would be perfect. But still for him history is merely a brilliant pageant, a heap of facts of which he knows neither the why nor the wherefore. This lack shows especially in soliloquies when man is pondering the most serious things. Shakespeare on such occasions is full of the most wonderful reflections, "the highest of all merit," but Scott rarely aspires to them, and when he does merely shows "shrewd good humor." It is so too with his observation of Nature. He thinks of it only in relation to the beautiful, never seeing it in relation with "still higher principles and with moral and religious truth." As a result, his scenery stands by itself; it is not "shown as the drapery of the thoughts." Again, Scott is not really a *moral* writer. (At this point one sees Wordsworth making way for Carlyle.) He is not immoral, because he never encourages immorality or is indecent, but he never does anything to reform

---

[6] *Athenaeum*, March 11, 1828, p. 217. See *The Life of F. D. Maurice, Chiefly Told in His Own Letters,* edited by his son, Frederick Maurice (2 vols., New York, 1884), I, 78.

[7] February 22, 1828, p. 134.

his age; "his works do scarcely anything toward making men wiser or better." Just as he has no power of reflection, but merely shrewd good humor, so here the most one can claim for him is "general and good-humored benevolence"; his mind is healthy and genial. His specific political opinions are also to be deprecated. They show his feudalistic bias and his failure to realize the evils of antiquated systems.

Scott stands, Maurice thinks, midway between great writers like Shakespeare and Homer who "exhibit the human mind" and the dealers in mere incident and sensation. Some of his work, it is true, would lift him higher than this middle ground, but for the most part he writes merely to amuse the crowd. The *Life of Napoleon,* his latest work, is merely a tedious novel. He has failed to appreciate the scope or meaning of his subject. For instance, "he seems never for a moment to imagine that the French Revolution was merely one of those shadows on the dial-plate of history which follow and measure, but cannot in themselves influence, the great onward movement of the human mind." Having thus shown his own grasp of the cosmos, and testified in favor of the sacred gospel of Progress, the critic closes on that note of apology now so characteristic of those who found it necessary to emphasize Scott's shortcomings, and gives him his due for "unaffected sincerity and genial kindness."

During these last years of Scott's career, the *Athenaeum* allowed space to several other general articles on Scott, none, however, so significant as the one just described. There is discussion[8] of the wide imitation of Scott on the Continent: by Sismondi in France, by Mme. Caroline Pichler in Germany (she is praised for her grave sentiments, independence of thought, and freedom of judgment, "not naturally to be expected from a female and particularly a native of Vienna"), by Manzoni in Italy, and now finally by the Spaniard de Trueba, to whom the article is really devoted. A year later[9] appear essays on "Sir Walter Scott and Goethe" and on "Scott's Novels — The New Edition of

[8] April 1, 4, 1828, pp. 310, 324.
[9] May 27, June 3, 1829, pp. 329, 337.

Waverley." One may easily hazard the guess that this is Maurice reiterating his theories. He says that Goethe's greatest quality, his "clear and all-embracing intelligence," is exactly what Scott lacks. Scott thinks little about his own mind and has no power of reflection. He has wit, not deep nor fine, but strong and copious, eloquence of a sort, a fancy for broad and vivid pictures and remarkable facility in composing them. But his genius really lies in filling "his conceptions with a spirit drawn from the form of ordinary human nature, and intelligible and interesting to all" and associated with "simplicity and uprightness . . . keen and unperverted sensibilities," moral energy and fresh social sympathies. On the other hand, he has no philosophical insight. He never showed in youth a tendency to muse on the mysterious and the infinite; he was never absorbed in complicated states of mind. He is popular because all his material comes from a common stock in which all have an interest, but he never realizes that men have a secret life within, which they do not display to the world — his books appeal for their glittering pageantry and the suspense concerning the outcome of the story.

In the second part of his essay the critic again elaborates the theme of Scott's shallowness, declaring that he knows little about human relations in society or the philosophical ideas of truth, beauty, duty, God, necessity, and freedom — he is merely a sort of "master of the ward-robe to the universe." Again he is compared, of course to his detriment, with Shakespeare, especially in *Hamlet,* but also with Godwin! This latter philosopher, "dark, hard, narrow," has, the critic admits, none of Scott's powers, and yet he shows man as under the dominion of "an encircling and constraining destiny." Nothing in Scott, it is said, not even the story of Ravenswood, comes back to mind so often as "the pale, stiff beings who dwell in the twilight cavern of Mr. Godwin's thought." Scott gives us bright and glittering toys, wonderful to play with; Godwin "clumsy and rusty medallions." Yet in Godwin there is "one grain of gold fit to be employed in forging a ring such as that of Solomon or that of Gyges." Scott has a thousand almost unequaled talents; Godwin "a single stern and dim

conception." The critic explains, however, that he does not condemn Scott, who never pretended to other talents than those he
actually possessed, and who has given mankind many gifts, but
he does condemn those who would make him a prophet or priest,
and exalt him above Homer, Cervantes, and Shakespeare.[10]
Such adulation is absurd. All there is in Scott is understood by
half the reading public of Europe, "and therefore cannot be very
deep or difficult." There follows a brief comment on *Anne of
Geierstein,* the newest of the novels. It is said that Scott's powers
are now known; readers know what to expect of him. *Anne,*
however, is the best novel he has written since *Quentin Durward.*
Indeed, it has more "pleasant writing, spirited dialogue, and
brilliant description" than any other, except Scott's own, since
Hope's *Anastasius* — "Oh that the sire of that most profligate
Greek would beget such another villain."

Scott's autobiographical account in the preface to the new
edition of the novels also leads to animadversions on his lack of
philosophy. The new preface is said to reveal no secrets. It shows
that Scott was never reflective, that he never "attempted to make
his life a harmonized and methodical work of art." The critic
expresses regret that Sir Walter never attended an English university, where he might have gained a philosophical point of
view, and where his obvious vagueness and inaccuracy might
have given way to "precision and fineness of thought," but finds
reason to thank God that at least he escaped the discipline of a
Scottish university!

The reviews of *Count Robert of Paris* and *Castle Dangerous* [11]
are clearly from another pen, more enthusiastic and less "philosophical." The first gives high praise to Scott's work in general.
It is said that no one has approached him in the field of the

---

[10] As a matter of fact, Scott was almost never exalted above them. He was
frequently equaled to Cervantes and sometimes to Homer in certain respects. The
comparison with Shakespeare which follows immediately (in the review of *Count
Robert*) is a great exception.

[11] *Athenaeum,* December 3, 1831, p. 777; December 10, 1831, p. 796. Note also a
most favorable review of *The Fair Maid of Perth,* e.g., "the true excellency of this
most exquisite novel" (May 21, 1828, p. 466).

historical novel. In the range of his common characters he surpasses Shakespeare, whose "peasants are all born fools and his
yeoman heroes of East Cheap," and who has no one to equal
Gurth or Dandie Dinmont. For both novels the reviewer shows
a somewhat surprising partiality. He finds *Count Robert* remarkably vivid and interesting in scene and action and affects
to see in Hereward the Saxon "the dawn of the British gentleman." So too with *Castle Dangerous,* the "stately superstructure"
of which he lauds, declaring, "in no instance has our great master
architect used his materials with better judgment." And at the
end he turns to praise of Scott's own character and spirit and
hope for his better health.

The *Athenaeum* series of essays is above all else interesting
for its statement, made nowhere else so clearly and fully at so
early a date, of what was to be the Victorian attitude toward
Scott. Political murmurings there had been, and complaints as
to many sorts of artistic failure; in fact, they had been the
general rule for some years, but no one before had pushed so
far and so consistently the thesis that Scott lacked depth and
"message." The best critics of Scott in his own time, Jeffrey and
Hazlitt, hardly considered such a point of view; they took the
novels as they were, saw in them the fruits of great genius, care-
lessly and lavishly dispensed, and did not take pause at the
absence of "grave sentiments" and earnest edification.[12] But here
an early apostle of the moral and utilitarian in literature, happening to light upon Scott, stole from Carlyle the thunder of his
essay of 1838. Doubtless it was Carlyle who established and gave
most vivid expression to this point of view, which persisted
throughout the rest of the century and is common enough even
now; yet Carlyle adds little, except in the power of expression,
to the kindly and condescending remarks of Maurice and other
Athenaeum essayists.

That Scott could, nevertheless, make a strong appeal to the
disciples of progress and even the radical professors of utili-

[12] Note, however, a passing hint at lack of depth by Hazlitt in his essay, "The
English Novelists." (See page 126.)

tarianism is amply demonstrated by Harriet Martineau's two essays on Scott. These she published in *Tait's Magazine* shortly before Sir Walter's death, and later included in her *Miscellanies* under the heading of "Philosophical Essays."[13] That so earnest and dogmatic a disciple of utilitarianism, who could enslave fiction to her service in such work as her *Illustrations of Political Economy,* should prove to be also a Scott enthusiast is at first blush almost beyond comprehension. She was, however, a devotee, and succeeded marvelously in interpreting Scott in the light of her principles so that he too is impressed into the service of her dogmas, and becomes, *mirabile dictu,* an exponent of utilitarianism. The first of her two essays, the one on Scott's genius, analyzes his personal character into the elements that Miss Martineau celebrated in her own attempts at fiction. She dilates on his early discipline — his suffering as a child, his wide reading and outdoor life. To her all this represents her favorite mode of education, that by natural forces and means as contrasted with the regular and formal process. The special qualities of his genius she analyzes and isolates. She first discovers his purity, in which he offers a refreshing contrast with Byron, and which she declares is natural and inherent, not the mere result of ignorance. He is modest, ranking his own work low, though she regretfully admits a touch of Toryism here — "He wrote a score of matchless romances for the sake of improving a patch of bad land." From these qualities, however, spring his frankness and discretion. She admires, too, his typical combination of mirth and pathos kept in true balance, except in the one instance of the Covenanters, which she hopes he repents. She finds in him likewise a fine cheerfulness, a "spring of joy" in his love of nature and his kindliness, though she is forced to regret that he lacked a deep faith in humanity as a whole and let his Toryism blind him in such matters as the Reform Bill. She admires his industry (which is a sign of his healthiness), his gusto,

[13] See *Tait's Edinburgh Magazine,* 2:445, 301 (1833) and Harriet Martineau, *Miscellanies* (2 vols., Boston, 1836), I, 1–56. These essays are here dated "Norwich, 1832."

which in turn must have fed and supported his cheerfulness, and the practical character of his conduct and conversation, that is to say, his reality, which pervades not only his everyday life but even the loftiest scenes of his novels. This list of personal characteristics is obvious enough; certainly most writers on the subject have found it inescapable. The only one to which serious exception may be taken is possibly the discipline; except at the very end of his life after his financial disaster Scott seems to have followed his own bent and indulged his tastes and inclinations much further than most human beings are able to. Her consideration and discussion of all these points is on the other hand colored by utilitarian notions, and produces altogether an effect and tone that must have been surprising to Sir Walter if the essay ever fell under his eye.

In the second essay, on the achievements of his genius, her social ideas are still more rampant. She glorifies him as a great teacher by practical example; he is more important than the whole phalanx of clergy, moral philosophers, and teachers. He "is the president of a college where nations may be numbered for individuals." He "has preached truth, simplicity, benevolence and retribution" all over the world, and is to be praised for "introducing the conception of nature as existing and following out its own growth in an atmosphere of convention," a favorite utilitarian doctrine which in its rigid practical applications led the sect into some of their worst pitfalls. By this she meant, as she explains, that Scott knew many ranks of people and really interpreted them. Here again, however, Scott's Toryism and aristocratic leanings make trouble for her argument. She regrets that he did not accord all ranks equal honor and has to admit his prejudice in favor of royalty. Still, she declares, he has shown the people the truth about courts and has exposed "priestcraft and fanaticism." In general, indeed, he has been of service in satirizing eccentricities and follies such as can be reached easily only through fiction.

It is a pity, she thinks, that in spreading the feeling of kindliness and joy that is so characteristic of him he did not extend

his field to take in humble life. This he actually does not show at
all, since his humble characters, even Jeanie Deans, owe nothing
of their special interest to their lowliness. He failed to see that
"true-heartedness" is found in perfection among humble folk
even more than in high life, and is intensified there by the reality
of existence and the absence of convention. Neither, unfortunately, did he have any conception of political freedom or the
permanent improvement of society — he really knew the poor
only as appendages of the rich.[14]

On the other hand — her last point — she thinks he has done
much for women, in a negative and unconscious way, by his
female characters, nearly all of whom are mere "womankind."
The very conventionality and insipidity of such characters, Miss
Martineau seems to believe, should open the eyes of readers to
the deplorable state of women in modern society. But Flora, Di
Vernon, Rebecca, and Jeanie supply inspiring instances of what
woman may be. In closing, after a recapitulation, she maintains
at some length that his greatest service lies in revealing how
much may be accomplished through the novel by way of instruction and benefit to society, and goes on to indicate how this discovery may be further capitalized and applied to the public good
in special instances. Thus it is clear that the overwhelming influence of Scott brought in not only a flood of romantic novels
and plays but also inspired, if such a word can be allowed, those
anything but romantic fictions, the *Illustrations of Political
Economy*.

[14] Obviously she failed to know or understand Scott in such matters.

CHAPTER VI

LETTERS AND JOURNALS;
NOVELISTS AND ESSAYISTS

THE MOST famous letters on Scott are those of J. L. Adolphus, *Letters to Richard Heber, Esq., M.P.*[1] These are of course not bona fide letters but merely formal, systematic criticism cast into the letter form. Actually they constitute the one important book on Scott in his own time. They were written while he was still in mid-career as a novelist and are cited with respect even now by modern critics.

Adolphus set out to prove by internal evidence that the author of *Marmion* and *The Lady of the Lake* must also be the author of the novels. This was of course practically a work of supererogation, considering that Scott's authorship of the novels was taken for granted in most quarters. Thus the elaborate machinery of parallel passages and other detective devices was hardly necessary. The book seems to be a kind of academic exercise undertaken as a labor of love. Indeed the author so describes it at the end and apologizes for its undue length on the ground of his fondness for the material. "Who," he says, "in speaking of a favorite author was ever able to confine himself within his proposed limits." He also remarks, "Too often, I confess, have illustrations been selected as much at least for beauty as for aptness." In its marshaling of evidence, Adolphus' book is certainly conclusive, and it is hard to see how anyone — if there was anyone — who still needed to be convinced could have withstood it. Scott himself read the book, was pleased by it, and had the author

---

[1] First published in London in 1821. References are to the 2d edition, 1822. Especially, see pages 14, 33, 43, 66 ff., 312.

at Abbotsford several times, but still smiled and said calmly that, though ingenious, the book proved nothing.

If proof of authorship had been its only point the book would now be of interest only as a literary curiosity. It goes far beyond its ostensible purpose, however. Practically all of his detail Adolphus presents from a critical point of view. Though an enthusiastic admirer of Scott he is fully awake to his numerous defects; in fact, his criticism has worn very well and still seems sound. In the matter of style especially he shows a clear-sighted detachment. He says that in general it does not attract attention — "it is the spirit, not the structure of the sentence that obtains our attention" — and draws comparisons with Hope's *Anastasius* (except for some of the Waverley novels the most successful novel of the time), where the style is in itself an obvious attraction. He notes the ordinary running level of Scott's style with the occasional rise to brilliant climaxes, where the writing is highly admirable, and is fully conscious of the "frequent offences against the simplest and most general rules of composition." Scott, he says, is a bad reviser. The dialogue he analyzes at length, and admits that in spite of its excellences it sometimes sinks to "bald verbosity" or becomes "weak and affected" to the point of absolute unreality. Earlier in the book he had pointed out Scott's pedantry in the use of technical military phrases even in conversations, which had "an artificial studied air" and "a quaintness hardly befitting the characters to which they are assigned."

In other matters, too, Adolphus demonstrates his careful and critical reading of the novels and his ability to worship without going blind. It is in his praise, however, that he is most interesting. He examines *The Bride of Lammermoor* carefully to show its high poetical quality, and to prove the author a man with the habit of mind of a poet. He asserts that "no writer has appeared in our age (and few have ever existed) who could vie with the author of *Marmion* in describing battles and marches except the author of *Waverley*." On such a point as breeding and manners he declared Scott to be far above the level of the average novelist, who was likely to be vulgar — Scott, he says, is "just and honorable in principle and conduct," has "elegant taste" and "a generosity of feeling united with exact judgment" which give him the power of expressing not merely "the right and fit but the graceful and exalted in human action" — indeed he points out later that these qualities prevent his perfect portrayal of scenes "of bold and unmitigated vulgarity." Altogether, Adolphus' criticism reminds one of Jeffrey. Both had a fine eye and a deep feeling for Scott's best qualities and yet at the same time realized with equal clearness the defects of method, at least, to which he was heir.

The less formal sources of contemporary opinion and feeling have been more fully exploited, perhaps, than the reviews and critical essays. Allusions to Scott's person and the novels and poems in diaries, letters, and recorded conversations, supposedly private and not intended for the publisher, are numerous and may be found, naturally, in large numbers in the various biographies from Lockhart down, or in such volumes as the memoirs of John Murray. Especially striking are the outbursts of ecstatic praise from readers who rushed to seize the novels as they fell, one by one, from the press. Charles Lamb is usually mentioned as the only notability of the time who was left completely unmoved by them, and his indifference is made light of on the grounds of his complete absorption in earlier literature. But the very mention of Lamb as the unique heretic [2] has heightened the impres-

[2] Of course there are other heretics, if not notable ones. Charles Kirkpatrick Sharpe, the eccentric antiquarian, a lifelong friend of Scott's and closely associated with him in his work on ballads, had the utmost contempt for the Waverley novels. He makes his opinions on novels perfectly clear in two letters of 1839. He approved Fielding, and Smollett for *Humphrey Clinker* (though otherwise he was "a caricaturist, with only vulgar, dirty humor to recommend him"), but he gave the palm to *Clarissa Harlowe*, "a perfect compendium of worldly wisdom," and, in view of Richardson's education, "the most wonderful thing ever composed." In Sharpe's own time nothing worth a pin had been written except *Castle Rackrent* and *The Heroine*. Having just read *Nicholas Nickleby*, he liked it better than any new novel he had ever read except the two just mentioned, though it was "a woeful falling off from Richardson and Fielding . . . and must die in a few years." Yet Dickens is "worth an hundred Sir W. Scotts, because he paints (extravagantly) *real* manners; Sir Walter what never was—is—or will be." See his *Letters*, edited by Alexander Allardyce (2 vols., Edinburgh, 1888), II, 516–19. Cf. also W. F. Gray, *Scott in Sunshine and Shadow* (London, 1931).

sion of Scott's absolute dominion. That Scott possessed such power over his readers, that they thought of him with love and admiration and welcomed a new Waverley novel with infinite delight, it would be futile to deny. As a matter of fact the generalization that everybody liked Scott is safe enough, and there is little use in trying to run down enough additional heretics to constitute what might be called a protestant sect. Quite typical of the prevailing rage, and less often quoted than most, are the two following instances. Henry Edward Fox at the age of nineteen confided to his journal: "I read *Kenilworth*. Nothing W. Scott writes can be bad (except the *Monastery*) but the impression it leaves is quite horrible and disgusting, for the manner of her death [Amy Robsart's, of course] is revolting to all feeling."[3] Harriet, Countess Granville, was also a devotee. At about the same period (September and October, 1820), she wrote to her friends, "We are all at *The Abbot*. I have only read the first volume. I delight in even the faults of his novels, *Ivanhoe* excepted." And a little later, "Today I perform alone upon a roast chicken, and mean to devour *Kenilworth* with it. There are different opinions. Charles Greville told me last night that he did not stir out or go to bed till five in the morning the day he began it."[4]

In spite of exceptions, "different opinions," and a virtuous youth's distaste for such horror as poor Amy's death, what further praises would an author have from his readers? It was for this sort of thing that Scott listened, and as long as he heard it in sufficient volume, he kept his own way, regardless of whether the professional critics sang high or low. Even more revealing is Hobhouse's comment on the last two novels of the series: "I have read poor Walter Scott's last romances, *Robert of Paris* and *Castle Dangerous;* incredibly inferior to almost all his other performances and smelling of apoplexy. Nevertheless, no one else

[3] *Journal of Henry Edward Fox* (London [1923]), p. 61. Note also page 193 for a comparison with Byron, to Scott's disadvantage; also page 121, for a devastating description of Lady Scott.
[4] *Letters of Harriet, Countess Granville* (2 vols., London, 1894), I, 181, September 15, 1820, and 186, October 8 or 9, 1820.

perhaps could produce so good and lively an historical fiction as either of these tales."[5]

Sydney Smith, a reader whose praise any writer of the time doubtless appreciated, confessed several times in his letters to his pleasure in the early novels. Writing Lord Lansdowne in 1819 he expressed disappointment at *The Bride of Lammermoor,* but nevertheless was "a great admirer of Sir Walter Scott" — when he took up a new novel, "turnips, sermons, and justice-business were all forgotten." Again, after *Ivanhoe* he wrote Constable, "Pray make the author go on. I am sure he has five or six more novels in him, therefore five or six holidays for the whole kingdom." He praised especially *Waverley, Old Mortality,* and *Ivanhoe;* in such later and weaker specimens as *The Abbot, The Pirate,* and *Peveril,* though he still finds words of favor, he was exasperated at the falling off.[6]

These are the rule. Of course not everyone was swept off his feet. As Lady Granville remarked, "There are different opinions." Yet readers who registered anything worse than a mild pleasure in the novels seem to be nonexistent. Crabb Robinson, the ubiquitous diarist of the period, having read *Waverley,* was by no means carried away, and altogether seems to have felt that the new writer was no improvement on Mrs. Radcliffe.[7] At least "his sense of the romantic and picturesque is not so delicate, or his execution so powerful," or "the incidents so dexterously contrived," though "his paintings of men and manners are more valuable." Besides, like most later readers, Robinson thought Waverley himself "a not very interesting personage" and won-

---

[5] See J. C. Hobhouse, Lord Broughton, *Recollections of a Long Life,* edited by his daughter, Lady Dorchester (6 vols., 1909–11), IV, 160, entry of December 30, 1831.

[6] Sydney Smith, *Life and Times* (4th and rev. ed., 1896), *passim.* Cf. G. W. E. Russell, *Sydney Smith* (London, 1905).

[7] Few modern critics take Mrs. Radcliffe very seriously, but Q. D. Leavis, in *Fiction and the Reading Public* (1932), would agree with Crabb Robinson that Scott is no genius but merely another Mrs. Radcliffe. Mrs. Leavis indeed admires Mrs. Radcliffe for qualities which most critics call defects. Compare Lady Louisa Stuart (see below, page 115), whose remarks now seem the natural ones to make. Wordsworth spoke of Scott as "of the Radcliffe school," but from another point of view. (See below, page 143.)

dered if his name was intended to indicate his wavering between two kings and two mistresses.[8]

That voracious reader, the exuberant Miss Mitford, whose gusto never failed her, was at best mildly enthusiastic, though as buoyant in style as ever. In October, 1814, she wrote to Sir William Elford to ask him if he had read *Waverley* and to give him her opinion. She knew it was Scott's "by a thousand indications — by all the faults and all the beauties — by the unspeakable and unrecollectable names — by the vile pedantry of French, Latin, Gaelic, and Italian — by the hanging the clever hero and marrying the stupid one . . . by the sweet lyric poetry — by the perfect costume — by the excellent keeping of the picture — by the liveliness and gaiety of the dialogues — and last but not least, by the entire and admirable individuality of every character in the book, high as well as low — the life and soul which animates them all with a distinct existence, and brings them before our eyes like the portraits of Fielding and Cervantes." She goes on to explain, however, that the foregoing gives a higher idea of the book than she really has, "though I do like it very much indeed"; and also that she likes Bradwardine best and Flora MacIvor least of all the characters.

Two months later she recurred to her aversion to Sir Walter's style — "that half French, half English, half Scotch, half Gaelic, half Latin, half Italian — that hotch-potch of languages — that movable Babel called *Waverley!* My dear Sir William, there is not in the whole book one single page of pure and vernacular English; there is not one single period, of which you forget the sense in admiration of the sound." After all, this alone restrains her from thoroughgoing enthusiasm. Sir Walter should have had a more classic style, and been more mindful of the elegances of the century which had just passed! She liked *Guy Mannering* better; in fact, "I am reading it with great pleasure," though she

---

[8] See Thomas Sadler, ed., *Diary, Reminiscences, and Correspondence of Henry Crabb Robinson* (2d ed., 3 vols., London, 1869), I, 474–75, February 5, 1815. Also Edith J. Morley, ed., *The Correspondence of Henry Crabb Robinson with the Wordsworth Circle, 1808–1866* (2 vols., Oxford, 1927).

is still a skeptic, and doubts if she will feel the same when she has finished it. Besides, she thinks it is not Scott's — *Waverley* was much more like him. A little later still she has come to the conclusion that Meg Merrilies is very melodramatic, and that the current admiration of her is merely a proof of the present vitiated taste. She has read *The Antiquary* too, but does not reveal her opinion. Eight years later, in 1824, she shows a much less qualified joy in Cooper's novels; she declares, "In my mind they are as good as anything Sir Walter Scott ever wrote"; and finds Long Tom in *The Pilot* "the finest thing since Parson Adams." It is clear that Miss Mitford does not join the procession with the rank and file of her contemporaries.[9]

Indeed, letters to friends who are urged to buy this or that new novel are the usual thing, coming from celebrities of Byron's caliber as well as from all sorts of more obscure people whose opinions taken altogether would represent the cultivated popular taste. There was one letter writer, however, whose opinions were especially significant for their insight and perspicuity and are quoted continually with approval by modern critics. This was Lady Louisa Stuart, whose shrewdness and force of expression are not at all surprising in a granddaughter of Lady Mary Wortley Montagu. Lady Louisa had become a good friend of Scott's soon after he began the novels; they met occasionally when she was a guest of the Duke of Buccleuch in Scotland, they corresponded when she was at home in London or the country, and she was one of that little group of intimates to whom Scott early confided the secret of his authorship — she herself says he told her in 1815.[10]

Lady Louisa read with great enthusiasm and appreciation, but closely and carefully and with due critical detachment. She is, for instance, capable of lecturing Sir Walter rather sharply for putting the word "sentimental" into the mouth of Claverhouse a

[9] See R. Brimley Johnson, ed., *Letters of Mary Russell Mitford* (London, 1925), *passim*.

[10] Except as noted, see *The Letters of Lady Louisa Stuart*, edited by R. Brimley Johnson (London, 1926), *passim*.

century or so before its birth in the writings of Sterne. This was the sort of thing that Scott cared little about, but the word disappeared when *Old Mortality* reached a second edition.[11] She felt, too, that considering the large number of his English readers Scott overdid the obscure Scotch dialect — even she with her Scotch connections had difficulty with it — but her most frequent criticism is of "huddled-up" plots. Again and again she alludes, good-naturedly always, to what both Scott and she seem to have regarded as a kind of congenital weakness. For instance, she writes of *Old Mortality,* "It surprises me by not sinking into flatness after the return of Morton from abroad; which was a very slippery place for *you,* who profess never knowing what you are going to write." Of *Redgauntlet* she writes to Sir Walter that she has read it twice, likes it very much, and sees a quick second edition, "though I could almost wonder why; for there is no story in it, no love, no hero — unless Redgauntlet himself, who would be such a one as the Devil in Milton." She tells him that *Wandering Willie's Tale* is in his best manner, but that Wandering Willie himself should have been used in the plot to better purpose. "I heard no more of him, that is to say, the aforesaid author grew tired and flung the cards into the bag as fast as he could. I know his provoking ways." She was also, she says, "a sincere partisan" of *Ivanhoe,* which disappointed many discriminating readers from the beginning. Still, she thought the book had many faults, notably the manner of the Templar's death, and in the matter of character, the undeniable fact that Rowena was "pretty much a 'sweet woman,' " and Athelstane too much a buffoon and "revived to so little purpose."

On the other hand, she insisted on the genius that distinguished all the novels. Even *The Monastery,* the first "failure" of the series, found a staunch defender in her. *The Abbot,* she

[11] Lady Louisa's point was well enough taken, although she is a little too late in her ascription of it to Sterne, at least as a novelist. See the *New English Dictionary.* The word does appear, however, in a very early letter of Sterne to Elizabeth Lumley (?1739-40). But according to L. P. Curtis (*Letters of Laurence Sterne,* Oxford, 1935, p. 14) so early an appearance of the word is one of several reasons for doubting the authenticity of this letter.

said, was good enough to send readers back to *The Monastery*, where they at last had their eyes open to its real excellences; and this was "a secret triumph to me." It was not, to be sure, as good as *Waverley* and certain others, but it had its "full share of what is in my mind the principal charm of them all — masterly touches of character." Only at *St. Ronan's Well* and the last "apoplectic" pair did her heart sink. Of the first she remarked, after reading the opening, "I apprehend a tumble down stairs and shall be as sorry as if I had written the rest myself," and of *Count Robert*, "Alas! alas! I have got 'Count Robert' and could cry over it." [12]

When it came to a question of Scott's use of history, Lady Louisa was a staunch defender. His kind of anachronism she thought fully justified. In *Peveril*, a novel for which she cared little anyway, she is irritated at his treatment of the Countess of Derby, "who was a heroine, but no virago . . . Fie upon him! he must be turned Whig with a witness." But this is an exception. Her usual feeling seems to have been that Scott did not pervert history, but, as she wrote apropos of *Old Mortality*, "elucidates it and would give a person partially acquainted with it the desire to be more so." Later, in 1820, she makes this same point again and amplifies it by a vivid and penetrating comparison with the work of Mrs. Radcliffe. This lady, she declares, abounds in the worst kind of anachronism — "the polished manners and senti-mental cant of modern times put in the fifteenth and sixteenth centuries. The enlightened philosophy likewise! young ladies arguing with their maids against their belief of ghosts and witches when a judge durst not have expressed his doubts of either upon the bench" — all in a "palavering style" made popular by Miss Aitken with her memoirs of Queen Elizabeth.

Like all other critics of good judgment, Lady Louisa recognized the superiority of the Scotch novels over the romances. Looking back at them in 1827, when the best of Scott's work had

[12] See Wilfred Partington, *Sir Walter's Post Bag* (London [1932]), p. 146, and (for allusions to *St. Ronan's Well* and *Count Robert*) Florence MacCunn, "Lady Louisa Stuart," *Blackwood's*, 185:554 (April, 1909). For allusions to *Old Mortality* in the second paragraph below, see *Familiar Letters of Sir Walter Scott*, I, 393.

long since been done, she gave the first place to *The Heart of Midlothian*. She had, however, set them in rank as they came out. *Waverley* was a favorite of hers, and when *Old Mortality* appeared in 1816, she set it above *Guy Mannering* and *The Antiquary* but not above *Waverley*, though she adds immediately, "As a whole, however, I believe it does bear the palm." She had high praise for it indeed. It was "super-excellent"—"it breaks up fresh ground and has all the raciness of originality." Its remarkable vividness of character and scene made her feel that she had been present at the action and had actually been swept off her feet, by Mause and Cuddie especially. She could not sleep after reading it. *The Bride of Lammermoor,* too, seemed to her one of the greatest. She wrote Scott in August, 1819, that she had had it by heart for five weeks, along with *A Legend of Montrose.* She told him that it had all the old power of fascination; Ravenswood was his best lover, and Annot Lyle's matin song had "the true notes of the old lyre." It was true that she recognized the old faults too —"but who does not read on"— and she declares with a deep feeling of affection that of all the twenty-four volumes so far published not one was to be spared. Lady Louisa's criticism of course is fragmentary and incomplete, but it has the peculiar authenticity and ring of reality that mark the true amateur, the vivacity that comes of having no professional responsibility and no duty to proceed through a formal routine. Besides, it is perhaps the best criterion we have of the feeling about the novels among the best readers — not critics.

§

The novelists of importance — and they were very few — all looked up to Scott as the Lilliputians looked up to Gulliver. The greatest, Jane Austen, is the only one who after a century is still "great"; in fact she is infinitely greater in our day than in her own. Jane Austen of course lived long enough to read only the first three or four of the Waverley series; *Waverley* and *The Antiquary* are the only ones we know she read. Although her allusions to Scott are casual and fragmentary, one seems justified in setting her down as an admirer of his. She had said earlier that she was not much impressed by *Marmion,* but after all she chose it as a gift to send to one of her naval brothers, in terms implying that she was doing him a great favor. When *Waverley* appeared, she straightway assumed, like nearly everyone else, that Scott was the author, and wrote (September, 1814) "Walter Scott has no business to write novels, especially good ones. It is not fair. He has fame and profit enough as a poet, and should not be taking the bread out of other people's mouths. I do not like him, and do not mean to like *Waverley* if I can help it, but fear I must." She adds, apropos of a new novel by Mrs. West, that she is determined not to like anything of hers, and knows she will have little trouble there. This characteristic passage from an intimate letter is Jane Austen's only significant comment on Scott as a novelist, but it shows clearly her conception of his importance and influence.[13]

In the estimation of the time Maria Edgeworth, not Jane Austen, was the only very important novelist aside from Scott, and of course her reputation was thoroughly established before he entered the field. There is no mistaking her idolatry of Scott. She had long worshipped at his altar and when *Waverley* was read aloud in a sort of advance copy in the Edgeworth family circle, she hastened to write him a long ecstatic letter [14] headed, in allusion to the anonymity, "Aut Scotus aut Diabolus," in which the new novel was praised to the skies for its description, its characters, its plot, with only a few little details of disapproval added as "proof positive" that the Edgeworths were no flatterers. But even these are so phrased as to turn into encomium. Her chief objection is to the Fielding-like addresses to the reader; "we cannot bear that an author of such high powers, of such original genius, should for a moment stoop to imitation." Nearly ten years later she wrote to a friend that they were delighted with

[13] See *Jane Austen's Letters to Her Sister Cassandra and Others,* edited by R. W. Chapman (2 vols., Oxford, 1932), II, 101, 134.

[14] For following references, see, except as noted, Augustus J. C. Hare, ed., *The Life and Letters of Maria Edgeworth* (Boston, 1895).

Peveril, "though there is too much of the dwarfs and the elfie." As for Finella (*sic*), Scott did not seem to know what he wanted to make of her and so left her indistinct. Miss Edgeworth has significant praise of *Rob Roy* too. It was read aloud to her for a second time, and she liked it "ten times better than at the first reading." "My eagerness for the story being satisfied, I could stop to admire the beauty of the writing: this happens to many, I believe, on a second perusal of Scott's works."

In these later years, of course, Maria Edgeworth became an intimate friend and correspondent of Scott and her admiration was deepened and strengthened. A letter of October 11, 1824, is especially interesting in the light of remarks by several modern critics, especially Chesterton. Scott had been praising Irish eloquence, which Miss Edgeworth denies superiority over the Scotch variety. She asks him how he can believe it finer when he remembers the thousand and one instances of Scotch eloquence in his own novels. She recalls Meg Merrilies, Effie Deans (did she mean Jeanie?) and Nanty Ewart — "Did no voice from [these] sound reproachfully in your ears as you wrote those words derogatory of Scotch eloquence?"[15] When he died she declared her "anguish . . . that such faculties, such a genius, such as is granted but once in an age, once in many ages, should have been extinguished of its light, of its power to enlighten and vivify the world, long before its natural term of setting! Whatever the errors may have been, oh what have been the unremitted, generous, alas! overstrained exertions of that noble nature."

Maria Edgeworth's reputation has fallen sadly in the last century; are modern readers drawn even to *Castle Rackrent,* to say nothing of *The Absentee* or *Belinda?* But in her own day her

[15] See Partington, *Private Letter Books,* p. 265. Joanna Baillie also passed on to Scott the contents of a letter of Miss Edgeworth's to her (July 2, 1816) praising highly *The Antiquary* and *Guy Mannering.* Miss Baillie herself expresses her great admiration for Meg Merrilies and Dandie Dinmont, and thinks *Guy Mannering* more steadily sustained. *Ibid.,* p. 126. Miss Baillie counted Scott her best friend and had the highest admiration for him and his work. She does not seem, however, to have left behind her much detailed comment on the novels. See Margaret S. Carhart, *The Life and Work of Joanna Baillie* (New Haven, 1923), *passim,* but especially pp. 34, 84, 87.

word carried great weight. Today Jane Austen's one humorous casual comment doubtless means infinitely more.

Another novelist of considerable repute in her own time was Susan Ferrier, and she too, even more than Maria Edgeworth, for she lived in Edinburgh, came under the spell of Scott's person. Her comments on the first novels, however, contrast sharply with Maria Edgeworth's. It is evident that they did not send her into raptures. In October, 1815, she declared in a letter that she has not read "anything fit to be named since *Guy Mannering*."[16] "I dare say you will be much delighted with that performance, as it seems to have given unbounded pleasure to everybody but me; but I do not like it half so well as *Waverley*, though I daresay it is a work of greater power." On the subject of the next novels she is worse than cool — "I've read *My Landlord's Tales* and can't abide them; but that's my shame, not their fault, for they are excessively admired by all persons of taste. . . . I thought my back would have broke at *Old Mortality*, such bumping up and down behind dragoons, and such scolding, and such fighting and such preaching. O, how my bones did ache!" But in 1823 she has grown more orthodox and less independent in taste and writes soberly and primly, "I am reading *Peveril*, and like it, as I do all that author's works, for the imagination, wit, and humor that pervade them," and still later (apparently in 1829), after she had come to know Abbotsford well, she speaks of Sir Walter Scott's patronage and interest as constituting her chief happiness. One may guess, however, that the romantic elements of the novels did not recommend themselves very strongly to her. Her own strain of humorous realism doubtless marked the limitations of her taste, and the later remarks seem to be dictated by a desire to be orthodox and by her veneration of Sir Walter, to whose intimacy she had been admitted.

Thomas Love Peacock was in general satiric on Scott, as he was on most of his great contemporaries. He thought Scott unreal and stagy, to be compared with spectacle and pantomime, and

---

[16] For following references, see J. A. Doyle, ed., *Memoir and Correspondence of Susan Ferrier, 1782–1854* (London, 1898).

guilty, like Wordsworth, Coleridge, Byron, and others, of going out of his way to dig up rubbish to manufacture into literature. But in the most serious and systematic remarks he ever made on Sir Walter, in his unfinished "Essay on Fashionable Literature," written shortly before 1820,[17] he described Sir Walter as having been since *The Lay of the Last Minstrel* "the most popular writer of his time, perhaps the most universally successful in his own day of any writer that ever lived." Scott pleases all classes; "the scholar lays aside his Plato, the statesman suspends his calculations, the young lady deserts her hoop . . . Mr. Scott's success has been attributed in great measure to his keeping clear of opinion. But he is far from being a writer who teaches nothing. On the contrary, he communicates fresh and valuable information. He is the historian of a peculiar and minute class of our countrymen who within a few years have completely passed away. He offers materials to the philosopher in depicting with the truth of life the features of human nature in a peculiar state of society before comparatively little known."

Of the novelists of the period, apart from Scott and Jane Austen, the one whose work has the best chance of interesting modern readers is John Galt, by virtue of *The Provost* and *The Annals of the Parish*. The kailyard school may have written itself threadbare in the century between Galt and Barrie, but the fresh vividness, spontaneous humor, and pathos, in these two books at least, still keep them green. Galt's realism of Scottish village life is quite unlike anything of Scott's in its effect; it is purely local; it has none of Scott's romantic implications of a broad national spirit and a deep romantic past. Yet Galt, too, regarded Scott as the hero of modern literature. In a hasty and perfunctorily written autobiography [18] — a running account of the incidents of his wandering, kaleidoscopic life between Asia Minor and Canada — Galt stops, apparently on impulse, to devote a whole chapter to the genius of Scott, beginning, "Since I have introduced

[17] Edited by A. B. Young and first published in *Notes and Queries*, July 2, 23, 1910. Cf. also Carl Van Doren, *Life of Thomas Love Peacock* (London, 1911). This essay may be dated by allusions to "Mr. Walter Scott" and also to *Rob Roy* (1818).
[18] *The Autobiography of John Galt* (2 vols., London, 1833). See especially II, 210.

the illustrious name of that superb genius . . . I may venture to express in what respects I not only consider him the first in his walk, but ranking with the greatest in any." He had been speaking of his own work and his own limitation of his novels to the humble purpose of moral edification, and had said that no man of common sense would think of entering into competition with Sir Walter on a more elevated and aesthetic plane.

Galt begins his critique by dismissing the bulk of Scott's poetry as "respectable mediocrity," but declares in the same breath that "in romance; he towers into unapproachable excellence." He admits that he gets more pleasure from the historical romances like *Ivanhoe* than from the more careful pictures of manners in novels like *The Antiquary;* in fact, he says, "*Ivanhoe* I regard as his masterpiece." He sets it with "*Hamlet,* or the *Paradise Lost,* or *Hudibras,* or the *Faëry Queen*"; and declares that it "can only be read to be duly valued, by passages"; "it is one of those sort of books in which bright truths and deep insights abound, and which can only be properly seen in quotations." Galt goes on to maintain that the least of Scott is "immeasurably superior" to the work of most men. Scott, he says, has a "necromancy of manner" which can endow with pleasure "matters from which the sober reason recoils," and is the only writer who "ever made the limning of crimes beautiful, and yet withheld from that beauty the power of captivating." He adds, "In this respect [the "necromancy" apparently] he excels, and in this I would say his great strength indisputably lies."

Galt speaks with scorn of that opinion of "the ignorant herd" who praise Scott for his mere pageantry and heraldry, which he says is generally faulty, but is after all insignificant in the total effect of his books. He takes pains to deny, too, that Scott's distinction lay in his volume, as many said, and to insist that it is rather in his "quality of excellence." He also takes occasion to reproduce two poems addressed to Scott, one on the appearance of *Marmion* and the other a high-flown "Apotheosis"[19] on the

[19] One may hazard the guess that the chapter was written for the sake of introducing these two effusions.

occasion of Scott's death, and ends with further remarks on Scott's literary genius and personal greatness, of which the most significant seems to be the following: "He was in the truest sense the describer of feudal manners and customs not as an antiquary, but as a poet. With no exception, either in prose or rhyme, he adhered to that character. In *The Antiquary* and *Saint Ronan's Well,* the peculiar spirit that was ever perched on his pen, presides with the same predominance as in *Ivanhoe.*"[20]

These critics are all realistic novelists, but their veneration of Scott is in general so great that one can hardly expect to find it increased among the more romantic brethren. Their song of praise is, however, equally loud. Jane Porter, who had pioneered in the historical novel just before Scott entered the field, wrote him a very humble letter in 1828 apologizing for undertaking a novel on the period of the Commonwealth and thus invading the field of *Woodstock* and *Peveril,* where really Sir Walter was "rightful Lord of the Soil."[21] Robert Maturin, a belated member of the Gothic school, but nevertheless its most powerful and imaginative practitioner, worships Scott as an idol. To be sure, he owed Scott a debt of gratitude. Scott had always befriended him, used his influence with publishers in Maturin's favor, written favorable reviews of his romances, and in general taken him under the wing of his patronage. Yet after due allowance for this personal relationship, it is clear enough that to Maturin Scott's genius seemed of the first water, unapproachable by any of his great contemporaries. His biographer, Idman,[22] says that he "loved Scott best of all authors, ancient or modern," and quotes remarks which Maturin is alleged to have made to a friend:

[20] Scott thought highly of Galt's Scotch realism, but an important reservation comes out in a letter to Henry Mackenzie: "I entirely agree with you that our Doric dialect is only beautiful when it is simple. Mr. Galt, though a man of very considerable powers, sometimes Out-Scottifies the Scotch dialect" — which will do in a broadly humorous character, but not in other sorts. Grierson, *Letters,* VIII, 146, January 2, 1824.

[21] See Partington, *Sir Walter's Post Bag,* p. 250.

[22] Niilo Idman, *Charles Robert Maturin, His Life and Works* (London, 1923), p. 132.

Yes, he has a most powerful genius, a genius that can adapt itself to the changes of times and feelings with the most extraordinary celerity, and with less than the labours of ordinary thought can reform and remodel the literature of the age. He is the greatest writer of his day. He writes not for England, but for all mankind; and he has embraced in his infinite vision all modes and systems of men and manners. What he does, he does appropriately; not seeking to display all the varieties of his mind in any one work, but only that which properly belongs to it; nothing is out of place; all is perfect, simple, and real; and he possesses the magical talent of explaining a whole character by a simple word of feeling; and of imparting to the meanest figure in his picture the interest of a principal.

Maturin indeed became an imitator of Scott; his last work belongs distinctly to the school of Scott rather than to that of Radcliffe. In this of course he was only one of a multitude. The smaller fry all rushed in in Scott's wake to capitalize the vogue of the historical novels. Those who would have imitated Mrs. Radcliffe had they been writing in the 1790's, now turned out not so much *Waverley's* and *Old Mortality's* as *Ivanhoe's* and *Talisman's*, which after all were just as novel, and were much easier. Scott himself felt that his imitators were spoiling his field and destroying his market with their cheap surplus. Of all these imitators none, it seems safe to say, is read today. A well-read person may have heard of G. P. R. James' solitary horseman, and he may possibly have read in early youth one or two of Harrison Ainsworth's thrillers, but to claim knowledge of Horace Smith (as a novelist, at least) and of Mrs. Bray one must be something of a special student, an explorer of ancient dust heaps. As one would expect, their opinions of Scott, wherever one finds them recorded, are invariably laudatory. Horace Smith in describing a meeting with Scott in Edinburgh uses such phrases as "his immortal works" and "our age's most illustrious writer," humbly dedicates *Reuben Apsley* to him, and, also humbly, writes him that *Brambletye House* is a "humble imitation" and that he is grateful for the mention of his name in the preface to *Woodstock*. G. P. R. James regarded himself definitely as a disciple of Scott. He lived for a time at Melrose and saw Scott often in his last years. The first novel he ever wrote he dedicated to Scott and he thought of him as "that truly great man."[23]

The poets were of course the great glory of the period — Wordsworth, Keats, Shelley, Byron, Coleridge. But the essayists, too, formed a notable company. To Lamb the Waverley novels meant little or nothing; he seems to have remained perfectly indifferent toward them. One might expect the same attitude in that other cockney critic, Leigh Hunt. Hunt had early written very sharply of what he considered (and with some justice) a too complacent attitude toward a villainous trick of Charles II which Scott had had occasion to mention in his *Dryden*. Yet later he regrets in his *Feast of the Poets* the lack of urbanity in this youthful attack. He had also taken exception, early in his career, to the picturesqueness of the verse narratives, *The Lay, Marmion,* and others, but in later casual allusions to Scott as a novelist he evinces a high opinion. In writing of Horace Smith, he says, "I would not insult either the modesty or the understanding of my friend while he was alive by comparing him with the author of *Old Mortality* and *Guy Mannering;* but I ventured to say, and I repeat, that the earliest of his novels, *Brambletye House,* ran a hard race with the novel of *Woodstock,* and that it contained more than one character not unworthy of the best volumes of Sir Walter." The opinion implied here is also to be found in his preface to his own poems (1832), where, in running over the "galaxy" of writers in the age just past, he speaks of "the wonderful works of Sir Walter Scott."[24]

De Quincey was emphatic in his admiration of the novels. He reviewed the German imposture *Walladmor* for the *London Magazine* in 1824 in an essay in which his casual allusions to Scott all imply a high regard. His most interesting comment, however, came very late in life in his essay on "Dr. Parr, or

[23] See Arthur Beavan, *James and Horace Smith* (London, 1899), pp. 199–204, 257 ff., and S. M. Ellis, *The Solitary Horseman; or, the Life and Adventures of G. P. R. James* (London, 1927).

[24] See *The Autobiography of Leigh Hunt,* edited by Roger Ingpen (2 vols., London, 1903), I, 212, 243. Cf. also Edmund Blunden, *Leigh Hunt and his Circle* (London, 1930), p. 246.

Whiggism in its Relations to Literature," written about 1857. Even when one discounts De Quincey's scornful anti-Whiggism, there is enough panegyric left to satisfy the most ardent partisan. De Quincey records Dr. Parr's dismissal of Scott's poetry as namby-pamby and says that can be forgiven, but refuses to condone a similar dismissal of the novels. Was any extremity of party violence, he says, to excuse Dr. Parr's "treating so great a man (as uniformly he did) as a miserable pretender to literature," and describing him as "an arrant charlatan and impostor"? De Quincey is willing to concede the poetry, "but he that can affect blindness to the brilliancy of his claims as a novelist and generally to the extraordinary grace of his prose, must be incapacitated for the meanest functions of a critic by original dulness of sensibility." "Mr. Bentham, Dr. Parr, and Mr. Douglas of Glasgow," he goes on, "are probably the three men in Europe who have found Sir Walter Scott a trifler." [25]

But above all others, prose writers or poets, the man of the age to whom Scott was most a living force, who steadily and consistently recurs to him and keeps him well in the forefront of his mind, is William Hazlitt.[26] In his function as a journalist critic Hazlitt wrote reviews of two of the novels, as well as the brilliant essay that finally appeared in *The Spirit of the Age,* but until his death, in all sorts of connections, he was continually alluding in one way or another to Sir Walter and his work. As one surveys all this matter certain points become perfectly clear. First of all, Hazlitt had a consistent and perfervid admiration for Scott's genius. When he thinks of the novels he goes into raptures. He is perfectly aware of obvious faults and flaws, but these matter little to him. He thrusts them aside and dismisses them. But on the other hand, Hazlitt, a radical, cannot forget Scott's Toryism, which in his eyes is a crime. For Scott as a man with political and social opinions he has an equally consistent and

[25] See *The Collected Writings of Thomas De Quincey,* edited by David Masson (14 vols., 1896), V, 69.
[26] For all references to Hazlitt, see *The Collected Works of William Hazlitt,* edited by A. R. Waller and Arnold Glover (12 vols., London, 1902–04).

perfervid scorn and contempt. The steady conflict between these two streams of feeling in Hazlitt's buoyant, fiery prose makes it the most interesting body of matter ever written about Sir Walter. And there is likewise a corollary of which Hazlitt never tires, one which he insists on stating again and again: the genius of Scott dwarfs and renders contemptible the genius of Byron.

Indeed, of all the criticism of the novels in Scott's own time, the finest and most brilliant is certainly Hazlitt's. Jeffrey, in his series of reviews, is admirably sound and penetrating, and writes with deep feeling, yet one looks in vain to him for the flaming energy and the stirring inspiration so characteristic of Hazlitt's genius. In his periodical writing, Hazlitt five times declares himself at length on Scott; in his lecture on "The English Novelists" in 1818, in reviews of *The Pirate* and of *Peveril of the Peak* in the *London Magazine*,[27] in the classic essay first published in *Colburn's* in 1824 and included the next year in *The Spirit of the Age,* and finally in the essay on "Scott, Racine and Shakespeare" in *The Plain Speaker* (1826).

In the lecture of 1818, written when Scott was producing his finest work, we discover that splendid enthusiasm and eager recognition of Sir Walter's genius which appears again in the later essay, and mingled with it the realization that while that genius after all had its limits, they were not the limits apt to be set by the fastidious. Here Hazlitt exclaims, "In knowledge, in variety, in facility, in truth to painting, in costume and scenery, in freshness of subject and in untired interest, in glancing lights and the graces of a style passing at will from grave to gay, from lively to severe, at once romantic and familiar, having the utmost force of imitation and apparent freedom of invention, these novels have the highest claims to admiration. What lack they yet? The author has all power given him from without — he has not, perhaps, an equal power from within. The intensity of the feeling is not equal to the distinctness of the imagery."

He has, Hazlitt continues, the art of concealing art; there

[27] *London Magazine,* January, 1822, and February, 1823; reprinted in Hazlitt, *Works,* XI.

seems indeed to be no art in the novels, and the author loses the credit due him, for he seems to transfer real life to his pages without transforming it. Of the characters Hazlitt declares, "He leaves them as he found them, but this is doing wonders," and after citing a long list of brilliant portraits, insists that it is impertinent to inquire whether they are creations or drawn from originals. "The picturesque and local scenery is as fresh as the lichen on the rock; the characters are a part of the scenery. If they are put in action it is a moving picture; if they speak we hear their dialect and the tones of their voice." Finally, though there may be rare instances of falling off, "if this author should not be supposed by fastidious critics to have original genius in the highest degree, he has other qualities which supply its place so well, his materials are so rich and varied, and he uses them so lavishly that the reader is no loser by the exchange" — he is inexhaustible. Here is wholehearted enthusiasm indeed. The only negative touch, the one regarding Scott's lack of intensity of feeling, while of great importance, is certainly not underscored in Hazlitt's mind either here or later.

The review of *The Pirate* in the *London Magazine* continues this strain of rapturous delight. It preserves perhaps better than any other written record the actual joy that thousands of Scott's contemporaries took in his novels, but which only Hazlitt was vocal enough to express in its full power. He begins, "This is not the best, nor is it the worst (the worst is good enough for us) of the Scotch Novels." He finds the story absorbing, though it is evident the author writes to gain time. "He has, they say, got a plum by his writings. What have not the public got by reading them? The course of exchange is and will be in our favor as long as he gives us one volume for ourselves and two for himself. Who is there that has not been the better, the wiser and happier man for these fine and inexhaustible productions of genius." When he is gone, "Ah! who will then call the mist from the hill? Who will make the circling eddies roar? . . . Who will summon the spirits of the northern air from their chill abodes, or make gleaming lake or hidden cavern teem with wizard or with elfin forms.

There is no one but the Scottish Prospero, but old Sir Walter, can do the trick aright." He notes the reworking of old materials in *The Pirate,* but asserts that it is weak only in comparison with some of his other novels. "Wert thou to live a thousand years and write a thousand romances, thou wouldst never, old True-penny, beat thy own *Heart of Midlothian!* It is for that we can forgive thee all that thou didst mean to write in the *Beacon,*[28] or hast written elsewhere, beneath the dignity of thy genius and knowledge of man's weaknesses, as well as better nature!"

Following this brief excursion into political prejudices, Hazlitt returns to his rhapsody — "Whatever he touches, we see the hand of a master. He has only to describe action, thoughts, scenes, and they everywhere speak, breathe, and live . . . the things are immediately there that we should see, hear, and feel. He is Nature's Secretary. He neither adds to, nor takes away from her book; and that makes him what he is, the most popular writer living." At last after citing a number of fine passages and also a half dozen slovenly sentences, he ends in the major key, "But let us have done with this; and leave it to the Editor of the *Quarterly Review* [one remembers Hazlitt's excoriation of Gifford] to take up the subject as a mighty important little discovery of his own!"

In the review of *Peveril,* political bitterness has almost completely swamped and destroyed Hazlitt's full-bodied pleasure in the novels; the essay is hardly more than a personal lampoon on Sir Walter. Hazlitt nevertheless considers *Peveril* an improvement on its predecessors. Scott had been sinking, but had risen again in *Nigel* and now, except for the fourth volume, is back at his proper level again. The book is linked in its subject matter with *Old Mortality,* but he does not do so well with the English Puritans as the Scotch, though he does proceed "with real pains and unabated vigor."

At this point political excitement overwhelms him. After

[28] A violently Tory journal (1821) of a very brief life, in which Scott had been originally concerned, though he came to disapprove it. It was in a duel over the *Beacon* that Boswell's son, Sir Alexander, was killed.

praise of Scott's "freedom from bigotry and prejudice" in his
novels, Hazlitt breaks out, "He is accused of being a thorough-
paced partisan in his own person — intolerant, mercenary, mean;
a professed toad-eater, a sturdy hack, a pitiful retailer or sub-
orner of infamous slanders, a literary Jack Ketch, who would
greedily sacrifice anyone of another way of thinking as a victim
to prejudice and power and yet would do it by other hands,
rather than appear in it himself." He goes on to imply that Scott
is really a hypocrite, though a man of prodigious talent, and after
a most extravagant comparison with Cobbett, wherein the latter
hero holds his own remarkably well — Hazlitt backs him for
"describing a Scotch heath or an American wilderness against
Sir Walter for a thousand pounds" and says that his style "is as
good, nay far better"—he declares that Cobbett has never been
a cat's-paw, "which is the *dernier resort* of humanity, into which
Sir Walter has retreated and shuts himself up in it impregnably
as in a fortress." This certainly is eloquent testimony to the
involvement of politics with other spheres of thought, and to the
utter destruction of all poise and natural feeling brought about
by the political intensity of the period. That Hazlitt could conceive of Scott as all he makes him out to be in the earlier review
and still think what he writes here is almost beyond belief.[29]

The same irritation breaks out again in the final essay on
Scott's genius, written in 1824 for Colburn's *New Monthly* and
republished in 1825 in *The Spirit of the Age*. After commenting
on Scott's absorption in the past and his carelessness of the future, a point of view in itself naturally antipathetic to Hazlitt,
and expressing his own low opinion of the early verse romances,
he breaks forth into his earlier strains of praise. "Not so of his
Novels and Romances" — in them Scott broke loose from all con-

[29] One should note Leonard Woolf's praise of Cobbett in "An Englishman"
(*Essays*, London, 1927): "First among Cobbett's virtues I place his English style.
I cannot imagine any English prose more suitable to be given as a pattern and
model to the ordinary man and woman. . . . plain, absolutely unaffected, vigorous and supple, beautiful." It fits the matter as "the satiny coat of a race horse
ripples over the muscles as he walks." In his sentences is the atmosphere of
the English country climate, language, and character. — Still, one need not
imagine in Cobbett a potential "Author of Waverley."

vention. "All is fresh, as from the hand of Nature." He lauds ecstatically their atmosphere and their character, though he makes decided reservations in the case of the newest novel, *St. Ronan's Well,* as material for which Scott was not suited. He lists characters from all the novels whom he regards as acquaintances—"What a list of names! What a host of associations! What a thing is human life! What a power is that of genius! What a world of thought and feeling is thus rescued from oblivion! . . . How many sad hearts has he soothed in pain and solitude . . . He writes as fast as they can read and he does not write himself down. He is always in the public eye and we do not tire of him. His worst is better than any other person's best . . . His works (taken together) are almost like a new edition of human nature. This is indeed to be an author!" And then after all Hazlitt must bear witness to his political faith. Again there is the earlier bitterness at Scott's political point of view — his anti-progressive and anti-radical tendencies; and finally he applies to Scott as a great genius Pope's attack on Addison, "Who would not weep if Atticus were he?" and continues, "we believe there is no other age or country of the world (but ours) in which such genius could have been so degraded." But these were temporary aberrations. Like Hazlitt's remarks on Scott's careless writing, which in this essay also become violently caustic, they do not becloud the fact of Hazlitt's full recognition of Scott's power. Indeed, where else has Scott been so eloquently praised?

In the essay on "Scott, Racine and Shakespeare" in *The Plain Speaker* (1826) Racine figures only slightly. The point of the essay is really to attack the overdone comparison or paralleling of Scott and Shakespeare in relation to creative ability. Enthusiastic as he was about Scott, this was a sticking point for Hazlitt, and he was evidently determined to show the futility of such a comparison. In turning to Scott in this essay, he begins with praise for such historic romances as *Ivanhoe* and *Quentin Durward,* particularly as indicating a much wider range than Scott had been supposed capable of.[30] *Ivanhoe,* especially, he declares

[30] But compare other remarks on *Ivanhoe* on page 138.

to be very nearly, if not quite, equal to the very best. But he denies that Scott possesses the gift of "sheer invention," and undertakes to prove his point by comparison with a much smaller writer, Mrs. Inchbald, who, he says, shows greater powers of invention and sheer originality in the trial scene at the climax of *Nature and Art* than Scott does in his famous trial scene in *The Heart of Midlothian*.

Then, passing to Shakespeare, he declares that Shakespeare *writes;* Scott *transcribes;* Shakespeare's great moments are *original;* Scott's are *compiled*. This is really the burden of the essay — the idea that Shakespeare's plays are actually created in his brain, while Scott's novels are, rather, an effective compilation of excellent materials gathered, stored away, and produced at the proper moment. Scott's great talent, according to Hazlitt here, lies in his not spoiling his fine materials. "Sir Walter is an imitator of nature and nothing more"; Shakespeare is infinitely more. Scott is not creative; his mind is merely full of information. To illustrate his point, Hazlitt cites Meg Merrilies' dying speech, "Lay my head to the East," which is thrilling, but after all a tradition, not an original conception with Scott. Further, he contrasts Meg Merrilies with the witches in *Macbeth* to show how Shakespeare passed beyond mere traditional folklore. Shakespeare gets at the essence; Scott manufactures in bulk — his imagination is matter-of-fact. "Sir Walter's forte is in the richness and variety of his materials and Shakespeare's in the working them up. Sir Walter is distinguished by the most amazing retentiveness of memory and vividness of conception of what would happen, be seen and felt by everybody in given circumstances; as Shakespeare is by inventiveness of genius, by a faculty of tracing and unfolding the most hidden yet powerful springs of action, scarce recognized by ourselves, and by an endless and felicitous range of poetical illustrations, added to a wide scope of reading and knowledge. Scott resembles Shakespeare "only in this . . . he thinks of his characters and never of himself, and pours out his works with such unconscious ease and prodigality of resources that he thinks nothing of them, and is even greater than his own fame." And finally: "The genius of Shakespeare is dramatic, that of Scott narrative or descriptive, that of Racine is didactic . . . Sir Walter Scott gives the external imagery or machinery of passion; Shakespeare the soul, and Racine the moral or argument of it."

The chief significance of this essay, beyond the obvious point that Hazlitt would not assent to the extravagant claims made by many of Sir Walter's admirers that he deserved a throne close to Shakespeare's, is his attempt to define the limitations of Scott's genius, which apparently he felt only when he compared him with Shakespeare. That he is making a safe enough point there is no denying. Shakespeare's name and Scott's are always being coupled, but, with rare and slight exceptions, never by responsible writers, as equals. The point is generally that Scott is supreme in this field or that, except for Shakespeare. Hazlitt recognized too, as he showed later in "Trifles Light as Air," 1829, the temerity of comparing any contemporary writer with Shakespeare. "The living," he said, "are merely candidates . . . for popular applause, the *dead* are a religion or they are nothing." But whether Hazlitt remains on safe ground and makes convincing use of such vague and intangible words as *creative* and *original* is another matter. Of course what Hazlitt is driving at is clear enough, but certainly he hardly does Scott justice when he employs such words as *compile,* and is his point about *tradition* a real one? Certainly, such "compiling," while it may not be literally "invention," is of a remarkably fine kind and easily shades off into originality. One may well take exception, too, to the comparison with Mrs. Inchbald, whose trial scene, fraught with deep feeling though it is, reminds one more than any other passage in her novels that she was a professional actress and thought not merely of dramatic, but of theatrical, effect.[31]

[31] Leslie Stephen in his essay on Hazlitt in *Hours in a Library* (2 vols., London, 1879–81) refers to "this grotesque theory" of Hazlitt's that Scott was not "original," that he built his novels out of great masses of information which he merely did not spoil. He also notes sarcastically Hazlitt's comparison of Scott with Godwin and Mrs. Inchbald, "who had, it seems, more invention though fewer facts."

One cannot help feeling that Hazlitt is establishing too high a standard of "originality" — restricting it and rarefying it too far. He gets at his own meaning much better when he speaks of Shakespeare's grasping the "essence"; and what he actually has in mind, apart from poetical expression itself, seems to be the fundamental and really dramatic grasp of character — "the most hidden yet powerful springs of character." It is akin doubtless to the reservations he made in the first essay — "he has not, perhaps an equal power from within. The intensity of the feeling is not equal to the distinctness of the imagery." It may be akin also to Walter Bagehot's feeling that Scott's characters were better furnished for this world than for the next and to the modern complaint about his superficial psychology and his lack of philosophy. But one should remember that Hazlitt is making such criticism with the very greatest, even Shakespeare, in mind. To many modern critics, perhaps even to Bagehot, much smaller fry have served to dwarf Scott.

These then are Hazlitt's opinions on Scott expressed at length, with some system and show of completeness. But one finds, too, many other interesting allusions to Scott scattered through Hazlitt's literary remains, in various essays, notes, and conversations. The total effect of all these scraps and passing comments is to reiterate and amplify or illustrate the judgments expressed in these five essays. There is the same enthusiastic appreciation of great genius, and the same angry gnashing of teeth at Tory depravity and hypocrisy — the same balancing of the literary genius against the man himself — repeated in various connections and under various lights.

Of outright panegyric there is a plenty, expressed directly or by comparisons with Shakespeare and other admirable figures or, more frequently, with one of Hazlitt's special objects of hatred, Lord Byron. As in the essays, Scott was for Hazlitt the author of the novels; the early poetry was nothing. In his essay on Byron, in *The Spirit of the Age,* he bursts out, "We had rather be Sir Walter Scott (meaning thereby the author of *Waverley*) than Lord Byron a hundred times over," and then goes on to develop a favorite idea. Scott represents Nature — he is transparent, dramatic, forgetful of self — "one of the greatest teachers of morality that ever lived, by emancipating the mind from petty, narrow, and bigoted prejudices." He never grumbles and quarrels, but is always "fair, natural, above-board." Byron, on the contrary, always self-centered, has to make over everything to suit his own point of view. Again in "Old English Writers and Speakers," in *The Plain Speaker,* he insists that Scott's popularity in France shows the rise of French taste as clearly as the popularity of Byron would show the opposite, and later in the same essay refers affectionately to Scott as the author of the Scotch novels, which he will continue to produce in quantity until some future Lord Byron asks, "Who reads Sir Walter Scott now?" Then, in speaking of *Redgauntlet* as the last and almost the worst of the series, though it is redeemed by Peter Peebles and Nanty Ewart and by the catch sung by Wandering Willie, his wife, and the boy, he goes out of his way to maintain that the catch has "more mirth and heartsease in it than is in all Don Juan or Mr. Moore's lyrics." "And why?" — because it is sincere; Scott is thinking of the matter and not of himself. He has "perfect indifference to self . . . He looks at Nature, sees it, hears it, feels it, and believes that it exists before it is printed, hotpressed, and labeled on the back, By the Author of Waverley." And still further, he asserts that there is no comparison between his prose and Byron's poems and that the only living writer he would venture to set beside him is Wordsworth.[32] A few years later, he speaks with contempt of Byron's dedication of *Cain* to Scott — "a pretty godfather to such a bantling."

Hazlitt could also use Scott as an example of perfection for a smaller writer. In a favorable review of Landor's *Imaginary Conversations* in the *Edinburgh* [33] he said of the character of Henry VIII that it was "transfused with all the truth and spirit of history — or of the author of Waverley." On the other hand he

[32] But compare the remarks on Cobbett. See page 129. For the allusion to *Cain,* see *Works,* XII, 179, "On Disagreeable People."

[33] *Edinburgh Review,* March, 1824; Hazlitt, *Works,* X.

could use him to damn a lesser man. In speaking of Godwin,[34] and how popular demand impelled him to go on spinning out his brains for more than was in them, he says, "There is only one living writer who can pass through this ordeal; and if he had barely written half what he has done, his reputation would have been none the less. His inexhaustible facility makes the willing world believe there is not much in it. Still, there is no alternative." He continues, apropos of Godwin's working up his material in *Cloudesley* too much, "This is the beauty of Sir Walter Scott: he takes a legend or an actual character as he finds it, while other writers think they have not performed their engagements and acquitted themselves with applause till they have slobbered over the plain face of nature with paint and varnish of their own . . . We know no other merit in the Author of Waverley than that he is never this opaque, obstrusive body, getting in the way and eclipsing the sun of truth and nature which shines with broad universal light through his different works. If we were to describe the secret of this author's success in three words, we should say that it consists in the *absence of egotism*." He had, by the way, made an earlier attempt to explain Scott's success. In "The Pleasures of Hating" [35] he said that the novels carry us back to the passions of barbarous ages and peoples: "As we read we throw aside the trammels of civilization, the flimsy veil of humanity," and are like dogs off on a hunt.

Scott served as a touchstone, too, in Hazlitt's analysis of Cooper.[36] He found Cooper mechanical, unimaginative, and unpoetical, and thought that he suffered from the lack of accumulated tradition which in Scotland served Scott so well. Of Scott as compared with Cooper, he wrote, "In our own unrivalled novelist, and the great exemplar of this kind of writing we see how ease and strength are united. Tradition and invention meet half-way; and nature scarce knows how to distinguish them . . . In art, in literature, in science, the least bit of nature is worth

[34] *Edinburgh Review*, April, 1830; *Works*, X.
[35] *The Plain Speaker*, in *Works*, VII.
[36] *Edinburgh Review*, October, 1829; *Works*, X, 312, 314.

all the plagiarism in the world. The great secret of Sir Walter Scott's enviable but unenvied success lies in his transcribing from nature instead of transcribing from books."

When Hazlitt wished to belabor such popular contemporary novelists as Theodore Hook and Disraeli, it was Scott he chose as a besom. In his essay on "The Dandy School"[37] he cries out, "Ever while you live go to a man of genius in preference to a dunce; for let his prejudices or his party be what they may, there is still a saving grace about him, for he himself has something else to trust to besides his subserviency to greatness to raise him from insignificance." A little later too [38] he fulminates against "three generations in succession thinking nothing of Garrick, Mrs. Siddons, and the author of *Waverley,* and preferring Mr. Theodore Hook before the quintessence of truth and nature," adding the remark that the vulgar, the mass, admire only vulgarity. Similarly, he set Scott over against his imitators, and contrasted their genius with his in the matter of originality and novelty. "We see what Sir Walter Scott has done . . . by turning up again to the day the rich accumulated mould of ancient manners and wild unexplored scenery of his native land; and we already see what some of his imitators have done."[39]

Of such apparent flaws as lapses in style and insipidity in heroes Hazlitt was perfectly cognizant. He had pointed out several times in his set essays on Scott the carelessness of Scott's writing, but it was his habit to dismiss such criticism as after all of slight importance. His casual comments on this point are in the same vein. The negligence is there, but Scott is a great writer still. In the *Conversations of Northcote* he declares,[40] "Nobody else could write so well — or so ill, in point of mere negligence" and Northcote goes so far as to insist that the novels must be by several hands, they vary so. In writing of "The Prose Style of Poets" in *The Plain Speaker* Hazlitt asserts that one could guess

[37] *Examiner,* November 18, 1827; *Works,* XI.
[38] "Actors and the Public," *Examiner,* March 16, 1828; *Works,* XI.
[39] "The Periodical Press," *Edinburgh Review,* May, 1823; *Works,* X.
[40] *Works,* VI, 386.

the author of *Waverley* to be "a writer of ambling verses from the desultory vacillation and want of firmness in the march of his style." "There is neither *momentum* nor elasticity in it; I mean as to the score or effect upon the ear. He has improved since in his other works: to be sure, he has had practice enough." But in Hazlitt's larger view, Scott was nevertheless a supreme writer, one of whom he could say, "We do not see how, in any circumstances, he could have written better than he does." [39] Nor did Scott's fluency and volume disturb Hazlitt. Rather he admired it, speaking of it on many occasions as a sign of genius, unlike many critics then and since who have found it regrettable. In the essay "On Application to Study" he wrote, "We have a great living instance among writers that the quality of a man's productions is not to be estimated in the inverse ratio of their quantity, I mean in the author of *Waverley*, the fecundity of whose pen is no less admirable than its felicity." And in the essay "On Envy" [41] he declares that the bulk of the Waverley novels hurts their effect actually because it makes them seem easy to do, prodigal, and careless, but that it is really not Scott's excellence readers tire of, but the imitations of him and attempts to emulate his fecundity. In the criticism of Godwin already noted, Hazlitt also contrasts the thinness of Godwin with the opulence and ease of Scott.

The very sore point of Scott's heroes Hazlitt likewise tended to brush aside. He even wrote the essay "Why the Heroes of Romance are Insipid" [42] to make the point that an insipid hero is only to be expected, and to explain that the hero is usually a kind of blank which the author leaves to the reader to fill in as he pleases out of his own imagination. Certainly it cannot be denied that the tradition of the stock hero and heroine as edifying models was so generally accepted that Scott may well have thought his readers quite capable of filling in the vaguest of outlines without any help from the author.

Except when he is contrasting him with Shakespeare, one

[41] Both these essays are in *The Plain Speaker*, in *Works*, VII.
[42] *Works*, XII, 59.

rarely finds derogatory remarks or qualified praise of Scott in Hazlitt's writing. In fact, the only striking instance is in a criticism of *Ivanhoe* while the novel was still new.[43] He recognized its inferiority to the earlier Scotch novels, but this very inferiority struck him as revealing Scott's limitations. *Ivanhoe* showed, Hazlitt said, the national and local limits of Scott's genius — he was clearly not at home in medieval England — his genius, "however lofty and however extensive, still has certain discernible limits; it is strictly national; it is traditional; it relies on actual manners and external badges of character; it insists on costume and dialect; is one of individual character and situation rather than of general nature" — a point of view that Hazlitt supports by citing Rob Roy as against Robin Hood. Occasionally, too, the idea that Scott was a mere copyist of nature rather than an originator takes a rather hostile form, as in a casual remark in a footnote where he speaks of Scott's forte as a sort of traditional literature in which "whatever he accumulates or scatters through his pages he leaves as he finds it, with very few marks of the master mind upon it."[44]

On the whole, however, Hazlitt was hostile to Scott only as a man; he could not forget that Scott was a Tory, a bootlicking sycophant, complaisant to the unspeakable Regent and tenacious of the old medieval tyrannies. In fact, he frequently sets his praise of Scott the novelist in such black and white opposition to his scorn of Scott the Tory that one can hardly help wondering whether he felt the sensational effect of it. Hazlitt is so impulsive and so fiery, however, that it is safer to believe him perfectly honest and unaffected. At any rate, the political bias is as clear in these scattered allusions as it was in the five full-length essays. Apparently it ran always close to the surface and was always ready to break through.

He can tell Northcote grudgingly that he admires Sir Walter "on this side of idolatry and Toryism," but a much more characteristic utterance, once the political fires are lit, is the one in

[43] *Dramatic Essays from the London Magazine*, April, 1820, in *Works*, VIII, 422. *Ivanhoe* had just been dramatized.

[44] *Works*, VII, 156n.

"Envy" in *The Plain Speaker:* "Who is there that admires the Author of Waverley more than I do? Who is there that despises Sir W—— S—— more? I do not like to think there should be a second instance of the same person's being 'The wisest, meanest of mankind,' and should be heartily glad if the greatest genius of the age should turn out to be an honest man." And he goes on to speak of "this misalliance between first rate intellect and want of principle." And even in the midst of the most laudatory criticism and enthusiasm rising into apostrophe he can stop for a moment to call Scott "an inspired butler," a "Yes and No My Lord" fellow in a noble family. Or he can describe perfect felicity as being like "Sir W. S.'s . . . when he sat down at the same table with the king," or refer to "the cold sweat of rankling malice, hypocrisy and servility . . . eh, Sir Walter?"[45]

As violent an outburst as any comes in an allusion to Scott's refusal to translate a poem by Lucien Bonaparte: "Such was the petty spite of this understrapper of greatness and of titles, himself since titled, the scale of whose intellect can be equalled by nothing but the pitifulness and the rancour of his prejudices."[46] Little touches of comic relief to Hazlitt's fanaticism are afforded by Northcote's occasional digs. Northcote, for instance, asks Hazlitt if he is not "more angry at Sir W—— S——'s success than at his servility," to which Hazlitt replies honestly, "I do not think so," or suggests that Hazlitt is glad that Scott is a Tory so that he can qualify his praise of him.[47] Whatever one may think of Scott's personal attitudes, even of his friendship with George IV, certainly malice, rancor, hypocrisy, and even servility are the last characteristics to charge him with. Such explosions, however, are interesting samples of Hazlitt's violence and enthusiasm which worked both for and against Sir Walter, as well as of the pervasive quality of party politics in all their virulent fury a century ago.

[45] See "Mrs. Siddons," *Examiner*, May 25, 1828, reprinted in *Works*, XI; and *Works*, XII, 272, 284.
[46] *Notes on a Journey through France and Italy* (first published in 1826), in *Works*, IX, 254.
[47] "Envy," *The Plain Speaker*, in *Works*, VII, 99, 105.

Yet the burden of emphasis falls on panegyric rather than abuse. In all his writing, whether in the essays devoted solely to Scott, or in passing allusions, it is there that Hazlitt himself places the emphasis, and the abuse, as one surveys the whole, sinks into the background. What one remembers are remarks like the following. "It is few who can get to the fountain head, the secret springs, of nature. Shakespeare did it always, and Sir Walter Scott frequently." Such a tone is frequent; in fact, it is the typical one. Hazlitt declares, "Not to like him [as the "Author of Waverley"] would be not to love myself or human nature, of which he has given so many interesting specimens: though for the sake of that same human nature, I have no liking to Sir Walter."[48] Indeed, in the midst of political diatribe he frequently reminds his readers that no one has cried up the Author of Waverley oftener than he, and will insist that he looks forward eagerly to reading the last new Waverley (if he could be sure it were!) and that "no one would be more glad than I to find it the best."[49] One may point out too that his latest remarks reveal best, perhaps, his enthusiasm and veneration. In the *Examiner* for May 25, 1828, he records the fact that Scott and Mrs. Siddons had been seen viewing a picture together — "Two such spectators the world cannot match again, the one by the common consent of mankind the foremost writer of his age, the other . . . the queen and mistress of the tragic scene." Then, begging pardon of Scott's great characters for turning from them and their creator to Mrs. Siddons, he launches into praise of the actress, but finally returns to Scott, and after a side thrust at his "servility," he breaks out into raptures and finally asks, "Who would not rather see Sir Walter Scott's fringed eyelids and storied forehead than the vacant brow of prince or peer."[50] And again in "Envy" in *The Atlas*, 1830, although objecting as usual to the comparisons with Shakespeare, he says, "No one envies the Author of Waverley because all admire him, and are

[48] See *Conversations of James Northcote, Esq., R. A.*, in *Works*, VI, 443; and "The New School of Reform," *The Plain Speaker*, in *Works*, VII.
[49] "On Reading Old Books," *The Plain Speaker*, in *Works*, VII.
[50] "Mrs. Siddons," in *Works*, XI, 381.

sensible that admire him how they will they can never admire him enough. We do not envy the sun for shining when we feel the benefit and see the light."[51]

It is such remarks that really set the tone of Hazlitt on Scott. These are the ideas that count most and that one remembers. The political hubbub of Whig or Radical or Tory has died down;[52] there is little in it now to stir the blood, but Hazlitt's instinct for the realities and permanencies of genius and art still lives, still has an authentic ring. One may make reservations, one may say that much water has run under the mill in the last century, as it certainly has, but even so, Hazlitt sounds as though he had a strong grasp on realities, and it is hard to believe that however great his admiration for later novelists might be (would he have been an enthusiast for the naturalists?) it would have destroyed or even have very sadly dimmed the fires of his joy in the Author of Waverley.

[51] *Works*, XII, 389.

[52] Yet even in the criticism of the last generation or so one finds a surprising amount of animosity against Scott because of his Toryism and his opposition to "progress."

CHAPTER VII

THE POETS OF THE PERIOD, ESPECIALLY COLERIDGE

MOST OF the eminent literary men of the period have left some record of the impression the novels made on them. In the case of Hazlitt, who was so active a professional critic, the bulk of comment is very large, and may be considered the most important body of criticism of Scott in his own time. Coleridge, among the poets, also spoke many times of the novels, sometimes with deep significance. These two are, among the great lights of the age, the ones who seem to have been most concerned with *Waverley* and its successors; Shelley may be set down as the one least concerned. Himself once upon a time a hopeful novelist, the author of *Zastrozzi* and *St. Irvyne,* he seems to have left nothing for his biographers to record about Scott's novels, although he had felt a youthful admiration for the early poems. Keats read the novels, but he can hardly be called enthusiastic about them.[1] He was, it is true, caught by the character of Meg Merrilies, and on his walking trip to Scotland was impelled to write the balled about her, but, as Amy Lowell points out, he had little interest in the novels in general. Indeed, as early as 1818 or 1819 he could write, "We have seen three literary kings in our time — Scott, Byron, and then the Scotch novels. All now appears to be dead — or I may mistake — literary bodies may still keep up the bustle which I do not hear." Only once does he enter into specific criticism and evaluation. In 1818 he wrote his

[1] See Maurice Buxton Forman, ed., *The Letters of John Keats,* (2 vols., London, 1931), I, 81, 278, 287; and Amy Lowell, *John Keats* (2 vols., Boston, 1925), II, 36.

brothers, in reply to a question, that Scott and Smollett were quite distinct in aim! "Scott endeavors to throw so interesting and romantic a coloring into common and low characters as to give them a touch of the sublime. Smollett on the contrary pulls down and levels what with other men would continue Romance." This sounds like high praise, but he goes on, "The Grand parts of Scott are within the reach of more minds than the finest humors in *Humphrey Clinker*." And also, one good thing of Fielding's, which he quotes, gives him more pleasure than "the whole novel of *The Antiquary*." He likewise quotes with approval from Hazlitt's lecture on Godwin in *English Comic Writers,* passages that emphasize Godwin's strength at Scott's expense. The total effect of this, while by no means damning, can hardly be called laudatory.

It is evident that Wordsworth too was at best lukewarm toward the novels. He and Scott met many times, and he valued Scott highly as a friend, a feeling to which "Yarrow Revisited" and the sonnet "A trouble, not of clouds or weeping rain" afford ample evidence. But of Scott as a poet he had a low opinion (though he thought him better than Campbell!) and he did not care much for the novels, though, like Keats, he uttered one critical dictum on the first ones. Having read *Waverley* and also *Guy Mannering* when it appeared, he wrote to R. P. Gillies of the second that a "very considerable talent was displayed in the performance and much of that sort of knowledge with which the author's mind is so richly stored. But the adventures I think are not well chosen or invented and they are still worse put together, and the characters with the exception of Meg Merrilies excite little interest. In the management of this lady the author has shown very considerable ability, but with that want of taste which is universal among modern novels of the Radcliffe school; which, as far as they are concerned, this is. I allude to the laborious manner in which everything is placed before your eyes for the production of picturesque effect." After explaining in some detail, Wordsworth adds that the general fate of novels is to be overrated at first and then undervalued. *Waverley,* he says, increased his opinion of Scott, and *Guy Mannering* has not detracted from it. He thought that the best part of *Waverley* was the description of Fergus MacIvor's character and of the Highland manners at his castle — these were presented with great spirit; but Bradwardine and his whole setting were "too peculiar and outré"; such a caricature needed more humor than Scott had at his command.[2]

It is apparent then that one must admit the Waverley novels to have been of little moment to these three great poets of the period. They evidently could have suffered their annihilation with little regret. In other poetical quarters, however, the partisan of Scott finds more encouragement. Byron, for instance, can always be counted on for extravagant praise. In spite of the early sarcasms of *English Bards and Scotch Reviewers,* the personal relations between Byron and Scott were always cordial. They met in London occasionally, there was some correspondence between them, an exchange of souvenirs, and on Byron's side an appreciation of Scott's review of *Childe Harold* in the *Quarterly.* Of the novels Byron always spoke better than well. There are for instance the lines from *Don Juan:*

> . . . as my friend Scott says, "I sound my warison
> Scott, the superlative of my comparative,
> Scott, who can paint your Christian knight or Saracen
> Serf, lord, man, with such skill as none would share it, if
> There had not been one Shakespeare and Voltaire
> Of one or both of whom he seems the heir.

Byron's opinion may also be gauged by the fact that in 1813 he called Scott the Monarch of Parnassus and set him at the apex of a pyramid of Poets. Even in 1821 he could say, "His poetry is as good as any now going." As for the novels, he seems to have been always eager to get them as they appeared, and was, too, always rereading them. Casual remarks about the novels in letters and

[2] See Edith J. Morley, ed., *Correspondence of Henry Crabb Robinson with the Wordsworth Circle, 1808–1866* (2 vols., Oxford, 1927), I, 24; also William Angus Knight, ed., *Letters of the Wordsworth Family from 1787 to 1855* (3 vols., Boston, 1907), II, 57. Cf. also II, 432, 502.

conversations are all to the same effect. Lady Blessington declared that Byron was always praising Scott both as a man and a genius, that he claimed to have read most of the novels three times, and said that Scott deserved all the admiration he got. When *Waverley* came out, Byron called it "the most interesting novel since I don't know when," and in 1820, writing for a consignment of new books, he said, ". . . all prose (bating travels and novels NOT by Scott) is welcome — especially Scott's *Tales of My Landlord.*" And in his journal for 1821 he said that he had read all the novels at least fifty times, characterizing the third series of *Tales of My Landlord* (*The Bride of Lammermoor* and *Montrose*) as "grand work — Scotch Fielding as well as great English poet — a wonderful man! I long to get drunk with him." A little later he writes, "Scott is certainly the most wonderful writer of the day. His novels are a new literature in themselves."[3]

Several of the lesser poets of the time have left records of their admiration for Scott. Southey of course was always Scott's friend and admirer. He wrote[4] to a friend in 1819 of his gratification at Scott's being "baronetted"; "if he be the author of the novels (as I am sure he is) no man has ever contributed so long and so largely to the amusement of his contemporaries." Years later, in 1827, he called the *Life of Napoleon* "a lame work," but insisted that it would not hurt the market for the novels and in the long run would affect Scott's reputation no more than Fielding's comedies had done his.[5]

Landor, whose opinion today would be much more highly prized than Southey's, was almost as enthusiastic as Byron. Like Byron, he had a high regard for the poetry, especially *Marmion;*

---

[3] See Thomas Moore, *The Life of Lord Byron, with His Letters and Journals, and Illustrative Notes* (London, 1844), pp. 206, 258, 279, 324, 355, 442, 458, 472, 477; cf. John Murray, ed., *Lord Byron's Correspondence* (2 vols., New York, 1922), II, 295. For the lines from *Don Juan* see Canto XV, stanza lix.

[4] See John Wood Warter, ed., *Selections from the Letters of Robert Southey* (4 vols., London, 1856), III, 117; IV, 42, 62.

[5] This is not a comparison of great point, since whatever one may think of Fielding's comedies, they were all over and done with well before he became a novelist.

in fact he was fond (like Hazlitt) of reiterating the fact that Scott was a far greater poet than Byron. Even as late as 1850 he could write, "Keats is our Ariel of poetry; Scott our Prospero. The one commands, the other captivates; the one controls all the elements, the other tempers and enlivens them." He always liked the novels, at first making *The Heart of Midlothian* his favorite, but later *Kenilworth*. In 1850, in the passage just quoted from, he writes, "I have been reading Scott's *Kenilworth* and think I shall prefer it on a second reading, either to *The Bride of Lammermoor* or my old favorite *The Heart of Midlothian*. It appears to me now to be quite a fine epic. We ought to glory in such men as Scott. The Germans would; and so should we, if hatred of our neighbor were not the religion of authors, and warfare the practice of borderers." It must be added, however, that though the cumulative effect of Landor's comments is to make Scott out a great genius, there is one significant passage that would place him on a lower level along with Byron, of whom Landor thought very little. In a letter to Crabb Robinson in 1834 he called the deaths of Byron and Scott "the patterings of rain before the storm" of the deaths of Coleridge and Goethe. Robinson in quoting this letter to Wordsworth speaks of "the *far greater* Goethe and Coleridge," and while the *far greater* is his own implication, one cannot deny that Landor's metaphor pretty well justifies it. But one should certainly not take such a remark by itself as indicating Landor's feeling about Scott. He notes indeed with approval Goethe's favorable opinion of Scott (Goethe even thought well of the *Napoleon*) — that he was the best narrator of his age.[6]

Another poet, Samuel Rogers, whose opinion once carried weight, was also not only Scott's friend but admirer, though he seems to have left behind him nothing in the way of specific com-

[6] See *Letters and Other Unpublished Writings of Walter Savage Landor,* edited by Stephen Wheeler (London, 1897), pp. 61, 63, 160–61; and John Forster, *Walter Savage Landor. A Biography* (2 vols., London, 1869), II, 527. For Landor's letter to Crabb Robinson see Thomas Sadler, ed., *Diary, Reminiscences, and Correspondence of Henry Crabb Robinson* (3 vols., 2d ed., 1869), III, 42; and for Robinson's letter to Wordsworth, *Correspondence of Henry Crabb Robinson with the Wordsworth Circle, 1808–1866,* I, 270.

ment or criticism. Crabb Robinson, indeed, notes (1823), with surprise it would seem, "Walter Scott is Rogers' friend, but Rogers did not oppose Flaxman's remark that his works have in no respect tended to improve the moral condition of mankind." But of course it is easy to imagine a dozen reasons why under various circumstances Rogers remained silent.[7]

But of all the poets, greater and lesser, who expressed themselves about Scott, the one who had the most to say was Coleridge. Did Coleridge really admire Scott? He is occasionally spoken of as a professed admirer, yet when one considers all his remarks on the novels together, one has grave doubts. He seems to have had two sets of views, possibly to fit two different moods, or possibly one free and outspoken for private utterance, and the other cautious and tactful for public. In interpreting his views, moreover, one is warned by his editors to remember that there rankled in Coleridge's memory the "thefts" from *Christabel*,[8] and also, to quote Mr. A. Turnbull, that he "was always hostile to the novel as enticing men away from serious study and reading." Be that as it may, Coleridge's critical opinions of the novels are certainly not of a piece.[9]

Coleridge's casual allusions to Scott are usually friendly and laudatory. In contrasting his own point of view with Scott's after the latter's death, he could refer to "dear Sir Walter Scott," and at about the same time he made the oft-quoted remark that when he was very ill he could read Scott's novels and them only. And even a decade earlier, in "Maxilian," he wrote of the Trossachs that they were "worthy to have made a Walter Scott, but

[7] Cf. R. Ellis Roberts, *Samuel Rogers and His Circle* (London, 1910), p. 171. Roberts says that the reason that Rogers did not reply to Flaxman was that "the sheer idiocy . . . prevented any but the rudest of replies." He also says (page 174) that Rogers did not really care for the novels; they did not seem to him "adult" literature. See Crabb Robinson's *Diary*, II, 255. Cf. also *ibid.*, II, 48, 248.

[8] For a frank admission by Scott on this point see a letter to Mrs. Hughes, where he says he got the stanza for *The Lay of the Last Minstrel* from hearing passages of *Christabel* recited by Dr. Stoddard. Grierson, *Letters*, VIII, 421, November 11, 1924.

[9] See Samuel Taylor Coleridge, *Biographia Epistolaris*, edited by Arthur Turnbull (2 vols., London, 1911), II, 215.

that a Walter Scott is only of God's making—*nascitur non fit."*
He could also resent an allusion to Cooper as "the American Sir
Walter" to the point of comparing it with the preposterous
designation of Klopstock as "the German Milton."[10]

A more coolly critical and reserved judgment is discoverable
in a letter to Alaric Watts in 1828,[11] in regard to contributions
by Scott to an elaborately printed annual. Evidently Coleridge
thought Scott's work unfitted to such a publication because of its
bulk and lack of "polish." "Of Sir Walter's power I have as high
admiration as you can have," he writes, "but assuredly polish of
style and that sort of prose which is in fact only another kind of
poetry, nay, of metrical composition, the metre *incognito* such
as Sterne's Le Fevre, Maria, Monk, etc., or of the finest things
in the *Mirror* — this is not Sir Walter's excellence. He needs
sea room — space for development of character by dialogue, etc.,
etc. — and even in his most successful works, the *Tale* is always
the worst part — clumsily evolved and made up of incidents that
are purely accidental." And he continues with an allusion to
"a cannon-gate tale on hot pressed rich paper, etc., etc." Even
such coolly tempered praise as this is hardly congruous with
comments in a letter to Edward Coleridge about a year earlier,[12]
obviously apropos of the crash of 1826: "My judgment is in
perfect coincidence with your remarks on Sir Walter; and when
I think of the wretched trash, that the Lust of Gain enduced
him to publish for the last three or four years, which must have
been manufactured for the greater part, even my feelings assist
in hardening me. I should indeed be sorry if any ultimate success
had attended the attempt to unite the Poet and the Worldling.
Heaven knows! I have enought to feel for without wasting my
Sympathy on a Scotchman suffering the penalty of his Scotchery."
Clearly it made a difference whether Coleridge was writing on
guard or off guard; whether he was addressing an ordinary cor-

[10] See *Table Talk*, August 4, November 1, 1833; "Maxilian" (*Blackwood's*,
January, 1822); Earl Leslie Griggs, ed., *Unpublished Letters of Samuel Taylor
Coleridge* (2 vols., London, 1932), II, 411–12.
[11] Griggs, *Unpublished Letters of Coleridge*, II, 420–21.
[12] *Ibid.*, II, 402.

respondent or a member of his own family or an intimate like Wordsworth.

His critical and detailed opinions on the novels are to be found chiefly in his letters to the young Londoner, Thomas Allsop, whom he met in 1818, and who became something of a Boswell to his later years. An amusing clue to Coleridge's state of mind regarding Scott, quite typical of his complicated mental predicaments, is revealed in a letter to Allsop on April 10, 1820.[13] The poet had been invited to meet Scott at a friend's, but says that he will not take the liberty of intruding, although he would like to, and "it would have highly gratified me" to have met him again, "perhaps the most extraordinary man, assuredly the most *extraordinary* writer, of his age." But in a postscript he wavers, and says that possibly he will accept the invitation, explaining, "I seem to feel that I *ought* to feel more desire to see an extra-ordinary man than I really do feel; and I do not wish to appear to two or three persons . . . as if I cherished any dislike to Scott respecting the *Christabel,* and generally an increasing dislike to appear out of the common and natural mode of thinking and acting."

All these delicate considerations, and respect for so "extra-ordinary" a man seem to be cast aside in a letter dated January, 1821, though there is good reason to believe that it was written a year earlier, and was incorrectly dated 1821 instead of 1820.[14] Here he dilates on the theme that neither philosophy nor poetry can ever be *popular* or succeed in their own time. On the other hand there never was a time like the present, he says, when books *held* to be excellent for poetry or philosophy sold so well, and when their authors were so highly regarded and paid. "Walter Scott's poems and novels (except only the two wretched abor-tions, *Ivanhoe* and the *Bride of Ravensmuir,* or whatever its name may be) supply both instance and solution of the present conditions and components of popularity, viz., to amuse without requiring any effort of thought and without exciting any deep

[13] *Biographia Epistolaris,* II, 178.
[14] *Ibid.,* II, 206. Compare the following paragraph.

emotion. The age seems *sore* from excess of stimulation; . . .
Compare *Waverley, Guy Mannering,* and Co. with works that
had an *immediate run* in the last generation, *Tristram Shandy,
Roderick Random, Sir Charles Grandison, Clarissa Harlowe,* and
Tom Jones (all of which became popular as soon as published,
and therefore are instances fairly in point) and you will be convinced that the difference in taste is real and not any fancy or
croaking of my own." Allsop also records[15] a conversation in
which Coleridge expresses again the same feeling: "Walter
Scott's novels are chargeable with . . . ministering to the
depraved appetite for excitement, and though in a far less degree
[than certain others] creating sympathy for the vicious and
infamous, solely because the fiend is *daring.* Not twenty lines
of Scott's poetry will ever reach posterity; it has relation to
nothing."[16]

These opinions are most carefully erased and a return effected
to the view of Scott as "extraordinary" in a long letter dated
April 8, 1820.[17] Mr. Turnbull suggests that this date is wrong,
and that April 18 is perhaps intended. At all events, it cannot
be far wrong, since Coleridge refers to *The Monastery,* which
was published early in March, as though it were the latest of the
series, and he had not yet had time to read it. The next novel,
The Abbot, appeared in September. The clear evidence of this
allusion would tend to cast doubt on the date of the irritable
letter of January, 1821, to which this letter would seem obviously
to be a reply. Possibly it was written in January, 1820, rather
than January, 1821.

"I occasioned you to misconceive me respecting Sir Walter
Scott," he writes, and goes on to explain that he had been thinking of the universal excitement and stimulation of mind aroused
by the extraordinary events of the time, and the consequent

---

[15] *Ibid.,* II, 220.

[16] For a perfectly frank and unrestrained expression of Coleridge's views on
Scott's poetry see a letter to Wordsworth in 1810 on *The Lady of the Lake.*
Here he cuts loose with a vengeance. Griggs, *Unpublished Letters of Coleridge,*
II, 37.

[17] *Biographia Epistolaris,* II, 182.

demand for *"relaxation, as rest* freed from the tedium of vacancy."* He thinks the popularity of the theaters shows this, as well as the great vogue of Scott. "I do hold him for a man of *very extraordinary* powers," Coleridge says, adding that he has read most of the novels twice and several three times "with undiminished pleasure and interest." He explains that in his reprobation of *The Bride of Lammermoor,* "with the exception, however, of the almost Shakespearean old witch-wives at the funeral," and of *Ivanhoe,* he "meant to imply the grounds of my admiration of the others, and the permanent nature of the interest which they excite. In a word, I am far from thinking that *Old Mortality* or *Guy Mannering* [his two favorites] would have been less admired in the age of Sterne, Fielding, and Richardson than they are in the present times; but only that Sterne, etc., would not have had the same immediate popularity in the present day as in their own less stimulated and therefore less languid reading world."

Coleridge even takes back his summary remark on the poems. Of them, he says, "I cannot speak so highly," but he praises them for fullness, variety, and "true picturesque unity" and declares that he had felt much pain in earlier years at ———'s "contemptuous assertions respecting Scott."

His criticism, he goes on to say, was "confined to the one point of the higher degree of intellectual activity implied in the reading and admiration of Fielding, Richardson, and Sterne; in moral, or . . . in *mannerly* manliness of taste the present age and its best writers have the decided advantage, and I sincerely trust that Walter Scott's readers would be as little disposed to relish the stupid lechery of the courtship of Widow Wadman, as Scott himself would be capable of presenting it." He admits, however, that he finds nowhere in Scott a character "approaching in genius, in truth of conception, or boldness and freshness of execution, to Parson Adams, Blifil, Strap, Lieutenant Bowling, Mr. Shandy, Uncle Toby and Trim, and Lovelace," nor can Scott's women equal the characters of Richardson or Smollett, "or Betty in Mrs. Bennet's *Beggar Girl.*" And though, "by the use of the Scotch dialect, by Ossianic mock-Highland motley-heroic, and by extracts from the printed sermons, memoirs, etc., of the fanatic preachers, there is a good deal of *false effect* and stage trick; still the number of characters *so good* produced by one man and in so rapid a succession must ever remain an illustrious phenomenon in literature, after all the subtractions for those borrowed from English and German sources, or compounded by blending two or three of the old drama into one, e. g., the Caleb in *The Bride of Lammermoor*."

Coleridge now comes to the point of putting his finger on the main source of Scott's success, his great merit and "felicity." Here is the most cogent and the most significant part of his letter. It lay, he says, in the very nature of the subject. The Waverley novels had caught the imagination, not merely because the struggle between Stuart and Calvinist was still a living memory; nor because the language was different enough to be poignant nor close enough to arouse sympathy; nor because the author was in *keeping* with his matter, and his characters were interesting as men, apart from antiquarianism, and were without moral anachronism (though *Ivanhoe* was "so wofully the contrary"). Underlying everything was the contest between loyalists and their opponents, "the contest between the two great moving principles of social humanity; religious adherence to the past . . . the desire and the admiration of permanence . . . and the passion for increase of knowledge, for truth as the offspring of reason — in short, the mighty instincts of *progression* and *free agency*." This subject Coleridge says can never be obsolete. It is not to be found in *Ivanhoe* — Saxon and Norman are nothing. If Scott had only taken as his subject the struggle between men of arts and men of arms in the time of Becket! But as it is, *Ivanhoe* is of the cast of the Minerva Library. He adds that he has not yet read *The Monastery*, but from hearsay suspects German borrowings in it, like the borrowings from Tieck in *Old Mortality*.

This is criticism worthy of Coleridge, and had much better be quoted than the later remarks generally cited to show his fondness for Scott, that when he was very ill he turned to the Waverley novels; for here certainly he justifies the novels as food for the vigorous and energetic, not mere time-killing relaxation for periods when the mind was on vacation or capable of nothing better. But what is one to do with all these letters taken together? Certainly such absolute and final statements as those first quoted are not to be explained away even by the most devious and subtle qualifications. It is as plain as a pikestaff what Coleridge felt when he wrote them, possibly in a moment of irritation. But in the other letter just summarized it is equally clear that when he wished to approach Scott in the proper mood, with sympathy and with a real desire to discover his secret, he was quite capable of striking the truth in its very center. For there is no denying that Coleridge drives through and beyond the conception of Scott as a great national writer, as a great exponent of national character, in itself splendid praise, and gives the clue to Scott as an artist whose foundations are broader than national, resting on one of the great dramatic contrasts of universal human nature. Though comparatively brief and informal, this letter deserves to be added to the criticism of Jeffrey and Hazlitt. These three really appreciated and understood Scott better than any others of their time, and after all, who is there among later critics who has added greatly to them?

Part II · 1832—1880

CHAPTER I

SCOTT'S CONTINUED POPULARITY

IN THE criticism of Scott during the half century after his death many crosscurrents and conflicting or even contradictory elements are discernible. There were not only the natural divergences of opinion between critics, but it is sometimes perfectly clear that the same writer was drawn two different ways, often suffering from a conflict between head and heart. When this happened the head generally yielded to the heart. The various attitudes toward Scott are not so eccentric or complicated, however, that they cannot be analyzed and charted, and related to commonly recognized influences of the age.

Naturally, for a few years following Scott's death, as well as a few preceding it, when he was killing himself to pay his debts, there was an obvious desire among critics to deal tenderly with him — to dilate on his gifts and to forget his defects — to recall *Waverley* and its successors, and to disregard the weaker novels of the 1820's. Sir Walter's person and his career have always been tremendously impressive; they were never more so than in these years. The *Edinburgh,* which had reviewed none of the novels since *Redgauntlet,* published in April, 1832,[1] when his Mediterranean cruise was being planned and his career seemed over, what was clearly intended as a valedictory essay, almost a funeral eulogy. Here the best face is put on everything. Admitted faults are minimized, and virtues exalted. He is declared the greatest master of fiction, approached in the past only by Cervantes, and in the present only by the author of *Anastasius!* His great influ-

[1] *Edinburgh Review,* 55:61 (April, 1832).

ence abroad, and his epoch-making innovations are remembered. He is said to be equaled only by Shakespeare in the number of his created characters, and to be surpassed only by the greatest of dramatists in their quality; we see and hear his people — Shakespeare's we know. He is great especially in creating representatives of a class, like the Puritans. His women, it is true, have grace and spirit, but less reality; yet would one have realistic portraits of women of the past? Would they be pleasant?[2] In his description of Nature, no one since Milton has been his peer. He is, too, a master of tragic pathos — *The Bride of Lammermoor* recalls the tragic fate of the Greeks, and the witches of *Macbeth*. And finally, while he never preaches a definite moral, he is always on the side of morality. His villains never become captivating, to "produce a brisk fermentation of mischief in many young and weak heads." Nor has he like Byron labored "to diminish our confidence in virtue and our abhorrence of vice." He has never been morbid or egotistic, but, like Homer and Shakespeare, has been "serene and unruffled."

Nor will the *Edinburgh* critic allow many of the common complaints against Sir Walter. The charge of reaction and feudalism he denies, insisting on Scott's real philanthropy and his far-sighted sympathy with the increase in wealth and comfort. No man, the writer declares, is impartial in dealing with historic events, but Sir Walter never carries his prejudices to the point of unfairness. Certain things must be forgiven him — his repetition of character, his wit, "clumsy, inelegant, and verbose," his introductions, and his careless style, but one should remember how much he has written. The critic will even go so far as to declare that many of the later novels, even those where the Scotch ground is deserted, are equal to the early ones, and will set *The Fair Maid of Perth* beside *Waverley*. Turning in his conclusion to the broadest considerations again, he recalls that Scott has lifted up the fallen novel, has taught the novelist to look to Nature, and has even shown "to what end history should be read and in what manner it should be written." Sir Walter, he

---

[2] Compare the modern realistic objection to Scott's unrealistic medievalism.

says, has created a method halfway between "the stately political history and the gossiping memoir," and has encouraged the reading of history, and of biographical and antiquarian research. And finally, though he declines prophecy, he reiterates his faith in Sir Walter's greatness as an innovator, and in the novels as enduring classics.

That most brilliant and philosophical young novelist, "The Author of Eugene Aram" (not to say of *Pelham* and several more), set the florid seal of his approval on the dead king in Colburn's *New Monthly*,[3] of which he was editor. At once, Bulwer calls Scott "the greatest — the most various — the most commanding genius of modern times." After resounding praise of his personal character he turns to his work. He decides that he is greatest as a poet, and thinks *Waverley* will decay before *Marmion;* the power he shows in his poetic style sinks to nothing in his prose. But the body of Bulwer's panegyric is nevertheless reserved to glorify Scott's humanity in his novels, and rests on a much sounder bottom, it cannot be denied, than did that of most of the critics of his generation. He picks up the charge that Scott had not imparted a useful moral to his fictions and had "dwelt with too inconsiderate an interest on the chivalric illusions of the past." To it he replies that the very pleasure and comfort of Scott's books is in itself of great moral value.

But more important from the moral point of view, he says, is that "Scott has been the first great genius — Fielding alone excepted — who invited our thorough and uncondescending sympathy to the wide mass of the human family." Where, he asks, does Shakespeare show a Jeanie Deans? Scott always has an interest in the people and always represents them truly. Here the political undercurrent, always so strong in the criticism of the time, boils to the surface. Bulwer points out that Scott, though a Tory, has done much more for the people than "liberals" like Byron, Shelley, or Moore. "Out of print, Scott might belong to a party — in print, mankind belonged to him." It is on this basis, not unwisely, that Bulwer defends Scott's morality.

[3] *Colburn's*, 35:300 (October, 1832).

Furthermore, he declares that Fielding, with much more learning and abstract philosophy, excels Sir Walter in only one character, Parson Adams. The only novelists Bulwer will range with him are Fielding, Le Sage, and Cervantes, and even these Scott excels in the aggregate of his work; not one of them has "manifested the same fertile and mighty genius as the author of the Waverley novels" — the gap Scott leaves in his death will always be felt. Bulwer writes of Scott pompously and sentimentally, as he was to do several times later, but after all he strikes a right note, and one that only too few of his contemporaries were to catch; his criticism is inspired beneath all its buckram with the same intuition that Jeffrey and Hazlitt had felt and that was to appear again among Scott's defenders of the twentieth century.

The *Edinburgh* essay and Bulwer's seem the most comprehensive and vigorous statements of the confession of faith in Scott to which the critics had turned after their dissatisfaction of a few years earlier. But it may be seen in several other places; for instance in a review of the last novels in *Fraser's* in 1832,[4] and in an essay by W. H. Prescott in the *North American* [5] of July, 1832, where Scott's worldliness is a little regretted, but his greatness as an inventor, his wide-ranging talents (he was no specialist), his natural eloquence, far better than the style of Fielding or Smollett, and above all his moral elevation of the novel are all highly praised. One does not, Prescott declares, have to read him in a corner, like Fielding or Smollett; there is nothing in him to blot; he furnishes "a pure and delectable repast for all members of the assembled family." This, indeed, was to be one of Scott's greatest glories in the decades to come.

Yet another echo of the praise that attended Sir Walter's decline and fall. *Colburn's* in 1836 [6] published an article on Sir Walter's review of himself in the *Quarterly* twenty years earlier. This is a kind of apology for such a questionable act — it is called a speck on the mirror of his character, and the writer wishes to

[4] See articles on historical romance, *Fraser's*, 5:6, 207 (February, March, 1832).
[5] *North American Review*, 35:187 (July, 1832).
[6] *Colburn's*, 46:79 (1836).

leave no doubt as to the state of his feelings. He declares at last that Scott "is a spirit whose influence will be felt upon the imagination, the morals, the feelings and the conduct of mankind, not England's — not Scotland's — not Ireland's — not any country's mankind, but upon the world's mankind to the latest posterity." There were of course still other eulogies in 1832 and the years following; perhaps one should mention the names of Talfourd, Robert Chambers, and Maginn,[7] all of whom wrote in unstinted praise, more or less in the terms of the *Edinburgh* and of Bulwer Lytton. Maginn, for instance, after panegyric with a strong Tory flavor, concludes, "A great light has been extinguished, a great glory lost to Israel, and we 'ne'er shall look upon his like again.' "[8] The same strain echoes in Allan Cunningham's *Biographical and Critical History of British Literature,* published in Paris in 1834, where the praise of Scott's artistic powers is superlative (except for his treatment of the supernatural and his heroes and heroines), and he is said to "stand without a rival at the head of Prose Fiction."

The feeling for Scott as a leader and model is revealed again in the *Edinburgh*,[9] where the low state of romance since Scott's death is regretted, and Harrison Ainsworth is reproved for declaring that the models for romance will henceforth be German or French; that Scott is not to his mind a romancer. Ainsworth is admonished that English romance will never be revived by such models and told that he had better come back to Shakespeare and Scott. It is certainly not an exaggeration to say that the prevailing feeling for Sir Walter is indicated in the subject of a series of three lectures given before a society of Chichester in 1833 and 1834 — "A Parallel of Shakespeare and Scott" — lectures which a writer in the *Monthly Review* praised highly, himself setting Scott only one degree below Shakespeare, and coupling them as "the two mighty enchanters."[10] Certainly there is nothing to be found in Great Britain at this time or for many

[7] See Allibone's *Critical Dictionary,* under Scott.
[8] *Fraser's,* 6:380 (October, 1832).   [9] *Edinburgh Review,* 65:180 (April, 1837).
[10] *Monthly Review,* 137:569 (1835).

years to come that compares with Chateaubriand's statement [11] that Scott has created a false type — novels historical and history romantic — and that he lacks the fine qualities of Manzoni and other modern novelists. But even Chateaubriand doubts his own judgment; he feels himself a foreigner, and believes also that the reputation Scott had established, so broad and deep, "suppose toujours des qualités du premier ordre"; his power to reach everyone as he did was in itself a great merit.

This mood was doubtless prolonged by the appearance in 1837 and 1838 of Lockhart's *Life,* which kept alive in many quarters down through the rest of the century a warmly personal and affectionate regard for Sir Walter. Indeed, a great part of the writing on Scott all through the middle of the century may be dismissed as sentimental revery or reminiscence, interesting as a sign of living public interest in Scott, and the continued effect of his genial and ingratiating character, the memory of which was kept alive by myriads of anecdotes from Lockhart and elsewhere. It must be confessed that for the very broadest public Scott seems to have been the man himself, the traditional hero of the last generation, and the poet, the author especially of *Marmion* and of *The Lady of the Lake,* whose haunts one could easily go to see from Edinburgh; and then, as far as novels went, of *Ivanhoe.* All these were works which critics from the beginning had thought inferior, but which had been from the beginning tremendously popular. Around him and these creations countless writers of delicate imagination spun sweet Victorian scenes and fancies which found a ready market in the more popular periodicals. And who can say that the influence of Lockhart's *Life* is not to be felt even today, a century after its appearance?

Considering the bulk of his work, it is rather surprising how little space Lockhart devoted to criticism of the novels. He had a very high regard for Nassau Senior's reviews and cited them frequently, sometimes at length, especially the last one written

---

[11] See *Essai sur la littérature anglaise,* in *Works* (12 vols., Paris, 1862–67), VI, 297.

for the obscure and short-lived *London Review*. Adolphus too he approved of heartily and occasionally drew upon him. But his own comments are of the briefest.

The most important point that emerges from them all together is his strong feeling that the Scotch novels had a distinction and a quality of genius that never marked the English or foreign ones. Of *The Antiquary* he said that it and its two predecessors had more of "a simple, unsought charm" than any of the later novels, and that nowhere else did Sir Walter get (what Lockhart set great store by) finer contrasts between humor and tragedy in his Scotch character. In praising *Ivanhoe* as a "work of art" he declares that it is probably Scott's greatest, but, he adds, no good critic would put it on a level with *Waverley, Guy Mannering,* or *The Heart of Midlothian.* But his strongest expression of this conviction comes in his remarks on *Anne of Geierstein*. None of the non-Scotch novels "belongs to the same pre-eminent class with those in which he paints and peoples his native landscape." Even the best English romances are not the equals of *Waverley* or *Old Mortality*.[12]

Indeed all the novels for which Lockhart reserves the highest praise, of which he speaks with the most feeling are Scotch ones; *Guy Mannering, Old Mortality, The Heart of Midlothian, The Bride of Lammermoor,* these in one way or another seem to him to show Scott at his finest, as do also even *The Pirate* and *Nigel;* but the superlatives he bestows on *Ivanhoe, Kenilworth,* and *The Talisman* as brilliant "works of art" always mark them as of another and inferior class.[13]

Certain of the series he accepts as more or less failures, though

---

[12] See Lockhart, V, 142; VI, 176; IX, 320.

[13] This is the usual attitude of the period toward the romances; they are inferior to the Scotch novels, but brilliant *tours de force*. One striking exception is to be found in a "Letter to Eusebius," *Blackwood's*, 59:408 (April, 1846). The critic has just reread *Guy Mannering* and *Ivanhoe*. The first he found perfect, the second, "in design commonplace — slovenly in diction — lengthened out by tiresome repetitions." None of the characters except Rebecca was successful. He says the novel is like a doubtful play of Shakespeare, which shows that a master hand has passed over it. Finally, indeed, he comes to the conclusion that there is more hope in the future for the poems than the novels.

only of the last two, *Count Robert* and *Castle Dangerous,* can he find nothing good to say. Having described his father-in-law's tortures in writing them, he records their publication and says that he will probably not return to the subject. But in all other cases, however serious the weakness, he is able to discover some compensating excellence. *The Black Dwarf,* "however imperfect and unworthy as a work of art, is to be placed high in the catalogue of his productions" for its delineation of "the dark feelings" springing from deformity, so typical of Byron, but to be found in Scott only here. In *A Legend of Montrose,* the character of Montrose is thin, but Dalgetty is the equal of Nicol Jarvie. Even *The Monastery,* the first great failure of the series, may be redeemed by its "beautiful natural scenery and sterling Scotch characters and manners," and, Lockhart concludes, the book may ultimately pass in the race other novels which made a better start but "in which he makes no use of Scottish materials." And even in *Peveril* — where he is most emphatic in dispraise (for instance, he says of Fenella, "an unfortunate conception; what is good in it is not original and the rest extravagant, absurd, and incredible"; and goes on to call the story "clumsy and perplexed" and the trial scenes merely conventional and unreal) — he cites Senior to support his claim that the book has many excellent characters. And so too with *Woodstock* and *The Fair Maid of Perth.* When reduced to it, he can even resort to comparison with other writers; no book of Scott's was so weak compared with its own kindred that it did not shine out when set beside the work of other authors. *Anne of Geierstein,* for instance, despite its many weaknesses, had qualities that remove it immeasurably "from any of its order produced in this country in our own age." Surely anyone who has dipped into Horace Smith,[14] G. P. R. James, or Mrs. Bray will feel that Lockhart was absolutely right.[15]

[14] Lamb was willing to compare his friend Horace Smith's *Brambletye House* with *Woodstock,* but to a modern reader this shows a great partiality. And the others mentioned are simply unreadable.

[15] References to Lockhart in this paragraph are as follows: *Count Robert,* X, 105; *The Black Dwarf,* V, 175; *Montrose,* VI, 87; *The Monastery,* VI, 255;

Thus the impression left by Lockhart's comments on the novels would certainly tend to increase the reverence and respect felt for them by the public. Lockhart had been close to Scott and had seen the novels develop and grow. His opinions were colored by Scott's own; in fact, they parallel them closely. He spoke positively and authoritatively. The numerous bits of intimate, first-hand knowledge about the novels also gave him authority. He told his readers that *The Antiquary* became Scott's own favorite, that he had put a good deal of himself into Monkbarns, and that the novel contained more of his own early associations than any other. In *Old Mortality* he had to lean on books heavily for the first time instead of on the dreams of his youth, and the success of the novel demanded for that reason more "energetic sympathy of imagination"; indeed, none of his books, according to Lockhart, ever inspired him to nobler emotions than he felt in creating his Covenanters. *Redgauntlet* too, we are told, was, like *The Antiquary,* strongly autobiographic; as a matter of fact it contains more of Scott's own personal experiences than all the other novels together. And *Woodstock* also had appealed especially to his intimate friends as reflecting his own misfortunes, the ill health of Lady Scott, the devotion of Anne and "old Maida, under the name of Bevis." Or there is the statement that so late a novel as *Anne of Geierstein* shows his innate good temper and the freshness of his sympathy with youth, with none of the selfishness of age; it reveals a man "young at heart" living strongly in the genial, vivid memories of his own youth and in close association with his own children.[16]

Then all these personal touches are buttressed by the extremely fine, deeply sympathetic analysis of Scott's personal character,[17] where Lockhart takes up the various faults alleged against Sir Walter — his romantic, "feudal" point of view, his

Peveril, VII, 116; *Woodstock,* VIII, 353; *The Fair Maid of Perth,* IX, 222; *Anne of Geierstein,* IX, 320.

[16] References to Lockhart in this paragraph are as follows: *The Antiquary,* V, 142; *Old Mortality,* V, 176; *Redgauntlet,* VII, 213; *Woodstock,* VIII, 353; *Anne of Geierstein,* IX, 321.

[17] X, 222 ff.

peculiar patriotism, his Toryism, his religion, his desire to acquire an estate and found a family — and shows how all these had seemed to those who knew him well, who had been close to him from day to day. It is the kind of analysis that one finds in the most sympathetic and appreciative of Scott's modern critics, in Professor Grierson or John Buchan, for instance, and might well be called a basis or source for all such essays on Scott's character as come later. And from the point of view of the novels by themselves, this was of great importance; for two generations at least the hero-worship of Scott was of the greatest service to his novels.

Reviews of Lockhart were to be found everywhere, concerning themselves of course with Scott's greatness as a writer, but still more with his greatness as a man. The general regard for the novels was so high at the moment that Lockhart, indeed, could have done little to increase it. Scott's own character, too, had been so tremendously admired for the last decade, ever since the financial crash, that the panegyrics evoked by the biography were not altogether new. Yet there came now redoubled cries that Sir Walter's own life was his greatest work, transcending his books in human importance — cries that were to be repeated all through the Victorian period, furnishing an excellent example of the insistence on moral values during that era.

The only discordant note of any great significance seems to be that of Fenimore Cooper, who while admitting Sir Walter as his "sovereign" had taken umbrage at Scott's remarks concerning his want of "manners" (Scott seems to have actually' meant "manner") and expressed himself violently in the *Knickerbocker* and elsewhere [18] on Sir Walter's snobbishness and Toryism, an attack that drew a savagely sarcastic rejoinder

[18] Note especially J. F. Cooper, ed., *Correspondence of James Fenimore Cooper* (2 vols., New Haven, 1922), I, 384, where he dilates on his bad impressions of Scott in his relations with the Ballantynes and Constable, and calls Lockhart a liar. Note also a letter to the *New Monthly* (I, 226) disclaiming any pretensions to be called a "rival of Sir Walter Scott" or "the American Walter Scott"; in fact, stating his intense dislike of such phrases. That he did have some jealousy of Scott seems to appear in his statement (I, 283) that his *Heidenmauer* "is better than two-thirds of Scott's" though not his own best. Cf. also Thomas R. Lounsbury, *James Fenimore Cooper* (Boston, 1883), p. 160.

from Maginn in *Fraser's*.[19] The *Dublin Review* also castigated Lockhart bitterly for his emphasis on his father-in-law's Toryism and anti-Catholic tendencies, which forced it in self-defense to call attention to Scott's general lack of fairness to Catholics and his "disgusting" novels *The Monastery* and *The Abbot*.[20] There were those too, like Cockburn, who felt that the *Life* detailed too fully what they considered small domestic trivialities, and that the whole story of the Ballantyne-Constable imbroglio should have been discreetly veiled.[21]

Macaulay too is chiefly remembered by writers on Scott for his refusal to review Lockhart for the *Edinburgh*. The staunchest of Whigs and the most eloquent expounder of "progress," Macaulay felt that he could not approve Scott's character sufficiently to undertake this office, yet at the same time he wrote, "I sincerely admire the greater parts of his works." He had felt the full impact of the Waverley novels in his youth,[22] and his debt to Scott in the matter of his own treatment of history is a commonplace. Indeed Macaulay's attitude is not unlike Hazlitt's. In both cases partisan politics lie at the bottom.[23]

[19] See *Knickerbocker Magazine*, 11:380 (1838); but also, for highly favorable comment on Lockhart, 10:259 (1837) and 12:508 (1838); and *Fraser's*, 19:371 (March, 1839), "Epaminondas Grubb, or Fenimore Cooper Versus the Memory of Sir Walter Scott."

[20] *Dublin Review*, 5:377 (October, 1838).

[21] It does not seem to have been generally noted that one of Scott's staunchest, indeed most violent, defenders in the storm raised by Lockhart's narrative of the publishing business was Charles Dickens, who contributed two articles to the *Examiner* on this subject, March 31 and September 29, 1839. These are summarized by William Forbes Gray in *Scott in Sunshine and Shadow* (1931), pp. 276 ff. They are reprinted in Dickens' *Miscellaneous Papers*, (2 vols., London, 1911). In both these articles Dickens sticks very close to his subject and does not enter upon any criticism of the novels. He writes, however, in a fiery, even violent style as an enthusiastic worshipper of Scott. The closest he comes to the novels is at the end of the second article: "Now we ask all those who have been cheered and delighted by the labors of this great man, who have hearts to feel or heads to understand his works, and in whose mouths the creations of his brain are familiar as household words" [what is their opinion of the merits of the quarrel].

[22] J. Cotter Morison, *Macaulay* (English Men of Letters series, London, 1882), pp. 112-15. See also, of course, George Otto Trevelyan, *Life and Letters of Lord Macaulay* (2 vols., 1876), especially I, 60-61.

[23] As also representative of this point of view, compare a review of Macaulay's *History of England* in the *Edinburgh*, 90:259 (July, 1849), thoroughly Whiggish

These adverse comments, however, create little effect amidst the almost universal chorus of praise. There can be no denying that Lockhart's *Life* has done Scott's fame a great service in preserving the tradition of his human and lovable yet heroic character and has bolstered up an interest in his books among later generations.

Indeed, really slashing criticism of Scott is practically non-existent in the Victorian period. There are reservations and vacillations, but the combined power of his personality, so well preserved in Lockhart, and of his works themselves with the tremendous weight of their original fame to back them up, was enough to make any critic cautious and soft-spoken, even if he was not naturally reverent and tender in his feelings. For the slashing style one has to wait until the 1890's and the invasion of French realism. Actually only one real exception has been noted — that of J. C. Jeaffreson, the most widely quoted of the mid-Victorian writers on the novel.[24] His comments on Scott recall the political fury of Hazlitt and the withering words of Carlyle, both of whom he had doubtless read. One might guess that he had seen Walter Bagehot's essay; they both wrote in 1858.

After a rapid biographical summary, Jeaffreson proclaims, "The *man* was a mass of contradictions; the writer incalculably great, though his achievements often provoke censure." He was "a narrow bigot whose principles were prejudices, and whose zeal a jealous hate of all opponents, yet he was a benevolent and philanthropic man." He read history from a prejudiced point of view; he was guilty of "intellectual cowardice and dishonesty and yet he was truthful and of high courage." He spoke a "Tory jargon," "altogether lacked earnestness of thought,"

and progressive, pro-Macaulay and anti-Hume. The writer declares that Scott was too much a royalist. He had in him no pride in Scottish liberty and no sympathy with the struggles of the people. He was always for the king and against the people; always for Mary, Charles, Claverhouse, and the Cavaliers. His Covenanters he made "absurd and repulsive"; indeed, Scott is to blame for the current contempt of those ancestors who won the Scotch their liberties.

[24] John Cordy Jeaffreson, *Novels and Novelists* (2 vols., London, 1858).

and "none of his works teach the strong man anything." He failed completely to grasp the genius of the times. We are "charmed with rich imagery, graceful descriptions, dramatic beauties of position [*sic*] and language and inexhaustible humor," but all this is for mere amusement; we remember Byron's "cries of anguish" and Shelley's yearning to soar higher.[25] Jeaffreson thinks he did his best; the lure of gain would never have kept him from higher things if he had been capable of them. There was nothing of the philosopher about him; he cared nothing for the truth — his zeal was all for the Tories, he had none for the Lord of Hosts. His goodwill was all for men's bodies; he cared nothing for their souls. His art became merely a trade. Yet he had a great and lasting influence. He showed writers how to avoid such "cumbrous plots" as that of *Tom Jones* and the weaknesses of Defoe and Sterne. "He lived to see better novelists than himself in the field [who were they, in Heaven's name?] but knew they used his instruments to secure their ends. By his success, also, he made the profession of writing respectable, and took from it the curse of poverty and disdain. After reading this, one must feel the absurdity of the remarks on Scott as a person, and must also wonder what Jeaffreson found to justify such a phrase as "the writer incalculably great," for certainly the details that follow nullify it. After 1890 one comes upon an occasional blast of this sort, but in 1858 and for many years after such a declaration was seemingly unique.

Indeed, to see how Scott was usually written about at this time in this type of book — that is, a rapid survey of novels or of literature in general — one may turn to James Hannay,[26] an author of excellent repute. One cannot imagine a wider contrast. Hannay emphasizes Scott's "genial and manly" temperament

[25] This, an obvious echo of Carlyle, is of course a frequent matter of sentimental regret among many sympathetic critics. To Jeaffreson's Byron and Shelley are occasionally added Burns. For instance, see *Fraser's*, N. S., 9:559 (May, 1874): "To Burns literature was something of a 'priesthood' lifting him above the mean element in which he lived, to Scott it was little more than a congenial trade."

[26] James Hannay, *A Course of English Literature* (London, 1866).

and says that "all his novels ought to be read by everybody who cares for novels." He has not merely one kind of merit, but has a vast range of power. His art moreover is based on his goodness, "that not too common quality." "He is not so deep as Shakespeare, but he is as deep as, and more lifelike than, any other person. For pictorial history he has done more than anybody but Shakespeare. His historical novels are a class by themselves, like Shakespeare's historical plays." It was Hannay, not Jeaffreson, who really expressed the feeling of the age.

Another well-known Victorian, Dr. John Brown, of *Rab and his Friends,* evinces an attitude that is common to innumerable commentators all through the century: "What has he not done for everyone of us? Who else ever, except Shakespeare, so diverted mankind, entertained and entertains a world so liberally, so wholesomely? We are fain to say, not even Shakespeare, for his is something deeper than diversion, something higher than pleasure, and yet who could care to split this hair?"[27]

This tender personal feeling is indeed characteristic of the allusions to Scott by the greatest of his successors in the field of the novel. None of them criticized his work in detail, but they all seem to have felt the deepest respect and affection for him. Dickens sprang to his defense in the Ballantyne controversy. George Eliot could stand unfavorable criticism of his novels no better than of her own.[28] Thackeray's biographers make it clear that *Rebecca and Rowena* was not a burlesque of *Ivanhoe,* that he was not attacking Scott as he attacked some of his colleagues in *Novels by Eminent Hands;* and in "The Peal of Bells" in the *Roundabout Papers* he muses over the long list of Waverley characters which he can head with "Amo," though he does, it is true, end by exalting Cooper's Leatherstocking above them all. And Trollope, though continually proving himself anti-heroic and anti-romantic, in his life of Thackeray speaks with

[27] In "Spare Hours," 2d series, *North British Review,* 39:379 (November, 1863), in a review of *Pet Marjorie,* i.e., Marjorie Fleming. Reprinted in *Horae Subsecivae.*

[28] See John Walter Cross, *George Eliot's Life as Related in Her Letters and Journals,* in *Works* (25 vols., Boston, 1908), XXIII, 18; XXIV, 112; XXV, 88.

all reverence of Scott and justifies Thackeray as a moralist by comparisons with Sir Walter.

Or, to cross the Atlantic, there are the reviews of Cunningham's *Life* of 1833 and Lockhart's in 1838, in the *North American Review*.[29] Both illustrate the fusion of interest in his character and works; it was impossible to consider the poems or novels apart from the goodness, kindliness, and geniality of his personal character, which had so charmed his whole generation. Both too are practically pure panegyric of Scott's character and work; imputed faults are mentioned only to be excused and easily forgiven, as "we know not whether the not infrequent carelessness [of his style] is felt by the reader as a blemish; it certainly is far more easily forgiven than the appearance of stateliness or art." In estimating his rank in literature, both articles would place him second only to Shakespeare. In the novel he was a great reformer and innovator; Richardson had, it is true, the power of "just and noble sentiment and a familiar knowledge of some affections of the heart," but he is now outmoded, while Fielding and Smollett had been "great in their own sphere, but that sphere was assuredly not high" — neither had had the least conception of soaring to the heights of poetical romance. And "with these exceptions and one or two others, the field was entirely barren." *Waverley* showed him to be a "Shakespeare in prose" and set him above all previous novelists; "he swept over the whole range of character with entire freedom as well as fidelity, ennobling the whole by high historical associations, and in a style . . . whose pure and classic flow was tinctured with just so much of poetic coloring as suited the purposes of romance."

As a matter of fact the *North American* maintained its allegiance unabated, twenty years later, in reviews of a new edition.[30] The critic emphasizes Scott's vigor and productive

[29] W. B. O. Peabody, *North American Review*, 36:289 (April, 1833); W. H. Prescott, 46:431 (April, 1838).

[30] Some early volumes of this edition (it appeared in installments) were reviewed in July, 1857 (85:271) and the complete edition in 1858 (87:293) by S. G. Brown. Note also in an article on Dickens by E. P. Whipple, 69:388 (October,

power and his sweeping innovation, and again compares him with Shakespeare, like whom he is said to be at once "thoroughly national and thoroughly cosmopolitan." Moreover, no one but Shakespeare has evolved so many vivid and living characters. It is true, the critic admits, that he has not risen to the heights of Shakespeare, Milton, or Dante, for he nowhere creates the perfect, the ideal, human being or tries to solve completely the problem of life, but — and here there is resort to a favorite refuge and defense — he must be praised for his uniformly high moral tone, and for never pandering to the low tastes and motives of human nature. It may be added that this writer is one of the very small company who would crown *Ivanhoe* as Scott's masterpiece.

The same attitude characterizes still another *North American* review six years later;[31] this time by no less a person than Henry James, now twenty-one years old, who is attacking contemptuously Nassau Senior's *Essays on Fiction*. He finds the book a group of antiquated essays, superficial and heavy, which might well have been left to collect dust. It will be remembered that Senior's essays on Scott had been dear to Lockhart a generation earlier, and were indeed the only ones he had quoted at length in his *Life*. It cannot be said that the youthful James was free from the trammels of the time; indeed he repeats most of the usual panegyric, and before he is through illustrates most of the Victorian attitudes, notably the common tendency to regret having "peeped and botanized" and to wash away all analysis in a flood of sentiment and affection. Senior, he says, "still loves

1849), a passage on Scott's influence, which the most enthusiastic critic would have found it hard to surpass. In a preliminary survey of the history of the novel, Whipple declares that all earlier forms "fled like mists before the sun, when Scott appeared with *Waverley*." Since then the novel has become extremely important and has exercised great influence on other fields of literature, especially history. No longer is it merely for the lazy; "under the impulse it received from Scott [it] became the illustrator of history, the mirror and satirist of manners, the vehicle of controverted opinions in philosophy, politics, and religion." It has even, he adds, taken the place of the drama and epic, but its success has drawn in "rogues and dunces," and also preachers who should have stuck to treatises.

[31] 99:580 (October, 1864).

[Scott] in spite of his defects, which, we think, will be the permanent attitude of posterity." In regard to haste and obvious defects he declares that Mrs. Henry Wood is even more prolific than Sir Walter and avoids many mistakes of his; yet "we still linger over those hasty pages." He calls Scott the first irresponsible novelist, the first who wrote merely to amuse, and says that since Shakespeare no writer had created so immense a gallery of portraits, nor on the whole had any portraits been so lifelike. They were, besides, "all instinct with something of the poetic fire." Then toward the end he suddenly throws criticism to the winds, declaring that Sir Walter, who never wrote for analysis, should not be criticized, but cherished and preserved. "There are moments of high strung sympathy with the spirit which is abroad when we might find [the novels] rather dull in parts, but they are capital books to have read," and so on in kindly panegyric, "thoroughly to enjoy him, we must become as credulous as children at twilight." This is not quite the lame and impotent conclusion it may seem; James is casting no slur on Scott as a writer of juveniles; he means merely to convey that the novels in their goodness and purity and power of inspiration appeal directly to unspoiled human nature.[32]

Clearly, the original waves of enthusiasm and personal affection might still roll as high as ever. No one could demand higher devotion to Scott than that expressed by a *Blackwood's* critic [33] in an essay on Scott presented in a series, "A Century of Great Poets." Scott "has made our past beautiful and dear; he has lighted up our country . . . surrounded us with the beautiful, the noble, and the fair." He was a national poet, a typical

---

[32] Doubtless James' opinion was modified during the next half century. Yet he could write in *English Hours* (London, 1905), p. 290, "Woe to the mere official critic, the critic who has never felt the *man*. You go on liking *The Antiquary* because it is Scott." And, he adds, *David Copperfield* and *Denis Duval* because they are Dickens and Thackeray. A remark in *Notes on Novelists* (London, 1914), p. 454, is less friendly. He is speaking of Mrs. Oliphant. "She had small patience with new-fangled attitudes or with a finical conscience. What was good enough for Sir Walter was good enough for her." And, "with her immensity of reading, as well as of observation and humor," she would have been good enough for Sir Walter.

[33] *Blackwood's*, 110:229 (August, 1871).

Scotchman. But his poems were only a preface; the novels were the basis of his "enduring glory." Apart from his heroes (who are weak, though so are many of Shakespeare's) the novels "opened a wonderful and enchanted world to the astonished public." Of *Waverley:* "In that wonderful flow of narrative the reader was carried along . . . finally to that scaffold and conclusion which he came to with a pang of the *hysterica passio* in his throat and at the same time that sense of inevitable and necessary fate which ennobles and saddens the Greek drama, all without time to breathe or pause or escape from the spell that had seized upon him." There is the highest praise for Scott's humor, his sympathy with his characters, "without which no man ever attains to real humor," a humor kind, delicate, "sweetened by the heart of sympathy within." Dickens, Thackeray, and Bulwer — each was a master of one sort of character; Scott "has a world of men under his belt." *The Heart of Midlothian,* with Jeanie Deans, is his masterpiece. The book has flaws, as his novels in general have, slight plots and weak heroes; but Scott, like Shakespeare, is sacred; "his very errors are dear to us." And he ends with an echo of Lockhart's judgment that *Ivanhoe,* though a brilliant piece of *bravura* and "the most animated sketch of ancient manners ever made . . . certainly the noblest in the English language," could not stand on a level, for character, with the great Scotch novels. No critic of 1820 gloried in Scott more freely than did this Scotch writer forty years after his death.

It is clear enough that Scott's character and personality were of tremendous service in keeping alive the fame of his novels and poems. Through most of the Victorian period, the acclaim of Scott as a man was as great as it had been in his own lifetime. Scotland, chiefly through his influence, had become a country for vacation tours, with Abbotsford and Loch Katrine and the Trossachs at the top of every list of sights that must be seen. The Victorians had no writer of their own (certainly not Dickens,[34]

[34] Compare the American *Southern Literary Messenger,* 22:291 (April, 1856), where an indignant and exclamatory lover of *Waverley* enters the lists against

even) for whom they felt the personal affection and tenderness and reverence that they lavished on this idol of the last age. Indeed, it is a continuance unabated of what Scott himself had known, but modified in quite characteristic Victorian fashion. It is tenderer, sweeter, and more sentimental; it is tamer and more domestic. The perusal of articles on Scott in the Victorian magazines for Victorian ladies and for the Victorian home soon makes this obvious enough.[35] Of course this too was of great service to his books and to the maintenance of an army of readers.

Aside from the critical estimates of his work, there was a steady flow of journalistic Scott material — pilgrimages to Abbotsford and the various localities of the novels, all sorts of anecdotes about him, his friends and his dogs (and his pet pig), conjectures as to the originals of his characters, sentimental musings on his heroines — these and scores of other subjects found ready admission to the pages of all sorts of periodicals, and testify to the general public interest in him, his books, and in fact in everything even remotely concerning him. Of course most of the journalistic matter reflecting this interest is, if not mere repetition, trivial and insignificant, and little worth raking from the files. As one reviews the whole mass of writing on Scott during this time, these various favorable elements in the situation — the tradition of his person, the purity of his page, and the theory that his poetic, national romance was superior to realism — more than offset the forces in opposition, that is, the very passing of time, with the rise of new and fascinating favorites, and the Victorian desire for moral earnestness and edification in general.

If there is much in this criticism that now seems soft and sentimental, there is also much that is fine in the genuine affection and reverence of these writers. It could, if expressed with proper restraint and dignity, become very impressive. To see it at its

a critic who in singing Dickens' praises had disparaged Scott in comparison.

[35] Note also Amy Cruse, *The Victorians and Their Reading* (Boston, 1935), *passim*, but pp. 294–95 especially, where the reverence for Scott in the average British household is recounted.

best one may turn to Edward Fitzgerald, or to Emerson, the most eminent of Scott's admirers in America. It is notable that the Waverley novels have appealed to many readers with special points of view or peculiar philosophies who approached them from some favorite angle or interpreted them as useful propaganda or illustration of special theory. Thus such diverse personalities as the utilitarian Harriet Martineau, the medievalist Ruskin, and the Catholics. Like them Emerson found in Scott qualities and ideas on which he always set a high value — simplicity, directness, lack of affectation, and a broad plain humanity. And so too Fitzgerald, breezy, romantic, and anti-realistic — a despiser of "Austens and Eliots."

Among notable Victorians the one who went beyond all others in his enthusiasm for Scott and who more than most Victorians was able to read him for pure delight and not the edification of a message, was probably Edward Fitzgerald.[36] His taste in novels as in other literature was very certain, very decided. It is clear from his innumerable allusions in letters that Richardson, Scott and Dickens were his favorites, and that among these Scott excited him most. Fielding and Thackeray he admired, but with distinct reservations. Jane Austen, George Eliot, Hawthorne — these he would not read.[37]

Fitzgerald continually read the Waverley novels, or, in his days of failing eyesight, had them read to him. In fact, most of his allusions to them come in the last dozen years of his life. Apparently any of them was capable of stirring him. He writes in 1871 with the greatest delight of reading *The Pirate* — "it

[36] For allusions and citations from Fitzgerald's letters, see, with two exceptions noted, William Aldis Wright, ed., *Letters of Edward Fitzgerald* (2 vols., London, 1910), II, 128–265, *passim*. W. F. Gray, in *Scott in Sunshine and Shadow*, deals with Fitzgerald's comments on Scott.

[37] ". . . I have been quite happy again with some of Scott's novels and Boswell's Johnson; both fresh as Dew. It is a great comfort to return to such books. I have also read Thackeray's *Pendennis* and *Newcomes* again — wonderful too — but not so comfortable." He goes on to say that Thackeray, Scott, and Johnson "Would have cogged well together." See Neilson Campbell Hannay, ed., *A Fitzgerald Friendship* (London, 1932), p. 73. For an interesting detailed analysis of Fitzgerald's literary taste see the life by A. C. Benson (London, 1905), Chapter VII.

is, I know, not one of the best" — and is glad to find how much
he still likes it; he is sure it is not "old prejudice" but "the
intrinsic merit and beauty of the book itself." "What a broad
Shakespearian Daylight over it all, and all with no effort." In
other letters he speaks in similar vein of *Kenilworth, Waverley,
The Bride of Lammermoor,* and *The Fortunes of Nigel.* For
instance, in 1882, "We are now in the midst of *The Fortunes
of Nigel* which I am (contrary to expectations) delighted with.
Sir Walter is not yet killed off by Austens and George Elliots
[*sic*], I do believe."[38]

Yet he also makes it clear that, like most other critics, he
thought the earlier novels the best. "They won't beat Sir Walter
in a hurry (I mean of course his earlier, Northern novels)." His
recognition of what is best in Scott comes out too in the scenes
he selects to admire and urges his friends to read. They are
invariably impressive for their dramatization of homely Scotch
scenes and common Scotch character; in an inn, perhaps, or
among the boats on a beach. In Fitzgerald's letters the paralleling
with Shakespeare is frequent, and comparisons with Homer and
his adored Cervantes also spring to his mind. Yet, on the other
hand, so is his violent prejudice against most of the nineteenth-
century novelists. He writes as it were with a chip on his shoulder
and will have his reader know, time and again, that no one has
shown himself since Scott's day who can bear away the palm from
him. "O, Sir Walter will fly over all their heads 'come aquila'
still!" Altogether Fitzgerald's enthusiasm, expressed in bits and
at odd moments, is refreshingly vivid and spontaneous. It has
about it the fine amateur quality that one feels in Lady Louisa
Stuart's letters of an earlier day. He himself remarks on occasion
that there are many things one may feel about Sir Walter without having to write an essay about them. Certainly here as in
many other places, *The Rubaiyat* for instance, he shows himself
very little the earnest Victorian. He could be a good friend of
Tennyson without admiring the Victorian prophet in him and

[38] See N. C. Hannay, *op. cit.,* p. 130.

he could be close to Carlyle and still refuse to dethrone Sir Walter for such a "cantankerous bigot" as John Knox.

On the American side of the Atlantic, Scott's most faithful spokesman was doubtless Ralph Waldo Emerson. All through Emerson's writing, in his books and journals and letters, there are continual allusions to Scott. While still a student he read some of the Waverley novels with delight, and a decade later on his first trip to England, the year after Scott's death, he said that the men he wished to see were Coleridge, Wordsworth, Landor, De Quincey, and Carlyle — no others, "for Scott was dead," unless it were the Duke of Wellington. Despite certain slighting remarks as a young man ("What did Walter Scott write without stint? — a rhymed traveller's guide to Scotland") he really thought well of Scott's poetry.[39] His son in notes on Emerson's centenary address on Scott at Boston in 1871,[40] says that his father had great fondness for Scott's poetry, that it was in his head continually, and that he was always quoting from it.

The novels, however, he set above the poetry. His finest praise was in the speech of 1871, when he said, "The tone of strength in *Waverley* at once announced the master, and was more than justified by the superior genius of the following romances, up to *The Bride of Lammermoor,* which almost goes back to Aeschylus for a counterpart as a painting of Fate,— leaving on every reader the impression of the highest and purest tragedy."[41]

[39] See *English Traits,* in *Works* (Centenary Edition, 12 vols., Boston, 1903–04), V, 4, 255.

[40] See *Works,* XI, 461. Another famous American writer, William Cullen Bryant, delivered a centenary address in New York in 1872, at the unveiling of a statue in Central Park. It was, naturally enough, panegyric, and does not undertake detailed criticism beyond a general claim of immortality for the novels on the basis of the crowd of characters in them. See Parke Godwin, ed., *Prose Writings of W. C. Bryant* (2 vols., New York, 1884), Vol. II.

[41] *The Bride of Lammermoor* seems to have been Emerson's favorite among the novels. His son says in the note already quoted that it was "the only dreary tale that Mr. Emerson could abide, except Griselda." He writes in his journal (1856): "Sue, Dumas, etc., when they begin a story do not know how it will end, but Walter Scott when he began *The Bride of Lammermoor* had no choice; nor Shakespeare in *Macbeth.*" Edward Waldo Emerson and Waldo Emerson Forbes, eds., *Journals of Ralph Waldo Emerson* (10 vols., Boston, 1909–14), IX, 25.

He went on to ascribe Scott's power over the public mind to the "singular union" of his aristocratic tendencies with "the eminent humanity which delighted in the sense and virtue and wit of the common people." Indeed, the common people in his books were drawn from actual acquaintances; he had "an extreme sympathy reaching down to every beggar and beggar's dog and horse and cow." In the number and variety of his characters he approached Shakespeare; while other novelists (Cervantes, Defoe, Richardson, Goldsmith, Sterne, Fielding) produced a few type figures, "Scott portrayed with equal strength and success every figure in his crowded company." There is also here the highest praise of Scott's "strong good sense" and humor: "He had no insanity or vice or blemish. He was a thoroughly upright, wise and great hearted man, and equal to whatever event or fortune should try him. Disasters only drove him to immense exertion. What an ornament and safeguard is humor! Far better than wit for a poet and writer. It is a genius itself, and so defends from the insanities."

Emerson thought of Scott as a great writer for youth, though clearly he did not mean to degrade him to the level of the writer of juveniles. In "Illusions"[42] he exclaims, "What a debt is his [the boy's] to imaginative books. He has no better friend or influence than Scott, Shakespeare, Plutarch, and Homer. The man lives to other objects, but who dare affirm that they are more real." And in his poem *The Harp* he has the phrase, "Scott, the delight of generous boys." Elsewhere he links Plutarch and Scott as writers whose approach is "human" rather than metaphysical, and thinks that Scott got his hold on the fathers through their sons.[43]

In the lecture on "Aristocracy" too, where he defines genius as the power to affect the imagination, to appeal to the whole world, he adds, "The eminent examples are Shakespeare, Cervantes, Bunyan, Burns, Scott, and now we must add Dickens."[44]

[42] See "Illusions," *The Conduct of Life,* in *Works,* VI, 312.
[43] *Works,* IX, 240; X, 314.
[44] *Works,* X, 54.

Even Scott's admitted habit of writing for his contemporary readers and letting the critics and the future take care of themselves appealed to Emerson. In the *Journal* he says, "We talked of Scott. There is some greatness in defying posterity and writing for the hour."[45]

It is obvious that Emerson placed Scott among the immortals, that he thought of him as one of the greatest of writers and a hero among men. The lack of a direct message that had so distressed Carlyle apparently did not worry his friend in America; Emerson saw in Scott a native dignity and simplicity and power which in themselves meant a high seriousness, where Carlyle had seen only triviality and an amusing surface. Emerson's praise may at times be exaggerated, and he is doubtless unfair to other novelists, yet the qualities that impressed him in Scott are after all the ones that the most sympathetic of his critics have at once grasped and appraised at their real value.[46]

There is no doubt of Scott's great popularity among Victorian readers or of his strong hold on the rank and file of the Victorian critics. Yet it is not to be expected that he would have it all his way. After the first few years when the period of funeral eulogies and the feeling of *nil nisi bonum* had passed, among some of the critics there began the process of turning Scott into a classic and appraising him more or less coolly and judicially. Sentiment subsided to the point where some critics felt that they could, at least tentatively and cautiously, probe defects and weaknesses and evaluate the novels analytically. Of the outright unfavorable there is nothing, if one excepts Jeaffreson, and a few remarks on anachronism. The utmost severity seems to consist in the disposition to be critical and to let Sir Walter take his chance with other writers, to stand aloof and let him seek his own level,

[45] *Works*, XI, 637. It is not often enough remembered that Scott believed he had written some pages that would live.

[46] Oscar W. Firkins says that Emerson's dislike of novels amounted to "a general incapacity," that "he abuses our kindness in his presumptuous interest in Scott," whom Firkins dismisses as juvenile, and that his fondness for Scott was due to his cordial response to "primitive virility, martial images and courtly, generous manners." *Ralph Waldo Emerson* (Boston, 1915), pp. 231–32.

and to ask how well he is holding his readers. Also inescapable is the regret over the lack of a philosophical thesis or a reforming or "progressive" tendency which had made the novel so valuable a social instrument in the hands of Dickens, Mrs. Gaskell, Kingsley, and George Eliot.

It was, after all, another age. It had a whole set of new ideas and ideals, about which it was intensely in earnest. It went in for progress and reform and uplift in a practical fashion far beyond anything Hazlitt dreamed of when he wrote about Scott in the early twenties. And it had a fine group of novelists to express its ideas — Dickens, Thackeray, George Eliot, the Brontës, Kingsley, Reade, and scores of minors, now forgotten, but good Victorians themselves, who exactly suited thousands of other good standard Victorians — writers like Mrs. Marsh, Holme Lee, Julia Kavanagh, Charlotte Yonge (all of whom were treated with respect in the dignified reviews), the most interesting of them women. These writers, great and small, dealt with the "realities" of life as the Victorians knew them. They were all "realists," Thackeray of course even cynically so. Over all these was the "gloss of novelty." Scott had to yield the limelight to them in spite of all his panegyrists might say, and to join and gradually merge into the group of great eighteenth-century classics, firmly enough seated on their respective thrones, but in the dim light of the background, figures of the past. There, of course, they waited to receive, after a little, Dickens and Thackeray and one or two more, when new ideas and new technics, most of them imported from across the Channel, should usher in still another age. Scott of course could not expect to be greeted with continual new bursts of astonished praise as he had been when his novels were new.

In the process of weighing, sorting, and appraising, the Victorian critics noticed all the faults that Scott's contemporaries had remarked and reiterated them frequently. To these they added the new one of a lack of message, of philosophy. Scott was never a preacher, and this the Victorians held against him and could not quite forgive him. The Georgians had not expected social gospels from their novelists; even radical critics like Hazlitt who quarreled with Sir Walter's Tory colors, did not demand one of him as the Victorians did from their purveyors of fiction. Hence, as one might expect, there is a great deal of talk all through the Victorian age of the lack of message, of earnestness, of direct inspiration and gospel, in Scott. This cry was raised by Carlyle, of course; one feels the undertone of it even in so judicious and detached a critic as Walter Bagehot, and among the smaller fry it is insistent. Among more important writers, however, Leslie Stephen spoke of it with something like contempt, and Ruskin too was a notable exception. But this was only because, like Miss Martineau, Ruskin found in Scott what he wanted to find, interpreting him as an apostle of the creed he himself was busy propagating.[47]

Possibly there is no better reflection of this Victorian earnestness and its application to Scott than an Oxford prize essay of 1862, *The Value and Influence of Works of Fiction*,[48] written by Thomas H. Green, when a young man in his middle twenties. He conceives the novel as a minor form of art, a wide, loose, popular form, possibly the forerunner of some higher development. Thus Scott (together with other novelists) is disparaged to begin with, reduced to the role of a John the Baptist preparing the way for some Messiah of the future. Green, moreover, subscribes to Carlyle's dictum that Scott approached men only from without, though, had it been otherwise, "he could not have uttered himself in the language of common life." Similarly

[47] It is only fair to point out, however, that the Victorian critics, and those of Scott's own time too, were mindful of the artistic dangers of didacticism and sometimes declaimed against them on principle. But after all it seems to have been a mere academic principle in the main and got little more than perfunctory lip service. A brilliant diatribe of James Russell Lowell in a review of Disraeli's *Tancred* which appeared in the *North American*, 65:215 (July, 1847) is startlingly unusual in its clarity of tone. The novel, he says, "no longer professes to amuse, but to instruct. This is the age of lectures. Even Punch has got into the professor's chair and donned the doctor's cap. The novel has become a quack advertisement in three volumes. Formerly we could detect the political economist at a reasonable distance and escape him by a well-contrived dodge. Now, no sanctuary is inviolate."

[48] Edited by F. N. Scott and republished at Ann Arbor, 1911.

his unfortunate Toryism and pseudo-feudalism was counteracted by "his genial human insight," which made him a reformer against his will and issued in his pictures of Scotch peasantry, his finest achievement. But Green contrasts the writers of Scott's period in the matter of "earnestness" with the Victorians, who could not have written as they did had they lived fifty years earlier. The very life about these later writers is more earnest, he says; it now has a sterner significance than "the coquetry and dissipation of the fashionable world or the dull courtesies of a country house."

Sidney Lanier's critical ideas on Scott are really based on the same conception. His interest is divided between the eighteenth-century novelists whom he despises as low, uninspiring, and unrefreshing, too much absorbed in vice, and his favorites, the "sweeter" group of Victorians led by George Eliot, whose praises he never tired of singing. He seems to feel that Scott may be passed over rapidly, though he deserves high praise. Lanier is of those who find the Waverley novels good for youth (though they could not charm the mature mind as George Eliot's could). They are, he exclaims, "among the most hale and strengthening waters in which the young soul ever bathed. They discuss no moral problems, they place us in no relation towards our fel-low that can be called moral at all, they belong to that part of us which is youthful, undebating, wholly unmoral — though not immoral — they are simply always young, always healthy, always miraculous." This is warm and pleasant, but he is anxious to get on to George Eliot and the realities.[49]

Thus in the midst of the sentimental panegyric,[50] affectionate and hero-worshipping, which made up most of the writing on Scott, there sounded more and more frequently such critical tones as these. Occasionally the note is somewhat sharper than in these last, there is an even stronger disposition to keep senti-

[49] *The English Novel* (New York, 1883). Published posthumously.
[50] For good typical instances note the appreciatory essays in *Harper's Magazine*, 43:511 (September, 1871), and the *Gentleman's*, N. S., 7:292, 485, at the time of the 1871 centenary. Here all unfavorable comment is confined to a few of the traditional, long-conceded defects.

mental attachments in check and sometimes to end with at least an implication that Sir Walter was not quite all he had once been thought to be, that his touch had lost a good deal of its magic, and that in many ways a close inspection and critical analysis was rather damaging.

On the publication of a one-shilling edition of the novels in 1863, as the copyrights began to expire, an essayist in the *Saturday Review* [51] asserted that this would prove a final test of Scott's popularity. He notices certain fundamental weaknesses in the novels. The characters, he contends, are drawn by one of the upper classes for the upper classes, who really constituted his readers, and his lower-class characters therefore were never judged by their equals. This sort of criticism is of course of very doubtful truth and value, both in the matter of fact and the deductions drawn from it. In addition, the critic continues, Scott does not belong to the highest class of writers; he has no gospel or message to deliver, although on the other hand, if no prophet, neither was he a Pharisee prating of a message. His success rested practically altogether on his love of antiquity and of nature. In religion, in art, even in history, which he merely ransacked for materials of amusement, he was superficial. He will probably be kept from shipwreck by his medievalism, which is now in 1863 a fad, and by his love of the out-of-doors. Moreover, his sympathy and qualities of heart make his work so attractive that his popularity can certainly never be followed by disgust, and as for the present, he is still beyond a doubt the favorite novelist of the country.

One of the 1871 essays, published in the New York *Nation,*[52] although written in a vein of tender and sentimental sympathy, when boiled down to its essential ideas is distinctly unencouraging. It opens, "Scott is now somewhat faded, it is common to say, and undeniably it is true to say so." The author believes that his fame is kept alive in large part by Scotch patriotism, and that the impression he made on his own time was so overwhelm-

[51] Reprinted in *Living Age,* 76:187 (January 24, 1863).
[52] 13:103 (August 17, 1871).

ing merely because the other novelists were so bad. Still it is
probable that the sifting and settling process of the last generation has brought his fame down to its proper level and that he
will remain as popular with later readers as he is in 1871. People
will go on finding fault with his shallow philosophy and his false
views of history and will regret many other things about him,
but — with a sudden change of front — there is no body of work
by any novelist since his day that can be said to equal the
Waverley novels, and especially the Scotch group, which is
clearly his stronghold.

A much more critical and analytical essay of this same period,
interesting for its more specific comparisons with the great Victorians, appeared in the *London Quarterly Review*.[53] Scott, it
is said, had all the great qualities of a story-teller, that is, the
gifts necessary to catch and hold the reader's interest, and in
addition is entitled to great credit as an innovator and for his
services to the novel as a literary form. Many later novels are
greater than Scott's; they come closer to the plane of Shakespeare,
and are much more artistic in form and expression than Scott's.
Scott's forte lay in the first place in the delineation of characters
more or less remarkable, and in awakening and maintaining an
interest in their careers; and in the second in throwing together
romantic circumstances, unusual but not improbable. (This is,
one may say, nothing more nor less than declaring that Scott
is a romanticist and deals with both romantic characters and
romantic action and setting.) On the other hand, Scott lacked
the power so notable in Jane Austen and George Eliot of making
ordinary people in ordinary circumstances interesting, but this
defect cannot destroy the charm of his "simple healthful love of
adventure." And even though he could not vivify the commonplace, he is much more to be admired than Thackeray or
Dickens. He kept clear of Thackeray's pitfalls, especially that
"cynic obliquity of gaze that led to much that is not admirable
in Thackeray," and he never lapsed into Dickens' coarseness and
caricature. Indeed, this critic desires nothing of Dickens for

[53] 38:35 (April, 1872).

Scott. He admires Scott's ability to describe manners in so many periods, but especially those closest to his own time; here again is the preference for the more realistic novels. He admires, too, Scott's fine portraits of characters in low life and suggests comparison between them and what he calls the travesties of Dickens. He differs from Carlyle's dictum that Scott's character drawing was external, that he never got at the heart of a character, maintaining that on occasion Scott could get well beneath the skin. He likes, too, his vivid antiquarian interest, but ends by declaring that *St. Ronan's Well* is one of the best novels ever written, a critical judgment which so far as it is possible to discover is unique. Scott's one attempt at contemporary realism, it is an especially surprising choice by a critic who has been extolling Scott's distinction in romantic fields and his failure in the commonplace.

Critical analysis of the novels as good as almost any in the period — writing that may well be set beside Bagehot's and Leslie Stephen's — is to be found in R. H. Hutton's *Life*.[54] Here is just and sympathetic praise without a trace of Victorian sensibility — indeed it is far more in the vein of 1910 or 1920 than in that of 1878 when it was written. Hutton's main ideas about the novels (in his tenth chapter) are pointed and easy to summarize. He thought their quality remarkably even, except for the last two, such differences as there were being due not to haste nor insufficient leisure but rather to other causes, especially the subject itself. He maintains even that the last but two, *Anne of Geierstein*, generally regarded as very weak, would have been as successful in 1814 as *Waverley*, and that *Waverley*, published in *Anne's* place, would have been equally depreciated. As for rapidity of writing, Hutton agrees with Sir Walter himself, that the very best work seems to have been the most rapid. Hutton said that Scott's chief interest was in "individuals as they are affected by the public strifes and social divisions of the age," and felt that while thoroughly romantic and always in need of a

[54] Richard Holt Hutton, *Sir Walter Scott* (English Men of Letters series, London, 1878). See especially Chapter X.

romantic setting, as witness his failure in *St. Ronan's Well,* where he was on ground more properly Jane Austen's, his treatment of unromantic materials was equally vigorous, and that altogether he had a largeness of conception never to be found in the domestic novel. On the old subject of heroes and heroines, Hutton is willing to admit their lack of color, but insists that Scott's treatment of his heroes is necessary if he is to show both sides of a quarrel as he generally wishes to do, and that judged simply by his male characters he is greater than Goethe — this of course in answer to Carlyle. With the women, it is true, his chivalry stood in the way of any real analysis. Hutton, in fact, sets little store by Carlyle. With Scott's best men and women, he says, Carlyle's dictum about painting only the surface has no validity, as his Mary Stuart and Elizabeth [55] prove clearly. As for his humor, it is sometimes heavy, notably in his "bores," yet in certain other types — his "dry" humor, and the highest form, where he skillfully blends the ludicrous and the pathetic — he is a master. His highest power of humor he reveals in Jeanie Deans, in spite of certain elephantine details. Yet Hutton will have no parallel with Shakespeare; Scott, he says, never approaches the "spiritual irony" of Shakespeare. Here is certainly discriminating and dispassionate judgment, sound and well considered — neither sunk in sentimental, affectionate revery nor overwhelmed by the equally emotional strictures of Carlyle.

[55] Critics generally approve the portrait of Elizabeth, but most of them (though not all) seem to think the one of Mary a failure.

CHAPTER II

VICTORIAN CRITICAL PREJUDICES

THERE IS no doubt of Scott's popularity during the early and mid-Victorian periods, nor of the respect and reverence felt for him by the reading public and the general run of the critics. Nor were the critics at a loss to discover rational and philosophic bases for their belief in Scott. For it is safe to say that the Victorian critics, by and large, tended to keep up the tradition that Scott was the greatest of British novelists. It had been felt by Jeffrey and other contemporary writers that his broad historical scenes, his national character, and his imagination and "poetic" quality had raised the novel as a form above the realm of private life, of the local and even parochial sphere, where the great eighteenth-century novelists had been content to leave it. Thus Scott had ennobled the novel, and thus he had shown himself a grander genius than his predecessors.

The temper of the Victorians inclined them to an acceptance of this point of view. Their own novelists, those of any account, (and need one take into account G. P. R. James and Harrison Ainsworth?) were all realists, except for brief excursions into romance like *Esmond* and *The Cloister and the Hearth* and *Romola,* and these after all are only superficially romantic. But still when they looked back through the eighteenth century to the beginnings of the novel, they felt that realism did not please them. It was too "low." The best realist of their own, the "cynical" Thackeray, was conscious of their restraints and said he had not the freedom to present Pendennis as Fielding had presented Tom Jones.[1] Even that daring rebel, Charlotte

---

[1] Yet would he have taken advantage of it if he had had it?

188

Brontë, said like a good Victorian that Fielding could stoop to carrion. The Victorians liked novels about their own daily life, but they demanded that that life be presented decently and "purely," with all conclusions comfortable, and that the seamy side of human nature be kept where it belonged, out of sight.

The most notable early Victorian denial of this typical point of view was made by G. H. Lewes, in "Recent Novels: French and English." [2] Lewes, a devotee of continental literature, who demanded above all else in the novel, "correct representation of life," declared Fielding and Jane Austen the greatest English novelists, and said he would rather have written *Tom Jones* or *Pride and Prejudice* than any of the Waverley series. Yet even Lewes agreed with his contemporaries in allowing Scott "greater invention, more varied powers, a more poetical and pictorial imagination," and character delineation true though not deep. Lewes refers to Sir Walter's powers of attraction as astonishing, and is willing to equal him with Ariosto, though not with Shakespeare, to whom, he thinks, Jane Austen comes much closer. And though Lewes was Fielding's most doughty champion among the Victorians, George Eliot, who should have known, said of her husband, "He loves Scott as well as I do"; and it is to be remembered that she herself always spoke of him with the highest respect and affection, and said, "It is a personal grief, a heart-wound to me, when I hear a depreciatory or slighting word about Scott." [3]

Mr. Frederic Blanchard [4] analyzes and illustrates this attitude in great detail. From his point of view as a loyal friend of Fielding, this is a sad era. Fielding had gradually fought his way up to his proper place as the greatest novelist, defeating the claims of Richardson, Sterne, and Smollett. Then early in the nineteenth century the vogue of the new romance, broader, grander, more poetical, had put him down from his rightful seat, and the mid-century, squeamish and fastidious, was even more prone

[2] *Fraser's,* 36:686 (December, 1847).
[3] See page 170.
[4] Frederic T. Blanchard, *Fielding the Novelist* (New Haven, 1926).

to deny him his rights. So Scott, the idealist, the painter of broad historic, poetic canvases, continued to be the idol.

A typical and really representative expression of the point of view that historical romance was intrinsically superior to the realistic novel is that of Archibald Alison, the historian, characterized by Leslie Stephen [5] as a very able mediocrity of thoroughly Tory prejudices. In his autobiography Alison speaks of Scott several times as the chief literary figure of the age, and tells impressively of having visited the grave of Scott, "the greatest of past novelists," and soon after receiving a visit from Bulwer Lytton "the greatest of the present." His chief and most magisterial utterance on Scott — and he could be fully as magisterial as Bulwer Lytton — was in an essay, "Historical Romance," [6] which he thinks deserves a place, as a type of wide range and scope, beside the plays of Shakespeare. Scott was its inventor; he exalted the novel from its former low state by raising it to this new form. The effect was "like sun bursting through clouds." "The hearts of men were taken by storm . . . It is not going too far to say that the romances of Sir Walter Scott have gone far to neutralize the dangers of the Reform Bill." Certainly, he maintained, they had extinguished the prejudices against the feudal and the medieval among educated people. Thus altogether the historical romance with its wide scope and its poetry was a superior, a more significant form than the mere novel of familiar life, and its inventor and chief exponent, Sir Walter Scott, was pre-eminent among novelists.

Two articles in the *North British Review* [7] illustrate well the attitude of many Victorians toward Sir Walter when they came to compare him with their own novelists. They shied away from thoroughgoing realism or from the "low" as it appeared in Dickens, and the theory that history lent dignity to the novel was very impressive to them. Hence the general refusal to accept Dickens as a really great genius and on the other hand the wor-

---

[5] In the article on Alison in the *Dictionary of National Biography*.

[6] *Blackwood's,* 58:341 (September, 1845). See also *Some Account of my Life and Writings*, edited by his daughter-in-law, Lady Alison (2 vols., Edinburgh, 1883).

[7] 3:77 (May, 1845); 15:422 (August, 1851).

ship in many quarters of Bulwer Lytton's meretricious romanticism. The first article, of May, 1845, is an attack on Dickens,[8] upon whom Scott is used as a cudgel. Dickens' vulgarity of style is emphasized; Scott in homely scenes and low company is never vulgar but remains himself a gentleman, "refreshing and instructive, . . . with his rich store of history and literary knowledge." Similarly, Dickens' low characters are almost always vulgar; Scott's never. And it is the same, the writer adds, in their dealings with sentiment. "Indeed it seems unavoidable that the high standard which is afforded by the novels of Scott should be perpetually referred to for trying all his followers in the same path of literature; and surely when it is remembered how eminently his romances are distinguished by shrewd practical good sense as well as by pure feeling and correct moral tone, by an unaffected and manly simplicity of style, notwithstanding the rich variety of knowledge overflowing, not displayed, in every page, he is well entitled to be regarded as the guide of the critic as well as the model of succeeding novelists." For such writers, then, Scott was a touchstone to try the realists who were never broad and dignified enough to stand the comparison.[9] As far as the remarks on the comparative dignity of Scott's and Dickens' low characters are concerned, one may point out that G. K. Chesterton, one of the most valiant and devoted of modern Dickensians, has said practically the same thing, though in a more penetrating way.[10]

The second article, of August, 1851, again asserts the commanding position of Sir Walter on "the throne which he occupies by well-nigh universal consent," but goes on to say

[8] The usual attitude toward Dickens in the more dignified periodicals was that he was vigorous and inventive and undoubtedly remarkable, but at the same time low, cheap, and vulgar, and that all his methods and devices were forced and exaggerated.

[9] Much the same sort of thing is done in an article on Diana Vernon in *Macmillan's*, 22:285 (August, 1870), where Diana is used to demolish the current fashionable heroine, especially of the *Guy Livingstone* type of novel. This current heroine is said to have eyes only for a great hero (preferably with a wife living) before whose glittering eye and immense moustache she loves to quail.

[10] See his essay "Charles Dickens," in Harold J. and Hugh Massingham, eds., *The Great Victorians* (London, 1932). Cf. page 315, below.

that he has been "nearly approached by one, the Scott of the present day, who surpasses him in depth of passion, in grandeur and sublimity of thought. For lofty conception of character developed in all its heroic unity there are few creations like *Rienzi, Zanoni,* and *Harold.*" Such statements reveal the unbelievable position that Bulwer held in the minds of many dignified critics at the mid-century,[11] but they also show the esteem accorded to historical romance itself. It was not popular, it is true. Trollope says that at about this time the publishers told him to send them no historical romances — "they are not worth a damn" — but the form was certainly regarded as noble.

It is this idea of the superiority of romance with its broad, historic scope that is really behind Bulwer's own praise of Scott. Bulwer himself, so prone to take a high tone, so ambitious to deal with ideas, to be wide-ranging and philosophical, so pretentious to take the historical novel from Scott warbling his native wood notes wild and raise it to an "intellectual" plane, naturally found in Sir Walter a genius superior to that of any realist. He himself dabbled in most of the types of fiction that were in vogue during his long career, but his natural predilections were for the grandiose, and it was the grandiose in him that inspired with awe those critics who even as late as the time of his death solemnly appraised him as a greater novelist than any other of his time — even Thackeray or Dickens. Bulwer was always fond of discussing and appraising, of formulating general

[11] Leslie Stephen, in his article on Bulwer in the *Dictionary of National Biography* gives the impression that Bulwer's fame was purely a popular one; that the critics never approved him. This is far from true. There were violent attacks on Bulwer, notably by *Fraser's* in the 1830's, but there were plenty of reviews in the most dignified periodicals down to the time of his death in 1873 which are couched in terms of deepest respect and admiration. See especially *Blackwood's,* 113:255, 356 (March, 1873), where the critic says, "Taking him all in all, no man of his generation has achieved the same brilliancy of success, or has so true a claim to be the leading and typical novelist of his day." He cannot be raised to Scott's level, the writer continues, but he has done more to keep Scott's tradition alive than any other novelist. And in *Blackwood's,* 115:248 (February, 1874) the reviewer of *Fables in Song,* by "Owen Meredith," Lytton's son, declared, "Neither Lord Lytton nor Mr. Thackeray reach the Shakespeare level, or even, in his broader aspect, the level of Scott; but they were both men of distinguished genius."

principles and laying down the law. Other important novelists, like Thackeray and Dickens, spoke casually of Scott with affection and reverence; Bulwer left on record magisterial pronouncements both early and late. He delivered his opinion with the deepest gravity when Scott died in 1832, and almost a generation later, in 1863, he uttered a final and highly characteristic judgment.[12]

This he begins with a perfectly sound statement of the necessity for perspective in criticism. He denies the value of contemporary criticism; deplores the shallowness and insipidity of what Scott's and Byron's contemporaries had to say about them, though they "naturally engaged the analytical examination of some of the finest intellects of their time"; and contends that the present date of 1863 is still too early to establish Scott definitively in his proper niche. He does, however, venture the prediction that present fads will pass and that in a century or two both Scott and Byron will be thought of not as old-fashioned but as ancient. He then proceeds to his main thesis in connection with Scott — "the ease and the breadth of his knowledge of the world." This he takes to be one cause at least of Scott's "unprecedented popularity as a novelist among all classes and in all civilized lands." He stresses again the point he had emphasized earlier that Scott was not metaphysical or philosophical, and also that he was not dramatic, like Shakespeare, though his narrative method was perfect, a point he illustrates with the scene from *The Bride of Lammermoor* the night before the Master disappears. This scene from "the grandest tragic romance our language possesses" he calls the perfection of tragedy in narrative, not dramatic, art.

He makes the point too that while Scott dissected the mind only sparingly, he carried knowledge of manners and of social life further than any novelist before him and "harmoniously, artistically poetised it." It is significant that even as late as this Bulwer should use *Ivanhoe* to illustrate Scott's genius. He de-

[12] For the first, cf. above, page 159; for the second, see *Caxtoniana*, XIX, *Blackwood's*, 94:267 (September, 1863).

clares that *Ivanhoe* especially catches the essence of the age it represents, and that the very types of character Scott chose would have occurred only to a writer of broad knowledge. His methods of idealization too Bulwer finds perfect. They go just far enough; "Scott's kings may be a little more kingly than a leveller finds them; still their foibles are not disguised and they are never stilted and over-purpled." He reiterates the chief point of his remarks of 1832, that Scott's humanity, always fresh and genial, preserved him from the dangers of political prejudice, which so obviously affected the history of such writers as Macaulay and Hume. Really, in his portraits of Claverhouse the Cavalier and Burley the Puritan he came closer to the truth than either the Whig or the Tory. A comparison with *Hudibras* also shows the height and impartiality of his art.[13]

At this point Bulwer's own notions and prejudices make themselves felt. He develops the point that Scott's rare knowledge of the world is exhibited in his permanent character types, in contrast even with Fielding's (including Parson Adams), which, though beautifully analyzed, are only temporary. And moreover Fielding when he is greatest is satirical, and hence likely to "debase high conceptions of humanity in pulling down the false pretenses of impostors." Scott, like Shakespeare, has little satire. He had the advantage of living in a noble age, with heroes like Napoleon and Wellington before him, an age too in which a greater respect for humanity had grown up, unfortunately accompanied, it is true, by a growing desire to erase respect for the old royal foundations and go back to a spurious worship of "old heathen republics."[14] In such a time, "Scott rose to unite the reverence for what is best in our own genuine antiquity with what is best in our own genuine modern modes of thought." This, Bulwer says, is really his chief merit and the main cause of his popularity throughout Europe. He was both conservative and liberal — "conservative in his conception

[13] This is a point which is insisted on in the best criticism of Scott today.
[14] Such statements reflect the change of complexion in Bulwer's politics. He had long since turned from the Liberals to the Conservatives.

and portraiture of those great elements of the Christian Past
which each Christian community of Europe has employed in its
progressive development; liberal in the respect he shows to all
that can advance our human destinies throughout the future —
to valor, to honor, to conscience. Though his intellect did not
lead him to philosophize, his grand all-comprehending human
heart achieved the large results of philosophy."

All this is of course quite typical of Bulwer, a sort of facile
harmonizing of the two opposed phases of Scott's genius, which
he pretends to have analyzed. One may be quite sure that Bulwer himself preferred his own thoroughly explicit "philosophy"
to the implied or latent idealism discoverable in Sir Walter's
"grand all-comprehending human heart." And it is a certainty
also that many of Bulwer's reverent readers did too; they lived
in an age that had no objection to large doses of the commodity.[15]

Quite possibly it was really a preference for the broad, sweeping style of romance that moved so different a person as Matthew

[15] Bulwer published in 1838 in the *Monthly Chronicle* an essay "On Art in
Fiction," in which Scott figures largely, in fact much more frequently than Fielding or any of the eighteenth-century novelists. It is notable that Bulwer is
especially attracted by *The Bride of Lammermoor*, to which he makes continual
reference. In this essay, where Bulwer is concerned with the ideal novel, Scott is
made out a much smaller genius than in the essays written especially on him.
Though Bulwer's typical theories all appear here, Scott is celebrated only for such
minor qualities as manners and landscape, and is seen to be seriously limited and
deficient in his treatment of the "passions" and "the metaphysical." This essay
shows very clearly how Bulwer's aspirations soared beyond Scott's range. See
Publications of the Modern Language Association, March, 1935, for a detailed
summary and analysis of this essay by H. H. Watts.

A less elaborate essay on prose fiction had appeared as a preface to a new
edition of his novel, *The Disowned*, in 1835. Here he had classified the novel
into the two main divisions, dramatic and narrative, with various subdivisions.
In the first class Scott is presented as the great master. His novels are said to
require very little work with the scissors to prepare them for the stage. The
characters too are really dramatic; they have an existence quite independent of
the plot in which they act. But when compared with Shakespeare it is evident
that Scott was concerned with externals, Shakespeare with the soul. We know
how Scott's characters *looked* better than Shakespeare's; but we know and understand Shakespeare's better. Yet in this type of novel Scott is supreme; if he is
ever surpassed, it will be by a writer with more philosophic power — one who
thus comes closer to Shakespeare. Perhaps it is not unfair to point out that
Bulwer's special pretension was exactly to this philosophic power of which he is
speaking here.

Arnold to write what seems to be his only very significant allusion to Scott, in a letter to Clough in March, 1853.[16] He had just been reading *Esmond,* which he said was "one of the most readable books I ever met" and, "Thackeray is certainly a first-rate journeyman, though not a great artist: — It gives you an insight into the heaven-born character of *Waverley* and *Indiana* and such like when you read the undeniably powerful but most un-heaven-born productions of the present people — Thackeray — the woman Stowe, etc."

Closely involved with the idea of the superiority of romance over realism in its breadth, dignity, and aspirations was the matter of morals and propriety. Realism was likely to be "low," cynical, demoralizing. Scott's every scene — nay, every word, might be read without apprehension in the most innocent family circle. Sir Walter, with his healthy outdoor atmosphere, his unquestionable morality, and his suitability for the fireside was so refreshing! This is a tone one would expect the minor and more conventional Victorian critic to take, as he frequently did. On the other hand, to the family circle Fielding and his colleagues — even Richardson — could not of course be admitted. Nor, if the truth were to be told, could, much of the time, Thackeray, so cynical, alas, or Charlotte Brontë with her subversive *Jane Eyre,* or even Dickens, though the latter kept his ear to the ground and tried to avoid offense.

Nor should it be forgotten that a novelist's private life had to be taken into account. Here of course Scott shone refulgent beside Fielding. His morals were blameless, he was a gentleman, he was successful, kings had delighted to honor him — he was in every way admirable. Fielding's life had been anything but edifying (so far as they knew), and Thackeray's picture of him made him out more shocking than ever. Altogether, the substitution of Scott for Fielding as king of the novelists, what Mr. Blanchard calls "the Scott heresy," is not at all surprising. The

[16] See *The Letters of Matthew Arnold to Arthur Hugh Clough,* edited by Howard Foster Lowry (London, 1932), p. 132. In his essays *On Translating Homer* Arnold shows a high regard for Scott as a ballad poet, but he does not seem to be considering him as a novelist.

Victorians certainly had a right to the theory that romance was superior to realism, but as for the rest, one is reminded of Carlyle's remarks on biographers in his essay on Scott, where he defends the personal details of Lockhart's *Life:* "How delicate, decent, is English Biography, bless its mealy mouth! A Damocles' sword of Respectability hangs forever over the poor English Life-writer (as it does over English Life in general) and reduces him to the verge of paralysis."

Thus it is clear that the Victorians were really torn two ways. The nature of their own time drew them toward realism, and especially a realism devoted to a message and a gospel, a realism that went about doing good. This they could not find in Scott, a fact they deplored. On the other hand, their sentimental predilections, their insistence on the right to inquire into an author's personal life and value his works partially at least on his moral record (this was an age, it may be recalled, when "lady novelists" were not allowed by the critics to discourse on themes permissible to the men) and above all their distrust and fear of free, thoroughgoing realism like Fielding's, together with the attendant theory of the superior status of "the poetic imagination" — all this led them to the conclusion that Scott was still their greatest novelist. After all, they were unwilling to depose him for Thackeray or Dickens or George Eliot, in spite of all gospels, and they were very sure about Fielding, Smollett, Sterne, and even "the saintly Samuel." The result of these opposing emotions appears, as will be seen, in distinctly divergent, and at times even contradictory, pronouncements. Again and again a writer will discuss Sir Walter's waning star and make gloomy predictions as to his future, only to beg pardon in his last paragraph and take back what he has been saying.

The moral emphasis is pervasive, but may be illustrated by a few striking instances. William Spalding, a very sedate professorial historian of English literature, could even make Scott's availability for family reading the sole subject of the one page devoted to him.[17] "The Waverley novels," he says, "have been

---

[17] William Spalding, *History of English Literature* (London, 1853).

excepted by many very cautious judges from the sentiment which banishes most works of prose fiction from the libraries of the young. The exemption seems to be justified by two considerations. These are not mere love stories, but pictures of human life, expressing broad and manly and practical views, and animated by sentiments which are cheerful and correct, if not very elevated and solemn; and further, most of them exhibit history in a light which is extremely effective in exciting curiosity and interest without degrading facts or characters to the sentimental level, or falsifying either of them beyond the lawful and necessary stretch of poetical embellishment." Though Spalding goes on to praise the realistic Scotch novels above the romances, it is evident that here is faint praise indeed — lukewarm and proper. Sir Walter is innocent pabulum for babes and sucklings, his novels fit to follow *Sandford and Merton* in the reading of the young. But what Spalding said in the way of praise in 1853 was to be echoed many times later, generally in condescension not far from contempt.

Another good instance of this strongly moral bias is to be found in the *Christian Examiner* of Boston.[18] Through the religious nature of the periodical may be prejudicial, the tone is not more extreme than that of articles published in more purely literary channels, for example those in the *Edinburgh* and the *North American* of 1832. The writer has no sympathy with adverse criticism of Sir Walter's work, and declares the Waverley novels an unequaled performance; whether of the highest genius or not, "they exhibit a fertility of resources, a readiness of conception and a power of facility and execution seldom or never equalled." But aside from all this, and here we strike the main point, both the life and work of Scott "are full of instruction and rich in moral uses." His honesty and his morality "without any parade of prudery and refinement" are the real source of his power. He is always a trustworthy guide who never imperils his readers with "overwrought sensibility"; in fact he is one of

[18] M. L. Hurlbut, "The Character and Genius of Scott," *Christian Examiner*, 26:101 (March, 1839).

the greatest benefactors of society in furnishing so wide a field for the imagination to range in. He teaches the lesson of the "compatability of high genius with plain practical good sense and the quiet virtues of domestic life." His genius and inspiration are the gifts of God, leading his readers to a finer and better life — "All sources whence such influences flow are hallowed."

Still another excellent instance of this moral point of view is to be found in a review of Lockhart in the *New York Review*.[19] The author even so early fears a falling off in Sir Walter's fame, yet his own faith is untouched. After the highest of praise in all points — a ranking with Cervantes, close to Shakespeare, and far above all English novelists — he comes in his conclusion to the main point, Scott's "healthy morality," his "common humanheartedness," and so forth. The elevation of plain Jeanie Deans to heroic rank is made in itself a kind of moral inspiration and victory. The novels, moreover, are "free from the grave reproach . . . of stimulating the passions with images of superhuman depravity and poisoning the moral sense by familiarity with unthought-of guilt"; the general tone of the novels is one of "unaffected purity and . . . sound morality." Clearly Scott's "healthy morality," which meant chiefly his avoidance of sex, and which was to prove a definite irritant to a later generation, was highly acceptable to this one.

Yet sometimes morality could be specially defined and twisted against Scott and in favor of the Victorians. Thus James A. Noble, the author of *Morality in English Fiction*,[20] excludes Scott from consideration as *unmoral*. Scott, he says, neither expounded nor attacked current morality; he merely accepted it. He was a raconteur pure and simple. Though highly gifted in character portrayal — here comes in the inevitable comparison with Shakespeare — his only care was to be picturesque; he was concerned with manners, not morals. Hence, since he did not care to go deeper, he has lost his hold on more thoughtful readers, and any revival of the earlier enthusiasm for him seems impossible.

[19] 7:137 (July, 1840).
[20] Liverpool [1886].

Noble's essay is actually concerned with Thackeray, Dickens, Kingsley, Charlotte Brontë, and George Eliot, and the development of his theme reveals the influence of the doctrine of earnestness and "uplift" — and of Carlyle; indeed, the author accepts almost completely Carlyle's estimate of Scott's morality.

The evaluations by typical literary historians of the period show how profoundly and thoroughly the Victorians were moved by all such considerations as those just described. They might talk about genius and art, but in the last analysis they came back to morality, and placed first an author's "influence for good." A "radical" like Lewes might emancipate himself from his age even as early as the 1840's, and men as distinguished as Bagehot and Leslie Stephen were not bogged in the morass, but the average critic was tied by a pretty short tether to a central stake of morality, and in any attempt to range was always abruptly snubbed. The result of this was that when he looked back over the whole range of the novel, he was brought logically to put Scott at the head of the list. The eighteenth-century men were morally disqualified, and the best Victorians, although they showed the desirable tendency to go about doing good, sometimes did it too realistically. Besides, they were not yet tested and seasoned, and the professional historian is always suspicious of his contemporaries.

The superlative praise of Scott to be found in such historians and academic critics issues also from the lips of Scott's contemporaries and from ours, but in neither case is it justified as the Victorians justified it. We may (as some of us seem to do) venture to compare Scott with Shakespeare, but we do not offer the same reasons for doing so that our forebears did. Mrs. Oliphant, for instance, was an able and energetic Victorian, an industrious and successful novelist herself, and a well-known critic. To see that she was Victorian in the usual, even the popular, sense, one needs only to read her novels, or her analysis of Charlotte Brontë's character. She is, however, by no means a merely simple soul, nor does she subscribe unhesitatingly to all the orthodox doctrine. Her dissection of poor Miss

Brontë is, though false, subtly elaborate and skillful, and is so specious that it might well impose on a reader who did not know the facts and realize her abuse of them. In her criticism of Scott [21] one must give her credit for deploring the habit of praising his "health" and "sanity," and his personal qualities generally, at the expense of his genius, when, as she declares, there is no other work worthy to be placed beside his. She also attacks in yeoman fashion the strictures of Carlyle, whom she considers Scott's original enemy, and his greatest, except for "the followers of that new school of analytical fiction which reigns at present [she is writing near the end of her life, in 1882] in England." Yet after all, when she comes to her own comments on the novels, one hears the voice of the author of *Margaret Maitland* of a generation earlier, or even the voice of the good Miss Maitland herself. She exalts Scott especially for his sympathy and understanding of the humble, finds a "higher grace" in his conception of Jeanie Deans' truth, and declares, "No poet of his period so elevated, so consecrated the truth." The defects of *The Heart of Midlothian* she admits, but asks where there is another book to put beside it, especially for the ideals it sets before its readers. In fact she passes from a long glorification of Jeanie's character to a moral justification of the whole series on a basis of the good they have done. And finally comes the almost inevitable mention of Shakespeare, this time in the patriotic key. Like a good Scotswoman, she says that no writer has done for his country what Scott did for his except Shakespeare and Dante.

One need not quarrel with Mrs. Oliphant and the many others who thus praise Scott for his understanding of the lowly and his ennobling representation of them. It is the peculiar idiom, the sentimental and pious twist given to the praise that one resents, for assuredly this side of Scott is one of his strongholds. If such criticism is set beside that of Bagehot or Leslie Stephen, or even of a few less distinguished critics, its softness at once becomes obvious. They show an intellectual reserve and critical

[21] Mrs. Margaret Oliphant, *Literary History of England, 1790–1825* (2 vols., New York, 1882). II. 142 ff.

poise which was by no means general. Julia Wedgwood, for instance, discusses many of these same points, but in a much sounder fashion.[22] She realizes to the full the importance in Scott of the fusion of personality and genius — a fusion so complete that there is no separating them — and is able to discuss it with understanding but without the sentiment to which most of her contemporaries yield. In the same dignified style she is able to handle a subject so dangerous to the sentimentalist as Scott's strong sense of common life and his understanding of common people. To this she traces the fine reality of his pathos. Her intellectual detachment appears too in her consideration of Scott as a representative of the past world, of "the reaction in favor of all that democracy undervalues and obliterates," and she makes one point that other critics seem to have missed — she notes that Rebecca reveals Scott's realization not only of the glory and brilliancy of war but of the misery and wretchedness it inflicted on the weak and oppressed. But such painstaking and thoughtful criticism is all too often prevented by the allurements of emotion unrestrained.

Or one may cite the 1870 edition of *Chambers' Cyclopedia* as typical in its strong admixture of the moral in its paeans: "That long array of immortal fictions [the Waverley novels] can only be compared with the dramas of Shakespeare, as presenting an endless variety of original characters, scenes, historical situations, and adventures. They are marked by the same universal and genial sympathies, allied to every form of humanity, and free from all selfish egotism or moral obliquity." After declaring that of course Scott does not rise to Shakespeare's level, and repeating the substance of Carlyle's comparison, the writer says, "Yet both were great moral teachers, without seeming to teach. They were brothers in character and genius, and they poured out their imaginative treasures with a calm easy strength and conscious mastery of which the world has seen no other examples." Again, in Bayard Tuckerman's *History of English*

[22] "Sir Walter Scott and the Romantic Reaction," *Contemporary Review*, 33:514 (October, 1878).

Prose Fiction,[23] the usual points about Scott are summarized, and the Waverley novels are spoken of as having attained "a supreme position in public estimation." Far from the least of the reasons for this are the moral ones. Scott, according to Tuckerman, not only "gave acute and healthful pleasure" but made the novel "the medium for moral and intellectual advancement." And, he adds, "The purity of thought which pervades all his writings, the never failing nobility of the views of life which he placed before his readers can have no other than an elevating influence."

The attitude of the pious wing toward the novel since Scott took it in hand and became its chief exemplar is reflected by Hugh Miller,[24] a voluminous contributor to religious publications about the middle of the century. He had characteristically taken the death of Scott's son, the second Sir Walter, in 1847, as the text of a moral essay on the vanity of human wishes and aspirations, but in 1856 he explains to his readers the use they ought to make of good novels. He says that novels and newspaper articles are now the most influential forms of literature, and novels especially, since with their serial publication "they are at once novels and newspaper articles too." Although he finds greater edification in Mrs. Oliphant, he praises the wonderful truth of the pictures of religion in Scott "save when carried away by Jacobite predilection," and concludes that since novels are bound to exercise great influence whether the pious approve or not, "all good people should by all means try whether they cannot conscientiously patronize the good ones."

Here is another phase of Scott's service to the novel. Jeffrey and many others had called attention to the doldrums from which Scott had freed the novel as a form, and in praising him had above all else emphasized his importance as an artistic and aesthetic innovator and regenerator. These earlier critics also of course, appreciated Scott's "purity" and good influence, but a professedly religious writer like Miller makes it clear how, gradually at least, the curse that lay upon novels was being mitigated

[23] New York, 1882.
[24] See "Our Novel Literature" (1856), in his collected essays (Edinburgh, 1862).

since the time of the good Sir Walter, and reveals the hope that
lay in the formerly despised novel as an instrument of grace.[25]
Occasional words falling from the lips of pious characters in
realistic novels of the time, from the earnest or the sweet or the
good, who frequently have read the Waverley novels not only
for delight but for moral improvement, show how high a respect was felt for Scott among those for whom aesthetic or artistic
considerations were meaningless or vain.

Another section of the Victorian world, smaller perhaps but
still important, found special reason to glorify Scott. The medievalists in religion and art, the objectors to the modern industrial world, saw a prophet and leader in him. Some of the historically minded, it is true, took exception to his freedom with
history, but men like Newman and Ruskin approached him with
the deepest sympathy, seeing in him a powerful conservative
bulwark against the leveling, democratizing forces of the new
age. Indeed, Ruskin is the most vocal and most eloquent exponent of this point of view.

During Scott's own lifetime there had been comparatively
little discussion of the historical quality of his novels, their accuracy and authenticity, or the nature of their medievalism.[26]
Among the Victorians, however, these points arose more frequently. They were gradually learning more from historians and
antiquarians about the realities of medieval life, and began to
be troubled about anachronisms in spirit as well as in detail. The
feeling of comparative dissatisfaction with the historical novels
such as *Ivanhoe* goes back of course to their very publication, but
the attack on the historical novel, and the distrust of and distaste for history in the novel, now so commonly expressed and
widely felt, is to be found in detailed, reasoned form fairly soon

[25] Compare the arguments in the *Port Folio* of Philadelphia that it was not
wrong to read novels. See also Cruse, *The Victorians and Their Reading*, Chapter
IV, "The Chapel Folks."

[26] With his contemporaries it was chiefly a question as to whether the novels
would be dangerous as discouraging the reading of actual histories. The usual
conclusion was that they would not, but would rather encourage it. It was often
felt that the effect of a given novel was to stimulate a historical study of the period
depicted. As has already been noted, however, there had been enough criticism of
historical fact in the novels so that Scott himself took some notice of it.

after Scott's death. To the very definite question "Walter Scott — Has History Gained by His Writings?"[27] the answer is a most emphatic and positive no. The author comes to the conclusion that Scott's history and historical influence in general are bad and false. This is especially true, the writer believes, since he uses all his artistic powers to conceal his falsity. It had not been true of Shakespeare, who creates little historical illusion and writes Elizabethan character large over all his people, while Scott makes every attempt at historical accuracy.

This argument is surely of little real validity, for to the average uncritical mind, and that is the only one with which such a theory could concern itself, Shakespeare's Prince Hal and Richard III would be even more impressive and convincing than Scott's Louis XI or Richard the Lion-Hearted, in spite of all Scott's "upholstery" and picturesque detail. This writer, however, has the typical fond regret of his time at having to say anything unpleasant about the great Sir Walter. He wishes that Scott might have written these great novels without the adulteration of false history; but he begins his article by describing the low reputation of the novel before Scott appeared, and telling how the situation was revolutionized in two years by Scott's "irresistible popularity"; and he ends with the protest, "God forbid that we should detract from the true fame of this great man," or make an "ungrateful return for the hours of delight we owe to him." Jeffrey's objection to *Ivanhoe* and its sort went more to the heart of the matter than this. The faults of the historical novel were yet to be stated with sufficient clarity, but when they were, little was added to Jeffrey's implications.

Much the same point of view, but expressed with the abruptness and lack of sentiment of a rigidly professional historian and of one further removed from Sir Walter's personal influence, is to be found in a review of an inquiry into the history of Amy Robsart.[28] The author opens with a summary dismissal of his-

[27] *Fraser's*, 36:345 (September, 1847).
[28] *American Bibliopolist*, 4:384 (July, 1872). A less violent attack on the history in *Kenilworth* is to be found in the *Eclectic Magazine* for January, 1867, taken from *London Society*. Scott is charged with following sensational gossip rather

torical novels as a class. He declares that an attack on Scott's
history is like fighting windmills. A scholarly investigation of
Amy Robsart shows how flimsy Scott's history really was. Scott
had no clear insight into any history, past or present, and cared
very little about it anyway. The day of the historical novel, of
Scott and Bulwer, is gone. As for *Kenilworth* and Amy Robsart,
the story could have been made as interesting and as brilliant
with the facts unchanged, but Scott did not try to get them and
had been deceived by false accounts. One should remember, too,
Freeman's destructive note on *Ivanhoe* in *The Norman Con-
quest,* accusing Scott of gross anachronism, not only in fact but
also in his confusion of ages, and his misunderstanding of the
very spirit of the age he was depicting.

Yet there is the other side of the shield to be considered. There
are of course the writers, beyond all count, who couple Shakespeare's histories and Scott's novels, setting the novels only a
degree or two lower than the plays, but far above anything else,
as popular agents in the dissemination of history. That is, there
is a continuation of the idea of Scott's contemporaries, in fact,
the idea of Scott himself. There are, too, the innumerable allusions to Scott's pervasive influence on history itself, in encouraging historians to give it life and color, Macaulay for instance
taking his cue from Scott.[29] There is stress on the historical value
of stirring among the people the interest that led to trips to the

than sober fact, more or less the same point made by the writer above. The
article ends, " . . . for the dark colorings of the character [Anthony Foster], as
for many of the incidents of his story, he drew so entirely upon his excited imagination and in so doing violated historic truth so grossly, as thereby to destroy
in the minds of even tolerably well informed readers much of the charm which
Kenilworth is calculated to produce." Yet in *Macmillan's,* 53:131 (December,
1885), there is a careful review of the research on Leicester and Amy Robsart, on
a basis of which the writer comes to an unqualified conclusion that Scott's assail-
ants, in all the most significant points, are arguing from very unstable grounds.

[29] His influence on historians was of course generally recognized, and was
usually spoken of as a matter of praise. The opposite point of view is to be seen
in an article on Thierry, the French historian, in the *North American,* 72:334
(April, 1851). The writer, A. W. Machen, in discussing Scott's influence, casts
doubt on the value as historical models of such works as *Ivanhoe* and *The Talisman,* however delightful they may be. The romancer, he thinks, leaps chasms
much more easily than the historian can, much too easily, in fact.

historic Border and to the Highlands. F. T. Palgrave,[30] speaking
of the works as a whole, prose and verse, would even make Scott's
chief claim to importance his "creation of the Celtic Highlands."
Before him, Palgrave says, the Celts were regarded with contempt as savages. This indeed was Scott's natural view, the one
he was born to, but he did much to wipe it out — a great boon
to Scotland. "If this be not first-rate power, it may be asked
where we are to find it." So good a critic as R. H. Hutton [31]
also thought a tremendous amount of real history was to be
learned from Scott, and that while he was mediocre in actual
history or biography, he revealed his unique power as soon as he
entered the realm of fiction.

Of like mind is the author of an essay, "The Literature of
Power" in the *North American*,[32] a defense of the imaginative
and fictional treatment of history. He insists that there is
"scarcely a single important period of British history which is
not reproduced in his [Scott's] novels better than anywhere else,"
and cites a long list of historic figures from the novels which
"together afford beyond comparison the noblest instance in all
literature of the power of the genius to make the past its own, to
evoke its personages and events and make them seem real and
living." An earlier *North American* writer, too, W. B. O. Peabody, always a great admirer, had declared in a review of a
current historical novel (*Calavar*) [33] that to see the truth one
had only to compare the James I of *Nigel* with the James I of
the best historians; the first was the living man, the second only
a picture.

But the most striking of all comments on this point is made
by the young Henry James.[34] He praises Scott for the "poetic
reverence" with which he approaches history, excluding "the
gross and ignoble in bygone times," and deplores in compari-

[30] See his preface to the Globe edition of Scott's *Poems* (London, 1917), originally published in 1866.
[31] *Sir Walter Scott* (English Men of Letters series, London, 1878).
[32] D. C. Brooks, 92:479 (April, 1861).
[33] *North American*, 40:255 (January, 1835).
[34] *North American*, 99:580 (October, 1864).

son the modern attitude. He says that Tennyson in his *Idylls* has followed the Scott tradition in this respect, but he shudders at the thought of so gross a realist as Charles Reade writing a novel on King Arthur! On the whole, there is no doubt which side of the matter the criticism of the age favored.

Many of the Victorian medievalists found in Scott a kindred spirit. His novels illustrated the older ideals they admired and could be used to confound the disciples of "progress" and modern industrialism. Ruskin, as has been said, was especially drawn to Scott. The note that Leslie Stephen had struck at the close of his essay was repeated by Ruskin in his "Fiction — Fair and Foul." [35] Ruskin, out of joint with modern industrial civilization, and preaching a return to the beauties of a bygone age, rides his hobby to his heart's content in a comparison between the Waverley novels and more modern fiction. The latter he dismisses as deeply begrimed with industrialism, the beginnings of which infected and tainted even Scott, who, he says, wrote some of his novels, for instance *Peveril of the Peak,* purely for the trade. But in general the Waverley novels seemed to Ruskin to be illumined by the beauty and integrity of the old pure chivalric standards, and by the dignity of the middle class of the older days, from which Scott sprang.

When Ruskin turns to consider the novels in detail, we find him like all the rest glorifying the early novels, although his typical explanation of their excellence is peculiar to himself. He finds a direct relationship between the quality of the novels and the author's health. Thus Scott's best work was done while he was, according to Ruskin, in the full vigor of good health before his illness of 1819. From *Waverley* to *The Heart of Midlothian* he was writing in health, but the second group of novels — *The Bride of Lammermoor, Ivanhoe, The Monastery, The Abbot, Kenilworth,* and *The Pirate* — bear the seal of the terrible illness he had endured. In this group Ruskin discovers "a prevailing melancholy and fantastic improbability," and scores especially

---

[35] *Nineteenth Century,* 7:941 (June, 1880). For Stephen's essays, see page 222 ff., below.

"the horrors of Ravenswood and the nonsense of *Ivanhoe*," which have been public favorites because of their operatic sensationalism. In the third and final group he finds the "two quite noble ones," *Redgauntlet* and *Nigel*, the only instances comparable to the fine first group, and like them written in health, and two others of high value, *Quentin Durward* and *Woodstock*, but also the slovenly and diffuse *Peveril*, a piece of hack work, the sickly *Tales of the Crusaders*, the broken and diseased *St. Ronan's Well*, and the last novels, written during the final collapse. Altogether, then, Scott produced a dozen fine novels. Ruskin enters at length into an examination of Scott's dialect as a test of his soundness and as showing the difference between "character and disease," a most elaborate analysis ramifying into all sorts of philosophical and moral implications.

Ruskin's taste in selecting his first list is sound and regular enough, but his argument was probably convincing to few beyond the circle of his own devotees. No one would deny that a strong vigorous man would produce better work than a feeble or sickly one, their endowments being otherwise equal, or that good health was desirable for good work. On the other hand who can say that the lapse into pure romanticism that came with *Ivanhoe* is really to be attributed to illness. There is the same difficulty with Scott's dialect. In its accuracy and appropriateness, it demonstrates, no doubt, his soundness, his closeness to life, but it will by no means bear the heavy weight of moral and philosophical significance that Ruskin piles upon it.

In *Modern Painters*, too, Ruskin pays Scott the highest compliment of which he was capable, in coupling him with Turner. Here he declares Scott the great representative in literature of the mind of the age, especially because of his humility — that is, he did not talk about the dignity of his work — and his careless ease. He continues, "The mass of sentimental literature, concerned with the analysis and description of emotion, headed by the poetry of Byron, is altogether of a lower rank than the literature which merely describes what it saw. The true Seer always feels as intensely as anyone else; but he does not much describe his feelings." Thus *Guy Mannering* is a greater work than *In Memoriam*. Certain faults, it is true, Scott did have; though "the greatest man born among us, and intended for the enduring type of us," he lacked faith, he dreamed idly over the past, evoking a false medievalism of quite different value from his realistic Scotch life, he failed to appreciate art, he was trivial in aim, yet melancholy. Still, he subjected himself to Nature and rose above the pathetic fallacy; he has an undercurrent of profound reflection which is left for the reader to find for himself; his enjoyment of nature is greater than that of any other poet, his humility teaches him happiness, and he has a natural love of color, of ancientness, of natural beauty, and of liberty.

Ruskin was constantly reiterating these typical theories and prejudices in casual allusions to Scott, of whom he was always fond, and whom he was always glad to praise at the expense of modern civilization and such representatives of it as George Eliot and Thackeray. These two especially he loathed as typifying the disease and gloom of modern life. Hence much of his extravagant praise of Scott; even the heroines and slovenly style are made out to be virtues, while undeniable failings are all ascribed to the malign influences of environment.[36]

That Scott should have appealed to a medievalist or antimodernist like Ruskin was to be expected. In general he has been celebrated by those who, though for other reasons than his, have turned their eyes back into the past. The ardent Catholic, for instance, finds like Ruskin an ally in Scott, though Scott himself had no Catholic inclinations; quite the contrary, in fact; the only question at all about his personal allegiance is which of two Protestant sects really had it. In the introduction to *The Abbot* he makes a typical declaration when he says, "Much is

---

[36] All these prepossessions of Ruskin's have been analyzed in the *Sewanee Review*, 30:130 (April, 1922), by Mr. H. H. Carter, who also scuttles Ruskin's beautiful theory of the relation between Scott's health and the quality of his work, when he points out that some of the novels Ruskin likes best were written between 1817 and 1819, a period when Sir Walter was frequently ill. For the passage from *Modern Painters*, see *Works of John Ruskin*, edited by E. T. Cook and Alexander Wedderburn (39 vols., 1903–12), V, 331 ff.

omitted illustrative of the impulse of enthusiasm in favor of the ancient religion," since people no longer "feel deep sympathy at this period with what was once the most powerful and animating principle in Europe, with the exception of that of the Reformation, by which it was successfully opposed."

Newman, while still Anglican,[37] referred to Scott as "a great poet of the North" who helped "prepare men for some closer and more practical approximation to Catholic truth." Newman, moreover, was capable of appreciating Scott on purely literary grounds; he had earlier praised Scott's characters for their individualities and diversities within common groups, such as the villains in *Kenilworth* and the fanatics in *Old Mortality*. He is said by his editors, however, not to have liked any novel that he did not consider ennobling; he was always very fond of Scott (as also, rather surprisingly perhaps, of Thackeray and Trollope), but he stood with Ruskin in rejecting George Eliot.[38] Keble, too, refers to Scott *passim* in his *Lectures on Poetry* in such terms as "the noblest poet of our age," and compares him with Homer and Pindar.[39] Conversely, of course, one occasionally comes upon bitter assertions of Scott's anti-Catholic bigotry in certain specific utterances and in such novels as *The Abbot* and *The Monastery*, as distinguished from the general pro-Catholic tendency of his medievalism. Such, for instance, are the plaints of the Irish critics against Lockhart's *Life*, cited elsewhere.

It is clear that the Catholics could take Scott either way. He himself was positively Protestant and as positively anti-Catholic; on the other hand, the whole impulse of his more historical novels was definitely encouraging to Catholicism, whether

[37] High Church readers naturally had the same point of view as the Catholics. Cf. Cruse, *The Victorians and Their Reading*, Chapters II, III.

[38] For references to Newman, see his *Apologia*, p. 96, and *Essays*, I, 19, 22, 268, in *The Works of Cardinal Newman* (40 unnumbered vols., London, 1908–18). Cf. also Wilfrid Ward, *Life of John Henry, Cardinal Newman* (2 vols., New York, 1912).

[39] There was a good deal of Catholic criticism in the next period, after 1880, practically all of it taking this point of view and following the lead of Newman and Keble.

Roman or Anglican. As for the vigilant Protestants, such tendencies seem to have escaped their eyes; Borrow is the only notable exception.

One of the most interesting and revealing expressions of the Anglo-Catholic feeling toward Scott appears in the elaborate and carefully studied essay written as a review of Lockhart's *Life* in the *British Critic*.[40] The writer conceives of Scott as a great poet, including the novels as poetry in all but the form of verse. He does full justice to the deep roots of Scott's romance in the tradition of Scottish life; in fact this is his main theme. He declares that Scott must be accepted as "a Primary Poet in every sense of the word," and that the early instinctive comparisons with Pindar, Homer, and Shakespeare are proved by the years to be sound.

But he reserves for his climax his theory of Scott as a bulwark of Conservatism, and a true son, though an imperfect one, of the Church. The preservation of old ideals through the storms of the Reform years and the rally that had followed them is "in good measure attributable to the chivalrous tone which his writings have diffused over the studies and tastes of those who are now in the prime of manhood. His rod, like that of a beneficent enchanter, has touched and guarded hundreds, both men and women, who would else have been *reforming* enthusiasts." Indeed, Sir Walter's liberal and progressive side, which is eagerly exploited by friendly modern critics, is for this reviewer a matter for apology and regret. And how wonderful, he says, if Scott could have been especially "the Poet of the Church." "Cum talis sis, utinam noster esses. What pity that these good and generous impulses, this energy of self-denial, had not the advantage of being hallowed by devotion to the cause most congenial, the only cause entirely worthy of them!" (i.e., "the Holy Catholic Church, unincumbered of Romanism"). Scott was evidently ripe for real conversion, had circumstances been favor-

---

[40] *British Critic and Quarterly Theological Review*, 24:423 (October, 1838). This was the organ of the Tractarians, and all its articles were given a definite Tractarian bearing. Newman had become its editor in 1836.

able; e.g., he "shrank from the rude and irreverent dealings of modern minute philosophy [with the supernatural]." But because of the effects of his early Presbyterian environment his conversion was incomplete, and lapses in his style and his own way of life (including his "occasional concessions to Liberalism") show the results upon him "of the cast and tone of religious opinion where his lot was cast." "We do consider it a sorrowful thing that the eye of such a mind should never have rested on the true form of the City of God; *quae si oculis ejus cerneretur, mirabiles amores excitaret*." Surely such a vision would not have cramped his hand but would have made him stronger and surer and would have brought him to absolute perfection. But, the critic concludes sadly, perhaps the perfect Catholic poet and artist is not to be hoped for; the Church, it may be, reserves all praises to herself by working through humbler instruments.

The diatribes of that robust Protestant, George Borrow, bear loud witness to the aid and comfort the Catholics were supposed to draw from the Waverley novels. In *Lavengro* Borrow accuses Scott of fostering a very silly and romantic medievalism and Catholicism. The Man in Black declares, "O Cavaliere Gualtiero, avete fatto molto in favore della Santa Sede." And through two chapters of the appendix to *The Romany Rye* he lets loose the vials of his wrath upon one who was the *fons et origo mali*, one to whom could be traced all the Popish and Jacobite nonsense that still persisted in the nineteenth century.[41]

[41] See *Lavengro,* Chapter 94, and *Romany Rye,* Chapters VI and VII of the Appendix. Borrow hated Scott for his politics, but admired him immeasurably as a literary genius, thus following in the footsteps of Hazlitt. He spoke of Scott at various times as "greater than Homer," and said he admired him especially for his poetry, though his admiration for the novels was very high. He also tells of "trudging away (in spite of rain and mist) to Dryburgh to pay my respects to the tomb of Walter Scott, a man with whose principles I have no sympathy, but for whose genius I have always entertained the most intense admiration." Like Hazlitt too, he enjoys thinking Scott as a "sycophant." See Herbert George Jenkins, *Life of George Borrow* (London, 1912), p. 393.

CHAPTER III

THE THREE CHIEF ESTIMATES: CARLYLE, BAGEHOT, LESLIE STEPHEN

OF THE innumerable critical essays of the time there are several to which still later writers have returned to get their bearings, and which are thus comparatively familiar. In this group are the essays by Carlyle, Walter Bagehot, and Leslie Stephen — all three of them landmarks and points of orientation. The general effect of these three essays is, considering the temper of the times, depreciatory; it was by no means from these spokesmen of theirs that the Victorians derived their fondness for Scott, though Carlyle, really the most damning of the three, may well have done much to nurture the personal tradition of Scott which was so important to the continuance of his fame.

Carlyle's was the first important voice to be heard in critical judgment after Sir Walter's death. As was said at the outset, Carlyle with characteristic finality summed him up and settled his fate with posterity. Carlyle cannot resist the appeal of Scott's personality; throughout the essay his admiration for a fine Scotchman, a fine human being, "a genuine man" is a vigorous and recurrent theme — "a right brave and strong man . . . a most composed, invincible man; in difficulty and distress knowing no discouragement . . . a most robust, healthy man . . . we will call him one of the *healthiest* of men." Indeed health is what Carlyle finds above all else in Scott, "a soul in right health," and he declares it the greatest of blessings that "when British Literature lay all puking and sprawling in Werterism, Byronism and other Sentimentalism, tearful or spasmodic, . . .

Nature was kind enough to send us two healthy men, of whom she might still say, not without pride, 'These also were made in England; such limbs do I still make there!' " This health of spirit Carlyle could discover among British literary men of the day only in Scott and in William Cobbett, in whom, it will be remembered, Hazlitt too had seen strong resemblances to Sir Walter, and whom Carlyle describes as "the pattern John Bull of his century, strong as the rhinoceros, and with singular humanities and genialities shining through his thick skin." And at the end he says of Scott, "No sounder piece of British manhood was put together in that eighteenth century of Time. Alas, his fine Scotch face, with its shaggy honesty, sagacity and goodness . . . we shall never forget it; we shall never see it again. Adieu, Sir Walter, pride of all Scotchmen, take our proud and sad farewell."

Yet, after all, when Carlyle turns to his hero's books he finds praise in a really high vein difficult. He could not report true greatness in them. "Sir Walter Scott's popularity was of a select sort rather; not a popularity of the populace. His admirers were at one time almost all the intelligent of civilized countries; and to the last included, and do still include, a great portion of that sort. Such fortune he had, and has continued to maintain for a space of some twenty or thirty years." But then, Carlyle explains, all popularity of whatever sort is a snare and a delusion, and passes like dew before the sun. It calls to mind the old cry of "One God, one Farinelli!", Lope de Vega, "the greatest of all popularities," and even August Kotzebue of *The Stranger.* He continues, "It seems to us there goes other stuff to the making of great men than can be detected here . . . His life was worldly; his ambitions were worldly. There is nothing spiritual in him; all is economical, material, of the earth earthy." Scott wrote for Abbotsford and a county family that was to be; this Carlyle, like Miss Martineau, found cause for regret and censure.

And when he comes to the novels themselves, what has Carlyle to say of them that would raise them far above bare mediocrity? "The great fact about them is that they were faster written and better paid for than any other books in the world." They are the perfection of literature for amusement; "a man might fling himself back, exclaiming, 'Be mine to lie on this sofa, and read everlasting Novels of Walter Scott.'" The novels are, again, "the perfection of extemporaneous writing," and there is in them, moreover, "genial, sunshiny freshness and picturesqueness . . . a deep sincere love of the beautiful in Nature and Man . . . in general *healthiness* of mind, these Novels prove Scott to have been amongst the foremost writers."

Nor is he "altogether deficient" in drawing character — his best Scotch characters seem deceptively alive; but alas, unlike Shakespeare, he could only "fashion them from the skin inwards, never getting near the heart of them!" And when he turns to still more serious considerations, Carlyle finds in the novels no freight of "opinions, emotions, principles, doubts, beliefs, beyond what the intelligent country gentleman can carry along with him." There is nothing of the true heroic, nothing for doctrine and edification, nothing for the sick and struggling heart. Too much of the interest in the novels depends on contrasts of costume, on upholstery, and when the present becomes quaint, as it soon will, they must lose their appeal. "Among the great of all ages, one sees no likelihood of a place for him."

When all is said, the most that Carlyle will claim for the novels is that they sated men with mere amusement and so set them to seeking something better, and that they awoke men's minds to the fact that the past was alive, that history was not a mere lumber of "protocols, state papers, controversies and abstractions of men." It is clear that for Carlyle the heart of a true book — the message, the driving moral force, the philosophy — did not beat in the novels. They lacked the saving salt without which they must perish. Miss Martineau, also a propagandist and an earnest worker before the Lord, had passed judgment and found the novels filled to overflowing with implied philosophy to suit utilitarian needs; in her sight, indeed, Sir Walter both in his person and his works was a great monument for the people to gaze upon, with rivers of healing flowing from his feet. But

Carlyle could not see the vision. To him there was nothing for
it but oblivion swiftly closing in. Thus he was the first (except
the early *Westminster* reviewer) to emphasize a lack of intellectual depth and moral significance in Scott; but he was not the
last, for it has been the business of many to reassert it and re-
demonstrate it in the century that has passed since his pronouncement.

Some of Carlyle's successors among the Victorian critics, however, demanded instruction and prophecy of Scott much more
crudely than Carlyle did. He has clearly enough in his mind the
idea of the novelist's duty to improve and edify, but he had not
yet seen fully what could be done when the theory was put into
practice, and Reade and Kingsley, with others of their tribe,
began to sugar-coat their lectures on sweatshops and prisons and
present them to the public thinly disguised as novels. Later
critics, with such examples before them, could see much better
than Carlyle how far Scott had fallen short as a laborer in the
vineyard. On the other hand, Carlyle's praise of Scott's "healthiness" became a regular cry with smaller critics. This they found
almost, if not quite, the finest thing about him, so that one
reads for the next two generations or so a plethora of advice
as to Scott's healthiness, not to say wholesomeness. As Carlyle
puts it, the idea has dignity and really important meaning; it
is surely one of the great qualities of Scott. It could be well
reiterated too by a critic like Leslie Stephen. But all too often
the smaller fry degraded it to mere Victorian respectability,
and praised Scott because he was not "low" like Fielding, or
morbid and sensational like the Gothic romances or some of
their own contemporary realists who looked too closely at the
seamy side of life. Again they said he could be safely placed in
the hands of the young, or read aloud without blushes.

Apparently the essay on Scott's genius that has worn the
best and found most favor with later critics who have gone back
to it is Walter Bagehot's, written two decades after Carlyle's
and a quarter century after Sir Walter's death.[1] As John Buchan

[1] *National Review*, 6:444 (April, 1858).

says, Bagehot writes of Scott with "his customary acumen and
good sense," but it is somewhat surprising that Mr. Buchan and
other ardent Scott enthusiasts should take so kindly to the
essay, for the effect of its cool and dispassionate analysis is certainly to place Scott in the second rank of genius at best. Here
are no comparisons with Shakespeare. Bagehot begins with an
assumption that Scott's popularity is passing, a fact he believes
due to the competition of new ideas and interests. He believes
that Scott suffers in this later generation because he makes his
love affairs of only incidental interest, being as much absorbed
in the setting as in the lovers. Neither has he those modern
desiderata, a thesis and a desire to depict the world in general.
Hence the reader's interest flags.

But Bagehot is able to put his finger on certain excellences
to which the novels owe their strength. This, he thinks, they
derive first of all from their "sensible" element, that is, Scott's
sagacity and knowledge of the world, his strongest "insensible"
feeling being his Jacobitism and Toryism. This "sensible" element shows itself in various ways; in his interest in and realization of a stratified and varied society, which he thought
democracy would level flat; in his treatment of "anomalous"
characters, eccentric figures which he could make natural, with
social niches into which they fitted easily; in his genial representation of the poor whose most attractive side he exploited without either idealizing and sentimentalizing them on the one
hand, nor on the other making them as coarse and vulgar as
possible; and finally in his sensible ideas of political economy
and his conception of a world where, Bagehot is convinced,
retribution comes in the long run.

The second chief quality of the novels he considers "the
romantic susceptibility of Scott's imagination." His heroines,
Bagehot admits, are not really successful, but he does find them
at least attractive. It is so too with the pictures of medieval life.
These represent the life of the past as it should be represented,
full of fanciful charm to the imagination, as are also his portraits of great historical heroes, such as Richard the Lion-

hearted and Queen Mary in *The Abbot,* pictured "as the
fond tradition of his countrymen exhibited her." Such an attitude and such impressions Bagehot defends, saying that they are
necessary to the success of the historical novel, in contradis-
tinction to actual history, which must proceed by careful
analysis, as a novel cannot. Developing these two great gifts,
then, this "sensible" insight and his romantic imagination, Scott
has, Bagehot concludes, given us fresh pictures of practical
human society, and has shown several periods of it in at least
their external manifestations.

So far so good. These merits Bagehot makes it clear he considers of great weight and importance; but they are, he says,
merits belonging to this world. Sir Walter's weakness or defect
springs from the fact that he does not show sufficiently qualities
which this world does not prize highly. One looks in vain for
any searching or probing inquiry into the roots of life, or
any tendency to philosophize; his world is the "healthy and
genial world of reflection, but it wants the charm of delicate
exactitude." His heroines, Bagehot says, have no souls — even
Jeanie Deans is not essentially feminine in the qualities that
attract readers to her — and his heroes are too commonplace.
In his delineation of the religious side of human nature too,
he is superficial; he had merely "the easy faith in the kindly
Dieu des bons gens." In depicting the Puritans, he caught only
the side that pleased him, the ludicrous one. Their superstitions
differed from his, and so he did not like them. In general, "he
omits to give us a delineation of the soul. We have mind, manners, animation, but it is the stir of this world . . . His heroes
and heroines are well dressed for this world, but not for another;
there is nothing even in their love which is suitable for immortality." In the matter of plot too, Bagehot believes that Scott
falls short of that highest order of genius which can conceive a
great plot, as in a unified vision. As for style, Scott's is excellent
in the mass, for it gives a vivid impression. Yet it leaves no
memory of phrase; there is nothing in him to quote. As a matter
of fact, he used the first sufficient words that came to mind, and

does not seem to have been sensible even in the works of others of "exquisite accuracy and inexplicable appropriateness."

Bagehot's essay is sound, well-considered, and penetrating criticism. It comes neither from an encomiast nor a detractor, those two classes of critics by whom, according to Mr. Buchan, Scott has been chiefly discussed and from whom he has suffered especially. One guesses at points that he has read both Harriet Martineau's and Carlyle's essays and has made them of service to him, but in his hands their theories, especially Miss Martineau's, become sharpened and clarified and set free from personal whim and vagary. Bagehot is able to view Scott from a purely literary point of view as neither Miss Martineau nor Carlyle, nor even Hazlitt, had been able to do. Even in his remarks on the Puritans Bagehot seems to feel neither political nor religious prejudices. His essay lacks the brilliant energy and the original fire of Hazlitt and Carlyle, both of them distinguished beyond his aspirations, but nevertheless he produced the first thoroughgoing, carefully considered, and well-poised analysis of Scott's genius in the Waverley novels.

Of course, as has been said before, it leaves Scott in the second rank of genius, for what else is the effect of the whole second half of the essay, to say nothing of the plain words about his plot-making? Bagehot is the first important critic to look back upon Scott as a literary classic of an earlier generation and to treat him with dispassionate aloofness, in a way that Hazlitt and Carlyle could not possibly do. Yet even Bagehot perhaps suffers somewhat from the interference of his own generation. He remarks with seeming disapproval that his own age demands philosophizing and a thesis, yet at the same time he requires more of it than Sir Walter can furnish, and one feels that he and Carlyle have a point in common. And is not his charge against Scott's characters an interesting and vivid restatement of Carlyle's comparison of them with Shakespeare's? It is notable that as we work down among the critics of a still later generation, who have had the benefit of a long era of novelists ever conscious of some particular point of view, and novels well-freighted, not to say water-logged, with philosophizings and theses, we find a decreasing tendency to worry about this point.[2]

A pronouncement that reminds one very much of Bagehot's, for its carefully considered thought and its avoidance for the most part of the clichés of the time, is Professor Masson's lecture on Scott.[3] Written to be delivered orally by a Scot, before a Scotch audience, this lecture has an energy of feeling rising from patriotic springs which one rather misses in Bagehot. Masson is chiefly absorbed in Scott's love of the past, and in his quality as a poetic historian, which rises, he says, to its greatest height in his Scotticism, "full, extensive and thorough." He emphasizes Scott's enormous contribution to literature in scene, character, and incident, declaring that he has given more material to the imagination than anyone since Shakespeare, and that no one in recent times has enjoyed so widely diffused an influence. Masson inquires into the quality of Sir Walter's medievalism, which was beginning to be questioned, and concludes that it was not really false but rather not speculative enough; Scott did not get at the ideas and modes of thinking of other times. He did not reproduce "the earnest and powerful thought of the medieval period" because his own philosophy of the human mind was not wide and deep enough to make such things "the objects of his anxious imagination," and for exactly the same reason would have failed in getting at the idea of the present. Such criticism of course suggests passages from Carlyle, Bagehot, and other Victorians, but Masson qualifies it. It is, he says, surprising that in spite of such a defect Scott should have succeeded so perfectly with his Scotch characters. "In their conception and execution I do not know that Scott *is* inferior to Shakespeare." In them he goes beyond what would seem to be his limits, and in them he has made Scotland famous. Modern critics of Scott might well recall Masson's essay more frequently.

[2] Although the "message" and thesis have persisted terrifically in great masses of modern novels, "artistic" theory and art-for-art's-sake have been dead against them. Compare, for instance, D. F. Hannigan's essay on Flaubert, alluded to below (page 264 n).

[3] David Masson, *British Novelists* (Cambridge, 1859).

In Leslie Stephen's essay [4] there is much less of pointed and clear-cut analysis than in Bagehot, although it is by no means lacking, and much more of personal musing. Its general effect is lukewarm. Stephen likes Scott and is inclined to be tender with him, but he really does not seem to think very highly of him.

He begins by stating his suspicion that Scott has lost some of his power, that "the warmth of our first love is departed," and it is beginning to be whispered that he is dull. Stephen reminds us that all writers with the passing of their own time lose "the gloss of novelty," and then poses the question of Scott's permanence. In fact, the essay is an attempt at prophecy, a reconsideration of the question Carlyle had settled so emphatically just a generation before. He believes that the novels have a possible chance in the future, but only in part, for it is beyond denial that they are adulterated with inferior materials and in spots are decidedly thin. Yet like many others he stops to consider Sir Walter's many attractions, and regrets the painful task of probing and sorting.

He recalls Carlyle's essay, especially the points that Scott had no message and wrote for money, declaring that these objections carry little weight with him. Later on, too, he minimizes Carlyle's talk about describing a character from the heart outward, a process he thinks impossible for any author. On the other hand, he makes much of the point that "Scott fails unmistakably in pure passion of all kinds," and says that Scott and Byron are complementary; if Sir Walter could have had Byron's "energetic passions" in addition to his own gifts he might have been a Shakespeare. But generally his "heroic" or dramatic characters are false, while his common figures, for instance Bailie Nicol Jarvie, are real. There is little, he thinks, to be said for figures as extravagant as Ravenswood or Madge Wildfire, but much for David Deans. Here of course we are back on familiar ground with Jeffrey and other contemporary critics who jumped in-

[4] *Cornhill*, 24:278 (September, 1871). It was the third number in his series, *Hours in a Library*.

stinctively to the conclusion that the Scotch novels were finer
than the romances, and that the best in Sir Walter was his
realistic Scotch character of the period before he wandered off
among his Gurths and Wambas and Sir Kenneths.

Stephen continues by recalling the imitation oak-carving at
Abbotsford which retained its powers of deceit so short a time,
and says that analogously the pure historical novels like *Ivanhoe*
have no life in them; they are all painted plaster and cannot
last—a mere debris. He digresses for a moment to smile at the
modern romantic Highlander, as invented and popularized by
Scott. Before him kilts and targets were in dark disrepute, the
dress of thieves; but under Sir Walter's patronage they became
a fit costume for George IV to don in compliment to his northern
subjects in Edinburgh. For *Ivanhoe* and the group of novels
of which it is representative, he thinks the only chance is a
sort of survival as books for boys, although boys generally prefer
books about cricket and boat races. Yet possibly it is worth
while for them to read *Ivanhoe*, even if it be granted that it
is no more than "amusing nonsense." Here we have almost,
though not quite, the first appearance of the thrust now the
most common of all those leveled against Scott, that he will do
for boys, perhaps, though he is no longer strong enough food
for the mature. Indeed most of Stephen's essay is based on the
long-familiar distinction between the more realistic and the
purely romantic novels, and the almost universal preference
for the former. The criticism of the "heroic" characters, the
reduction of *Ivanhoe* to the status of a juvenile, his succeeding
remarks on the proper period for historical novels, and his final
list of the novels that he thinks may still appeal to a later
generation, are all restatements in detail of the well-established
dictum that the best of Scott is to be found in his novels before
Ivanhoe.

Stephen declares that sixty years before the author's own lifetime, that is the period of *Waverley* in Scott's case, is about the
proper distance for a historical setting. It is near enough to be
real, and may suggest the tale of a living grandfather, and is

at the same time far enough removed from the sharply defined present to have the desired romantic haze. Accordingly he thinks that the eighteenth-century novels have the best chance of success, and of these he selects as the finest *Waverley, The Antiquary, Guy Mannering, Old Mortality,* and *The Bride of Lammermoor.* All these, he says, depend on scenery and society Scott himself had known. Of *The Heart of Midlothian,* which since Stephen's time has emerged with a fair degree of clearness as the most highly regarded by later critics, he does not think so well. He admits that it has some passages of Scott's finest quality, but finds it disabled and defaced by a greater preponderance of Scott's worse style, a critical stand that cannot well be denied when one recalls the dead weight of the opening chapters and the purely conventional and artificial melodrama of the last section, which follows so anticlimactically upon Jeanie's success in London.

One may mention here that Stephen's opinion of *The Heart of Midlothian* improved in time. In a lecture delivered many years later [5] his tone was much more enthusiastic and appreciative. He now maintained that *The Heart of Midlothian* was Scott's most impressive book, and even went so far as to declare that if it had been sustained to the end it would have been the finest novel ever written. This overwhelming distinction he derives from its fine pictures of the relationship between father and daughter.[6]

The essay of 1871 continues with a passage on Scott's poetry, which while admittedly not of the first order Stephen defends as having the "charm of unaffected and spontaneous love of nature," and being "still the best interpreter of the sound healthy love of wild scenery"; it is "a good thing to have a

[5] See the *Critic,* 13:107 (September 1, 1888).

[6] In later casual allusions he shows much greater enthusiasm than in the 1871 essay. In his essay on Disraeli's novels (also in *Hours in a Library*) he says, apropos of men of action and men of literature, that he would rather have written the Waverley novels "than have won Waterloo or even Trafalgar." For the defense of Scott against Hugo, see his letter to Stevenson. Also, in "The Story of Scott's Ruin" (*Cornhill,* 75:448, April, 1897), he shows that a quarter-century had deepened and intensified his feeling for Scott.

breath from the Cheviots," such as Sir Walter alone can furnish.
And finally, setting Scott beside the contemporary novelists,
who were often praised at his expense, Stephen castigates the
"healthy animalism" and muscular Christianity of such popular heroes as Amyas Leigh and Guy Livingstone, insisting that
a comparison between their world and Scott's brings out the
difference between sham and reality and indicates that "Scott
may still have a lesson or two to preach to this generation."

Bagehot and Leslie Stephen produced the two most notable
essays on Scott except Carlyle's during the half century after
his death. In the general impression that they leave, both run
counter to the feeling of the age. Neither Bagehot nor Stephen
is really under the influence of Scott's personality; the little
touches of sentiment in Leslie Stephen are by no means of an
intensity hard to control. Upon the warmth and sentiment of
Hazlitt and Carlyle follows the cool and judicious appraisal of
a crowned classic, over whose head a whole generation has
passed. The age in general was still warm and tender toward
Scott's memory and strongly inclined to consider him the greatest of novelists. These two critics are not only cool and judicious;
they show a very distinct tendency to uncrown the hero and set
him down below the giants, though it is not clear that they have
other candidates among novelists to take his place. For these
intellectual Victorians, at any rate, the Wizard of the North had
lost his magic.

§

During the half century after Scott's death it is apparent that
there were certain distinct tendencies in the criticism of Scott.
There can be no doubt of the more popular attitude. In his
lifetime Scott had become one of the great figures in the life
of the British Isles, among literary and artistic men the greatest.
The Duke of Wellington was the great national hero of the
early century, and one is not at all surprised to find such a statement as that "the Duke" and Sir Walter were the two great
Britons of the time. The halo that accumulated about his head

during his career and whose light was increased and intensified by the heroic struggle of his last years did not vanish with him at his death. In fact, it is by no means dissipated today, although of course few halos can maintain their original brightness for a century. But it can be said that for fifty years or so Scott's glory in the popular mind seems to have been very little diminished. It was the custom to speak of him with great affection and respect, indeed to treat him as almost sacrosanct, and at least as a great public benefactor whom it was ungrateful and churlish to criticize. He was made to be revered and cherished, not criticized.

Great streams of vacationists made summer tours to Abbotsford and the Trossachs. In fact, does not every arranged tour to Scotland even today include Abbotsford, whose nineteenth-century Gothic is now anything but imposing, and whose only attraction is the tradition of its builder? And the magazines continued to publish all varieties of picturesque materials for popular consumption. Even among the more critical writers this attitude has its effects. There is apt to be a tone of apology and a regret that unfavorable remarks have to be made.

Still, criticism was more damaging and more searching and systematic than it had been in Scott's own time. His own contemporaries could see as clearly as we his obvious weaknesses. They knew, the more discriminating of them, that he was apt to be diffuse, that his young ladies and gentlemen were dull and flat, and that the historical romances lacked the fine distinction of the first group. These flaws were of course harped upon during the Victorian period, and came to be taken for granted. In addition there began to be doubts as to Scott's historical soundness, more definitely expressed than in his own time. But above all, the Victorians regretted his lack of a message, of a conscious and systematic philosophy, and were afraid that he was, in spite of all his charms, superficial. These are criticisms which originate in Carlyle and become more pronounced as the period advances. They are quite understandable when one considers the earnestness and conscientiousness of the Victorian novelists in delivering to their patrons a full weight of clearly ticketed ideas and practical propaganda. On such a basis of competition Scott was bound to fall back in the running. It was felt too by some that much had been learned about the technic of the novel since Scott's time and that his method was ponderous and slow and unsophisticated.

Nevertheless, when all was said and done, he had qualities and conveyed impressions that the Victorians looked for in vain among their own novelists. After all, these later people were a little dangerous. Thackeray, though very keen and shrewd and beyond a doubt authentic, was cynical and depressing; London society was as he showed it but it was not pleasant to be told so. Charlotte Brontë, who had created such a furor with *Jane Eyre,* was full of dangerous upsetting ideas that might easily create a bad frame of mind among the younger generation, especially the young ladies; and Dickens in spite of being very funny and very pathetic, dealt with such low, coarse characters!

When one realized this, it was refreshing to turn back again to old Sir Walter. Here were no subversive ideas. Here was nothing to put notions into the heads of youths and maidens, and not a word that could not be read aloud in the family circle. His moral tone was always unimpeachable, and he always seemed healthy and natural and free, after so many scenes in London clubs and drawing-rooms, to say nothing of East End sweatshops and thieves' resorts, and even Manchester and Sheffield factories. Or to put it in the form of artistic principle, the genius that conceived a *Waverley* and a *Heart of Midlothian* and perhaps even an *Ivanhoe* was of a higher sort, because of its wider range and greater canvas, than that which expressed itself in a *Vanity Fair,* an *Oliver Twist,* and even a *Middlemarch.*

There seems to have been a good deal of this feeling during the period, and perhaps one should not be surprised to find it. The intellectual Victorian grown somewhat free of the Scott tradition applied his critical faculties to Scott and found what he considered grave defects, prejudicial to permanence; but in the end he seemed to feel that it was not quite gentlemanly to desert the cause and betray the person of one who had given him so much pleasure in youth and even now was capable of furnishing delightful vicarious excursions into the Highlands or the picturesque "Mile" of the Edinburgh of a century before.

And finally, one may repeat, utterly damning criticism is non-existent. As yet there was no one to say flatly and finally that Scott's day was done. Hazlitt as early as 1824 had dismissed the poems as ephemeral, but there had been no one willing to echo plainly Carlyle's melancholy predictions. Some of them might have their suspicions that he was a second-rater in some ways and that his contemporaries had been over-enthusiastic, but a library without Scott or a Scott unread was not yet conceivable.

Part III · Since 1880

CHAPTER I
FOREIGN INFLUENCES; THE READING PUBLIC

WHEN ONE comes down past 1880 in the history of the novel he gets into a new world. There is now in the novel, both in practice and in criticism, a fundamental change. Some of it doubtless came from George Eliot. Certainly with her the novel turned intellectual in a conscious, professional way quite different from the intellectualism of Thackeray, which was distinctly of an amateurish, gentlemanly sort. As Lord David Cecil says,[1] she was a highbrow as John Stuart Mill, Spencer, and Matthew Arnold were highbrows. The novel had been written for edifying entertainment; it had been "light reading." But George Eliot took herself with intense seriousness and was so taken by her readers; she came to be "the Sibyl," the prophetess. Spencer found her novels and hers only suitable for admission into the London Library. The novel was no longer entertainment; it was indeed a vehicle for a conscious and systematic body of ideas, a philosophy. This new attitude in George Eliot was continued in her successors, in Hardy and Meredith[2] for

[1] Lord David Cecil, *Early Victorian Novelists* (Indianapolis, 1935), Chapters I, VIII.

[2] Hardy of course could appeal to a much wider public than Meredith because of the general nature of his books. For his ideas on the function of the novel see "Profitable Reading of Fiction" in the *Forum*, 5:57 (March, 1888). Here he admits reading for relaxation, but goes on to the discussion at length of reading for "intellectual or moral profit to active and undulled spirits." In this essay he declares that beauty of form is neglected in the criticism of novels, and cites as an instance of it *The Bride of Lammermoor* (as well as the first thirty chapters of *Vanity Fair*, and *Clarissa*). A remark in the *Edinburgh Review*, 181:33 (January, 1895), on Meredith, is illuminating: "We have always maintained that the primary function of novel-writing is to entertain, and that no novelist has the right to demand such severe and sustained effort."

instance. As Cecil says, certainly the modern serious novel is anything but light reading. In its philosophy, in its subtle and complicated explorations into psychology and the equally subtle and elaborate technical devices which it has developed to present those explorations it baffles the common reader if he ventures to approach it.

But George Eliot was of course not answerable for all this. More important doubtless were the French. From them came the drift toward a new and more thorough-paced realism and a relaxation of the moral bonds which all through the mid-century had been viselike. The French (and Henry James) had discovered the technic of writing novels. They had found out how to make the novel neat and compact; they had devised all sorts of subtle tricks to use in the management of plot and the analysis of character. They, and the Russians even more, had shown what psychological analysis really was, and had made it clear that the novelist could do his duty only by holding himself aloof from his characters, by being cool, dispassionate, and scientific as he watched his puppets perform. Where was the famous character analysis of Thackeray and George Eliot when it was set up against that of these modern masters? How damaging was the effect of their sentimental digressions and moral musings! And then, in addition, there was the idea of *le mot juste.* To be held worthy of critical consideration the novel must be filed and polished phrase by phrase like a sonnet. Finally, in point of view the novel was not to be romantic, it was to be realistic — but with a realism, a naturalism, wholly "artistic" and unmoral, that would have made Thackeray [3] gasp and was to bind itself to the minute "actualities" of life beyond anything that even Daniel Defoe had dreamed of. Balzac, then Flaubert and Maupassant and Zola — these and many others were gradually showing the English what the novel might really be and really do.

An amusing suggestion regarding the relationships between French and English literatures, at least as far as "emancipation,"

[3] As a matter of fact, Thackeray read *Mme. Bovary* and was disgusted by it.

realism, and morals are concerned, drops from the pen of F. Marion Crawford, himself a highly popular — and perfectly proper — American novelist at the end of the century. Very early in the period he points out [4] the comparative influence of the *jeune fille* in Anglo-Saxondom and on the Continent. The English girl, he says, has the run of literature and the theater, so that novels and plays have to be written with her in mind. And, he continues, "if we do not write for the young girl, who will? We have not the advantage possessed by the French of satisfying the demands of young people by translations from works in other languages. The young girl in France as a matter of fact reads Walter Scott, Bulwer and Dickens, while her mother diverts her leisure with the more lively productions of Paul Bourget, Guy de Maupassant, or possibly Balzac." It is obvious that things have changed since the solicitous days of 1893.[5] The Anglo-Saxon *jeune fille* still has the run of literature and the theater, but nothing is modified for her eyes or ears, and if her young French sisters are as carefully sheltered as ever one imagines the careful picking and choosing of the French translators who seek to add a little novelty to the list of Scott, Bulwer, and Dickens. This passage also throws light on the criticism of Scott by present writers that he does not deal with sex, and thus omits from his scheme of things one of the most important motives, perhaps the most important, of human nature.

In this new age Scott suffered not only from the new ideas of what the novel should contain and how it should be written, but also from the fading of his personal appeal. It may be admitted that under any circumstances the spell of his personality would become less potent as his figure grew more distant with the passing years, and that critics would no longer feel a prick of conscience when they spoke coolly or disparagingly of the novels or poems. The fires of personal affection might

[4] F. Marion Crawford, *The Novel — What It Is* (London, 1893).

[5] It was still possible for an organ like the *Edinburgh Review* to declare of the love passages in *Richard Feverel* that they "must quicken the pulses of a girl's heart, yet there is nothing that is mischievously suggestive or that need bring the blushes to her cheek." *Edinburgh Review*, January, 1895; cf. above, page 231 n.

be stirred and revived momentarily by the publication of his journal and letters, and occasional warm expressions of devotion, even in the older Victorian style of direct apostrophe (witness Sir Edmund Gosse), might crop out here and there, but the appeal to personality could no longer be the mainstay it had been. Readers would no longer take up the novels because of tenderness and devotion to the author. And as for the old Victorian sentimental reminiscence and anecdote and description of Loch Katrine at eve when the stag had drunk his fill, that as a fact had gone out. Apparently the market for that sort of thing had fallen off badly. Tours to the Trossachs and to Abbotsford continued no doubt to constitute a profitable business, but the desire to cherish and reverence had, at least comparatively, lost its force.[6] The new generation of critics was coming to feel as a matter of principle that the confusion of a writer's personal charms with an appraisal of his genius or an analysis of his work was dangerous and misleading, that it was doubtless a mark of Victorian sentimentality. That is, criticism was becoming more scientific, more sophisticated, and from this angle, too, one of Sir Walter's strong defenses was crumbling. A writer's books were no longer to be loved because he himself was lovable and charming.

That the new trend was fully recognizable as early as 1880 is made obvious by a review of a new edition of Lockhart in that year.[7] The reviewer, commenting on the supposed decline of Scott's popularity, attributes it in general to the reaction against any writer who has been long admired; the same thing, he says, is happening to Macaulay, Dickens, Tennyson. But more especially there is the modern change in taste, the modern interest in analysis and realism and the commonplace. With these things the writer, who reflects the Victorian belief in the superior station of romance above realism, was not in sympathy, for he goes on to say that they all constitute a kind of fad, that Scott

[6] It is often implied that the old sentimental attachment still flourishes in Scotland. Mr. Alan McKillop, in his address at Rice Institute in 1933, said he was disappointed when he tried to discover it.

[7] *Atlantic Monthly*, 46:313 (September, 1880).

and other writers will return, and that Scott himself is "the last purely imaginative writer of English fiction," marked by a unique "majestic abundance of power" and "a sort of grandeur and massive strength, such as he alone has possessed in modern times." Here, expressed very early,[8] is the conception of the present age as decadent, absorbed in technic and in scientific analysis and in abnormalities, as a kind of Twilight of the Gods— a conception commonly held by the more nostalgic and aggrieved of modern critics who wait, more or less patiently, the arrival of a saner and purer day.

The result was hard not only on Scott but on the mid-Victorians. Beside the novelists of the new school they were all formless and chaotic, amateurish and naive in technic, and they obviously wrote most of the time by the page or even the chapter, having never heard of *le mot juste*. Similarly their realism and their psychology and their philosophy (whether because there was too much or too little) left a great deal to be desired. The result was a strong feeling that the earlier gods of the novel were outmoded; the moral emancipation offered by the French, coupled with their technical finesse, was too much for these earlier writers to compete with. One is reminded of the similar situation when the critics and dramatists of the Restoration, glorying in their new sophistication, looked back on Shakespeare and his fellows, warbling their native wood-notes wild. This new attitude is pervasive and inescapable. It comes out in bold statement and in continuous implication, and is attested by such a question as

[8] Mr. Ford M. Ford says, "But the European 'influence' was as yet [1891] quite subterranean. It was, as it were, practiced in the cellars of the time, this reading of the works of the great Russians and the great French." The appearance of *The Yellow Book* meant that criticism was released from attention to the "botched and amateurish" work of the older novelists. Since 1894 there have been a few novels a year worth noticing, and a few novelists who paid some attention to style. But before the nineties there was nothing except the work of Trollope. See Ford Madox Ford, *Henry James. A Critical Study* (London, 1913), pp. 76, 79. On the moral side, for details of the furious war waged against French naturalism and Zola especially, see C. R. Decker, "Zola's Literary Reputation in England," *Publications of the Modern Language Association*, 49:1140 (1934). The attacks on Zola began under the lead of Swinburne in the late seventies and the amazing prosecution of Vizetelly followed in the eighties. Of course, one only needs to recall the early history of Ibsen in England and the first stages of Shaw's career.

that of W. H. Mallock, "Are Scott, Dickens, and Thackeray Obsolete?"[9]

Yet it is undeniable that the criticism of Scott in the late nineteenth and twentieth centuries leaves the general impression of being as favorable as any he has ever had. In fact, much of it is militantly aggressive. This is due of course to the feeling among his champions that his great virtues are neglected, and that the devotees of new gods are seeking to oust him. Much has been written about Scott during this period, most of it highly enthusiastic; yet it would be futile to claim that most critics, especially in these later years, have been friendly or even interested in him. He has been ardently defended by a determined group of writers, strongly academic, conservative, and anti-modernistic for the most part, and ignored by the rest.

But the effect of favorable criticism under such circumstances is striking. In Scott's time, when the very heavens resounded with his praises, the utterance of any critic, however admiring, who insisted on flaws, sounds rather chill and judicial. On the contrary, in our own time, when Scott is popularly dismissed as outmoded, and the critics sing his praises, the effect is to elevate him higher than ever. And surely praise a century later is more telling than the praise of one's own time. Quite naturally a modern reader is much more startled and impressed at hearing Virginia Woolf intimate that Scott may be mentioned in the same breath with Shakespeare, than when he gets the same suggestion from Francis Jeffrey. However that may be, the general tone of most modern English and American critics who have written about him has been even militantly and aggressively pro-Scott, and if Arnold Bennett was right in his definition of a classic author as one whose life is maintained by a passionate few, then Scott would seem for the present to be a true classic, for certainly he has had lately a band of ardent defenders to insist that no place was too high for him. As A. T. Sheppard remarks, the fact that Scott is so often attacked and defended proves that "he still lives and is likely to live."[10]

[9] See page 246.   [10] "The Historical Novel," *Quarterly Review*, 259:245 (1932).

Many of Scott's later supporters start indeed from the assumption that he is neglected both by the critics and the public. They are as likely as not to begin an essay with the offhand, casual assertion that no one any longer reads Scott. And there are occasional writers who hail this as a sign of sense and good taste, feeling that time has at last done justice to the naive and childish talents of Sir Walter — no one now reads him and, it is added, why should they?[11] Still, there is not much of this, perhaps because it is considered obvious and negative and hardly worth discussing. One need not lash a dead horse.

The much more common attitude of those who do take the trouble to write about Scott is that current literary taste makes too little of him and needs to be set right. To the assumption that he goes unread because there is nothing in him to interest the modern reader comes the reply that this is absurd and utterly false, or if true means merely that modern taste is perverted and distorted, and to find out its mistake need only wait for the whirligig of time to bring in its revenges.[12]

Andrew Lang, who seems to have carried as much weight in journalistic criticism in 1900 as Arnold Bennett did lately, is especially bitter when he considers the effect of new modes on his hero.[13] He speaks sarcastically of current taste and the "especial contempt for Scott," whose works are not those "of a passionate, a squalid, or a totally uneducated genius," the productions of a "Peeping Tom who studies woman in her dressing

[11] Note the cool condescension of such an organ as the *Nation* in its brief notices of the centenary of 1932. According to the *Nation* (October 5), Scott means nothing, one way or another; and (October 26) he was light and superficial, the Edgar Wallace of his day. See the *Nation*, 135:297, 403. Similarly, Mr. Denys Thompson, in an essay "Our Debt to Lamb" (in *Determinations*, London, 1934), speaks of Scott's centenary (1932) as merely "a rich seam for literary racketeers" with "superfluous biographies," and a chance for "your modern novelist-purveyor of soporifics" to justify himself. It should have been used, Mr. Thompson continues, rather as a splendid opening to show the degeneration of the reading public, which the Waverley novels seduced from poetry.

[12] Apparently it was believed in 1927 that it had. In that year there was started in Edinburgh the *Sir Walter Scott Quarterly*. This periodical was apparently to serve Scott as the *Dickensian* serves Dickens, but it survived for only four issues. It is notable that it was not undertaken in a defiant or protective mood; its editor declares at the outset that a Scott renaissance is under way.

[13] Andrew Lang, *Sir Walter Scott* (London, 1906), pp. 105, 126, and Conclusion.

room and tries to spy or smell out the secrets of the eternally feminine." Scott, he says, is not a stylist searching for the exact word, "usually the least natural word for any mortal to use in the circumstances." He cannot draw a young, beautiful, wicked woman; his limitations now militate against a high appreciation of his work by the admirers of M. Guy de Maupassant and M. Catulle Mendès. Scott could not have treated their themes; "he had funds enough to draw upon in human life and character without hunting for personages and situations in dark, malodorous corners." Yet he is not to be deprived of his unfading laurels by change in fashion, his own limitations, or "feather headed folly or leaden stupidity"; to judge by new editions, the novels are "not less popular now than are, for their little span, the most successful flights of all-daring ignorance and bombastic presumption." This is certainly not distinguished criticism, but it strikes a note frequently heard during the quarter century preceding, as well as the one that followed.[14]

Considering the general situation, then, it is not surprising that the current defenders of Scott should continue the old laudatory comparisons with Homer, Shakespeare, and Cervantes, and should also write him up by writing others down. Mr. John Buchan, Lord David Cecil, Professors Elton, Seccombe, Ker, to name but a few, are by no means timid and apologetic. They carry the war into the enemy's country. The great Victorians are stood up beside Scott to the dimming of their glory, and all the gods great and little of the later generations are submitted to the same ordeal. Two centenary articles of 1932 illustrate this well enough. In a very vivid, lively essay A. M. Mackenzie[15] brings in a whole list of names from Thackeray down to D. H. Lawrence, Joyce, and Dorothy Richardson to prove the futility and error in the current depreciation

[14] The name of Andrew Lang is anathema to certain current critics; see Q. D. Leavis, *Fiction and the Reading Public* (London, 1932), and Donald and Catherine Carswell, "The Crisis in Criticism," *Nineteenth Century*, 113:107 (January, 1933). The Carswells trace the degeneration of reviewing since 1875 to the baneful influence of Lang and W. R. Nicoll, who, they say, catered with enormous success to the puritanical tastes of the broadened reading public.

[15] *Mercury*, 25:270 (January, 1932).

of Sir Walter; and Mr. M. O. Smith defends Scott at the expense of George Eliot and Thackeray, the French realists, and even the great Russians.[16] For the modern critic this last is the supreme test. There is no doubt that in his eyes Tolstoi and Dostoevski and Turgeniev (the last much less now than a generation ago) are the "giants," the "Titans"; there are no other modern novelists, English or Continental, whose names he breathes with equal awe and reverence. For such critics as Virginia Woolf and Percy Lubbock, Tolstoi is the greatest of all novelists, *War and Peace* the greatest of all novels. Hence the coupling of Scott's name with theirs becomes the highest praise and the most audacious of critical expedients; yet Mr. Buchan and others besides do not shirk it.

In the modern handbooks and textbooks on the novel Scott seems to have suffered little from the inroads of the new criticism. These books, written invariably by professors, are of course concerned largely with information about the novels and also stress quite naturally Scott's tremendous influence as an innovator; yet they always offer the student an estimate or comparative evaluation. They generally detail the admitted flaws in style, characterization of heroes and heroines, and so on, but they never fail to emphasize Scott's greatness as a man and a creative genius. They vary, as one might expect, in their degrees of admiration and enthusiasm, but there is not one that does not show a considerable amount of both, the highest encomiasts being perhaps Sir Walter Raleigh and Saintsbury. Surely, if Scott's reputation were to be moulded by these writers, he would still be a popular idol and a favorite with the critics.[17]

[16] "Scott and his Modern Rivals," *Queen's Quarterly*, 39:603 (November, 1932), a special Scott Centenary number.

[17] The books consulted are: Walter Raleigh, *The English Novel*, 1894 (5th ed., New York, 1904); W. L. Cross, *The English Novel* (New York, 1899), the account which in its compact fullness perhaps remains the best; Harold Williams, *Two Centuries of the English Novel* (London, 1911); Saintsbury, *The English Novel* (London, 1913); W. L. Phelps, *The Advance of the English Novel* (New York, 1918); Cornelius Weygandt, *A Century of the English Novel* (New York, 1925); G. C. Knight, *The Novel in English* (New York, 1931); Robert M. Lovett and H. S. Hughes, *History of the Novel in England* (Boston, 1932); and Pelham Edgar, *The Art of the Novel* (New York, 1933).

Although his final conclusions do not leave Scott where his warmest friends would have him, Mr. E. A. Baker's running analysis of the novels in his monumental history [18] would certainly induce the highest respect for Sir Walter as a novelist. The weight of his praise is on the realism of the Scotch novels, yet he approaches the best of the romances — *Ivanhoe, Kenilworth, Quentin Durward* — with much more sympathy than do most modern critics, setting them apparently not so very far below the first series. He also develops his critical theories of Scott entirely without reference to the modern atmosphere, possibly thinking it of no import in the perspective of the academic literary historian. He is, however, almost unique in this respect.

In speaking of the novels one by one, he puts his finger on what have seemed to modern critics Scott's greatest successes, and his praise at many points is superlative. He calls attention to the brilliant climaxes in *Guy Mannering* and the complete sympathy Scott shows with all his people, even with outcasts, the socially disreputable. He lauds the perfect realism of Edie Ochiltree and the Mucklebackits in *The Antiquary*, as also of Nicol Jarvie, Andrew Fairservice, and Diana Vernon in *Rob Roy*. He calls *Old Mortality* a historical monument, and *The Heart of Midlothian* a national epic, adding to the two great scenes usually cited the one between Jeanie and Effie in prison, about which he agrees with Adolphus that it might entitle Scott to "sit down at the feet of Shakespeare." In *The Bride of Lammermoor* he sees the perfect Gothic novel which many had tried but no one attained, and declares like several others that the hags in the churchyard can stand in competition with Shakespeare. As has already been said, his praise of the romances is ungrudging, but in the later novels his highest praise is kept for Clara Mowbray in *St. Ronan's Well* — a really

[18] See E. A. Baker, *op. cit.*, VI, 122–226. This is the longest systematic analysis in one piece of purely critical writing that the Waverley novels have ever had. It consists of a series of chapters on the novels in chronological order, with detailed analysis of all of them up to 1825, and a final general chapter. For Mr. Baker's remarks on Scott's treatment of character, his philosophy and history, see below, page 306.

tragic heroine, an Antigone — and for the perfect blending of the public and private sides of *Redgauntlet,* as well as for Peter Peebles and *Wandering Willie's Tale.* It is true that many of these points have been favorites with earlier critics, but in his development of them Mr. Baker has the advantage of a much closer and more minute study of the novels than most of the critics have given them (John Buchan is a notable exception). He also devotes much more space to the novels than any other writer has, and writing in a compact, highly condensed style, is able to pile up a formidable mass of detail. It is perhaps also an advantage to assume a calm aloofness from current theories of the novel; at least it saves one from imputations of propaganda and crusading.

Quite apart from the critical analysis of Scott's work, the apportionment of praise and blame, the weighing and considering, is the matter of his relations with the reading public, the degree of his actual popularity. How much has he really been read at various periods during the last century, and by whom? And what have been the influences that have controlled the ebb and flow of public taste? One may draw what conclusions he likes from the pronouncements of critics on these points, though if he relies on them he is almost certain to emerge in a state of confusion. There are, on the other hand, some plain, authentic statements of fact and some statistics that lead to quite definite conclusions. And finally there is a good deal to be said about social conditions and the relation between writers and the public in general to explain the present status of Scott and most of the other "standard novelists."

It is easy enough to collect positive statements by critical writers about Scott's popularity at any time during the last century. The only difficulty is that since about 1840 they are consistently contradictory, either partially or absolutely. It is clear that they are in practically all cases based on mere conjecture or personal impression. Yet the writers who are willing to be positive are numerous. Of course during Scott's lifetime, in the midst of his production, the evidence of this sort is clear and conclusive. Everyone united in exclaiming over his tremendous and universal appeal to all levels of the reading public. Indeed his popularity satisfied him and his friends beyond all expectations, and has always been considered by literary historians dazzling, even unique. Certainly no writer before had ever enjoyed such success, and there is no doubt that the resounding periods which the critics enjoyed writing about seeing his books in the hands of old and young, of grave and gay, on the savant's desk and the lady's work table, were amply justified.

But from the time of his death, or soon after, confusion and disagreement begin. From then on one finds all sorts of statements concerning Scott's hold on readers, the degree to which he could still fascinate them. One reads that his glamour is fading, that his public is gradually deserting him, and that there is little hope of long life for his novels. Then one also reads that his appeal is as strong as ever, that his readers are still legion. Probably both sets of opinions are based on an equal amount of concrete evidence, or rather lack of it. Such conflicting statements may be found down to the very present and generally seem to spring from mere feelings or notions.

A series of comments in the *North American Review* [19] running well down into the Victorian era show the feeling in the camp of the true-blue loyalists, for the *North American* remained one of Scott's staunchest supporters. In reviewing Cunningham's *Life* in 1833 and Lockhart's in 1838 it had spoken of him in superlatives and had not even raised the question of his popularity. At that time it was apparently taken for granted, and to discuss it seemed superfluous. In 1857, however, in brief comment on a new edition of the novels, the *North American* speaks of their "undiminished claims on the whole reading public and the position which they still hold unchallenged at the head of their department of literature." "Why is it," the critic says, "that the pioneer author always remains unrivalled in the kind he creates," as Homer and Aeschylus have done. And the

---

[19] *North American Review,* 36:289 (April, 1833), W. B. O. Peabody; 46:431 (April, 1838), W. H. Prescott; 85:271 (July, 1857), A. P. Peabody; 87:293 (October, 1858), S. G. Brown; 99:580 (October, 1864), Henry James.

next year, 1858, in a review of a new American edition of Scott it is declared that the market for his work is as strong as ever, that the popularity of the Wizard of the North is unabated, being no less now than a third of a century since, and that time will never reverse the decision that his novels were the most striking literary phenomenon of the age. As for the competition of later novelists, none dares dispute his crown; "Scott is still the monarch of novelists"; though equaled in single points, he is unmatched in his total effect. Obviously the reviewer thought Dickens and Thackeray were not dangerous rivals. Nor apparently was George Eliot, for six years later, reviewing Nassau Senior's essays, Henry James declares, "The popularity which Mr. Senior celebrated forty years ago has in no measure subsided," though he does add that Scott has suffered the attenuating process of becoming a "standard author," a remark that would seem to throw cold water on what he has just said, else what does it mean? He continues by asserting that the facility often charged against Scott really springs from a transcendent strength, which gives his work a permanence such as Mrs. Henry Wood could not hope for, though she was as prolific as Scott had been. He is of course no longer a novelty, his technic is known — *Ivanhoe* written now would no longer be surprising; and besides there has been since Scott much ingenuity in the novel and plenty of genius. Dickens, Thackeray, Kingsley, Reade, and George Eliot "have all overtaken the author of *Waverley*" and "Sir Edward Bulwer has produced several historical tales which, to use an expressive vulgarism, have 'gone down' very extensively. And yet old-fashioned, ponderous Sir Walter holds his own."

As early as 1840, however, there are whispers that Sir Walter's glory may be departing, and fears that a later age may not grant him his due. In an interesting review [20] of Lockhart's *Life,* which is throughout entirely sympathetic and laudatory, without a touch of adverse criticism, the writer admits sadly, "That he outlived the glory of his popularity is undoubted," and fears

[20] *New York Review,* 7:137 (July, 1840).

that his later and inferior work may set the level of his fame. Perhaps the most impressive statement of this feeling, unless it be Leslie Stephen's, is in an essay in the *Quarterly* of 1868.[21] This is really a review of Lockhart, delayed thirty years to await Lockhart's own passing, since his close association with the *Quarterly* made an earlier review ethically impossible. It is actually a long biographical essay on Scott and is thoroughly sympathetic and reverent, the declared purpose being to re-awaken the present delinquent generation to the glories of Scott's life and work. At the beginning it is stated that Scott seems in danger of passing, "we cannot conceive why — out of the knowledge of the rising generation." There are, to be sure, cheap railway editions to be read and thrown away, "but the instances are rare, we suspect, in which even among educated persons, young men or young women under five and twenty know anything at all either of what Scott wrote or of what he did." This is deplorable, a public misfortune. There is no surer test than the reading of the young of the educated classes. When Scott is cast aside so that young ladies and gentlemen "may break their hearts over the sorrows of bigamists and adulterers" (and there were many such in mid-Victorian fiction, from *Jane Eyre* to the novels of Mrs. Braddon, who specialized in bigamy), one has doubts as to "the moral sense of the age."

Walter Bagehot in 1858 opens his very carefully considered essay with an allusion to the passing of Scott's original popularity, obscured as he is by new writers and new interests, and in 1863 another essayist [22] declares Scott still the favorite novelist of his country, but seems doubtful of his future, although he believes his popularity can never be followed by disgust, as it is in some cases. One of the centenary writers of 1871 [23] remarks, "Scott is now somewhat faded it is common to say, and undeniably it is true to say so," and Leslie Stephen on the same occasion suspects that Scott's power is waning, "the warmth of our first love departed," and has heard whispers that he is dull.

[21] *Quarterly Review*, 124:1 (January, 1868).
[22] *Saturday Review*. See above, page 184.   [23] *Nation*, 13:103 (August 17, 1871).

In the nineties we find statements that his position is fixed and unassailable, that his novels have sold by the million since his death, with the implication that they still do, and that they delight both young and old.[24] But in the same decade there is D. F. Hannigan's [25] contemptuous belief that by the turn of the century Scott will be remembered by only three or four novels. And so it goes. There is little to be made of all this, except possibly the gradual subsidence of popularity which almost any classic must suffer as its "gloss of novelty" wears off. Scott must in the nature of things have yielded some of his place to Dickens, Thackeray, George Eliot, and others, and must have been affected by new modes. At best, that is the most he could have hoped for; it would be absurd to hope or believe that the Waverley novels could continue to astonish and delight the world in 1871 or in 1914 as they did in 1820.

On the other hand, there was still so much writing about him in this period, his personality and the characters and scenes of his poems and novels were kept so steadily before the public, and in so affectionate and sentimental a light, that he must have been, through most of the century at least, very widely read. The cool and intellectual criticism of Leslie Stephen and Walter Bagehot is certainly proof of nothing more than the gradual settling process which was inescapable. The idea of Scott as a writer for boys, which is now widespread and indicates a much greater attenuation than that of the Victorian era, had not yet arisen. The first hint of any such attitude is given by Henry James in 1864, and is actually sympathetic. Certainly when he speaks of becoming as credulous as children at twilight in order to enjoy Scott thoroughly, he does not mean to be disparaging. The whole tone of his essay indicates a sentimental attachment of which this is really the crowning glory. In Leslie Stephen's essay of 1871 *Ivanhoe* and its like are called boys' books, but there is certainly no hint of calmly sweeping the whole series

[24] See a review of Scott's *Journal* in the *Quarterly Review*, 171:386 (October, 1890), and by W. Fraser Rae in the *Temple Bar*, 90:477 (December, 1890).

[25] See page 265.

into the limbo of rather antiquated and clumsy "juveniles," where there is a distinct feeling today that they belong.

A late nineteenth-century writer who interested himself especially in the matter of Scott's popularity was W. H. Mallock.[26] He declares positively that Scott and Dickens are more popular than ever before, a statement he supports by referring to the large number of new editions of both writers, and the thriving market for their books. Those who say that they are not read live, he thinks, among people who do not read them, or who read them long ago and do not discuss them in daily conversation. Scott he believes has a wider appeal than Dickens, and in Scotland is appreciated by the poorest peasants, whereas Dickens, despite his low-class characters, fails to appeal to that class. Judging from his own experience, however, he asserts that in England the broad reading public, both young and old, show complete familiarity with both Scott and Dickens, whose popularity he traces to their strong undercurrent of nationalism. Thackeray, on the other hand, never so broadly popular, also lacks their stamina, Mallock believes, because of the special and very local world in which his stories move, a world already vanished or vanishing.

When one comes down into the twentieth century, one gets the impression that Scott's faithful adherents have been hearing on every side that he is no longer read, or that at best he is only a writer for boys. Wilfrid Ward [27] is one of the many friends of Scott who believe that he is now little read. Yet at the same time there are many statements, as confident as ever, of continuous and unwaning popularity. Andrew Lang, for instance, evidently unimpressed by talk that Scott is unread, says in 1901 [28] that whether he is read or not, he sells, like Shakespeare, in endless editions. Mr. Woodberry in 1905 [29] proclaims the undying popu-

---

[26] "Are Scott, Dickens and Thackeray Obsolete?" *Forum*, 14:503 (December, 1892).

[27] *Dublin Review*, 155:281 (October, 1914).

[28] In a review of Hudson's *Life of Scott*, in the *Critic*, 38:338 (April, 1901).

[29] *McClure's Magazine*, 25:165 (June, 1905). Reprinted in *Great Writers* (New York, 1907).

larity of the novels, read by millions, he says, and unaffected by criticism; and another writer in the *Nation* in 1914,[30] the date of Wilfrid Ward's essay, speaks of the novels "as flourishing in undiminished popularity" and, apropos of the charge that they carry no message, "How brazen then for *Waverley* and his fellows to be marching along after a hundred years, their eyes not dim, nor their natural force abated" — possibly a little generous sentiment for *Waverley's* centenary. And a decade later we have Virginia Woolf declaring that while Scott no longer influences even the most impressionable writer, yet no books are so widely read and enjoyed with "uncritical and silent enjoyment"; and on the other hand, Mr. C. R. L. Fletcher, rebuking the "farrago" of Stalker's *Life,* speaks of the comparative neglect of Scott by younger readers today, which he thinks inexplicable.[31]

It is possible, however, to collect quite a little accurate, even statistical, information about the sales of Scott's novels at least down through the nineteenth century, so that one may after all come to fairly definite conclusions on the reading of them through that period.

Concerning the original sale of the novels, Lockhart gives perfectly definite statistics. After the novels were under way Scott published in the standard three-volume form at a guinea and a half, or ten shillings sixpence a volume, a form which he is said to have established and which weighed down and cramped the novel until nearly 1900. Considering the size of the reading public and the extremely high price of the books, which led among people of slight or moderate means to their being bought in clubs or to their being read aloud at so much per head per evening,[32] the sales were huge; for the times unheard-of. They seem small, however, compared with Dickens' sales, which ran as high as seventy thousand for his earlier books two decades

---

[30] *Nation*, 99:124 (July 30, 1914).

[31] *New Republic*, 41:42 (December 3, 1924), and *Quarterly Review*, 244:16 (January, 1925).

[32] This arrangement persisted. Forster tells the story of a charwoman who attended a regular paying tea at her lodging house to hear the reading of the parts of *Dombey and Son* as they came out.

later, with the publication in shilling parts. Scott at his best, with the more expensive form of publication, attained to what Lockhart calls a "triumphant twelve or fourteen thousand." This figure was approached as a climax with a gradual climb from *Waverley* to *Ivanhoe*. In the early twenties a decline began, which brought the sales down to the lower figure of eight to ten thousand. The sales of *Woodstock* (1826),[33] for which Scott received £8,228 cash, were helped perhaps by the wide publicity of Sir Walter's financial failure and were unexpectedly large; but the following novels fell off again, although Scott never had anything that might be called a market failure. The last two novels, the weakest of the series, had immediate sales of only 3,400 each, a figure that Sir Walter, who had a low opinion of them, found highly gratifying. At the end there was also a distinct revival of interest in all the novels, due to the publication of the widely advertised collected edition, the "Magnum Opus."[34]

For the times this was a magnificent, a unique record. To see its significance one should compare it, not with Dickens' sales in shilling parts, the greatest in the next generation, but with those of a very popular novelist like G. P. R. James, whose American publishers considered him their most profitable speculation, and who at the crest of his wave in the thirties and forties sold the first rights to his novels at five or six hundred pounds.[35]

[33] It sold for £8400, with clear profits to Scott's trustees of £6075. Lockhart wrote Scott on March 13, 1826, that he had been worried about *Woodstock*, the failure of which would have been most unhappy. He lists a number of passages in it which he thinks are in Scott's best form. Grierson, *Letters*, IX, 395, 475n.

[34] Cadell's correspondence with Scott in 1828 and 1829 shows how great Sir Walter's commercial value still was. The canny Cadell knew now as later that he had here a gold mine in the Magnum Opus. He was greatly worried lest other work, illness, or death should interfere with it. He urges the author on to steady, unremitting labor, warning him that he must keep before the public, and dangling before him promises of fabulous amounts that the Magnum Opus would produce, to more than pay off his debts. There is a plan too for a new series of three novels at six months intervals, to be paid for at the rate of £4200 each, and notice of arrangements to speed up printing and binding by importing hands from Glasgow. See Partington, *Private Letter Books*, pp. 360 ff., and *Sir Walter's Post Bag*, pp. 278 ff.

[35] See Stewart M. Ellis, *The Solitary Horseman*, p. 120.

A graph of Scott's original profits would possibly confirm the opinion of the critics, or at least bring the popular opinion into line with it, for they have universally preferred the early group of Scott novels where Scott found his greatest profits. The great exception to such a statement would of course be *Ivanhoe,* which enjoyed very high sales, and which has never been highly praised by more critical readers. One might guess, however, that if that person called the average reader were asked casually what Scott wrote he would answer first *The Lady of the Lake, Marmion,* and *Ivanhoe.*[36]

For the period following Scott's death there is also definite information concerning the sales of the novels. Soon after 1832 the copyrights were sold by the estate to Cadell; and Lockhart reports the excellent profits, the small fortune in fact, that the publisher drew from this investment before 1850. Jeffrey in 1844 [37] says that Cadell told him that during the preceding year he had sold sixty thousand volumes and that the demand "had been for some time sensibly on the increase." Moreover, when Cadell's estate was settled in 1851, the *Athenaeum* [38] carried a full back-page advertisement of the sale of the Waverley copyrights as the most important copyright material ever offered for

---

[36] Arthur S. Collins, in *The Profession of Letters* (London, 1928), Chapter II, shows how great were the rewards for popular writers in all literary fields at this time. Literature had become an independent profession, free from a system of patronage. But in general the amounts received by Scott are out of all proportion with the payments made to other novelists. The ratio is more like that between his profits and those of G. P. R. James, just noted.

Scott himself has left very clear testimony concerning the greatly improved position of authors in this period. In 1821 a Royal Society of Literature was projected which was to subsidize works of genius with £100. Scott advised strongly against any such arrangement. He declared that any author of genius could now make a good living, that for the kind of work the Society proposed to reward with £100 any bookseller would give £1000, possibly £2000, and that authors of any eminence commonly made profits of £3000 or £4000 from a single work. He thought that an author could now count on an income of from £500 to £5000 a year, according to his talents and industry. The only writers of genius he knew who were in straitened circumstances and who could be helped under such a plan were Coleridge and Maturin. See Grierson, *Letters,* VI, 398. Some of these figures seem unduly optimistic; yet the general situation is clear.

[37] Francis Jeffrey, *op. cit.*

[38] March 15, 1851.

sale — "the abundant resources of this valuable property," etc., etc.[39]

If one may judge at all from the sale of a biography, the remark of W. Chambers, who edited and republished in 1871 the *Life* of Scott that his brother, Robert Chambers, had originally written immediately after Scott's death, should be highly significant. He says that this *Life* had had a sale of 180,000 copies, a great figure, even if one made allowance for its being "issued at a small price for popular reading."[40] Surely one may conclude that a public which bought the *Life* in this fashion was still reading the novels.

On the expiration of the copyrights in the early sixties, moreover, publishers rushed into the market with new, cheap editions, "railway editions," to catch what they apparently considered an enthusiastic public. In France, too, he was still widely read until the middle of the century, one publisher alone having sold 1,400,000 volumes of the novels.[41] Yet another amazing bit of statistical information, which brings Scott's popularity safely down to the end of the century, is vouched for by John Murray, who says that in 1892 a well-known Edinburgh printer told him that though he had printed editions of Scott for only one publisher he had paid in wages for them in thirty years fully £40,000.[42] It seems safe to assume, then, that for at least two generations after 1832 his novels and his poems too were read by greater numbers than ever. If this is so, the steady growth of the reading public doubtless more than compensated for the falling off one might expect as the attraction of novelty faded.

Yet it is difficult to believe that for the past generation, and especially for the past ten or fifteen years, Scott has been widely

[39] See Grierson, *Letters*, IX, 401n, for an analysis of Cadell's dealings with Scott's family. It is apparent that he drove a very good bargain with them and that they really came out at the little end of the horn. It is implied that a generous man like Constable would not have taken such advantage of them. Lockhart, however, actually thanked Cadell in 1847 for what he took to be generosity.

[40] See the preface to the edition of 1871.

[41] See M. G. Devonshire, *The English Novel in France, 1830–1870* (London, 1929), Chapter VIII.

[42] See *Times Literary Supplement*, July 6, 1922, p. 444.

read, despite the claims that have been made for him by the more friendly critics.

As a matter of fact, references in the last generation or so to publishers' profits and new editions as proof of popularity are not very convincing. Everyone knows that a few of the novels, *Ivanhoe* first of all, and *Kenilworth* and *The Talisman,* are republished in huge cheap editions for use as texts in secondary schools, and that a few of the Scotch novels are sold in the same way for consumption in colleges and universities.[43] But no one familiar with their use would be too sure that this proved Scott's "undiminished popularity." Indeed pupils are generally required to read what they would otherwise let alone. And certainly what popularity there is among young readers is limited to the group of romances, as one might of course expect. One hears tales, for instance, of conscientious school librarians who have successfully introduced *Ivanhoe* or *Quentin Durward* to school children and have had the satisfaction of getting their copies worn to shreds, only to have *The Heart of Midlothian* or *Old Mortality* returned to them almost at once, perfectly fresh and clean after the first few pages.[44] Although there are no available statistics on the subject, it is hard not to believe that most of the publishers' profits come from these school editions. Nor is an argument based on sales of library editions much more convincing. Every school, university, or public library of any size must have one or more "sets" of Scott, as of all the other established classics. There must be, moreover, a steady demand from those who desire a library ready-made, to fill so many feet of shelf space. For such purposes who would spring to mind sooner than Walter Scott and the other "standard" novelists, unless it were Shakespeare and the *Britannica?* It might be added too that

[43] Mr. C. R. L. Fletcher, *op. cit.,* refers to the enormously lucrative republication of Scott in school editions. This, he thinks, is of little help to Scott.

[44] Leslie Stephen suspected as early as 1871 that boys preferred books about cricket and boat races to *Ivanhoe,* and there are plenty of later anecdotes which would indicate that children cannot be got to swallow even *Ivanhoe.* Mrs. Leavis (*Fiction and the Reading Public*) tells for instance of a best-selling novelist whose boys would not look at Scott and Dickens, but consumed "the magazines and Edgar" (i.e., Wallace).

even the possession of a complete library edition by a cultivated reader does not necessarily imply the enthusiastic perusal that some of the later critics profess to believe in. As Canon Ainger had rather shrewdly guessed,[45] Scott might be widely bought, but not so widely read. After all, in the absence of any real data, one is forced into a position of doubt. Scott has enthusiastic readers, that is sure; but the assumption that he is still widely and popularly read is difficult to accept. It is easy enough for one who is writing in praise of Scott to declare that he still has thousands (or even millions) of friends, and equally easy for another in a mood of irritation or dislike to dismiss him as obsolete and forgotten. But a consideration of the taste of the reading public at present discourages any faith in a really wide and popular reading of Scott, or for that matter of any of the classic novelists.

Of course the whole matter has its sociological bases. In his own time Scott had the benefit of a blazing novelty and comparatively no competition. The reading public, while wider than that of the eighteenth century, was still compact, and was still serious, still highly cultivated. It appreciated moral values and erudition and dignified manners. It sought and found in the new novels not only delight but also edification. That is, from the point of view of the twentieth century, Scott's public was an infinitely superior one.

Yet from the point of view of the eighteenth century, democratization was already doing its evil work. Coleridge [46] thought the public had degenerated, that it had been enervated by the sensational events through which it had lived, and that popular literature to succeed in his period had to be made easier and simpler than it had been in the days of Fielding, Smollett, and Sterne, who, as Coleridge said, demand more of their readers than Scott does. And also it is beyond question that there was a great market for even easier fiction — and more sentimental and more sensational — than Scott's. The minor fiction of the later

[45] See the essay on Scott in *Lectures and Essays* (2 vols., London, 1905).
[46] See pages 150–51.

eighteenth century as well as the early nineteenth shows that. So also do the satires on the Gothic novels and on current sentimentalism, and occasional remarks that Scott was too dull for many patrons of the circulating libraries.[47] The Minerva Press was a flourishing institution. There is also the charge from a pious source that habitual novel-readers did not find Sir Walter voluptuous enough.[48]

This condition was modified but not radically changed in the Victorian era. The reading public steadily grew broader, and the appetite for sentiment and sensation naturally grew sharper. Ainsworth, Mrs. Braddon, Mrs. Henry Wood, Mrs. Archer Clive, Wilkie Collins, Charles Reade, and even Dickens — the literature furnished by such writers is more violent, or more highly spiced, or its sentiment more highly saturated, than that of their predecessors. Certainly the popular literature of 1800 or 1820 seems in general more polite, more proper, more genteel than the great masses that were ground out for the early Victorians, although of course they had plenty of innocuous and sweetly pretty novels too. Yet apparently these modified conditions did not affect Scott badly. Nor did the great new rivals who arose to attract attention away from him. Scott's momentum carried him along for a good half century after his death; figures of sales and other similar evidence support such a belief. To great crowds of Victorians of all levels Scott was still a delight. His technic did not yet seem cumbersome and boring, nor his morality and manners insipid and superficial. To the Victorians he was a great classic, and his success among

[47] See Amy Cruse, *The Englishman and His Books in the Early Nineteenth Century* (London, 1930). Miss Cruse has a chapter demonstrating the popularity of the Waverley novels, but also others on the circulating library and the Minerva Press, which show that Scott by no means crowded out other novelists. There were, no doubt, plenty of readers who desired a lower level than that of Scott. One of the Minerva Press novels, Mrs. Bennett's *Beggar Girl* (a book praised by Coleridge, see page 151) is said to have sold 2000 copies at 36s. on the day of publication. See *The Englishman and His Books*, page 107. And Charles Knight in *Passages from a Working Life* (3 vols., London, 1864–65), I, 221, says, "Novel reading was general. Miss Porter and Miss Edgeworth and Mrs. Radcliffe still held their ancient empire and were not driven out by the Waverley Novels."

[48] See the *Christian Observer*, quoted above, page 83.

them as a classic was fully as brilliant as it had been among his contemporaries as a novelty. The rhetoric about finding his books on the savant's desk and the lady's table was still in order. And except for shadings and reservations, critics and public were in accord. Indeed to the Victorian critic the very fact of popularity, if he thought it sprang from wholesome sources, that is, if the novelist were a power for good, was a weighty argument.

But since the period of the *fin de siècle* there has been a great change in all these matters. Most of those who write and talk about literature have, it seems safe to say, been cool and indifferent toward Scott, or even contemptuous. At least this is the assumption of Scott's defenders, as has already been noticed. To these critics the argument of popularity and the power for good, for "inspiration," not only carries no weight; it is anathema. Professor Schücking in discussing this point recalls the glorification of the popular voice in the romantic period; Schiller as a young man thought the people elevated art and the artist himself tended to lower it. Grillparzer considered the public a jury that passed or condemned works of art according to sound human understanding and natural feeling. Much more characteristic of the modern critical attitude is Nietzsche's "They applaud; what nonsense have I been talking?" [49]

The modern period opened strongly on the note of art for art's sake [50] and has continued definitely in the same key. The moral point of view has been almost universally abhorred, and the artistic detachment, elaborate experiments in technic, and scientific naturalism that have been the *sine qua non* have alienated the great mass of the reading public. The artists who have enrolled wholeheartedly in this school have written for a very narrow audience; they have ignored the great public.[51] And the critics have been strongly on their side.

[49] Levin L. Schücking, *Die Soziologie der Literarischen Geschmacksbildung* (Leipzig, 1931), p. 78.

[50] Cf. Schücking, *op. cit.*, Chapter IV; also Holbrook Jackson, *The Eighteen Nineties* (New York, 1922), *passim*.

[51] This narrow public may be considered in two ways, of course, according to one's prepossessions; either as the only public worth having, or as a mere clique.

The situation has been analyzed by various interested writers. Schücking declares that naturalism dug a gulf between the people and art. Naturally, he says, art for art's sake appeals little to the general public, which expects art to do certain things for it — especially to idealize, to present heroes and heroines, to be beautiful and inspiring, and certainly to be perfectly easy of comprehension. Mrs. Leavis makes practically the same point, describing the situation of Henry James and the later experimentalists. We have had, she points out, a group of novelists who are practicing a highly serious art and who have no connection with the general public; their sales run at most to four thousand copies. Mr. Joseph W. Beach [52] also calls attention to the cleft between the public and the novelist, and indicates its causes. In his opinion extreme subjectivity both in the earlier "well-made" novels of Henry James and the later and very different "modernist" types has made wide popularity impossible. So also has the emphasis on the pathological, the complicated forms of technic, which make for very difficult reading, and the hard ruthlessness of much modern fiction, which repels the common reader as inhumane.

It is clear enough that the novelists of such a school or schools and the critics who support them would be apt to have little sympathy with Scott. And even writers like Galsworthy and Arnold Bennett, who have been financial successes and have appealed to the upper levels of the broad public, even though they may not have penetrated into the rarest atmosphere have not seemed to care for Scott or to be interested in him. Galsworthy gave an address on the novel at the Sorbonne in which he did not even mention Scott. Arnold Bennett in his *Journal* looks at Scott only to envy his rapidity of production. But Bennett was entirely absorbed in his study of French models and felt that the English classics were in general formless and chaotic, and Galsworthy, too, was devoted to Continental models. There is of course Mr. Hugh Walpole and there is also Mr.

[52] Joseph Warren Beach, *The Twentieth Century Novel* (New York, 1932), Chapter XLIII.

Priestley, the latter a recognized Victorian and Dickensian dealer in humors. The only one of the very upper circle of "experimentalists" who speaks out for Scott is Virginia Woolf. Mr. E. M. Forster, for instance, says quite frankly, "For my own part I do not care for him," and will allow Sir Walter but one "genuine basis" for praise, the gift of story-telling.[53]

And if the novelists and critics and the very highest level of readers will not have him, neither, there is just as good reason to suppose, will the public, which has found plenty of writers to give it exactly what it wants and has not had to rely for its entertainment on the English classics or the modern experimentalists. What was done for the Victorians in the way of intensifying sensation and sentiment is as nothing compared with what has been done since. All the arts and wiles of commercial journalism have been exercised to the limit to satisfy the tastes of a huge public in Anglo-Saxon countries, where everyone can read and practically everyone does read, if not books, at least magazines. The reviews of the best sellers and the most rapid glance at the covers, even, of the scores of magazines in the corner emporiums make it clear what sort of competition Scott and the other classic novelists are facing. What chance has not only Scott but Fielding or Thackeray or George Eliot or even Dickens, the most easily popular of them all, against such attractions? Absolutely none, of course. It is impossible to believe that a considerable portion of the general public really reads any of the older classics. Whatever one may believe about causes and effects, the fact remains that even the poorest and most illiterate of Scott's original readers, even the auditors in the reading clubs, had a more serious and sober idea of the purpose of reading that the lower ranges of the reading public, that is, the great mass, have today.

[53] E. M. Forster, *Aspects of the Novel* (London, 1927). Mr. Forster paraphrases *The Antiquary* so as to show "its simple devices." But it is notable that he and the modern partisans of Scott do not meet at all in the argument. In his paraphrase Edie Ochiltree appears only as an agent in plot, and the only one of the Mucklebackits he mentions is the melodramatic Elspeth. To Scott's partisans this is nothing; they see Edie Ochiltree as a great character apart from plot, and are absorbed in the pathos of the mourning scenes in the Mucklebackit cabin.

Yet that is not to say that the Waverley novels are not read. It is even possible that Scott is read for pleasure by as many people today as when he first appeared. He had originally "his triumphant twelve or fourteen thousand" and was an astounding best seller. But the ordinary best seller today startles no one with sales running above one hundred thousand; he is a very common phenomenon.[54] With such a public Scott may easily have as many readers as a century ago. Scattered throughout the British empire and America, they would make little show. One occasionally finds among his acquaintances habitual readers of Scott, and some inquiry at American public libraries reveals the fact that he has a respectable circulation aside from school assignments. The more enthusiastic statements of his devotees must be discounted; yet so also must the others that no one reads him. He may be neglected by all levels of the public; on the other hand, there are quite certainly enough individuals from various levels who do read him to justify one in believing him a living classic.

[54] According to Alexander Woollcott (*McCall's*, October, 1934) the ten supreme best-sellers of the past decade ranged from 350,000 to 1,200,000.

CHAPTER II

DEPRECIATION AND DEFENSE

AS HAS already been said, neglect and indifference to Scott is in the atmosphere; it is generally taken for granted. Yet of downright contempt for him and positively destructive or annihilating criticism, systematically expressed, there seems to have been very little. In fact, for authoritative and important assertions that Scott is second-rate or worse as a novelist one must go to the Continent. Taine in the early 1860's had been hard on the Waverley novels, and such later critics as Brandes and Croce, both of whom are widely known and read in translation in England and America, have also been anything but laudatory. Croce says, indeed, that since Taine the Continental critic has had his eyes open to Scott's mediocrity. This is doubtless what one would expect. To highly sophisticated foreign readers whose ideas of the novel have been determined by the Russians and the French naturalists, Scott might well seem unintellectual and unphilosophical, piously bourgeois in his treatment of sex, clumsy and blundering in his technic; altogether, naïve and superficial. Such an impression is to be seen clearly in the comments of Brandes and Croce. Taine had, besides, his own peculiar prejudice against realism; and Brandes, who makes the most of Sir Walter's artistic shortcomings, was, like so many modern critics, an apostle of progress, and on that score would regard the Waverley novels askance.

Taine is quite orthodox in preferring the Scotch novels to the historical romances. Of these he spoke with calm contempt as false and superficial history, concocted for pretty stage effects to please patriotic English lords and to suit the sensibilities of ladies and young girls, showing them a Moyen Âge and Renaissance softened and sweetened. For Scott's realism, as far as it went, he has only praise, comparing him for his detail and his genial, affable spirit with Teniers and Addison and calling him the Homer of modern bourgeois life. But even at its best, in Scott and the great Victorians, Taine found realism essentially second-rate, a bourgeois literature produced for the bourgeois, distinguished by its excessive concern with petty detail and moral instruction, a literature of slight attraction to lovers of the beautiful in art, whatever might be its appeal to the utilitarian soul.

There had been no criticism of Scott like this in England, and there has been very little since, though the preference for romance over realism, in principle at least, was a favorite Victorian tenet. Its coolness and aloofness, its minimizing of Scott's most cherished gifts, are to be found in the pages of none of the Victorian critics, and of very few later ones. Brandes and Croce, however, echo fairly closely the judgments of Taine. For them Scott's importance has been reduced to a merely historical one. He was, they willingly admit, an important innovator, a discoverer of a new formula in the novel, and he exercised a tremendous influence on his own time, but his work is now obsolete and can hardly be taken seriously.

Brandes,[1] it is true, is kind to Scott, but while he makes concessions, still brings one back, as Taine does, to a conclusion of essential mediocrity. The Waverley novels, Brandes says, "are the mature productions of an inexhaustible gift of story telling and an extraordinary talent for description, both of men and things. They mark a distinct advance in two matters, the understanding of history and the representation of the life of the middle and lower classes." Scott, not Chateaubriand, was the real discoverer of local color. He did not see into individual character very deeply, but understood people as a nation or a

[1] Georg Brandes, *Naturalism in England,* which contains a chapter on Scott, was originally published in 1875 but seems to have been reworked for publication in English as volume four of *Main Currents in Nineteenth Century Literature* (6 vols., New York, 1901–05).

clan perfectly. In his novels the domestic details of private life, presented with vigorous realism, replaced the typical eighteenth-century series of tavern scenes, and the English were willing to forgive "his terrible prolixity" because of his graphic force. He was "one of the greatest character portrayers in all literature." Romanticism has produced nothing finer than Diana Vernon and Jeanie Deans and Louis XI. This is the sum of virtues which Brandes will allow Scott, and one begins to think that if only second-rate he must be close to the borders of greatness.

Brandes, however, has much to throw into the opposite scale. He shows far less disposition than most English critics to condone his "one great malpractice — inartistic hurry." He deplores too, as few English critics until lately would have done, the fact that there is nothing in Scott to give offense — the very point which the Victorians were apt to make his stronghold. He calls the novels soulful but idealless, and remarking on Scott's careful avoidance of the erotic, says he cared more about morals than art. Brandes objects that Scott also tones down all the coarse elements of past ages, and one recalls that this too was a point that a Victorian critic cited in his favor. He must, Brandes goes on, be given credit as an innovator, but is now antiquated himself; in fact, all critics view the historical novel askance. Above other weaknesses, however, Brandes stresses the fact that Scott demands nothing of himself or his readers in style, conciseness, and quick apprehension. A lasting classic, he says, must "not only be poetically planned but artistically elaborated in every detail."[2] As for Scott — even his finest scene, the trial in *The Heart of Midlothian,* loses half its effect because of prolixity. With only half his talent, but twice his culture and self-criticism, he would have made less stir but would have lasted longer. He has suffered too because he was entirely unaffected by the march of science — a grave danger for any modern author. Now to what has he fallen! A century ago he was a

[2] According to this, almost none of the older English novels will be lasting classics.

tremendous force with a host of great followers; now he is "the favorite author of boys and girls of fourteen, an author whom all grown-up people have read and no grown-up people read."

This is brilliant, and it is impossible not to admit the facts that underlie Brandes' points. The basis of argument lies, of course, in the weight and significance to be attached to them. The friendly modern English critic does not deny the faults that Brandes stresses, but he does minimize them, and refuses to demote Scott from the company of the first-rate on their account. This is especially notable in the case of style and management, which Brandes makes all-important, and which the British or American critic is apt to mention as obvious but after all of small account, a typical difference in attitude, possibly, between the Continental and the English point of view.

Brandes' criticism seems gentle and tolerant, compared with that of Croce, who, writing in 1923,[3] says that no writer of the first half of the nineteenth century could have failed to set Scott among stars of the first magnitude, and that eulogy and enthusiasm did not arise only from the middle stratum of the reading public, as Goethe's praise, for instance, makes manifest. But, he continues, all this glory is a thing of the past; since Taine, critical judgment has been fierce and inappreciative. Above all, the novels are too long, and the Continental reader feels their artificiality and the mechanical methods by which they advance. The production of the novels makes Scott seem like a captain of industry trying to supply a demand; one admires the power of invention and the assiduity which enabled him to produce two or three novels a year and thereby to acquire Abbotsford. His biography, which has been the glory and delight of the English critic, is for Croce merely the story of his finances, a document in the spirit of *Self-Help* and other thrifty works by the prudent Samuel Smiles. In their relations to literary

[3] *Dial*, 75:325 (October, 1923). This essay was reprinted in *European Literature in the Nineteenth Century* (London, 1924). It had also been reprinted in the *Living Age*, 317:99 (April, 1923), from a South American source.

history he finds the novels a manifestation of the historic-moral-political sentiment that had arisen in reaction against eighteenth-century rationalism and the Jacobinism of the French Revolution, a movement that Scott luckily exploited. Of his contrivance of stories and his skill in plotting, too, a department in which other critics have found little to praise in him, Croce has a low opinion, declaring that Scott's plots would be laughed at today and that Goethe's admiration of them matters little, considering his own weakness in this particular. Croce is especially irritated at a panegyric by Sir Edmund Gosse, and skillfully enough points out the doubt and uncertainty of its conclusion that if others fail Sir Walter, England will still be true to him, another patriotic cry quite reminiscent of many Victorian critics. The art of the novels Croce declares to be superficial, and in *Ivanhoe*, which he takes as an instance, he says it is impossible to find any "epic sentiment, love, religion, or any other feeling." At times there is a hint of real drama, as in the scenes between the Templar and Rebecca, or in occasional passages in *Old Mortality*, but on the whole his "good-natured smile . . . is really the most frankly poetic trait the novelist possesses." *The Heart of Midlothian*, which is his best novel, is so simply because it is impregnated with good nature; one cannot help liking the characters. Look for Scott's outbursts of good-will, humanity, and smiling simplicity, Croce admonishes. "All the rest is either labor or erudition; but from these spots shines his modest poesy" — for this alone can we be courteous to a writer who delighted older generations. [4]

[4] It is possible to adduce modern Continental critics, or at least French academic ones, who still think of Scott as a great genius, quite apart from his function as innovator. Compare the comments of Chevalley, Maigron, and Cazamian, whose work is widely known in England and America, to judge from frequent allusion and quotation. Cazamian is especially interesting as recognizing all the modern charges against Scott and dismissing them as of no great importance — as "his genuine simplicity and unpretentiousness are restful after the strained objectivity of recent schools." In compact and carefully considered analysis, Cazamian even discovers in Scott a supple and complicated art of presenting character, an art "which has at its roots a full sense of life, with all its complexities, and an alert attention to all the perceptible elements through which the solution of its problems reveals itself, in a spontaneously concrete appreciation of the qualities and

Really, no one of great importance seems to have gone out of his way, at least in England and America, to try to demolish Scott. The only striking example of consistent and thorough hostility in periodical criticism is apparently that of D. F. Hannigan, who twice at least bore violent witness against Scott. His first outburst came in 1891,[5] as one of the flood of articles poured fourth upon the publication of Scott's *Journal*. He believes that Scott was always after hard cash; that he was really a philistine, and never an idealist. Though some of his personal qualities may be admirable, nothing can be said for his literary ones. His code was narrow and his prejudices intense — all modern progress was to him an absurdity. His formula of the historical novel is obsolete; the future historical novel is not to be modeled on either *Waverley* or *Ivanhoe*. The interest in chivalry which he aroused is also passé and has been replaced by "the love of humanity — the instinct of democratic progress." And finally, "We can reverence his memory and pity his foibles . . . but we no longer regard him with the fetish-worship which made our grandfathers and grandmothers blind to his shortcomings."[6]

Mr. Hannigan reasserted these principles in the *Westminster*

paradoxes of things." Scott's romanticism, he also says, has a soundness, a fusion with the life of every day, an immunity from fever, not to be found even in the poetry of Wordsworth. Considering its French source and the cool detachment of its method, Cazamian's high valuation is extremely impressive. See Emile Legouis and Louis Cazamian, *A History of English Literature* (New York, 1929). M. G. Devonshire, *op. cit.*, p. 129, objects to Maigron's criticism because of his partiality to the romances of the *Ivanhoe* type; she thinks he reduces Scott's genius to a merely antiquarian level. She much prefers the criticism of Chasles, the chief contemporary reviewer of Scott.

[5] *Westminster Review*, 135:265 (1891).

[6] For an indignant reply to this article see the *Saturday Review*, 71:286 (March 7, 1891). To judge from style and point of view, the same writer contributed to the *Saturday Review* of May 4, 1889 (67:521) a sarcastic reply to Howells (cf. page 285 below), who had been making the point that, though great, Scott was hardly to be compared with Flaubert or Tolstoi; and also to the issue of June 13, 1891 (71:716) a burlesque modern review of *The Heart of Midlothian*, treating Scott condescendingly as a new author, making satiric comparisons with Howells and Meredith, and noting plagiarisms from Mrs. Poyser in *Adam Bede*. This writer expresses well the resentment and irritation felt by many at the inroads of the Continental novelists and the defection to them of many English critics and novelists as well, who took them as models.

Review in 1895,[7] having been stirred to anger by a long panegyric in the *Quarterly*. The *Quarterly* writer refuses to see any real weakness in Scott at all, and praises the novels from first to last most fulsomely. Hannigan, taking umbrage at this unrestrained enthusiasm, and in apparent enmity toward the *Quarterly* ("a venerable review which only sees the light four times every year"), describes the essay as intended "to galvanize these now half-forgotten novels into life by an elaborate article." According to Mr. Hannigan, Scott is merely mediocre or worse. His medievalism is all stage costume, and even the famous Rebecca is a stick. Scott did not create historical romance; Defoe is incomparably greater than he in the field. What he did create was the costume novel; he has "scarcely more vitality than the contents of a museum," an opinion in which he cites Taine for support. *Notre Dame de Paris, Salammbô,*[8] and even *Henry Esmond,* "though not of a high order," are far above Scott. Even Dickens was better at history. None of the historical romances is now, to quote Leslie Stephen, more than a debris. One may admit that he has some slight virtues, especially his power to portray oddities; and *The Heart of Midlothian,* but for its ending, might compare with Fielding and George Eliot, if not with Balzac or Flaubert. The celebrated Jeanie Deans is for the most part a lay figure. *The Antiquary* is perhaps a comparatively good novel. But in general Scott has no depth — there was "never

[7] *Westminster Review,* 144:17 (July, 1895). For the *Quarterly* article referred to see 180:431 (April, 1895).

[8] Hannigan was a translator of French novels into English and obviously a violent partisan of the new school. An essay of his on Flaubert is an admirable statement of the various ideas of the new school, especially the perfervid worship of art for art's sake. His scorn of "purpose" in fiction carries him to the statement, "the silly idea of Dickens that a novel might be useful . . . would have been the best proof that [Dickens] was a sorry botch, for whom literature was not an art, but an ignoble trade." One surprising point is his praise of George Eliot, "the queen of English fiction," as a "purely impersonal artist." Here too is the aristocratic, exclusive attitude and the scorn of the "ignobile vulgus" (cf. Schücking, *op. cit.*), represented among English novelists, he says, only by Meredith. Flaubert, he concludes, will be the master for all coming novelists ("I mean those worthy of the name and not mere constructors of puerile romances") and "Salammbô will be read by all persons of culture with delight when Scott's 'plaster-of-Paris romances' have become mere lumber." *Westminster Review,* 144:383 (September, 1895).

a more unreal story written" than *The Bride of Lammermoor,*
for instance; and in his superficiality of character study he
reminds one of Dickens, who was "the most artificial and in
many respects the most worthless of all novelists." Scott's insight
did, however, pierce a little deeper than Dickens'. But the Banim
brothers,[9] Carleton, and Lever compare favorably with Scott; and
Sheridan Le Fanu (one notes an Irish loyalty) knew more about
life in bygone days. In short, Scott was shallow and clumsy, his
medievalism was all upholstery, and the twentieth century will
know him by only three or four novels at most. Here is of course
manifest crankiness and whim, though it is significant that the
ideas spring from an admiration of the French novelists, and that
great store is set by Taine.

The most unfavorable criticism of Scott by later British
writers may be found in two books chiefly biographical and both
of them recent: *The Intimate Life of Sir Walter Scott* by Archibald Stalker, 1921, and *Scott and His Circle* by Donald Carswell,
1930. The first depreciates Scott to the limit, both in the chief
events of his life, which Mr. Stalker derives from ignoble
motives, and in the quality of his work. Scott, however, is
damned in good company, for Mr. Stalker finds the classics in
general "dull and heavy," although he is willing to allow Scott
an occasional excellence, and even praises him absurdly on occasion, as when he declares that Scott was the first writer since
Shakespeare to make literature interesting.

Mr. Carswell's book, a brilliant biographical essay on Scott,
with shorter ones on Hogg, Lockhart, and Joanna Baillie, inter-
prets Scott's part in the Ballantyne-Constable collapse in the
least favorable light, and is also vitriolic on Lockhart. At the
end Mr. Carswell dismisses Scott, after speaking of his lack of
reality and his pursuit of incompatibles, as "a professional man
who aspired to be a feudal lord and could not keep his fingers
out of trade; a Jacobite whose devotion to the House of Hanover

[9] A writer on Irish novels in the *Edinburgh Review*, 52:410 (January, 1831),
had referred to the Banim novels as weak imitations of Scott, declaring that his
imitators in general could not follow him easily and naturally, and even imitated
his weaknesses or turned his virtues into defects.

became a byword; an enthusiastic admirer of the material progress of his age who would not accept its social and political
consequences; an Anglophobe in principle who in practice
found England altogether admirable; an historian who knew
everything about history except its meaning [10] . . . His writings
are as bare of ideas as his conversation was." And, he never really
understood anything.

Even Mr. Carswell, however, calls him the "simplest, sincerest,
and greatest of all romantics," and, having satisfied his craving
for brilliant antitheses, finds it expedient to allow Scott a number of gifts that seem remarkable for a second-rater. He ends
with phrases that make one wonder at his earlier bitterness:
"But if he conspicuously lacked the higher intellectual qualities,
he had the endowment most suited to express his genius — an
inexhaustible invention, a formidable memory, a sharp, though
superficial eye for character, a gusto for the human pageant, and
a power of application that enabled him in ten years to produce
more than Dickens produced in twenty. . . . It is enough to
say that in the history of prose fiction there are but two epoch
makers — Cervantes, who did the ancient and beloved art of pure
story-telling to a cruel death, and Walter Scott, who brought it
to a glorious resurrection." But even with the sting thus removed
from its tail, such criticism seems exaggerated and partisan. It
is easy enough again to recognize the facts and situations from
which it springs; it is not so easy to accept its weighing and its
interpretation as sound and inevitable.[11]

[10] Compare R. S. Rait, below, page 326.

[11] Mr. Carswell's book provoked a number of acid reviews, and one little
controversy. It was reviewed in the *Times Literary Supplement* by Professor Grierson, who analyzed it as a piece of special pleading against Scott — twistings,
inferences, and guesses being presented as authentic fact. Mr. Carswell replied
to this, declaring himself a thoroughgoing admirer of Scott, who had been attacked
merely because he would not canonize and adulate sufficiently. To this Mr. Grierson replied maintaining the point of the original review and adding that Mr.
Carswell was merely writing in the biographical style of the day, and that doubtless the impression he gave differed from what he intended or yet realized; that
instead of detachment he seemed to have animus. In a second letter Mr. Carswell
stuck to his position and complained of "heresy hunting." See the *Times Literary
Supplement*, August 28 – September 25, 1930, pp. 681, 716, 735, 758. The *New
Statesman*, 35:420 (July 5, 1930) accused him of being patronizing and conde-

Even more extravagant are the opinions of Mr. Ford Madox Ford,[12] who, writing from motives one can only guess at (*English Novel,* 1929), calmly crowns Marryat as the king of English novelists and allows him for company only Richardson, Smollett, Jane Austen, and Trollope. Fielding he dismisses as contemptible, immoral, and hypocritical, Dickens and Thackeray as powerful, blundering amateurs, and Scott as of no real importance. "Obviously," he says, "even Scott's *Antiquary* is worth consideration if one had the time," that is, if reading and golf fall into the same category. One can "agreeably narcotize himself still with *Rob Roy* or *The Tower of London* or *The Woman in White* or say *Rudder Grange.*" But after all, Mr. Ford thinks, or so he says, that the English in general have written "nuvvles" rather than novels, and have produced little worthy of the serious attention of an adult Frenchman or, for that matter, of the attention of any mature person who has passed his sixteenth birthday.

It is worth noting that none of these hostile critics, except perhaps Mr. Ford or Mr. Hannigan, can escape Scott's importance as an innovator. Even Mr. Carswell becomes as eloquent on this point as he is in detailing the disgraceful anomalies of Sir Walter's character. But it is left for a French critic, M. Abel Chevalley, to show forth most eloquently the grandeur of Sir Walter from this one point of view and to present him in phrases that align him with the greatest. He declares, "Il anoblit le roman en y portant l'éclat des genres jusqu'alors dits nobles. . . . Walter Scott est parmi les auteurs, comme un pair du royaume. Avant lui, rien n'était indigne du roman. Après, il n'est plus rien dont le roman ne soit digne." He gave the novel the grandeur of epic poetry. He was not a psychologist and he had many faults, but he saw the pageant and spectacle of life — what

scending in the current biographical manner in a tone "at once ridiculous and exasperating"; "the man does not live who can afford to treat him [Scott] *de haut en bas.*" The *Nation and Athenaeum,* however, taking account of such reviews, thought these objections due to national prejudices. "To one unaffected by national prejudice it would seem that his portrait is spirited and just." 48:464 (January 3, 1931).

[12] Ford Madox Ford, *The English Novel* (Philadelphia, 1929).

the mass of the people see; this was the secret of his popularity. And under his leadership the novel translated history and replaced poetry.[13] Ordinarily, the argument of great influence in the past and distinction as an innovator means little to a later generation. There is no colder praise. But words like these carry an emotion and feeling far beyond such usual cold deductions of the literary historian.

So vivid a person as W. E. Henley, to judge from the little he wrote about Scott, also seems to have felt warmly toward him, though he speaks of him chiefly as an innovator. In his essay "Byron's World" he celebrates the friendship of Byron and Scott, "those two radiant and distinguished spirits," and in his "Note on Romanticism" praises him as a great leader in the romantic revival, who, while he was "a Great First Cause" of much that was dismal in his imitators, was also "the inspiration of not a little of what is best and most enduring among the results of the Romantic Revolution."[14]

Stevenson is sometimes spoken of as a detractor of Scott, and was for a time himself held up as Scott's superior in romance.[15] As a matter of fact, he was by no means a hostile critic. Standing on the threshold between the Victorian and modern periods, he shows interesting reflections of the new Continental influences. He early developed an admiration for the French. In romance he exalted Hugo at the expense of Scott, declaring that the French romantic "enclosed Scott in Homer." He was so enthusiastic indeed as to draw from Leslie Stephen[16] the remonstrance

[13] Abel Chevalley, *Le Roman anglais de notre temps* (London, 1921). Cf. also Maigron, *op. cit.*

[14] See *The Works of W. E. Henley* (7 vols., London, 1908), IV, VI.

[15] It was, of course, the custom a generation ago at the height of Stevenson's popularity to insist on his superiority to Scott. Yet his biographers and critics in general deplore this fashion as being in the end detrimental to Stevenson's fame. See especially J. A. Hammerton, *Stevensoniana* (rev. ed., Edinburgh, 1910). John A. Steuart, *Robert Louis Stevenson, A Critical Biography* (2 vols., Boston, 1924), II, 256, apropos of a rash statement by R. L. S. that Scott never knew the Highlands, asserts that it was three or four times as true of Stevenson; that Alan Breck himself springs out of *Rob Roy* and Dumas.

[16] *Cornhill*, 30:179 (August, 1874); for Stephen's letter, see *Letters of Robert Louis Stevenson*, edited by Sidney Colvin (4 vols., New York, 1911), I, 155 n.

that after all Hugo lacked conspicuously certain fine qualities to be found in Sir Walter. Stevenson was also a devotee of Flaubert and Daudet, and his meticulous phrasing, his experiments as a "sedulous ape," his devotion to the idea of *le mot juste* are perhaps better remembered now than anything else about his writing. Many times he spoke sharply of Scott's slovenliness and carelessness — the most famous instance doubtless being the allusion to *Guy Mannering* in "A Gossip on Romance."

Yet even in the early eighties he seems to have transferred his allegiance from Flaubert and Daudet (he is said never to have really known the Russians except for *Crime and Punishment*) to Scott and Dumas.[17] As Graham Balfour remarks, the hard things Stevenson says about Scott are always on the technical side. Almost in the same breath he can complain about endless, trailing sentences and break into praise of "the King of the Romantics." He passes from "the slap-dash and the shoddy," which he thought more and more pervasive in the later books, to the striking admission, "Those who avoid (or seek to avoid) Scott's facility are apt to be continually straining and torturing their style to get in more of life. And to many the extra significance does not relieve the strain."[18] And if the shelves of English novels in his library were dominated by James and Meredith, the Waverleys stood close by. Toward the end of his life he could say that three novelists had had the real creator's brush — Scott, Balzac, Thackeray.[19]

Taking all his comments and allusions together, one feels that this attraction to Scott is natural and instinctive, fundamental, and that the fuming about technic comes from an overlay or veneer of French doctrine. Indeed the conflicting strains of natural impulse and training show in his choice among the novels. *Guy Mannering, Rob Roy,* and *The Antiquary* he main-

[17] See Steuart, *op. cit.*, II, 32–33.
[18] See Graham Balfour, *Life of Robert Louis Stevenson* (2 vols., New York, 1901), I, 117 n.; Colvin, *op. cit.*, II, 211 (as also for citation in next paragraph).
[19] See Steuart, *op. cit.*, II, 266, and Colvin, *op. cit.*, IV, 13.

tains are "all . . . worth three *Waverley's.*" Yet he goes on, "I think *Kenilworth* better than *Waverley, Nigel,* too; and *Quentin Durward* about as good. But it shows a true piece of insight to prefer *Waverley,* for it *is* different; and though not quite coherent, better worked in parts than almost any other; surely more carefully."

Stevenson had too a tremendous admiration for Scott himself as he was to be found in Lockhart; indeed, in several letters of 1883–84, when he had just been reading Lockhart, he speaks of the *Life* as an overwhelming book, too heartbreaking to read every day — the novels themselves, he says, were better for that.

The bulk of the hostile criticism is after all very slight, but it is beyond a doubt representative of a great many critics and readers who, taking Scott's mediocrity for granted, are quite indifferent toward him. It may be motivated somewhat by personal whim, and there are traces, as in Brandes and Hannigan, of social theories — the "march of progress" idea — but obviously of the greatest importance is the influence of the new ideas, chiefly French, concerning the art of the novel. By the writers just cited these theories have been used as touchstones to demonstrate Scott's insignificance, and it cannot be denied that in discussion and conversation if not in written criticism Scott must have been frequently tried and summarily condemned on a basis of them, for writers in Scott's favor usually seem to think that they are fighting single-handed against a multitude.[20]

Again and again one comes upon writers who either explicitly or implicitly take account of the later demands upon the novel in matter, style, and method, dismiss them as exaggerated or as a passing phase, and assert Scott's greatness, not to say supremacy, as valiantly as ever. That is, these critics almost always assume that Scott is generally out of favor, but that this is merely a sad commentary on the perverted state of modern taste. In fact, this is very often the point of departure in modern criticism of Scott.

It goes without saying that the more sentimental and personal

[20] Cf. Hugh Walpole on this point, page 283.

criticism of the mid-Victorians lingered on into these later years, though growing gradually less and less noticeable. And this criticism too, as one might expect, shows the influence of the new ideas, either in its militancy or in its tone of regret. Here belongs the *Quarterly* essayist who had so stirred the ire of Mr. Hannigan in the early nineties.[21] He declares that none of the severe attacks leveled at Scott from time to time have affected him in the least. He undertakes to defend absolutely all the novels, even the romances, argues that Scott is a great writer of tragedy, that his treatment of love is beyond attack, couples his name continually with Shakespeare's, and disparages George Eliot for Scott's benefit. He attacks Hazlitt as Scott's arch-enemy, a notion that becomes clear at the end when he discloses a strong Tory and Anglo-Catholic bias; and he declares in a peroration, "As all past attempts to dethrone the Waverley novels from the eminence to which they were raised by popular acclaim have been complete failures, such, we may safely predict, will be the fate of all future efforts."

Swinburne also shows the effect of what seemed to be a growing coolness toward Sir Walter.[22] One expects fierce partisanship from Swinburne, and he is not disappointed. Irritated by the depreciation or neglect of Scott which he felt in the literary atmosphere, Swinburne took occasion to crown Sir Walter with his due meed of praise, and to launch thunderbolts at the disloyal and unfaithful. In referring to the *Journal* he says, "If there is one thing of which a reasonable man might have felt reasonably confident, it is that nothing could heighten the admiration or deepen the affection felt by him for the name and the memory of Sir Walter Scott," and the *Journal* he takes as a final illustration and attestation of a character almost incomparably lovable, admirable, and noble, a gift altogether beyond price. Even the later novels find a determined, possibly a willful supporter in Swinburne, who cries that "no more stupid and beetle-headed falsehood ever crawled into hearing and hardened

[21] See page 264.
[22] In a review of Scott's *Journal. Fortnightly Review*, 55:681 (May 1, 1891).

into tradition than that which condemned his last works to compassionate oblivion or contempt," and insists that only *Castle Dangerous* shows anything like a serious or positive sign of decay. *The Two Drovers* and *The Highland Widow* he says are masterpieces of tragedy in miniature. Then turning to exponents of later schools, he declares pugnaciously, "There will be many Jameses — nay, there will be many Hawthornes, ere such another Scott," and says that while obviously he cannot be equaled to Shakespeare, he, if anyone, might be compared with him as a creator of men and an inventor of circumstance. The critics he dismisses along with the Jameses and the Hawthornes. He says, "The leavings, the scrapings, the parings of his genius and his intelligence would suffice to equip a dozen students or critics of the unproductive sort." He even seems to think that Scott's name itself has been made a handicap to his books, for he professes to believe that it is only because it is Scott's that *Count Robert of Paris* is ignored. A few details in Scott's personal attitude he fails to approve, notably his apology for Byron and what Swinburne thinks a lack of due respect for himself and his work. He concludes *fortissimo,* "While the language in which he wrote endures, while the human nature to which he addressed himself exists, there can be no end of the delight, the thanksgiving and the honour with which men will salute, aloud or in silence, the utterance or the remembrance of his name."

One need not look far for other expressions of the sentimental reverence of early Victorian days, some of them marked by a confession of faith unsurpassed even in the primitive days of the cult. Another reviewer of the *Journal,*[23] for instance, concludes, "His position is alike firm and lofty; it can neither be forfeited nor raised, any more than a dead man or woman who is beatified can cease to be a Saint or attain another dignity." On the same occasion, W. Fraser Rae declares,[24] though not so solemnly, that Scott's novels, which have sold by the million since his death, "delight the school boy who reads them for the story and the intelligent man or woman who reads them for

[23] *Quarterly Review,* 171:386 (1890).　　　[24] *Temple Bar.* See above, page 245.

their graphic pictures of bygone days and of nature and human nature under varied aspects."

The same strain is sung by a reviewer of the *Letters:* "With every new record, this honor of his name, which is our honor and great glory among the nations, continually rises and grows greater. He has not only the noblest character, the warmest heart, the greatest genius, but is the most natural and spontaneous man we know."[25] And, the writer adds, he stands second only to Shakespeare. With this group perhaps belongs an essayist of 1897,[26] who takes as a text A. J. Balfour's assertion that Scott had surpassed all others "in the matter of his inimitable stories," and finally celebrates the "great strain of wildness and fire . . . that electrified into living and moving forms all the massive contents of that great mind." Another member of the right wing with decidedly old-fashioned views is A. H. Millar, who, writing of Scott's *Letters,*[27] has nothing but praise of the highest sort to offer, especially for the edifying story of his life. He often doubts, he says, the use of biography. He doesn't care to read of George Eliot's "strange revolt against the fundamental customs of modern society," believes Carlyle's biography would hardly increase his fame, and wonders who would care to read of Fielding's "wretched record of debauchery" or "the melancholy details of Swift's home circle" or "the prurient incidents in Smollett's career."[28] But it is not so with Scott's life, which will bear searching scrutiny, and furnishes a sharp contrast to practically all the rest.

During the last years of the century one also finds, though much less frequently, those sentimental reveries on Scott which had come so easily to the popular magazine writers of the preceding generation. Quite in their vein are two papers by John Dennis,[29] very late specimens of their sort, conventional and insipid appeals "to young readers" to attract them to Scott's

---

[25] *Blackwood's,* 155:15 (January, 1894).   [26] *Spectator,* 78:762 (May 29, 1897).
[27] *Scottish Review,* 23:225 (April, 1894).
[28] This is what comes of identifying Fielding with Tom Jones and other characters, and Smollett with Roderick Random.
[29] *Good Words,* 31:756, 817 (1890).

character and induce them to read his work by explaining to them how good he was and how much good both he and his books had done. Ancient allegiance and good old distrust of the Gallic break out in a short note of praise of *Quentin Durward*.[30] The writer admits that were it his cue he could find plenty of fault with Scott, but it is rather his desire to show that "the glamor of adventure is over all," and to maintain that though Zola sneers at Scott, there is more pleasure and profit in this one book of Sir Walter's than in all of Zola. Criticism in this tone uttered under distinguished auspices is to be found as late as 1910,[31] in an essay on Scott's friends and critics, where the author, after admitting all the usual complaints about the novels, claims pre-eminence for him on the ground of his great gallery of characters, and especially for his avoidance of the seamy side and the freshness and wholesomeness of his moral tone in depicting them.

Frederic Harrison and Sir Edmund Gosse seem to be the most notable representatives of the older, perfervid Victorian tenderness and veneration surviving in a later era. Harrison [32] speaks of Scott in terms of the utmost awe. "His unique glory is to have definitely succeeded in the ideal reproduction of historic types so as to preserve at once beauty, life, and truth, a task which neither Ariosto nor Tasso, nor Corneille and Racine, nor Alfieri, nor Goethe and Schiller — no! nor even Shakespeare himself entirely achieved." He says, "In Europe as in England, Walter Scott remains as yet the last in the series of the great creative spirits of the human race"; no successor has the "same grand type of mind, or has now a lasting place in the roll of the immortals." From this he proceeds to launch thunderbolts against a younger generation of "juvenile fops" which rejects Scott for literary garbage, and at the end of his chapter bursts forth, "And this glorious and most human, and most historical of poets . . . this manliest and truest and widest of romancers, we neglect for some hothouse

---

[30] *Gentleman's Magazine*, 272:323 (1892).
[31] *Blackwood's*, 187:187 (February, 1910).
[32] Frederic Harrison, *The Choice of Books* (London, 1886).

hybrid of psychological analysis, for the wretched imitators of Balzac, and the jackanapes phrasemongering of some Osric of the day who assures us that Scott is an absolute Philistine."

Nor does Sir Edmund Gosse flag below his somewhat older contemporary. He declares [33] that it is impossible to speak of Scott critically; his novels are "a cherished part of the heritage of the English-speaking race," with all their "noble geniality — perennial freshness — variety — magnificent train of events." Sir Edmund willingly admits flaws in the novels, but challenges the world to produce a purer talent, or a more consistent one, maintaining that only two of the whole series (he neglects to name them, but doubtless the two last) need be wished away. Abroad, he admits, Sir Walter has been defeated by Balzac, "but on British soil there is as yet no sign of any diminution of his honor or popularity," and in reply to the foreign critics who fail to understand a loyalty to a writer whose art is in some ways obsolete, he explains that it is Sir Walter's fineness of spirit, "the character of an English gentleman," that keeps him going.

All this, however, is in the tone of the passing generation; twentieth-century partisans of Scott may be and are equally loyal, but in their expression of affection they are certainly more restrained. It is not often in these later years that one comes upon such expressions of sentiment as those of F. M. Romanes,[34] who, in disposing most contemptuously of Stalker's *Life,* speaks of Scott as a writer who inspires real affection much more than admiration, and says, "We love him, we could not do without him." Highly personal and affectionate, and still in the mid-Victorian moral atmosphere, H. D. Sedgwick [35] would make Scott the prophet of "honor, loyalty, truth," a great civilizing force, surer and more permanent in literature as a power for good than the preachers like Carlyle, ranking indeed among the greatest moral prophets in literature.

[33] Richard Garnett and Edmund Gosse, *English Literature* (4 vols., New York, 1903), Vol. IV, *From Johnson to Tennyson.*

[34] *Dublin Review,* 169:237 (October, 1921).

[35] *Atlantic Monthly,* 90:755 (December, 1902). Reprinted in *Essays on Great Writers* (Boston, 1903). Cf. below, page 298.

But the latest and perhaps the most Victorian of all such recent criticisms of Scott is one written by George Maclean Harper in 1932,[36] which has the authentic ring of earlier generations, and except for latter-day allusions might be much more probably dated 1860 or 1870. Professor Harper exalts Scott for his sunny spirit and his happiness: "his books [are] like glorious summer days: there may be clouds and rain, but sunshine and warmth and color and the songs of birds prevail." He does not, like Galsworthy, Dreiser, and Bennett, worship the Muse of Dreariness. Millions have received not only pleasure but noble impulses from his books. In teaching the art of gentility he is almost the equal of Thackeray (Mr. Harper is one of those who would make *Henry Esmond* the greatest of all novels) and while not the peer of Shakespeare belongs at the head of the novelists, where his closest companions would be Thackeray and Dickens and perhaps Hardy. Here indeed is the old sentiment, naked and unashamed.[37]

[36] *Quarterly Review*, 259:344 (October, 1932).

[37] A surprising and rather significant book, considering its origin and time, is C. A. Young, *The Waverley Novels, An Appreciation* (Glasgow, 1907). It was written for honors at Oxford in 1901, when the author was only twenty-one years old. He was Scotch, educated at Stirling and the University of Glasgow, and had taken walking tours through the Scott country. He is accordingly deeply patriotic. His criticism is "orthodox" in the manner of the thorough Scott partisan; he praises for the usual excellences and admits the usual defects. Yet there is very little of the Victorian sentimental vein in him. He is full of information from the letters and journal and from the novels themselves, his criticism and analysis are solid, and he does full justice to Scott's realism, while at the same time undertaking a defense of the historical novel as a type and of Scott's more historical romances. His work would really make an excellent handbook on the novels, and while not deeply original in its main ideas, is fresher and more original than much that has been written by mature writers. It is certainly a brilliant performance for a boy of twenty-one. One of the most significant points about it is that so brilliant and apparently well-read a person should show no influence of the new fiction, in which his only notable reference is to Meredith. His critical reading on Scott is worth noting, too; he alludes especially to Carlyle, Leslie Stephen, Bagehot, Taine, Hutton, and C. H. Herford (*The Age of Wordsworth*). Occasionally one strikes a badly chosen illustration (the worst is a defense of Bois Guilbert as a great tragic figure and of his death as a grand tragic and moral climax) and the conclusion has more emphasis on morality than he would give it today. But the book shows the appeal that Scott might make as late as 1900 to a brilliant, distinguished young man, an appeal not based on mere sentiment or patriotism.

Such criticism as this, chiefly on an emotional and sentimental basis, represents the survival of an original but long-enduring worship of Scott to which the extreme reaction is represented by those adverse critics lately described. Allied with it is the criticism of Catholic writers. Obviously the scientific and moral points of view in the later novel are repellent to them and drive them straight back to older writers and especially to Scott. Earlier Catholics had regarded Sir Walter with mixed emotions. As a medievalist and a conservative he was on their side; his romance cultivated the ideals they cherished. Yet he was himself a thoroughgoing Protestant, and had been, they thought, both ignorant and unsympathetic when he had brought Catholicism into his novels. The first of these feelings was, however, the stronger, and it is the one that survives among their successors, supported especially by Newman's affection for Scott and his novels. One writer in the Catholic magazine *The Month* [38] even goes so far as to limit Scott's anti-Catholic prejudice to a general feeling against "enthusiasm" in religion, and to insist, in his final climax, that "if the British public has slowly awakened to the fact that every monk is not necessarily a lazy hypocrite, nor every Catholic layman a Jesuit in disguise, the change is, in no small degree, owing to the influence of Walter Scott."

The two most notable Catholic spokesmen for Scott in these latter days seem to have been H. F. Walton and W. H. Kent.[39] These two take more or less the same stand. Mr. Walton speaks of the current contempt of Scott "by the foolish few carried away by the taste for subtlety engendered by much study of the psychological novel and . . . by the knack of belittling genius," and declares that in spite of "the Protestantism and the spirit of his age which must in any case have chained him to earth," his novels must appeal to Catholic readers especially for "their absolute freedom from everything foul and debasing, their sane

[38] T. E. Ranken, "Sir Walter Scott and Medieval Catholicism," *The Month*, 101:146 (February, 1903).
[39] *The Month*, 92:457, 568 (1898); the *Catholic World*, 100:155 (November, 1914).

and wholesome purity of thought and tone." Scott, Mr. Walton says, lights on fundamental virtues, like fidelity. He knew the seamy side of life but unlike the modern novelist did not emphasize it, and so is accused of limitations. Yet the pure in heart shall see God, which is after all the *summum bonum*. Mr. Walton dismisses "the sounding brass" of Carlyle and the "tinkling cymbal" of Leslie Stephen, and with them Ruskin, who really failed in understanding when he depreciated the medieval novels, which especially show Scott's interest in the Catholic. Scott would have been a Catholic, and a fine one, but for his environment; all his instincts and aspirations prove it. As it was, he forged the first link in the chain that has led to the Catholic revival in England; "the influence of the Waverley Novels marks the turn of that tide which since his day has borne so many to the foot of the Fisherman's Throne." Yet Scott himself in his Protestantism was as "an infant crying in the night, with no language but a cry" or as one "unconsciously, inarticulately craving the shadow of a great rock in a weary land."

Father Kent also conceives of Scott as a great though unconscious collaborator with Newman. Newman, he says, declared that the novels, set over against the eighteenth century, were "almost as oracles of Truth confronting the ministers of error and sin," and he thinks that Newman's prayers for Scott were answered in the conversion of his descendants to Catholicism. He brings in the militantly Protestant Borrow also, to prove Scott's essential Catholicism, citing the well-known allusions in *Lavengro* and *The Romany Rye,* as well as Borrow's comment on Newman's first sermon in the Oxford movement, "Why, the simpleton had been pilfering from Walter Scott's novels." Father Kent also cites Thomas Arnold's [40] contention that Scott, Johnson, and Burke had been the three great bulwarks against the new destructive, revolutionary spirit, and maintains, like Mr. Walton, that Scott, though never a propagandist, naturally and unobtrusively exerted a fine moral influence; he has "the

[40] The (at times) Catholic brother of Matthew Arnold. He wrote a belated review of Lockhart in the *Rambler,* May, 1860, largely as a reply to Carlyle.

beauty of fair thoughts and noble ideals and harmony with everlasting law." Thus, for the enlightened, he merits a higher place than the modern literature which "a mere sensuous criticism would set above him."[41]

The consciousness of a hostile or at least indifferent atmosphere pervades even the most significant and thoughtful, well-balanced comment on Scott during the last few decades — the criticism lying between the two extremes of depreciation and affectionate eulogy. It is practically all of it more or less argumentative in tone, starting as it does from the assumption already noted that the reading public no longer appreciates his greatness. Sometimes this is more or less tacit; in other cases it shows itself in an almost fierce resentment. It is distinctly laudatory, and its desire is clearly to restore Scott to his earlier dominant position. There can be no doubt that the consensus of the best present-day discussion recalls the tone of Jeffrey and the early enthusiasts. There is, however, a difference. These later friends of Scott admit as obvious the charges that were first preferred against him in his own day and were emphasized and developed by Victorian critics, but sweeping them aside dismiss them as insignificant and easily to be forgiven, taking it for granted that the intelligent reader is not to be kept by such things from a recognition of great, even the greatest, art. The defensive or protective, apologetic attitude of these later champions of Scott, so surprisingly pervasive, comes, as has been said, from a feeling in the air rather than from a bulk of positive and aggressive criticism on the other side.

The usual modern essay or discussion of Scott follows more or less closely a regular pattern. It either asserts that he is read as much as ever or that he is grievously neglected. It lists the

<hr />

[41] Two other Catholic articles in the *Dublin Review*, 108:72, 109:333 (January and October, 1891), may be cited, one by Thomas Canning on "Catholicism in the Waverley Novels," and the other a review of Scott's journal. The first lists a series of anachronisms and other errors of which Scott is guilty in dealing with things Catholic, yet claims him as essentially Catholic in spirit and a potent force in breaking down anti-Catholic prejudice. The second also emphasizes the pro-Catholic values of Scott's medievalism and romanticism in general, and sees a dispensation of Providence in the present Catholic ownership of Abbotsford.

stock charges against him in regard to his style and construction, his lack of depth and idea, his failure in characterization, and either minimizes or denies them. And finally it arraigns modern taste, warning readers or novelists, or both, to beware lest their ears be stuffed with their own wisdom. With variety in order and illustration, this is the procedure of the modern critic of Scott. A few instances from the many possible ones may be chosen to serve at this point.

Francis H. Stoddard, who published a textbook on the novel in 1900,[42] admits that it is the fashion of the present day to make light of Walter Scott's claims to genius and quotes "a recent critic" to the effect that Scott wrote for a duller and slower-witted generation,[43] and while great as compared with previous novelists and still good to amuse the young, suffered from a multitude of faults both of mind and technic, almost the worst of which were his false aristocratic ideals and old Tory prejudices of caste. But Stoddard declares, "A sad day will it be when the fiery spirit and the poetic romance of *Waverley, Kenilworth, Quentin Durward, Ivanhoe* and *Guy Mannering* fail to find an answer in our spirits and emotions." Stoddard is unlike most modern critics, however, in his interest in the more purely romantic and historic side of Scott, which he thinks is closer to fact than his theory would indicate. He seems chiefly concerned to defend Sir Walter's methods in dealing with history, ignoring his more realistic Scotch novels.

Even more representative is Wilfrid Ward, writing in the *Dublin Review* (1914) on the centenary of *Waverley*.[44] Mr. Ward is of those who believe that the novels are now little read. "The critics find fault," he says; they think Scott tedious and long-winded, "wanting in finish and subtlety of conception, of delineation and of analysis." There is no use, he admits, in denying the value of modern technic; but the modern age is unhealthily cramped by its critical faculty and its over-

[42] Francis H. Stoddard, *The Evolution of the English Novel* (New York, 1900).
[43] The irony of such a statement as this will be appreciated by any one who has read Q. D. Leavis, *Fiction and the Reading Public.*
[44] *Dublin Review*, 155:281 (October, 1914).

sophistication, is too much interested in detail to appreciate the broad, sweeping, healthy, vigorous pictures of Scott. It is really, he thinks, a "loss of youth and health" that dims modern eyes to Scott's greatness. The clever modern writer may be much smaller than Scott, with his greatness of original conception. "The jaded palate of our generation is too fastidious to enjoy Scott's simple great pictures" — a feeling that Mr. Ward shares with Chesterton.[45] Moreover, Scott is eloquent, and to modern taste eloquence seems vulgar. Like many other modern writers, Mr. Ward goes back to Carlyle to declare that the latter failed to understand the deep essential loyalties of Scott's nature, or to appreciate his dramatic, not didactic, presentation of them in the novels. Thus Mr. Ward's essay is typical; it is chiefly argument in rebuttal, with Carlyle and the devotees of modern technic treated as Scott's chief enemies.

Other essays in this tone and following this method may be cited. Mr. C. L. Moore begins an essay on Scott, "The Jupiter of Novelists,"[46] by denying the usual charges, especially externality and lack of profundity, which he says are at once disproved by a reading of the novels, and goes on to declare that despite haste and slips, hundreds of passages reveal a power unequaled by modern realists, that even his "failures" are enough to make a "tolerably first-rate reputation," and that all his successors must yield to him in "novelty, variety, vitality and energizing power."

Charges that there are beams in modern eyes, that the age is critical rather than creative, and therefore narrow and short-sighted, abound. Canon Ainger makes the point in his lecture on Scott (1898) especially in regard to the modern obsession with style, and he implies much about modern taste when he declares that Scott wrote for multitudes and not for a clique, and hence need not perish with a clique. Lord Ernle thinks that Scott, like the great Victorians, who after all wrote in more or less the same tradition, and like him were under the domination

[45] Mr. Ward's criticism has here no especially Catholic tinge, but of course he was well known as a Catholic oracle.

[46] *Dial*, 56:329 (April 16, 1914).

of conventional morality and propriety, is neglected today because of the careful art and technic of the novel, the cult of *le mot précis,* and so forth. Mr. Vernon Rendall carries the war into the enemy's camp in an aggressive defense of Scott. Like Lord Ernle he says that Scott was not really very old-fashioned until the end of the century. The complaint of tedium he asserts comes from an age "which has taken to itself brevity and smartness and might own Mr. Jingle as its model, supported by a row of ineffable asterisks." Moreover, he adds, talk in the modern novel is not necessarily better than old-fashioned narrative; and the later novelists too have their peculiar undesirable qualities.[47]

Professor W. P. Trent opens a critical analysis of *The Heart of Midlothian* with a protest against the contempt of Scott which he labels "conventional" — the habit of speaking of Scott as good for boys, and the naive belief that he has been surpassed by Stevenson. Another of Scott's professorial defenders, and one of his staunchest and most effective, Oliver Elton, in asserting Scott's pre-eminence even when contrasted with the best of his modern successors, Hardy and Meredith, makes the point that the older critics, who lack the modern point of view, after all come the closest to Scott; the typical modernist is too much obsessed with "style," "the phrase," and "philosophy."[48]

To such witnesses may be added also a number of modern novelists who seem anxious to strike a good blow for Sir Walter. Some of these, like Virginia Woolf, have themselves gone in strongly for the most modern of methods, but, except for Mr. Ford, always *sui generis,* they seem to doubt the finality of the modern ideas. Mrs. Woolf, who has written what is possibly the most brilliant tribute to Scott in recent years,[49] bothers little to attack the moderns, though she lightly dismisses the charges

[47] See as follows: Alfred Ainger's essay on Scott (1898) in *Lectures and Essays* (2 vols., London, 1905); Rowland E. Prothero, Lord Ernle, *The Light Reading of our Ancestors* (London, 1927); Vernon Rendall, "Scott and the Waverley Novels," *Nineteenth Century,* 96:531 (October, 1924).

[48] W. P. Trent, *Sewanee Review,* 17:153 (April, 1909); Oliver Elton, *Survey of English Literature, 1780–1830* (2 vols., London, 1912).

[49] Virginia Woolf, *op. cit.*

against his style and holds up beside him Stevenson, who she says is a cleverer phrase-maker but an infinitely smaller artist. Maurice Hewlett, himself a romanticist, one might expect to be sympathetic, as indeed he is. Stirred by the jeers of Mark Twain and also by disparaging remarks on Scott's style by George Moore (who in *The Confessions of a Young Man* praised Scott's gusto with gusto, but later called him "pompous and garrulous"), Hewlett[50] declares that other great novelists, even Fielding, are also vulnerable to attacks of this sort, and that such critics fail to see the greatness of the material under the convention and artificiality of style (a point of view earlier expressed by Canon Ainger). Scott, he says, can be Homeric, and, like Homer, may be allowed to nod.

Hugh Walpole[51] expatiates on the low estate to which Scott has fallen. He remarks on the contempt expressed by a prominent English author unnamed, and implies that Scott is less regarded than any of the other classic novelists — even such minors as Galt, Susan Ferrier, and Wilkie Collins attract more interest, he thinks.[52] "Scott alone of all past British novelists seemed to have no defender, no champion even born of an irritated opposition" — notions that give point and emphasis to Mr. Walpole's defense but that after all are hardly tenable. Mr. Walpole proceeds to sarcasm on modern sophistication about "art," and to praise of Scott for his breadth and variety, his "gift of world creation," which he says is "especially valuable now when the English novel is tending to be either too clever to be true or too stupid to be tolerated." "Perhaps we know too much; Scott maybe knew too little, about art, I mean, and the way that novels ought to be written, and how to leave out all the verbs and yet make your prose intelligible; or how, still better, to leave out almost everything and so make your prose unintelligible. He had not read so many books about theories, but

[50] "Mark on Sir Walter," *Sewanee Review*, 29:130 (April, 1921). For George Moore's later attitude see *Avowals*, Chapter I.

[51] In "A Note on Sir Walter," *Nation and Athenaeum*, 35:201 (May 17, 1924).

[52] It is easily demonstrable that Scott is discussed infinitely more than Galt, Miss Ferrier, or Collins. And if he has few readers, they have still fewer.

he knew facts and he loved life, and that same love blows creatively through every page that he wrote."

In the issue of the following week, this essay drew lively applause from a vivacious "Septuagenarian" who at the same time pointed out most pertinently that classic novels like Scott's, or any others for that matter, cannot compete with contemporary productions at any time. But how will it be in 1974, he asks. Contemporary novels fade and die. Some of Scott's too are dead, but his best are apt to overtake and pass contemporary novels in time, even in their own time. And another popular novelist has insisted [53] that to deny Scott's genius in fiction is only to condemn oneself as holding some hopelessly narrow view of the art.

The refusal to accept the modern idea of the novel as ultimate was voiced as early as 1903 by as important a realist as George Gissing. In *The Private Papers of Henry Ryecroft*,[54] considering the current obsession with technic in art, he reiterates "the venerable truth that an artist is born and not made" which he thinks will bear repeating "in times which have heard disdainful criticism of Scott on the ground that he had no artistic conscience, that he scribbled without a thought of style, that he never elaborated his scheme before beginning — as Flaubert, of course you know, invariably did." He mentions Shakespeare, Cervantes, and Thackeray as other "sinners against art" who were "none the less among the world's supreme artists, for they lived, in a sense, in a degree, unintelligible to these critics of theirs, and their work is an expression, satisfying and abiding, of the zest of life."

Chesterton's brilliant essay, "The Position of Sir Walter Scott,"[55] is also written with modern prejudices in mind; in fact, the essay is really an attack upon them. Chesterton contends that romance, held in contempt at present, is really not a matter of material but rather "a state of the soul." The length of the novels, their leisurely movement, Scott's fondness for "trap-

---

[53] J. B. Priestley, *The English Novel* (London, 1927).

[54] See "Spring," Section XX.

[55] G. K. Chesterton, *Varied Types* (London, 1903), republished as *Twelve Types* (London, 1906).

pings," all these points Chesterton turns into virtues and uses to glorify Scott and to depreciate modern taste. But above all he praises Scott's love of eloquence, which has been lost in the modern analytical and self-conscious novel; "that ancient sea of human passion upon which high words and great phrases are the resplendent foam is just now at a low ebb." Henry James, for instance, is "concerned with that delicate and fascinating speech which burrows deeper and deeper like a mole; but we have wholly forgotten that speech which mounts higher and higher like a wave and falls in a crashing peroration."[56] But the arraignment is strongest at the end. Chesterton, mindful of the *fin de siècle*, says Scott "stands for the great mass of natural manliness which must be absorbed into art unless art is to be a mere luxury and freak," and even asserts that an appreciation of Scott might almost be used as a test of decadence.

The views of William Dean Howells on Scott, expressed at about this same time,[57] are perhaps worth quoting rather fully. Howells was the leading American exponent of a realism which, though now distinctly worn and faded, was certainly attractive to the upper levels of the reading public. In spite of his "modern" realistic leanings, which appear clearly enough in his judgments, and his citation of Tolstoi and Turgeniev to prove Sir Walter's relative unimportance, it cannot be said that Scott fares very badly at his hands. Yet his tone differs from that of the critics just cited. They admit few regrets for Sir Walter's lack of the modern novelist's virtues; Mr. Howells on the other hand is sad to think what the Waverley novels might have been, had their author had the advantage of modern example. The chief points of his criticism are familiar enough. He thinks that the Scotch stories had a reality that disappeared in the later romances, though these show a developing sense of form. The Scotch stories, too, are still enjoyable for adult readers; the others are

[56] In the matter of eloquence, Chesterton is arguing from the ground which other, and the most effective, modern champions of Scott have considered his real stronghold. Compare the arguments of Verrall, Buchan, Cecil, and others.

[57] In a series of articles on heroines in nineteenth-century fiction in *Harper's Bazaar*, 33:775 and 903 (July 28 and August 11, 1900).

only for young boys. The characters in the romances are all of them types, he thinks — Ivanhoe, Rowena, and even the favorite Rebecca, whom he quotes to prove that she is quite capable on occasion of talking like an elderly novelist. He likes *The Bride of Lammermoor* and Lucy Ashton — after Jeanie Deans, however — judging her a really tragic character. He quotes the scene where Ravenswood gets back his love token. "In spite of the slovenly construction, the repetitions, the touches of melodrama, the whole want of artistic delicacy and precision, the spirit of an immensely affecting tragedy is here present. Lucy's part . . . could not be the work of less than a master." Mr. Howells finds her, however, his only lady with reality. Scott is more at home with his lower-class types. For *The Heart of Midlothian* he keeps his highest praise. Rather strangely he finds Effie Deans real and consistent to the end, and in the case of Jeanie he points out little touches in the famous scenes of the trial and with the Queen that give reality. Of the trial scene he says (like Brandes) [58] that it succeeds despite "the loose, inaccurate and ineffectual languaging"; it is great because of greatness of conception. He expresses very explicitly his dissatisfaction with Scott's style; "in the prose of his novels he was shapeless, heavy, tautological, infirm, wandering, melodramatic and over-literary," and he grieves to think what Tolstoi or Turgeniev might have done with the trial scene.[59] The fault, on the other hand, was of the age, which was itself over-literary, though Mr. Howells thinks Scott helped to make it more so. At the end he emphasizes Scott's genius by a comparison with Cooper, who he says lacked "that depth of humanity which one always feels under Scott's turbid surfaces . . . the sweet play of his humor, the sudden flashes of his inspiration." Despite the implications of his Russian allusions, Mr. Howells does very well by Sir Walter.

[58] See page 260.

[59] J. W. Beach (*op. cit.*, pp. 16–18) says of the trial scenes, "This is the stuff of drama; emotional stuff of the highest power; and these scenes can hardly be read even by a fastidious reader brought up on Conrad or Stevenson without some sense of their force." But Scott should have let the story tell itself. He uses too many "elegantly patronizing terms of conventional pity"—guideposts for suitable emotion in the reader.

CHAPTER III

STYLE, PHILOSOPHY, AND CHARACTER

THE UNDERLYING influence of modern "artistic" theory in all this criticism is easy enough to see, whether it leads to a point of view like that of Howells or that of Wilfrid Ward or Hugh Walpole. All modern conceptions of the novel are so strongly colored by the theory and practice of the last two generations that any other point of departure is almost impossible. The result is, to repeat what has already been said, that practically all this later writing on Scott is directly argumentative. The charges against him are retried and he is partially or wholly absolved from blame on the score of his style, his philosophy, his delineation of character, and even his treatment of history, points that now as always are brought up against him. But the treatment of historical fact means little to most modern critics, since it is of slight moment in the Scotch novels, which nowadays to nine out of ten readers mean Scott.

Actually the debatable ground is usually divided between two points, style and philosophy, the latter comprehending not only underlying idea and moral and spiritual significance, but also inevitably the treatment of character, for it is only through his characters that Scott's fundamental ideas, his "essential loyalties," are expressed. Philosophy (or at least a "message") and style, the two have been in great demand in the novel — the first in one way or another for a century and the second for fifty years — and Scott's modern defenders try to justify their hero and qualify him for modern acceptance by demonstrating that he is a philosopher and also a stylist, at least when he cares to be or is especially inspired. There is practically always the assumption, doubtless justified, that Scott is in need of a kind of reinstatment, which will be granted him only if he can be shown to write well and to be freighted with significant ideas.

A few defenders of Scott brush the matter of style aside with a wave of the hand, saying that it is irrelevant and does not matter, but the more general procedure is to admit what always was admitted, namely, that there are *longueurs* in Scott, dull stretches and careless prolixity, at the same time insisting that he is capable of rising to a high, even the highest, plane when a great moment arrives. The first point of view is taken by Canon Ainger, who says that Scott's ordinary style is hardly to be defended, that he really had none, writing too much and too fast, but that after all the individual back of the style is much more important; you can shatter Scott's style, but the individuality and charm behind it still remain. He must be taken as a whole.

Professor Woodberry takes somewhat the same line. He says that with Scott the virtues of mere craft count for little. His construction is loose, his composition rapid and careless; yet there is in him the sheer power of genius, with its inevitable and brilliant mastery of the situation. Is not this the point of Virginia Woolf's dictum that he wrote in pages, not sentences, but had style at his command? She says too that Stevenson, while better at phrases, is no match for Scott in total impression and compares a great storm in Scott with one in Stevenson which she says would not wet through the soles of a lady's slippers. Even Stevenson himself, in "A Gossip on Romance," irritated as he is by Scott's sentences, is thoroughly appreciative of the essential genius underlying romantic conceptions for which the phrases seem an unworthy vehicle, and calls him "the King of the Romantics." So too Paul Elmer More, who dismisses Scott's "slovenliness" by saying that we are used to it in fiction and need not mind it; Professor Seccombe, who declares the criticism of his style and construction mere irrelevancy obscuring the greatness of his genius, and Professor W. P. Trent, who says that a failure in style may be admitted, but thinks it altogether a secondary matter; there are many slips a college freshman could correct, but without improvement. And A. A. Jack, remarking, "But Scott [unlike all other novelists] has no manner; he opens his eyes and jots down quietly everything he sees," seems to find a transparent impersonality which makes style unimportant.[1]

Many critics, however, are unwilling to let it go at this, but prefer to undertake a positive defense of Sir Walter as a stylist. And many who do not discuss the point as such really argue for it when they defend his presentation of character, especially in dialogue; in proving his greatness as a delineator of character, they demonstrate likewise his genius with words and phrases.

Beyond a doubt the most striking defense of Scott's style is in a fine essay of A. W. Verrall.[2] Like most critics, Mr. Verrall admits a flatness and prolixity in ordinary passages. Moreover, he will not answer for the false language of the "romances." He insists, however, that in the Scotch novels the flatness of Scott's ordinary style merely fills gaps between climaxes where the writing is perfect. With a French minuteness of detail, he analyzes phrase by phrase certain chosen passages to demonstrate Scott's infinitely subtle tact in phrasing and his power of reproducing in dialogue the characteristics of the speaker. He finally arrives at the conclusion that "Scott, in his way and at his hours, is a very great stylist, supreme and hardly to be surpassed," though his manner of working and his profusion give room for faults and the misrepresentation of his genius in this respect. Mr. Verrall's method of minute analysis is effective; to the careful and open-minded reader it must be impressive. A writer who can when inspired write as Mr. Verrall shows that Scott writes, cannot be dismissed as pedestrian.

To Mr. Verrall's analysis may be appended another unusual and subtle method of attack developed by Ernest Weekley, the philologist.[3] Mr. Weekley, after scornful allusion to the current

[1] For references in this paragraph, see as follows: A. Ainger, op. cit.; G. E. Woodberry, op. cit.; P. E. More, cf. below, page 324; T. E. Seccombe, cf. below, page 299; W. P. Trent, op. cit.; A. A. Jack, Essays on the Novel (London, 1897), p. 73.

[2] Quarterly, 213:33 (July, 1910).   [3] Atlantic, 148:595 (November, 1931).

depreciation of Scott, demonstrates the fact that after Shakespeare Scott has probably contributed more words and phrases to the English vocabulary than anyone else, and that in addition he has re-established many words from Shakespeare in common usage, and has established new meanings or shades of meaning for old words. It would be difficult to explain how a merely dry or slovenly writer, a man with little or no distinction of style, could have such an effect upon the language in which he wrote.

Another critic willing to meet squarely the current objections to Scott's style is Mr. Oliver Elton,[4] who believes with Scott's contemporary, Adolphus, that the style of the novels, though diffuse (a fact he believes needlessly over-emphasized), is lucid, clear, and effortless, notes the epical and dramatic effects it gets in historical passages, the excellence of the special style he developed for kings and queens, and points out as an excellent example how the writing in *The Heart of Midlothian,* as soon as Scott gets his bearings and becomes concrete, "ceases to lumber and becomes easy, classical and strong." He accounts for certain qualities irritating to modern readers by the requirements of gentility in the age; Scott's instincts as a gentleman often prevented him from speaking out, and, too, he was required to be stiff and formal in the conversation and the love-making of the upper classes. There is no doubt that this is true.[5] Mr. Oscar Firkins has illustrated it better than anyone else in showing how there lay upon Jane Austen at this same time the cold hand of the eighteenth-century tradition that heroes and heroines were to furnish their readers models of deportment and conversation.[6]

But the critics have never spent much time on any of the young ladies and gentlemen and latterly that little has been

[4] *Op. cit.* Cf. A. A. Jack, on the preceding page.

[5] Alan D. McKillop (*op. cit.*) has a defense of Scott's style similar to that of this last group of critics. After declaring that Scott's carelessness is exaggerated for the modern reader by the clevernesses of the short story writers, who he says will never be able to impose their methods on the main stream of the novel, he analyzes Scott's style into various levels ranging from "elephantine . . . late eighteenth century prose" to the pure Scottish vernacular, where of course Scott's dignity and power come out fully. He traces the rise and fall of these various shades of style through *Waverley.*

[6] In Oscar W. Firkins, *Jane Austen* (New York, 1920).

devoted rather to apology and explanation than to positive defense or praise. Like the romantic novels themselves, the heroes and heroines have been almost forgotten in the praise of the realism of the Scotch novels. The usual explanation of the flatness of the heroes and heroines is Scott's lack of interest in love; he was interested in the historical or national material he was exploiting, and added his love stories to give it coherence. This is the line taken by Mr. Seccombe, who excuses the heroes and heroines on the ground that the novels are not primarily love stories, although he considers many of these characters good, and even believes the insipidity of the heroes to be intentional and deliberate. A. A. Jack argues in much the same way. In defense of the historic novel on the ground of its almost insuperable difficulties, he asserts that there is after all much to be said for the heroines, but his defense actually retreats into apology. Scott, he says, found plenty of pink-and-white girls in real life, put them in his books, and then paid little attention to them, leaving them to become mere details in the broad landscape.[7] As has already been said, Scott's manners and traditions prevented him from dealing freely with ladies; the innermost thoughts, instincts, and feelings of a lady were things no gentleman could intrude on. While this is quite possible — in fact, Charles Reade and Thackeray make a specific point of it in their novels a generation later — one cannot help feeling that the first and more obvious reason was really at the bottom of Scott's treatment of these figures. He was interested in other things, and drew his heroes and heroines according to easy formulas of long standing, of such long standing indeed that it was only too easy to be casual and perfunctory with them.

Like Verrall and Mr. Elton, whose remarks on Scott he admires greatly, Mr. John Buchan, who rose to a gallant defense of Sir Walter against all comers in 1924,[8] is not satisfied with so

---

[7] Compare Harriet Martineau's strange argument (page 106) that this itself was a great service to women, since it called attention to their insignificance and unimportance in modern life.

[8] See "Some Notes on Sir Walter Scott," The English Association, Pamphlet No. 58, enlarged and reworked as Chapter 13 of his *Sir Walter Scott* (London, 1932).

easy an attitude as Professor Trent's. He recalls Scott's own admission about his "hurried frankness of composition" and parries the various charges in regard to style, especially the one of his polite, literary banality, with the declaration that other distinguished writers have been similarly guilty — Hardy, for instance, with his stiff, pedantic phrases. Moreover, arguing in Verrall's fashion, he says of Scott that at his best "he attains to a style as perfect and unforgettable as Shakespeare's, and it is most subtly compounded."

As for general construction Mr. Buchan's argument is much the same. While an excellent plan can be claimed only for *Old Mortality* and *The Bride of Lammermoor,* usually the main theme is well managed, though there may be confusing secondary ones. And also "The great dramatic moment arrives and Scott rises to it with the ease and certainty of genius." Mr. Buchan quotes Scott's own defense that the removal of the "padding" would spoil the effect of the good parts, and draws various interesting analogies. One should not expect a fruit tree to bear all fruit and no leaves; in many paintings a prosaic object, a *punctum indifferens,* is valuable for its contrast; and "pedestrian salt" is necessary to give proper flavor to romance. In the reworking of his paper, Mr. Buchan even challenges comparisons with Tolstoi and Dostoevski. They throw into their books, he says, great masses of data, adopting a scientific rather than an artistic point of view, whereas Scott "presents the manifold of experience winnowed and sifted and free of inessentials."

As far as Mr. Buchan's complaint that all writers have their bad moments is concerned, one can grant that easily enough, but is it not drawing a red herring across the trail? As Mr. Buchan says, "Dickens has appalling lapses of style; so has Thackeray, so has George Meredith," and he adds as a climax that Mr. Hardy has too. But the point is that, granting the obvious truth of such statements, faults of style have never made the trouble for these writers that they have for Scott; none of them has been so continuously dinned at upon this score as has Scott. Hardy's pedantic phrases of course irritate the cultivated reader as Scott's high-flown clichés do, but they do not have the same effect on him as Scott's page upon page of padding, or even, on occasion, chapter after chapter, before he saw clearly what course he was to send his story on. And it may be remembered too, apropos of Professor Elton's counterthrust about modern artistic style, that while it is justified no doubt, Jeffrey and his colleagues a century ago, who had not suffered from the theories of Flaubert and other modern stylists, were apt to chafe at Sir Walter's style even in the midst of their panegyric, and to wish that he would write more carefully and read over at least once what he had written.[9]

Lord David Cecil, another valiant defender of Scott, in an elaborate and very carefully considered centenary essay [10] does anything but apologize for Scott's style. Scott he insists writes on a grand scale and triumphs over his faults. He gets great effects from poor material, and without trickery or cleverness; and as for pictorial power Hardy is his only rival. Though not a stylist — he would never be studied for his style — when he dramatizes the lower classes he is magnificent, perfectly natural, yet as expressive as poetry, whereas other ventures into the same field, Synge's for instance, lose their reality when they rise to poetic levels. Lord David notes especially "tirades of tragic eloquence" like Meg Merrilies' (Verrall's specimen) and the great force of the Biblical language in *Old Mortality* and *The Heart of Midlothian,* as well as little fleeting touches of eloquence in a phrase or line. It is here, he says, that Scott's genius appears in its most concentrated form; the realistic novelists express such

[9] Hugh Walpole notes that proof was corrected, if manuscript was not. See the *Times Literary Supplement,* June 22, 1922, p. 413.

[10] See "Walter Scott," *Atlantic Monthly,* 150:277, 485 (September and October, 1932), published also in book form as *Sir Walter Scott* (London, 1933). In the introduction to *Short Stories by Sir Walter Scott* (World's Classics Series, London, 1934), Lord David emphasizes especially the contrast between Scott's strength as a creator and his weakness as a craftsman. He declares him a master of character, incident and setting, of the comic and the pathetic. "No other English novelist is both so variously and so powerfully gifted," and, in the matter of style, his "power of realistic eloquence is his supreme title to fame." There is, he says, nothing like it elsewhere in English fiction; the only parallels are in the plays of Shakespeare.

moments of tragic emotion in a word or two; the art of the tragic poet is beyond their daring.

However seriously his defenders may take imputations against his style and construction, they rate as much more serious those against his depth, his ideas, his philosophy, and, associated with these, his handling of character. The charges of bad writing go back to the very beginning of the novels themselves; it was with the revelation to the Victorians that life was real and earnest that the complaints about philosophy, which to most of them meant a "message," began to appear. It has already been noted that Harriet Martineau, as earnest a Victorian as ever lived, found the novels nearly a decade before Victoria's accession saturated with edification, but that Carlyle in 1838 gave definite form to the charge that there was in them none of the philosophy or idea necessary to keep them alive, that Scott could not persist, being no Prophet-Preacher, and that his very characters, sad as it was to say so, had no heart or soul — that Sir Walter got no deeper with humanity than its skin. All through the Victorian age this worried the critics, although Leslie Stephen said it did not worry him; they could not find in Scott what it was easy enough to discover in their own writers and what they were coming to believe was the justification and salt of that literary form so long despised as trivial, the novel. The same objection is also to be found in foreign critics like Brandes and Croce, who are not earnest Victorians and who demand more than a "message," but who find Sir Walter merely simple and childish, too immature for ideas or philosophy, and in such native parallels as Mr. Carswell, with his declaration that Scott's books were as bare of ideas as was his conversation.

It is indeed a common device of Scott's modern defenders when they come to the matter of philosophy and ideas to recur to Carlyle and use him as a kind of convenient springboard into the argument. Just as the hostile quote him with approbation, the friendly conceive him as Scott's greatest enemy in the past and feel that he must be disposed of. Generally the attack on Carlyle is directed at his obvious point of weakness —

his quality as a preacher, his demand for a message or gospel. Again and again in modern criticism has the validity of such a demand been denied, as has also the more dangerous charge that Scott never got at the heart of his characters as Shakespeare did. Stephen Gwynn [11] formulates as strikingly as anyone the answer to this point in Carlyle's attack when he says that Scott's best characters reveal their hearts in speech and action. They are not Hamlets and Othellos, he admits, but we know them as we know Hamlet and Othello, by what they say and do, by "the sudden act or the swift word, in which the whole nature is revealed."

Possibly the most systematic examination of Carlyle's essay, including the personal motives underlying it, is that by Professor Grierson,[12] who analyzes Carlyle's strictures one by one to show that they may all be answered, and who also emphasizes the fact that Carlyle, temperamentally bitter and melancholy, could hardly speak kindly of any successful person because of his own long wait for success. In addition Mr. Grierson points out that Carlyle was in most ways unfitted to sympathize with Scott, not only because of his general moral earnestness, but because of such matters as his Presbyterianism, toward which Scott was at least cool, while Carlyle saw in it the most poetical quality of Scotland. And yet, Mr. Grierson says, Scott could see the whole country steeped in poetry. And finally he asks a question which many critics have thought a telling one, in reply to Carlyle's own questions about Scott; does Carlyle give more help in a crisis than Sir Walter? Certainly Carlyle out of the past and the Continental realists and naturalists in the present have been established by Scott's friends as his chief enemies.

Practically all the modern English critics who have written on Scott repudiate such judgments as Carlyle's. Some of them, it is true, will not go so far as to make Sir Walter a philosopher of the greatest depth and range, but others find his books permeated and suffused with moral and spiritual significances. These later

[11] Stephen Gwynn, *The Life of Sir Walter Scott* (London, 1930), pp. 278 ff.
[12] "Scott and Carlyle," *Essays and Studies*, The English Association, 1928.

critics, for whom the Victorian novel is an old story, and to some of whom Thackeray, Dickens, and George Eliot seem even more faded than Scott, no longer demand that the thesis or the idea that the novelist is propagating should be writ large in boldface type across the face of his work. They are more willing than their forebears of the last two generations to discover ideas and theories, a philosophy of life, and moral, social, and political attitudes expressed unconsciously or by indirection. Indeed such a method, if method it may be called, is more satisfactory and artistic to the typical latter-day critic than the quite conscious preaching and moralizing tendencies of the great Victorian novelists, to say nothing of the Kingsleys and Reades.

Thus the true modern is irritated by Thackeray's direct appeals to his reader, and by George Eliot's eternal obsession with her theory of the act and its consequences and the various "isms" that infect her pretentious later novels. Is it not the fashion to find the essence of her genius in *Scenes of Clerical Life,* the simplest and most unphilosophic, the least consciously edifying, of all her fictions? Certainly there are those who would find as much philosophy and more fine art in *Amos Barton* than in the obvious and carefully detailed moralizings even of *Adam Bede,* to say nothing of the Sunday school moral contrast of *Romola.* Or to come still closer home, do we approve the effect of a message or thesis when an author allows it to dictate to him as Hardy did in *Tess* or *Jude the Obscure* or Meredith in the climax of *Richard Feverel?* And is not even such a classic model of naturalism as Zola too didactic today? No modern novelist would venture to rise to such endings as he gives to *L'Assommoir* and *Nana.*

The modern interest in the "art" or technic of the novel, although it might lead, as Professor Elton thinks it has, to precious and finicking criticism of Scott's style, would on the other hand certainly induce sympathy with an author who had no lesson to teach, or at least no lesson packed up and ticketed as such. Certainly the modern serious novelist will avoid above all things "the message"; his idea of dramatic detachment forbids it. Accordingly it is the cue of the modern critic who wishes to make a case for Scott to find in him almost, and sometimes quite as much philosophy and moral significance as Miss Martineau discovered a century ago, and he finds it, he maintains, in the way that suits him best, suggested and implied in the action and the characters of the novels.

The most thoroughgoing expositions of this point of view have been written in the last decade or two, but earlier expressions of it do come to light; for instance, there is Professor Saintsbury,[13] who said in 1894 that Scott has enough "realistic" detail to set up half a dozen psychological novelists, and quotes casually but with approval the French critic Milsand, to the effect that Scott had more philosophy than a good share of the modern "philosophical novelists." Another critic, writing in the *Spectator* at about the same time,[14] praises Scott's characteristic glow and color but finds this romantic quality mingled with "the criticism of a broad sagacity and the business insight of a shrewd realist."

This is also the chief point of T. S. Omond [15] when he makes Scott the archetype of Romanticism because of his balance, serenity, and sanity. Like M. Cazamian he feels the tendency of romanticism to run off into excesses — "storm and stress, wildness and horror, Werther-like sentimentalism and Byronic misanthropy" — and appreciates the value of Scott's stability. It seems to be the point of view also of W. J. Courthope,[16] who declares Scott's works "the most enduring creations of the romantic school," since he "adhered most tenaciously to the social common sense and the inherited life of his nation and kept the firmest check upon the caprices of his own individual genius. . . . [He was] the best representative among English men of letters of conservatism in its most generous form." Thus Courthope, a strong conservative, who agrees with Johnson that

[13] *Macmillan's*, 70:321 (September, 1894).

[14] *Spectator*, 78:762 (May 29, 1897).

[15] Thomas S. Omond, *The Romantic Triumph* (New York, 1900), pp. 75 ff.

[16] See "The Revival of Romance," *National Review*, 5:220 (April, 1885), republished in *The Liberal Movement in English Literature* (London, 1885).

Rousseau deserved transportation, and feels the typical eighteenth-century aversion to romantic dreaminess, goes on quite naturally to a denunciation of the essay by "our radical Diogenes," Carlyle.

P. A. Graham, reviewing Hudson's not too sympathetic life of Scott,[17] lights on Hudson's judgment that Scott's novels were without idea or philosophy. He says that the modern reader now looks only to the novel for his philosophy, a situation that precludes treating the novel as a delight or pageant, and while he does not himself feel that Scott is a philosopher, he exclaims that "on this somewhat lower plane, [one is] amazed at the wide loving sympathy that could enter into and reproduce so many, so widely different types of humanity. Take the creation of any other imaginative writer, and how dwarfed it looks beside those long galleries of Scott." Evidently Mr. Graham intends this as a substitute. "on a somewhat lower plane" for what is called "philosophy." Nevertheless he refers to Scott as "our greatest novelist," and objects to Hudson's criticism in general, as the product of an "ism" that would destroy Scott and obliterate all Dumas and all fairy tales. On his own account he denies Hudson's contention that mature people cannot read Scott, and says, "The years have robbed Dickens of any shred of interest, have palled Thackeray, have made George Eliot unreadable, but still to open Scott at any place and almost in any mood is to unseal a fountain of pleasure, and this notwithstanding a growing and poignant sense of his limitations." This is perhaps special pleading, and over-enthusiastic, notably in its obliteration of the Victorian novelists merely for the sake of Scott, but it does indicate the growing tendency to refuse to let Scott be dismissed as empty merely because he does not preach an organized and detailed philosophical system.

This attitude comes out still more clearly in H. D. Sedgwick's essay in the *Atlantic* in 1902.[18] In its moral and sentimental tone Mr. Sedgwick's essay is reminiscent of Victorianism, and

[17] *Academy*, 60:109 (February 2, 1901).
[18] *Op. cit.*

loses some of its force as a defense of Scott by its underlying implication, carefully avoided in direct expression, that Scott is for the young. The essay concludes, however, with a defense of Scott against Carlyle's charge that the novels have no philosophical or moral force. Mr. Sedgwick speaks of the inspiration that Scott has been to young men to do noble deeds and think high thoughts. "As a power for good, who shall come next to Shakespeare, Dante and Cervantes, if not Walter Scott?" He calls Scott's a great theatrical imagination, claims for him poetry beyond any other novelist, as well as a "shrewd practical understanding," and maintains that even "the melodramatic theatre indicates certain fundamental truths of human nature." The whole argument is in fact quite typical; the writer cares little that Scott is not an earnest preacher or moralist ("literature, not preaching, has been the great civilizer") and answers those who find in this fact an insurmountable weakness by appealing to the general effect and drift of his work.

For a more aggressive and combative statement of the point of view one may turn to Professor Elton and Professor Seccombe.[19] Mr. Elton places Scott at least on a level with Balzac, and insists that he keeps his pre-eminence when contrasted with the chief English novelists of the last period, especially Meredith and Hardy. In the matter of style, he considers modern critics obsessed with the idea of "philosophy" and defends Scott against them by maintaining his power in the portrayal of life: "He draws the surface; we are tempted to think he is not deep because he does this and because he does not hurt and sting. But he does not draw the surface superficially . . . He draws it as a master. Nothing is so hard . . . except to go deeper still, which is Shakespeare's way." And, he adds, declaring that it is easy enough to see what he did not do, but not so easy to see what he did. "It is by the mass and the excellence of such art that Scott keeps his supremacy in Britain."

Professor Seccombe, probably irritated by the prevalent

---

[19] Oliver Elton, *op. cit.*, and William R. Nicoll and Thomas Seccombe, *History of English Literature* (3 vols., New York, 1907), III, 953.

theory that Scott can be absorbed and drained dry by young boys who gallop through him for mere story, demands rigorously that we should read Scott six times, "for the story, for the dialogue, for the historical perspective, for the learning, which is great, for the wisdom, which is still greater, for the consummate knowledge of human character, which is greatest of all. And so, in the fullness of time if we persevere, we shall duly arrive at the refutation of the absurd libel that Scott has no message, is no teacher. He teaches by the same methods as Shakespeare— namely, by the representation of human nature in action." And in estimating Scott's mind, he finds two predominant qualities, "the marvellous creative energy of his imagination working upon the raw material of history; and the extraordinary knowledge and sagacity with which this imagination is ballasted."[20]

Or again, one may cite W. P. Ker, who in an address on Scott delivered at the Sorbonne in 1919,[21] would defend him against those who say he has no depth, that he is all upholstery and trappings and lets real character go. Like Mr. Elton, Professor Ker invites a comparison with Balzac, even before a French audience, noting at the same time Balzac's extremely high praise of Scott, especially for his characters. He also points out that there has been an enormous amount of criticism of Scott's religion and politics — from the bitter remarks of Hazlitt, to whose praise of Scott, however, he does full justice, to those of Mark Twain, out of which Mr. Ker gets much amusement.[22] All such critics he characterizes as valiant adherents of the

[20] Seccombe again championed Scott on the centenary of *Waverley* (*Contemporary Review*, 106:26, July, 1914), celebrating his spontaneity and natural creation, which he says are unburdened with the laboriousness or sense of working up material to be found in some of his successors, like Reade or Shorthouse. (But is *John Inglesant* laborious?) He is so far an enthusiast as also to undertake the defense of Scott's heroes, and to declare his heroines "unsurpassed as a group out of Meredith or Shakespeare." He also contributed centenary essays to the *Times Literary Supplement* on the novels from *Waverley* to *Kenilworth*. These are reprinted in the *Scott Centenary Articles* (London, 1932).

[21] See "Sir Walter Scott," in *Collected Essays of W. P. Ker*, edited by Charles Whibley (2 vols., London, 1925), Vol. I. See also *Living Age*, 302:751 (September 20, 1919).

[22] See below, page 318.

"march of intellect" idea. Finally he makes the point that Scott should be thought of all together, in his own life, his method of work, and the whole bulk of his production. This is, of course, a pertinent reminder, for there is hardly a great writer in the whole range of English literature whose own personality has been so completely caught up into the public imagination and fused with the popular conception and estimation of his work. The criticism of Scott's work never is and never can be carried on without continual recurrence to the facts and conditions of his own life. Mr. Ker's suggestion, which is merely repeated from many Victorian critics who had a sentimental attachment to Scott and his works, is in itself an answer to many of the adverse criticisms of Scott. One cannot reasonably deny many of the facts urged against him, but many of the facts seem to fade and lose their significance when considered as mere details of the whole microcosm of his life and work.

The most explicit and systematic answers to the grave charges of lack of philosophy and depth of meaning have been given by Mr. John Erskine and Mr. John Buchan, both of whom frankly and plainly cast their ideas into the form of an argument against the assumptions of Scott's shallowness and moral insignificance. Mr. Erskine [23] states his belief at once that Scott had more philosophy than many brilliant so-called philosophers, and that of a saner and sounder sort. He then proceeds to integrate out of the details of Scott's life and the steady and consistent implications of his novels, a philosophical system so definite and orderly that the modern reader who craves philosophy need no longer fear to compare Sir Walter even with Hardy and Meredith.

Mr. Erskine finds expressed throughout all Scott — both in his personal action and his written word — an obvious stoicism, an idea of human character as "fixed and ultimate" and an idea of fate (he quotes Emerson's "Deep in the man sits fast his fate") that links him with Sophocles and Euripides, a fate not of mere

<hr>

[23] *Columbia University Quarterly,* 17:40 (December, 1914).

superstitious fatalism, but springing from ingrained and fixed traits of character. Arguing on this basis, Mr. Erskine finally arrives at the triumphant conclusion, "I hold with those who call him the wisest and the greatest man of English letters in the nineteenth century and he is incomparably our greatest novelist."

Having established his hero, he then turns to rend his opponents. Scott, he says, is a good protective against most modern romances and "social cure-alls which still offer to make us good and happy, at low cost, with just a little rearranging of environment." A good stroke at Mr. Ker's group of enthusiasts for the "march of intellect"!

The temptation to make out such a case for Scott is understandable, as is the desire to prove that he can meet the modern favorites on their own ground and produce as systematic a philosophy as any of them. Nevertheless, despite the brilliance and spirit of the argument, one cannot help wondering what Scott himself would have thought of it, and if he would not have been both gratified and surprised to find himself the parent of so fine a system, and the lineal descendant of Sophocles and Euripides. After all, a knife cuts both ways, and the champion as well as the detractor can well afford to remember how Scott lived his daily life, his simplicity and modesty and lack of pretension.

Mr. Buchan [24] is equally convinced of Scott's depth, but his argument is simpler and less spectacular. As he says, it is charged against Scott that he does not strike deep into character, does not seem to see into the soul, and, what implies the same limitation but implies it more gravely, that he wrote merely to amuse; according to Carlyle, his was "the task of harmlessly amusing indolent languid men." These charges are to be found expressed in one way or another not only in Carlyle but in Hazlitt and Bagehot, not to mention many later writers. As Mr. Buchan says, it is suggested by Hazlitt, when he looks in vain in Scott for

[24] John Buchan, *op. cit.*, and also the reworking of this paper as Chapter XIII in his *Sir Walter Scott*.

"what the heart whispers to itself in secret," and it is at the core of Bagehot's declaration that one finds in Scott plenty of the stir of this world, but that his people, well furnished for this, have about them nothing of the other world.

In answering these charges, which he says, if true, would exclude Scott from the first rank of greatness and leave him a mere skillful entertainer, Mr. Buchan admits the foundations of the strictures, but insists that they merely imply limitations such as are to be expected even in Shakespeare. Scott's world, he says, is one "founded on common sense and honest sentiment." It is not highly intellectual; a Hamlet was beyond his range. And it is the same with religious matters and with the characters, not of women but of ladies whom his ideas of propriety would not allow him to watch too closely. Yet on the other hand, Mr. Buchan says, granting all this, he has produced a great host of characters in the Scotch novels "who are as completely realized in their minds as they are vividly depicted in their bodies," and he cites in detail Scott's handling of Steenie Steenson in *Wandering Willie's Tale* as an example of subtlety of psychology and insight into character. Mr. Buchan thinks too that critics have been deceived by Scott's dramatic method, and his self-effacement, which they have contrasted with the page-long analyses and discussions of later novelists, into thinking that Scott was incapable of analysis. He also declares that the modern passion for the pathological has been misleading; Scott, he says, touches it lightly and fleetingly and gets its essence, and then goes on to better things. Besides, he adds, James Hogg could do the pathological like a modern realist — is he therefore to be assumed Sir Walter's equal in the study of character?

The second phrasing of the charge Mr. Buchan answers first of all by appealing to what he has already said about character. He charges Carlyle, as most of us would, with demanding too earnestly a message or a creed, and he replies most aptly to that moralist's complaint that "the sick heart will find no healing" in Scott with Hazlitt's exclamation, "How many sad hearts have been soothed in pain and solitude!" Mr. Buchan refuses to accept

Bagehot's dictum that Scott lacks "consecrating power." Indeed, he declares, Scott's "consecrating power" is higher than that of any other English novelist, higher than that of Balzac, as high as Tolstoi's or Dostoevski's at their best. His instinct for real tragedy is unfailing — "the failure of something not ignoble through inherent weakness or a change of circumstance to which it cannot adapt itself." His world was gay but also solemn, and he can make his characters seem like puppets under the hand of the eternal. "[His] purpose, which lay deep in his consciousness was to inculcate 'reverence and godly fear.' " The basis of his philosophy is "the eternity and the wisdom of the divine ordering of things," and in the struggle of this world against divine ordinance he counseled submission, peace, and fortitude — "the classic reconciliation" based on a recognition of the goodness of eternal law.

His people are triumphant; the novels "restore faith in humanity by revealing its forgotten graces and depths." [25] They have the classic catharsis. Sir Walter has the special gift of blending tragedy and comedy, of uniting mirth and pity, as did Homer and Cervantes. He has a noble austerity in his reading of characters. "He can penetrate to the greatness of the humble, the divine spark in the clod." No one has expounded the poor as he has in characters like Edie Ochiltree and Jeanie Deans. His Bessie Maclure has what Stevenson called in Dostoevski a "lovely goodness." Like Dostoevski "he loves mankind without reservation, is incapable of hate, and finds nothing created altogether common or unclean." The struggles of his characters,

[25] Hugh Walpole in "A Centenary Estimate," *English Review*, 55:350 (October, 1932) says the "novels were all concerned with nobility of conduct, and nobility in the simplest way." Professor Grierson, in an address at Columbia (see the *University Quarterly*, 25:9, March, 1933), says that the ultimate values in his novels are fidelity to principles and honor, and the two Christian virtues, charity and submission to the will of God; and he notes that Scott rejected as unworthy and even degrading an ending based on "virtue rewarded" and poetic justice for Rebecca. M. W. Wallace (see a centenary essay in the *University of Toronto Quarterly*, 2:111, October, 1932), in listing Scott's qualities of greatness, comes in climactic order, after his story-telling power and his interest in common people, to his philosophy of endurance and resignation, as expressed in the novels and reflected in his own life.

likewise, are not as usual between two temperaments but between an individual temperament and a tradition. In these struggles Scott rises easily into tragedy, as the modern realistic novelist cannot.

Mr. Buchan finds in Scott "that enlargement and purification of life which is the test of great literature; he makes the world at once more solemn and more sunlit." The solemnity he finds in such tragic figures as Ravenswood, Fergus MacIvor, and Redgauntlet, and in the tremendous force of the witches in *The Bride of Lammermoor;* the sunlight in the comedy of which Scott was also so obviously a master. And he asks in his conclusion, "Is there nothing here for comfort and edification? Is there no more than the utterance of the intelligent country gentleman?" Are not the characters of Jeanie Deans and Edie Ochiltree fraught with human significance? Scott made such figures sublime, without betraying the truth. "It is Scott, the Tory county gentleman, the worldling, whom some would have us discard as superficial, that lifts them into the clear air of the heroic." This is one of the most impressive of the modern tributes to Scott. It is obviously written *con amore* and with a real and natural interest in the subject. The author tells us in the beginning that he was fired to the task by the rereading of what he liked best in Scott, and by the feeling that the books themselves refuted the charges brought against them, and his approach to the subject as well as his freshness from the reading brings conviction to his argument.

Lord David Cecil's defense [26] of Scott's philosophy and treatment of character is a little less direct. He approaches the matter in a discussion of Scott's range, which, he says, includes "all that part of experience which concerns man as a product of his local environment and his historic past . . . in relation to the circumstances and traditions—political, social, religious, natural— of the society in which he lives." Like Mr. Buchan, Lord David emphasizes the roundness of Scott's best characters — the combination of the tragic and comic; the great characters all have

[26] *Op. cit.*

a comic or even a grotesque side, and the humorous characters have their serious sides, and both are consistent in all their phases. His best characters spring from their environment, and are interesting as appearing in it. They are, too, all parochial, since otherwise they would lose their local quality.[27]

Under Mr. E. A. Baker's searching scrutiny of Sir Walter's philosophy and his treatment of character, the novels do not come out so well. For Mr. Baker Fielding is the supreme master; Scott is continually being compared with him and cannot stand the comparison. "As historian of manners and humorous delineator of character, he is of the Fielding school," but he falls short of Fielding in artistic conscience and ability to plan, and, even more importantly, in his power to reveal "the wider bearings of individual acts," a power which he reveals only in flashes. He "had neither the probing curiosity of the analyst nor the philosophical vision of such as Fielding." He saw parts or details, but not the whole; diversities but not universalities of human nature; eccentricities and humors, not normalities; characters but not character. "The deeper and more tragic ironies" he could not handle; true comedy like that of Fielding, as well as tragedy, lay outside his orbit. He deals with adventure, the unexpected and surprising, what *happens to* the characters; hence his feeble heroes, his weak plots, and his common lack of deep and really dramatic conflict,[28] which appears only once, in

---

[27] One may compare with this the remarks of Edwin Muir in the *Spectator*, 149:364 (September 24, 1932). Mr. Muir praises Scott for his creation of scores of fine characters, but says he gave them a pasteboard world to live in — "flesh and blood as solid as Fielding's, pasteboard as flimsy as Bulwer Lytton's." The general effect of this essay is less favorable to Scott than Mr. Muir's remarks in his *Structure of the Novel* (London, 1928). There he emphasizes the inherent weakness of lavishing all the interest on secondary characters whose function in plot is negligible, but he says that once an important character (Jeanie Deans) becomes the chief actor, "and Scott writes the greatest of his novels." Moreover, his public figures are better than those of anyone else, Dumas or Thackeray, for instance; and "He is a fine novelist of action and a great portrayer of character." In these two departments he is not so strong as, respectively, Dumas and Smollett, but he is greater than either. To appreciate how rich Scott's genius really was, one must make great allowances for his vehicle.

[28] This idea is interestingly applied to Scott's treatment of history. See below, page 321 n.

the character of Jeanie Deans. Carlyle's dictum about the characters is at bottom true, though it is exaggerated, and though it
fails to make allowance for Scott's great diversity. Even such
fine characters as Edie Ochiltree and Meg Merrilies elude him;
he cannot follow them to the end. Hazlitt was right too in declaring that Scott was not thoroughly original, but a copyist of
nature. And as far as a philosophical system is concerned, what
others have thought a fine and heroic stoicism is here seen, in
agreement with Louis Reynaud, merely as a shallow determin-
ism. His characters are not free but bound by their heredity and
environment; he himself believed in accepting the place one is
born to, and his principles were really matters of habit and up-
bringing. Thus Mr. Baker restates and amplifies the argument
of Walter Bagehot; indeed his sympathy with Bagehot, on Scott
at least (not at all on Fielding) is made manifest by frequent
citation, and Scott is set down on a lower level than his modern
apologists will accept for him. The crux of the matter really
lies in Mr. Baker's feeling of a lack of unity in Scott, of his
"world of characters" as a mass of individuals whom he does not
really fuse into a world at all; the other writers lately cited obviously believe that a real fusion takes place and that the mass of
individuals merge to form a unified world; one, moreover, gov-
erned by deeper and nobler motives than a mere adherence to
convention and habit.

For most modern readers probably the defense of Scott's
greatness by appeal to his characters, individually or in crowds,
to illustrate his knowledge and grasp of human life — his feeling
for character, not mere costume — is the most effective and convincing method. But just as the modern critic writing on the
Waverley novels disregards the romances and considers only the
Scotch series, so also, of course, he disregards the heroes and
heroines and the polite characters in general, and draws his
illustrations, with certain exceptions, from Scott's common
people. Heroes and heroines especially are likely to be quite perfunctorily dismissed, except perhaps for "the famous Rebecca"
and Diana Vernon (Jeanie Deans, of course, is not a heroine as

she is not a lady), and it is at once made clear that Scott's great characters are his peasants and his fisher-folk. It is through his dramatic presentation of them, through their high eloquence, and their implicit philosophy that his genius finds its way to expression, an idea which is by no means new in this later generation.[29]

Again and again one is told that a mere reading of the books is enough to refute those who, like Carlyle, say that Scott is superficial; or one is exhorted to go and read them again to see if it is not so. This is really important in Mr. Buchan's essay; he is ready to deny the conventional charges, and most of all the one about shallowness and insignificance, with plenty of fresh illustration. Many writers not only cite fine single characters, but remind one of the broad scope not only of scene but of character in the novels, their crowds of people, the energy and spirit and vitality with which those crowds stream before us. In this flood of humanity Scott reveals his greatness and depth. The writers who take this point of view are the ones whose enthusiasm for Scott seems the deepest and most real.

This is the basis of argument in G. E. Woodberry's essay on Scott,[30] where the "Scotch world" of the novels is always kept before the reader. Mr. Woodberry says that the novels contain Scotland as Cervantes' do Spain, and that their significance lies primarily in their representation ŏf social, not private, life; they are like chronicle plays, with an interest in the stream of public events. There is "a larger world round about the story." As with all the greatest writers, the stage is crowded, the world is full of

---

[29] Note, however, as one striking exception, a series of articles in *Macmillan's*, 62:257, 63:443, 64:453 (1890–91) on Scott's heroines, an attempt at sentimental appreciation. The author has to make a good many exceptions and reservations, however. The thesis is developed that Scott wished to show in his heroines that passion and principle may exist together. He probably did, as it was a proper convention; but he did not seem to find it an inspiring theme, nor have many of his readers. Note also in the *Atlantic* for January, 1892 (69:139) an article on the age of Scott's heroines, showing that although young, they generally have grown up in the companionship of much older men and so are unusually mature. If critics have been little concerned with the heroines, they have been even less so with the heroes.

[30] *Op. cit.*

people. Moreover, their reality lies not so much in their being drawn from actual originals; Scott's brain was packed with the very life of the Scotch people — the novels are an "amalgam of memory." The very emotional forces are national — not love, for which Scott cared little, but the passion of loyalty and the religious enthusiasm of the Covenanters. And on the private side of life Scott is master of a sorrow and a dark brooding spirit that are typically Scotch. In this Scotch world everything is homogeneous and in keeping; there are "free action, bold character, primitive customs, . . . high feeling and enterprise such as . . . no author since Homer [has depicted] with the same breadth and elevation." His creative power places him "among the greatest imaginative prose writers in the world and makes him the first of romancers as Shakespeare is the first of dramatists." He gets immediate effect simply and without effort, and like Shakespeare and Homer, creates crowds. In presenting character "he achieves expression in its highest form, the expression of a soul using its human powers in earthly life." This is truly creative; it is "not the scientific exhibition of the development of character, not the analytic examination of psychology and motivation, for which inferior talent suffices, but the revealing flash of genius which shows the fair soul in the fair act."[31] In such criticism Mr. Woodberry is obviously ignoring the modern demands of technic; to him they mean little. And in the matter of intellect, he is quite willing to admit that Scott was not much interested in it. He even goes so far as to say that "his unconscious subordination of the intellectual . . . is one great cornerstone of his sanity and wholesomeness."

A. A. Jack [32] too, like many other critics, would make Scott our "first" novelist, on the basis, it would seem, of his characters. Though surpassed in many single novels like *Esmond,* Jack says, his great volume, wide range, and steady excellence make him pre-eminent, a prose Shakespeare. And in analyzing what he considers the best of the novels (all of them from the Scotch series) he is really demonstrating that Scott is first of all a novelist

---

[31] Cf. Stephen Gwynn, *op. cit.* See above, page 295.   [32] *Op. cit.*

of character. He shows, for instance, how both *Rob Roy* and *The Heart of Midlothian* are saved by the tremendous force of character in them, by the humanity and reality of their people. Yet Jack, unlike Woodberry, has reservations. He can still say, for instance, that "the world in its perplexity" did not lie open to Scott.

Canon Ainger [33] also bases his high claims for Scott on his representation of life through his best characters, the humble ones. These, he says, were drawn from life, but too many of his others — his Helen Macgregors and Rashleigh Osbaldistones — come from melodrama, a fact the sophisticated have held against him. Yet, Canon Ainger would assert, all the melodrama in plot and character matters little, and is forgotten and swept aside by "the indefeasible charm of the story, the attractiveness of its leading characters, the pathos, the romantic touch, the transcendent humor," out of which arise Sir Walter's sure claim to permanence, and our feeling that he was "human," that he wrote for the multitudes of humanity, not for a clique with whose passing he too would pass. Here too, of course, is obvious again the resentment against the trend of modern criticism.

The same reliance upon character is shown by Hugh Walpole in his frequent defenses of Scott. In his Rede Lecture at Cambridge in 1925, he asked, "Is there in the region of intricate psychology in this our day that boasts so especially of its preeminence in that direction anything more truly discerned than the Bennet family in *Pride and Prejudice* and the contrasted Jeanie and Effie Deans of *The Heart of Midlothian?*" The year before Mr. Walpole had insisted that Scott had created a world full of real characters, characters who have life independent of the melodrama or the weak plots in which they act, and who reveal to the reader every part of life in a variety of scene and character which proves Scott's rare "gift of world creation." And again in the "Centenary Estimate" just quoted he praises Scott as, above all, "a supreme creator of human character" and declares that he could if he had wished, to judge from his journal

[33] *Op. cit.*

and letters, which reveal unexpected subtleties and introspections, have produced a *Mme. Bovary* or a *Tess*.[34]

Other modern novelists feel this power of "world creation" to be of the highest significance. Mr. J. B. Priestley writes: [35] "The stir and bustle of life, the march of events, the humor and pathos and heroism in high places and low places, the varied scene, the panorama of hill and dale and crowded street . . . this is what Scott gives us, pours out with the generosity of a god. His work is like a vast city, and that is why it is so easy to criticize adversely. . . . He had a massive knowledge of human nature, particularly as it is seen in the ordinary hurly-burly of life." He praises his "abundant and lifelike creation" and says that, as with Shakespeare, his world of comedy and tragedy "is shaped by his own robust sense and coloured by his generous feelings and his eloquence; and it is one of the largest, manliest, noblest that the Novel can show us. . . . The Novel, in Scott's hands, broadened out to mirror a whole roaring world, great events, and crowds on the march."

But it is left to Virginia Woolf to defend Scott most brilliantly in this vein. She speaks [36] especially of the common people (in the Scotch novels, of course) who are to her splendid, with their dialect and their metaphors, their "immense vivacity." Mrs. Woolf says that we know what Scott's characters thought as though they were real people, by various means, and that they vary from reading to reading like real people. Are they, she asks, characters merely for our naive childish moments? Within them is "a host of observations, subtle and profound enough, should we trouble to spread them out; and next this transparent stream through which we see stones, weeds and minnows at the bottom, becomes without warning the sea, the deep, the inscrutable, the universal ocean on which we put out with the greatest only."

[34] See the Rede Lecture by Hugh Walpole, published as *The English Novel* (Cambridge, 1925); *Nation and Athenaeum*, 35:201 (May 17, 1924); and above, page 304 n.

[35] J. B. Priestley, *The English Novel*.

[36] Virginia Woolf, *op. cit.*

And even in the more romantic elements Mrs. Woolf is willing to take greater delight than most. Here too, she says, Scott's greatness lies especially in the talk of his characters. "His romance is Nature's romance. It is the romance of hunted men hiding in woods at night, of brigs standing out to sea, of waves breaking in the moonlight, of solitary sands and distant horsemen, of violence and suspense. This survives; this, which is not so profound or so moving as the other, but if we remember the excitement of the moment, the flying beauty of the landscape, and the abundance and the freedom and the groups round inn-tables, and the talk — above all, the talk — hostlers talking, old beggars talking, gypsies talking, post-mistresses talking, as if they would talk their hearts out, then how can we deny him a place among the highest?"[37]

Other writers enough have been willing to see in Scott's humanity variety and breadth, but it has sometimes been the breadth of a shallow river, not of Mrs. Woolf's illimitable ocean. Concerned with one thing or another, in their Victorian earnestness or their modern rage for psychology, they have declared that Scott saw the pageant of life, but knew nothing of its problems. W. J. Dawson, for instance, by no means hostile or disdainful, speaks [38] of Scott's geniality, good sense, and human sympathy, but thinks he lacked psychology, except occasionally in his humbler characters. And in general, "he sees the pageant of life, but not its mystery." That is, his limitations reduce him as they had in the eyes of Carlyle, and even Bagehot and Croce, to little more than pleasant mediocrity. Mrs. Woolf's words imply much more than that; they carry one back to Hazlitt when his political fury was asleep and his heart too was stirred by the currents of life he felt in the new novels.

In such criticism is implied a general and pervasive understanding of humanity, intuitive and uncalculated, simple and

[37] In her novel *To The Lighthouse* (1927) Mrs. Woolf has Professor Ramsay read with deep feeling and veneration a passage from *The Antiquary* and then declare that it is beyond the grasp of other novelists. This passage and that quoted above are identical in their feeling toward Scott.

[38] William J. Dawson, *Makers of English Fiction* (London, 1905).

natural, which, as Mr. Woodberry says, indicates genius much more than the conscious processes of "psychology" for which inferior talents suffice. Several modern critics have emphasized this aspect of Scott's genius in its moral and social implications to prove the undercurrent of philosophical idea in his writing. Hazlitt, living in Scott's own time and terrifically excited by political tempest, sometimes forgot his impression of Scott's deep humanity, and many another admiring contemporary and Victorian shook his head sadly over Sir Walter's perverse and stupid Toryism. As Mr. Ker said, the "march of progress" apostles have often manifested disapproval. But with the increase in perspective and the fading of local and temporary political animosity, it has become clear to many that Sir Walter's essential humanity was more significant and more representative of his spirit than were his party sympathies.

No one has ever suggested that he was a great political thinker, though it has often been explained that his fondness for the past, for a varied and definitely graded society, for all that was represented in Abbotsford, would naturally predispose him against the democratic forces of his own time and align him with the Tories. Politically his attitude toward the people was the feudal one of *noblesse oblige*, a benign paternalism. But in his Scotch novels he wrote as he acted in life, not as a benevolent despot looking down upon his humble dependents but rather as one who has met even the lowest on terms of equality and been received with an intimacy never accorded a superior.[39]

He knew the common people of Scotland as though he were of them, and he caught from them for his books not only their dialect, their superstitions and picturesque local customs, but their essential spirits, their hearts and souls. Nor was it merely in their more romantic aspects that he saw them. Mr. Buchan does full justice to Scott's intense interest in the more practical and economic side of their lives, pointing out the normal common people in the background of all the earlier novels and "the

[39] That he actually did so there is plenty of proof in his letters and journal and in numberless anecdotes.

full and sagacious pictures of social and economic conditions." He shows too how in his own life he was constantly concerned with such matters, "how human beings made a livelihood, how social change was to be combined with social persistence." Of the crofting system in the Orkneys, for instance, he said that large farms were the only salvation, "but he could not face the dispossession of the small folk." That is, he saw clearly that in such affairs there were other important considerations than merely economic ones.[40] The best contemporary critics in discussing Scott himself make much of the realistic, practical side of his nature, which was always balanced against the more obvious romantic side. Professor Grierson makes this dualism the chief theme of his introduction to Scott's *Letters,* presenting it more fully and more clearly than anyone else has as the key to Scott's character.

To many modern writers who either imply or proclaim this interest in the people, it seems much better warrant to a claim of idea and philosophy than the more pretentious methods of other novelists whose philosophical significance no one would think of questioning. It is from this point of view, again, that the modern critic so commonly picks up Carlyle's essay to refute it. Even W. J. Dawson, who, as has just been said, shows a by no means overwhelming enthusiasm for Scott, makes the excellent point that Sir Walter was really a democrat and loved the common people, that he did not vulgarize them as Dickens, a professed democrat, did, and that his popularity, having a firm basis in his human sympathies, is likely to endure. The best expression of the idea, however, is Mr. Chesterton's. He says that of the nineteenth-century writers "there is none in the noblest sense more democratic than Walter Scott." Really all his characters are kings in disguise. The preposterous Nicol Jarvie in a crisis becomes more of a man in stature. "Molière makes M. Jourdain talk prose; but Scott made him talk poetry." His poor men rise in rhetoric, talk nobly in the crisis, become more "classical." "Scott keeps the natural diction of Bailie Jarvie, but

[40] Buchan, *Sir Walter Scott,* p. 126.

insensibly sobers and uplifts that style until it reaches a plain and appropriate eloquence." This idea Mr. Chesterton reiterates when he declares that Scott had a far finer sense of the dignity of the common man than Dickens, for the latter cast his poor man into the mould of the cocky, impertinent Comic Servant in order to make him score off his masters.[41] This harmonizes well with the ideas of Mrs. Woolf, and it is closely akin to the thesis of Verrall, with his penetrating analysis of the magnificent and thrilling speeches of Meg Merrilies.

[41] G. K. Chesterton, *Charles Dickens. A Critical Study* (New York, 1906), pp. 246–52, and "Charles Dickens," in Massingham, *Great Victorians*.

CHAPTER IV

SCOTT'S TREATMENT OF HISTORY

MOST OF the fault found with Sir Walter has had to do with his style and construction or with his philosophy. Yet there is also of course the matter of his history, less absorbing to the critics but still a fertile subject. It has been repeated all too frequently in these pages that the historical romances set in remote periods have never pleased the critics as well as have the Scotch novels. Hugh Walpole, for instance, can say that Scott's claims as a historical (i.e., medieval) novelist, though enough to make a great reputation, are of relatively slight importance. But of course in these latter days the historical novel has had few friends anyway; most critics have considered it a well-nigh impossible form.

This modern distrust, however, has a source quite different from that of earlier generations. In Scott's time critics seriously considered the question as to whether the novels would seduce regular readers of history away from more solid works, but generally came to the conclusion that they would actually encourage further historical reading, and would besides bring historical knowledge to many who would otherwise remain utterly in the outer darkness.[1] Most of the Victorians felt likewise, regarding Scott as a great popular historian, though some few attacked the Waverley series and historical novels in general

---

[1] Excellent points are made by Lovett and Hughes (*op. cit.*) concerning Scott's importance in connection with history. They would ascribe the great strength of his appeal to his own generation chiefly to the fact that history, not yet replaced by natural science, was the central intellectual interest. To Scott's influence they would also ascribe the requirement of historical background in the highest forms of poetry, drama, and fiction all through the century; and they remark Scott's importance as giving a romantic appeal to the Tory reaction.

as inaccurate and superficial, a dangerous infection or contamination of history. But the modern dislike of the form comes not
from a concern for the muse of history but rather from the
strong modern tendency toward realism, from the absolute conviction that the true field of a novelist is the life of his own time.
It is an almost universally accepted dogma that as soon as a
novelist departs from his own ground and his own time his
vision becomes confused and blurred. In writing historical
novels he is undertaking the impossible. This has been felt
since the days of *Ivanhoe,* but it does not seem to have become
a dogma and developed into a commonplace until the rise of
French naturalism and its attendant theory.[2]

There is also, to be sure, the charge against Scott's history in
the narrow factual sense, less important indeed, but still more
than a detail. There were a few complaints of anachronism and

[2] For a typical and thoroughly representative statement of this attitude see
Brander Matthews, *The Historical Novel and Other Essays* (New York, 1901).
Matthews agrees with the French critics that the author must deal with his own
time; he cannot go back. In speaking of Scott he defends the Scotch novels as
having comparatively little infusion of historical scene, and as not being, therefore, strictly historical novels. He does not make the best argument for them;
that is, that their period of the eighteenth, and even late seventeenth, century
differed little from the period of Scott's own youth, at least in the essentials of
character and manners with which Scott was chiefly concerned. It is rather surprising to find as sympathetic an essay as Herbert Butterfield's *Historical Novel*
(Cambridge, 1924), but Mr. Butterfield is actually concerned with the functions
of the ideal historical novelist in contrast with those of the professional historian.
His essay is hardly at all a criticism of actual examples, but rather a statement
of the ideally great value of the historical novel.

Ernest Bernbaum, in "The Views of the Great Critics on the Historical Novel,"
Publications of the Modern Language Association, 41:424 (June, 1926), traces the
distrust of the historical novel in the later nineteenth century to the prevalent
empirical, scientific skepticism with its insistence on accuracy, and thinks it quite
possible to evolve a philosophical criticism in support of the form. Mr. Bernbaum
attacks Leslie Stephen and Brandes especially for indulging their peculiar prepossessions and prejudices.

Alfred T. Sheppard's *Art and Practice of Historical Fiction* (London, 1930),
which seems to be the most extensive recent treatment of the subject, is also a
defense and an apology. It consists of a history of the form, before Scott as well
as after, and a discussion of the various problems faced by the historical novelist.
It is notable for allusions to scores of historical novelists and hundreds of their
novels. There is high praise of Scott as "King of the Romantics," in Stevenson's
phrase, and a long list of tributes to him (pages 43 ff.), some of which are not repeated in the present work.

misrepresentation in the original reviews, but there were more in the next period. The Victorians began to be meticulous about historical fact and interpretation in the novels, and the professional historians occasionally set the readers of the novels right in points of fact. Thus *Kenilworth* especially was riddled with holes.[3] Other critics, too, from Hazlitt to Mark Twain and even later, have been more or less incensed by what seemed to them Scott's false and misleading influence, his shallowness or his unregenerate Toryism; and, as has been seen, one can find such brilliant and caustic epigrams as that "he was an historian who knew everything about history but its meaning." Of all the democratic and radical fulminations against Sir Walter probably that of Mark Twain is the most famous. Mark Twain could wax eloquent enough over Scott's merely literary vapidity,[4] but when he turned to politics he outdid himself. In *Life on the Mississippi* he makes poor Sir Walter responsible for the gimcrack Gothic of the Louisiana state capitol, the flowery style of Southern newspaper reporters, and finally for all the benighted feudalism and reaction of Southern life. Indeed he says that Scott did so much to form Southern character that he was "in great measure responsible for the war."[5]

[3] Cf. pages 205 ff., above.

[4] See *Mark Twain's Letters*, edited by Albert Bigelow Paine (2 vols., New York, 1917). Paine says (page 736), "Mark Twain could never get up much enthusiasm for the writings of Scott. His praise of *Quentin Durward* is about the only approval he ever accorded to the works of the great romanticist." This remark has reference to two letters to Brander Matthews. Mark Twain had just been reading *Guy Mannering* with infinite disgust. After a series of questions implying that Scott was worthless, he writes, "Can you read him? and keep your respect for him? Of course a person could in *his* day — an era of sentimentality and sloppy romantics. . . . He *was* great, in his day, and to his proper audience; and so was God in Jewish times for that matter, but why should either of them rank high now," etc., etc. Of *Guy Mannering*: "that curious, curious book with its mob of squalid shadows jabbering around a single flesh-and-blood being — Dinmont; a book crazily put together out of the very refuse of the romance-artist's stage properties — finished it and took up *Quentin Durward,* and finished that. — It was like leaving the dead to mingle with the living . . . I wonder who wrote *Quentin Durward?*"

[5] Mark Twain's theories are echoed and elaborated by H. J. Eckenrode in "Sir Walter Scott in the South," *North American Review,* 206:595 (1917), where the South is declared to be naturally strongly democratic and progressive, the original center of American philosophical democracy. As such it was corrupted and de-

As for the medievalism in the novels, a writer in the *Nation* for 1893 [6] makes an important point and one that was coming to be recognized even a generation earlier, namely, that it seems weak to us because we know much more about it than did Scott's age. This is quite true. Jeffrey felt the failure of the characters in *Ivanhoe,* but the modern cultivated reader probably knows much more about the spirit of the Middle Ages than Jeffrey could. Yet whatever the professional historian may feel, the literary critic usually makes light of such objections or takes no notice of them whatever. The universal preference for the Scotch novels over the more distant historical ones is based not on the argument of mistaken notions of history, anachronism, and so forth, but rather on the fundamental impossibility of revivifying a long-past age, and of breathing into Gurths and Wambas the same life that the author could give to Bailie Nicol Jarvie or Dandie Dinmont. That is, it is a matter of disbelief in the historical novel, which the literary critic refuses to take very seriously anyway.

It is indeed rather surprising to find thoroughgoing defense of several of the romances in the *Times Literary Supplement* of the last decade.[7] The first of these, by W. P. Ker, published just

stroyed by the disillusionment of the French Revolution and by Scott's medievalism. Southern "chivalry" and its attendant qualities all sprang from Scott. The South became medieval and lost touch with the times, and the North took the lead, though it was never productive of great personalities. The writer concludes, "The American nation would be farther along the road to the solution of the great problems of human life if the Southern planters had not lost faith in democracy and sought inspiration in the unsubstantial visions of Sir Walter Scott." His special bent and his conception of Scott's character can be judged from such remarks as, "Probably no epoch of human existence has been much drearier than the Middle Ages"; and, "Scott had a pathetic trust in the efficacy of mere rank; if the king had touched him for the king's evil, his faith would have made him whole." But one should compare with this Grace W. Landrum, "Sir Walter Scott and His Literary Rivals in the Old South," *American Literature,* 2:256 (November, 1930). According to her, Scott had powerful rivals in romance, especially Byron and Bulwer. It is also clear that there was much unfavorable criticism and that the realistic side of the novels attracted more attention than the romantic. Altogether, Scott's influence was not toward a foolish romanticism; Mark Twain was greatly mistaken.— For the passages on Scott in *Life on the Mississippi,* see Chapters 40, 45, and 46.

  [6] *Nation,* 56:370 (May 18, 1893).
  [7] Written on their centenaries and republished in 1932 as *Centenary Essays.*

before his death, sings the praises of *Quentin Durward*. Mr. Ker's selection of *Durward* is comparatively fortunate, for Louis XI has always been accepted, along with James I in *Nigel,* as one of Scott's great figures, though Mr. Ker does praise also the hero and several of the minor characters. Later writers in this series are even more enthusiastic over the charms of such romances as the *Tales of the Crusaders, Count Robert of Paris,* and *The Fair Maid of Perth*. In these later years, however, the romances have found for the most part only lukewarm defenders.

This group is now indeed more likely to be mentioned rather as an important influence, as for instance by Professor Maynadier, who has studied the effect of *Ivanhoe* and its successors on the style of the nineteenth-century historian.[8] Professor Baldensperger [9] has shown how vast and sweeping was the influence of Scott's idea throughout Europe in 1827, especially in the impulse it gave to the ideal of a "world literature" and a broad historical outlook. An earlier writer [10] had even declared that the idea disclosed in *Waverley* in 1814, that is, the vivifying of history, was destined to exercise a greater influence on mankind than the fall of Napoleon, and that the validity and excellence of Scott's method, true to "the truth of history," is to be tested by the superiority of his creation to the raw material it came from, as in his portrait of James I and his pictures of Alsatia, in comparison with Shadwell and other sources. It is, of course, futile to deny Scott's importance as an innovator in the novel and in the writing of history. His most contemptuous detractors freely admit it, and we even have it charged against him as a religious or political crime of the first magnitude by violent opponents like Borrow and Mark Twain.

In a way, then, there is little opposition between the historians, who are chiefly concerned with the historical facts of the medieval and sixteenth- and seventeenth-century novels, and the literary critics, simply because the latter usually dismiss prac-

[8] "Ivanhoe and Its Consequences," in *Essays in Memory of Barrett Wendell* (Cambridge, 1926).
[9] *Revue de littérature comparée*, 7:47 (January, 1927).
[10] *Blackwood's*, 196:276 (August, 1914).

tically all these novels of older periods as inferior, and confine their criticism for the most part to the Scotch novels, where history is not so much a matter of public event and character as of national quality and temper. Thus to the historian's indignant request that we consider the errors of *Ivanhoe,* we have the countersuggestion that we try to appreciate the national character and Scotch coloring of *Rob Roy* and *The Heart of Midlothian.* It is not often that one finds such unalloyed enthusiasm as that of an Anglo-Catholic and Tory critic who, refusing to admit the validity and force of any unfavorable criticism of Scott, defends all the historical novels, even the feudal group, declaring that the faults found with *Ivanhoe* are insignificant, and are of moment only to the antiquarians; or of another *Quarterly* reviewer of 1897, who declares reverently and affectionately that history owes a great debt to Sir Walter for his fine characters of great figures — kings, statesmen, judges [11] — as well as for his portrayal of national manners and his wide knowledge of the lower orders of society.[12] Thus T. F. Henderson, in the *Cambridge History of English Literature* is more representative when he says[13] "that immortal gallery of Scotch

[11] E. A. Baker (*op. cit.*) makes an interesting and, it would seem, an original point concerning Scott's presentation of great historical characters. He notes that Scott is sparing in his drafts on actual history, that he avoids great episodes where history is in the making and keeps to the historical fringes or outskirts. This is closely related to the more fundamental idea that the novels deal with adventure rather than with action springing from the impulses of character, "the drama of human will at odds with circumstances," and that hence they are not in the real sense dramatic. He thinks this appears especially in Scott's great historical figures, who are never presented in crises involving great decisions as they are in Shakespeare. That is, Scott did not show history in the making, but characters as made by history. He could draw pictures of these great characters but was unable to present them in decisive action or reveal their deep-laid purposes. They *look* great but do not *act* greatly, for instance Louis XI and James I; the latter "displays his mannerisms and absurdities, but not his political ability." This treatment of character, Mr. Baker thinks, is reflected in Scott himself, who is said to have had dogged pertinacity, but not the will to form and execute great schemes. The theory is obviously related also to the idea Mr. Baker borrows from Reynaud that Scott was "sourdement déterministe"; neither he nor his characters had real freedom of action. Mr. Baker's choice of Jane Austen's Darcy as a contrasting man of action hardly seems convincing, considering the general effect of his character and the scope of the action he is involved in.

[12] *Quarterly Review,* 180:431 (April, 1895); 186:464 (October, 1897).

[13] "Sir Walter Scott," *Cambridge History of English Literature,* XII, Chapter I.

characters . . . is the most unequivocal testimony to his great-ness" and quite readily admits Scott's failure in many historical characters like Mary Stuart,[14] Claverhouse, and Montrose. Nearly always even the most favorable criticism of the historical novels is heavily qualified. They are, to begin with, put in a class by themselves below the others, and even then are apologized for and hedged about with damaging admissions. Thus Professor Henderson declares that Scott's power of reviving the past, at least as he saw it, was one of his great gifts, though his vision of the past was not always accurate, and though many of his details of fact and character come as a shock to the person who knows history.

It is the same with other critics, who however much they may find to praise in the romances, finally leave them in an inferior position. Thus Oliver Elton finds something to say even for the weakest. It is true, he says, that in the medieval novels, "to the religious and speculative note, the note of criticism or satire . . . he hardly responded at all," but Scott did love thoroughly "not only the lighter charm of romance" — ceremony and cos-tume — but also the soul of chivalry and adventure, as he drew it from Chaucer and Froissart. It is significant too that Elton's highest praise is reserved for one of the most modern of the group, *The Fortunes of Nigel,* and the character of James I. Nowhere does he speak disparagingly of Scott, but one reads be-tween the lines that he cares comparatively little for *Ivanhoe.*

H. A. Beers [15] had earlier taken much the same attitude. He praises Scott for giving life to history, which with the eighteenth-century historians had been a matter of formulae and ideas, and treating it dramatically and picturesquely. But of his medie-valism Beers says that he saw only its showy side, the battles and pageantry. He did not get at the spirit of chivalry; his books are quite unlike those of the period itself. This is merely, according

[14] Compare Maigron's enthusiasm, though chiefly on literary grounds, for the character of Mary Stuart. Many critics too have admired the portrait of Claver-house in *Old Mortality.*

[15] Henry A. Beers, *History of English Romanticism in the Nineteenth Century* (New York, 1901), Chapter I.

to Beers, declaring that Scott's medievalism is incomplete, though the best we have. Yet, after all, to say that Scott grasped only the externals, though no one has done better, is not so very different from the depreciatory argument that Scott's medievalism is all upholstery.

Saintsbury, who defends the historical novel in a series of three essays,[16] does so chiefly on a basis of technic and innovation. He tosses off lightly the charges against Scott's historical detail, and declares his belief that the novels usually, though not always, gained by the liberties the author took. But for him the great thing was Scott's perfect success with a form that had been bungled for two thousand years. Scott had the proper predisposition of interests and the historical preparation; "the Historical Novel had to be created, and Scott had to create it." He goes on in detail to praise Scott's tact in handling the dialogue, the fine background of reading he had for *Nigel* and *Woodstock*, and his grasp of the all-important law that the hero and heroine and the thread of story must be fictional. But it is clear that this, distinguishing as it is, is not the kind of praise awarded to the Scotch novels.[17]

Even Brandes, whose general conclusions on the novels are so damaging, is willing to give Scott great credit as an innovator in his treatment of history. Taking them together, Scotch novels and romances, he allows them high importance for the advance they marked in the understanding of history and the representation of lower- and middle-class life; and in a list of characters on whom he bestows the highest praise he includes not only Diana Vernon and Jeanie Deans but Louis XI. Yet he adds that it becomes increasingly clear how far Scott's historical impressions (medieval, that is) are from the reality; for instance, how he toned down the coarse elements.

After all, it is hard for the modern critic to become really enthusiastic and to speak with conviction until he strikes the

[16] In *Macmillan's*, "Scott and Dumas," 70:321 (September, 1894).
[17] For other typical defenses of Scott in the matter of history, especially anachronism, see A. Lang, *op. cit.*, and H. D. Sedgwick, *op. cit.*

Scotch novels and Scotch history. Paul Elmer More [18] is able to praise wholeheartedly the historical quality of the Scotch novels, which he says are for mature readers while the historical novels are for boys. Prose romances cannot live, he says, "unless firmly grounded in realism" as the Scotch novels are, or unless, like Hawthorne's, they are "surcharged with spiritual meanings." He explains that having attempted to read a new history of Scotland by Andrew Lang, he had found the novels the only guiding ray of light through the mazes and involutions of that work; only where they illustrated the history could he follow and understand it. He says that they owe much of their life to their national quality, and he even believes that any novelist is to be judged ultimately by his portraiture not of persons but of a people. This conception is now very common, it would seem, whether one thinks of *Robinson Crusoe* or *Tom Jones,* or of *The Forsyte Saga, The Old Wives Tale,* or *Babbitt.* It is not unusual to find the greatest significance of novels in their quality as historical documents, in their value as records of national life. Obviously Mr. More would find the history he sought in *Waverley* or *The Antiquary* rather than in *Ivanhoe* or *Quentin Durward.* The focussing of Mr. More's interest on the Scotch novels is apparent in his conclusion. The Scotch temperament deriving from Scotch landscape and Celtic blood, full of peculiar shades and contradictions — that Scott catches it in all its nuances, he says, is proof of his realistic powers; here is romance walking "hand in hand with the soberest realities."

When one takes all the latter-day discussion of Scott's history together, it is clear that it is this kind of history — the living history of Scotland caught by Scott at first hand — that now holds the critic's attention and commands his admiration. Mr. More, who entitles his essay "The Scotch Novels and Scotch History," is evidently not concerned with Sir Walter's notions of the Crusades or the court of Queen Elizabeth. The same is really true of Woodberry, of whom one gets the impression that

[18] "The Scotch Novels and Scotch History," in *Shelburne Essays* (3d series, New York, 1907).

he is writing out of a passionate fondness for Scott, whom he has known always, but that he has forgotten *Ivanhoe* and *Kenilworth* and really remembers the Waverley novels as Scotch. And so it is with most other writers. This is what the sifting process of time has done for Scott. The older critics did not feel that they could pass by the romances quite so lightly; they had to take them into account. But their successors have no such feeling. As a result we have no longer any great interest in the romances or in Scott's medievalism, or at most such as Beers and Elton express. We do find, it is true, an occasional glowing tribute to the portraits of Louis XI or James I, but most of the critics are too absorbed in their contemplation of Jeanie Deans or Dandie Dinmont or the witches of *The Bride of Lammermoor* to pay much attention to this other gallery. In fact, there have been those to protest that the high excellence of these Scotch figures has worked an unmerited hardship on Scott's portraits of kings and queens and other historic personages.

The feeling that the Scotch novels are great historical documents, while it is not at all new, is much stronger than ever before. It has close connections, of course, with the current conceptions of Scott's philosophy and ideas. Indeed, just as most of the really penetrating discussions of his style turn very soon into considerations of his depth and wisdom and philosophical connotations, so also do the finer discussions of his history converge to the same point. That is, fundamentally of course, there is no real separation between questions of style, philosophy, and history. Scott's history is very little a matter of mere factual accuracy; in his best work, the Scotch novels, it is a matter of the deeper realities of Scotch character. From this point of view the only significant charge brought against him is one made by his own contemporaries with considerable violence that, blinded by his Tory, aristocratic prejudices, he failed to understand and appreciate the religious fervor of the old Covenanters. He himself was his ablest defender on this point. But the objection, were it sustained, would seriously undermine the position his later apologists claim for him, for it would impugn his understanding of one of the most essential strains in the Scottish character.

Thus Mr. More's essay takes a line that has been followed by the most thoughtful and most effective modern critics. One of the most interesting articles in the short-lived *Sir Walter Scott Quarterly* (1927–28), "Sir Walter's Pageant of Scottish History" by R. S. Rait, historiographer of Scotland, celebrates Scott's deep understanding of Scotland. Professor Rait declares that Scott understood Scotch history better than anyone who has ever lived. In one place or another he deals with most of the great Scottish figures, but above these is his conception of the people. He told Washington Irving that the character of a people was not to be learned from its fine folks, and his really humble characters eclipse the great ones. His work, Professor Rait says, "is never merely a pageant of Scottish history; it is always a pageant of Scottish life."

Professor Rait again defended Scott as a historian in his essay "Walter Scott and Thomas McCrie" (in *Sir Walter Scott Today*), where, having studied minutely the historical background of *Old Mortality*, he is able to show that in all essentials Scott is scrupulously fair to the Covenanters and is even unfair to Claverhouse, to whom his traditional sympathies would naturally attract him. Mr. Grierson in his introduction marks the importance of this essay as demonstrating Sir Walter's fairness and regard for justice; "the suspicion with which his common sense kept watch over the impulses of his romantic imagination, of his own sympathies and prejudices, has made him to some extent even unfair to those whom in his heart he loved and admired [i.e., in regard to Claverhouse and in certain respects Mary Stuart]. . . . It was not in his novels, but alas! in his affairs . . . that Scott gave a too free rein to the impulses of his romantic imagination." From the beginning those who have read the Scotch novels have known that Scott was not a Tory partisan in the novels. Hazlitt, for instance, could hardly have written of them as he did, had this been true. Yet there is occasionally in modern criticism the suggestion that this poise and balance is merely prudent trimming, that Sir Walter was simply a Tory canny enough to keep in with the Whigs, a Jacobite shrewd enough to curry favor with the Hanoverians.

No one, however, has shown more clearly than Professor Grierson the nature of Scott's function as a historical novelist, or explained more significantly the value of his realism in romance. He makes the point that what Scott actually did was to enlarge the range of the realistic novel by bringing the past within its scope, by giving historical material the attractions of the eighteenth-century novel. Thus his real affinity is with Defoe, Fielding, Smollett, not with Walpole nor Mrs. Radcliffe.[19] Superstition, for instance, he introduced not for its own sake but to reveal the mind of the superstitious peasant. One remembers Lady Louisa Stuart's remark, "This recalls Defoe." And what he did with history, Mr. Grierson continues, was not to present it as in a dream, that is, to charm the reader back into the past, but to bring the past up into the present. He draws an illuminating contrast between Scott's method and that used in a modern Spanish novel of the period of Philip II, where the author actually gets into the age and seems to share its feelings and assume its moral point of view, so that debauchery and murder seem trivial crimes beside indulgence toward heretics and Jews.[20] Scott

[19] The idea of Scott as in the line of the eighteenth-century realists is of course by no means a new one. It was suggested frequently by his contemporaries when they looked at his more realistic side. It fell into abeyance in the Victorian period when critics saw chiefly contrasts and oppositions, but it has been systematically developed by several modern critics. One of the most brilliant statements of it is that of Charles H. Herford (*The Age of Wordsworth*, London, 1897, pp. 109 ff.), who calls Scott "the last and greatest of the race of realists and humorists who created the English novel." The usual objections to the novels he brushes aside as trifling "in the presence of creative power so colossal"; and, from the historical point of view, he declares that Scott used his great realistic and humorous powers, together with his romantic feeling for picturesque color and contrast, to record Scotland imperishably, as no other country has been recorded by the labor of one man, in "the very stuff of its people, the very genius of its soil."

[20] This was the point of view of Balzac, who wished to apply Scott's minutely detailed historical description not only to the life of his own time, nineteenth-century France, but also to the past, but who tried when he went back into the past, as in the *Contes drôlatiques*, "to write and feel and think as if he were a Frenchman of the sixteenth century, a contemporary of Rabelais." See R. H. Gordon, *op. cit.* Scott's readers are never allowed to forget that he is a nineteenth-century gentleman and historian.

on the other hand never lapses from the point of view of the present. Mr. Grierson does not claim for him the power to reproduce the past, to give the *frisson historique* as could Hugo, Balzac, Flaubert, or William Morris. What he could do was to create the feeling that the past had once been a present, like today; that human nature was always the same. For instance, there is the highly realistic atmosphere of *Waverley*, a Jacobite novel in which Flora is the only romantic Jacobite. In a realistic, humorous picture Scott makes the assumptions "that the men of the past were like those of today, that then as now in any great political movement you would find all sorts of men engaged, and for the most diverse reasons, that the true idealists would be few, the self-seeking numerous, and perhaps even more numerous those who, like Edward, go with the tide." [21]

Thus again Sir Walter is closely allied to Defoe, and his romance is solidly founded on realism. Here, as with Mr. More, is a conception of the novels as embodying a romance "which walks hand in hand with the soberest realities." Earlier critics valued Scott's realism and celebrated him for his services to history, but it was not until these later days, it would seem, that his critics, concerned almost altogether with the Scotch novels, have caught so fully the meaning of the novels as history.

[21] See a centenary address reprinted in the *Columbia University Quarterly*, 25:9 (March, 1933), and the introduction to his edition of Scott's letters (1932 ff.), pp. lxxii ff.

Part IV · Recapitulation

RECAPITULATION

OUT OF THE mass of commentary on the Waverley novels that has accumulated in the last century and more, certain definite and incontrovertible facts, as well as many debatable ones, emerge. There is no doubt at all of Scott's tremendous popularity with a broad reading public until nearly 1900, nor of his secure position with the critics for as long or nearly as long. One may dismiss as a critical commonplace his popularity in his own time, with the reminder, however, that it included, on the authority of Carlyle and others, the very highest and most critical levels of the reading public. The merely popular best-selling novelist of today does not presumably include among his devoted readers men like Goethe, Hazlitt, DeQuincey, Byron, Jeffrey, and Coleridge; neither did he (or she) attract and hold such readers a century ago. And from the written records it is clear that Scott maintained his position, despite strong competition and the fading of novelty, for two generations or so after his death. The Victorians continued to read him with real interest, and they wrote about him in letters and memoirs and in their critical literature much as had his contemporaries. They even exclaimed and wondered over the prodigality and sweep of his genius, his nobility of spirit, and his sound humanity. He had become a classic, but he had not turned into marble. To the Victorians he was very much alive.

Indeed it is not putting it too strongly to say that from 1814 until nearly 1900 he was generally regarded as the greatest of English novelists, and at least the peer of the greatest Continental classics, that is, Cervantes and Le Sage. Of course the group we refer to as the French and Russians were unread and unknown in England, outside very narrow circles, until almost the end of the century. With his contemporaries Scott had all the advantages of the innovator. His novels were so different in all respects from any they had known that they were swept off their feet. They refused for a moment to allow any of the great eighteenth-century writers to place near him. Fielding might be wittier, Richardson certainly explored more thoroughly the female heart, but all that was nothing. None of them dealt with human life on the scale he did, none of them was either so broadly learned or so deeply wise, none of them so humane. Of course none of them was so pure or so good. And their view of life was provincial, parochial; his was national.

As for his romanticism in itself, quite naturally he was often thrown into contrast with Byron by his contemporaries. Many of course preferred him on moral grounds, but there were notable critics like Hazlitt and Landor whose preference had an aesthetic basis; critics who contrasted his simplicity and sincerity with the hectic extravagance and self-consciousness of Byron. Still, he was most frequently contrasted with the novelists, practically always to his advantage.

Such views persisted among the Victorian critics. *Tom Jones* was admired by the more broad-minded especially for its technic, and so was *Clarissa,* but there were too many charges to be listed against such books. There was too much immorality and indecency; there was also the narrow scope. Scott was epic and national; they must still be thought narrow and local. The romantic novel must necessarily be a higher and finer type, nobler and more inspiring. Nor did their own novelists stand the comparison better than the early ones. Here too as with the eighteenth-century writers there was the clog of realism. Dickens was never really accepted by his more critical contemporaries; they thought he had amazing talents, but he was vulgar and low, a mere caricaturist of London types. His devoted readers were of the middle and lower levels. Thackeray of course was of a higher order, but he too lacked the aspiration, the romantic wings of Scott. He was depressing, he was cynical; after all, surely not altogether a force for good. George Eliot could really muster the best case. She was regarded by the critical with a reverence like that paid to Scott, as a great moral leader, but she never captured the popular imagination as Scott did, and her reputation among the intellectual began to decline almost as soon as it reached its zenith. At her highest in the seventies she was by the nineties probably the worst off of any of the great Victorians.

After all, the new novelists of the Victorian era had their share of attention from the critics and the public at large, but there was not one of them who was generally and steadily referred to with the reverent respect, for either aesthetic or moral virtues, that was accorded Scott. The Victorians might feel the lack of a definite, tangible philosophy or of a practical message easily applicable to their own social problems, but when it came to the point, there was no one of their own who could quite fill his shoes. Really the Victorian period, as far as he was concerned, was merely an extension of his own time. Until nearly 1900, again, Scott would certainly have come out far in the lead in any contest for supremacy in the field of the novel. Occasionally a Victorian critic might proclaim *Henry Esmond* or *Tom Jones* a greater masterpiece than any one of the Waverleys, or Parson Adams a greater creation than any of Scott's, yet he could not bring himself to exalt Thackeray or Fielding above Sir Walter.

Is it not true that the widely popular writer must be romantic? He must be hopeful and inspiring, optimistic in his view of life, and he must write with ease and abandon. The love and the adventure and action count too, but the moral qualities are even more important. Dickens is the other most naturally popular English novelist and he too, beneath a very thin surface of realism, is a romantic. But none of the rest is fitted for a really wide popularity—the kind attained by *Robinson Crusoe,* which, though realistic enough in some of its aspects is romantic in its surface and in its moral implications, or *The Vicar of Wakefield,* a novel of highly romantic sentiment. But Thackeray and Fielding, satirical and critical, and George Eliot, a professional philosopher, could never be so widely popular. In many periods they might appeal to the critics more strongly than the romantics would, but in the Victorian age theory itself favored the romantics.

The continual comparison with Shakespeare from the very beginning is one of the most striking features of Scott criticism, and one of the best indications of where Scott stood for almost a century. The highest compliment that any English critic can pay a writer is to link his name with Shakespeare's. Shakespeare's place is apart, of course, yet to indicate that there is any basis for comparison, even at a distance, or in some single quality, is a supreme compliment, a device for suggesting superlative genius. One is not so greatly surprised to find this high reverence among Scott's contemporaries; the innumerable anecdotes about the reception of the novels prepare one for that, but to find it persisting among Victorians and even among twentieth-century writers — that does give one pause.

Indeed, it is easy enough to cite a list of responsible critics of the last generation who like to set him next to Shakespeare in some way. We find Saintsbury, for instance, declaring in 1894 that "the consensus of the best critics would put him next to Shakespeare as a creator of individual character of the miscellaneous human sort" (though below Shakespeare, Fielding, and Thackeray "in a subtle intimacy and massive completeness of execution"). Or, among critics with a moral bias, such a question as H. D. Sedgwick's, "As a power for good, who shall come next to Shakespeare, Dante, and Cervantes, if not Walter Scott?" is not untypical. "Like Shakespeare, he had the instinctive power of intellectual creation"[1] — one soon comes to expect this sort of allusion, or Woodberry's still bolder parallel, that as Shakespeare is the first of dramatists, Scott is the first of romancers. Mr. Paul Elmer More prefers his witches to Shakespeare's, and also declares that Scott is at times closer to Shakespeare than any other author, though ordinarily more in the vein of the lesser Elizabethans. Thomas Seccombe believes that we should regret the loss of the novels and songs only as we should the loss of Shakespeare. And Virginia Woolf's figure of the wide sea where

[1] *Quarterly*, 186:464 (October, 1897).

only the greatest can take us certainly implies for any English reader a comparison with Shakespeare. Even so late a critic as Lord David Cecil, whose writing is highly analytical and certainly not suffused with tender emotions, can say, "Scott may be the most imperfect of English novelists, but he is the only one whose great moments can be compared with Shakespeare's."[2]

Here too the comparison springs most frequently from Scott's ease and prodigality in the creation of character and his instinctive, natural understanding and sympathy — his broad and tolerant humanity. Of course any critic may, if he is deeply enthusiastic about his subject, compare him with Shakespeare. Jane Austen, Fielding, George Eliot, and others have been so honored, but surely Shakespeare's name does not spring out on the pages devoted to them so persistently, so regularly, as it does here.

And if his friends do not hesitate to mention Shakespeare's name, they are even more fluent in making him the peer, at least, of all the other great writers with whom there is any point at all in comparing him. With Homer of course the ease of comparison is obvious if a critic wishes to emphasize Scott's epic quality, but there are also Cervantes and Le Sage and Balzac and in these later days Tolstoi and Dostoevski and Flaubert. Altogether, as far as other names could be drafted, they have been set beside Scott's to his glory.

The attitude toward Scott's limitations has also from the beginning been clear and definite. There has been lately the feeling that the recognition of his flaws was recent, that the advance in the technic of the novel and its intellectual pretensions in general had made Scott and (to a less degree, perhaps) most of the older novelists seem clumsy and childish. But this is not true. The sense of his defects may have been intensified, but they were quite apparent to his contemporaries, who took him to task for them from the very first. From *Waverley* on he was charged with careless, diffuse writing, bad plot construction, conventional, flat heroes and heroines. He himself took note

[2] See the introduction to his edition of *Short Stories by Sir Walter Scott* (Oxford, 1934).

of all these charges and answered them or at least commented on them. With them was of course involved the question of artistic conscience and of commercialism, which Scott also took note of, and which was echoed regretfully by the Victorians and contemptuously by modern critics who seem to think that Scott's motives were few and simple — that he wrote altogether for money to squander on a pretentious estate.

It is not to be denied that his standard of success in the case of any given novel was the volume of sales. He did have his eye on the public and his thoughts on Abbotsford. In general he cared little what the criticis said so long as the sales kept up. This is impressed on the reader of Lockhart again and again. It weighed heavily upon the thoughts of the admiring Miss Martineau, and it caused Carlyle many a shaking of the head. But this was not the whole story. The reader of Lockhart and of the journal and letters knows that Scott wrote for love if ever any one did, that the stuff of the novels until the last few years was what he should naturally have written about, though with admixtures of foreign matter that the conventions of the time forced him, he thought, to add, especially conventional love stories with proper heroes and heroines upon whom he spent as little time as possible. The matter of speed and carelessness some of the contemporary critics were as caustic about as the later ones, but he was convinced that he had to write fast — carefully outlined plots, and sentences and phrases ground out in the sweat of his brow, were not for him; he froze into lifelessness when he tried them.

And while he wrote to please the present, he was conscious of the genius of some of his pages and felt that future generations would know of him. He declared that for him at any rate the most copious writers had been the best, and he believed that success in one's own time did not necessarily imply a merely temporary fame. Indeed Scott was not simply the manufacturing best seller who was willing to work under high pressure to exploit a market and make hay while the sun shone. It looked that way sometimes, but after all he was a man of genius with something unique to give, and to give in tremendous amounts, and he had according to his temperament to pour it out freely and get on to the new creations that came crowding on the heels of those that were shaping under his hand.

There is another point that should be taken into account. Scott's genius coined money for him and he was delighted. The money that rolled in on him exposed him to situations, to temptations, and to faulty judgments that no man of letters had had to face before. Many of the eighteenth-century writers too had been concerned about money, because they had to rake and scrape to keep the wolf from the door. Scott came at the beginning of an age in which it was increasingly easy to make a good living at literature, even to become wealthy. Considering the size of his public, Scott's success was the most amazing of the century, but many popular writers after him — James, Ainsworth, Dickens, Reade, Trollope, Thackeray, even the high-brow George Eliot, to mention only a few, none of them mere best sellers — made excellent, even large incomes, though as a rule nothing to compare with the huge successes of later authors like Bennett, Wells, and Galsworthy. On the other hand, difficult writers like Meredith and Conrad, who came to be regarded as great, but were never popular, were released from financial worry only at the end of their careers. But the "successful" writers of the nineteenth and twentieth centuries have had to be concerned with money. They no longer had to take the crumbs thrown them by the booksellers; they treated with their publishers *de haut en bas,* as Scott did, and drove the best bargains they could, either themselves or through their agents (one should remember the famous Pinker who cuts such a figure in Arnold Bennett's journals). In their memoirs and letters there is a great deal about money, investments, and business. Financial affairs are prominent in Forster's *Dickens,* just as they are in Lockhart's *Scott,* and at least it can be said that Scott was more dignified and composed in his dealings than the naive and impulsive Charles Dickens was in his. There are no records in Lockhart comparable to those of Dickens' tantrums — especially the one over the returns of *The Christmas Carol,* which though a huge popular success was a financial disappointment. Thackeray too was deeply concerned with his profits. He wished to live luxuriously and to leave his daughters able to do so after his death. Charles Reade threw himself into business with all the gusto and ingenuity of a modern business man. Trollope furnishes the reader of his *Autobiography* with complete financial statistics, and in our own times there is the shining example of Arnold Bennett, whose life is a "success" story to be bound up in the same volume with Henry Ford's or Lord Northcliffe's. These successful writers were all more or less worldly; they had to be. The more money they made the more they had to concern themselves with worldly affairs. And as has been contended before, Scott's ambition to establish a distinguished family in a great house at Abbotsford was by no means the sordid ambition it can easily be made out to be. It was excessively romantic and from the romantic point of view may be regarded with great sympathy.[3] The climactic argument against him in this regard has been the Ballantyne-Constable affair, and the latest and most judicial analysis of that, the one made by a Scotch lawyer at the instance of Professor Grierson, leaves one with the impression that he is to be charged with nothing worse than poor judgment in business.[4]

There is also the charge of political narrowness and animosity. This was to be expected in his own time. Suggestions of Toryism were infuriating to a man like Hazlitt and irritating to so determined a progressive as Macaulay in the next generation. In fact they were deplored by many of the Victorians, who were not only enamoured of progress, but were made to realize by their own

---

[3] Scott's feeling about Abbotsford is made clear enough in his letters, especially in the phrases "my romance of a house," "a sort of romance in architecture," "a place to dream of, not to tell," which appear continually in his letters of 1825. See, *inter alia,* Grierson, *Letters,* VII, 367; VIII, 129.

[4] It is of course possible to brush aside all such argument and to contend as Frank Swinnerton does in *The Georgian Scene* (New York, 1934), p. 310, that a novelist should be professional, not amateur; that the opposite of professionalism is dilettantism. Mr. Swinnerton thinks that the successful novelists of the past have been quite justified in taking the money that came to them and did not need to worry about the prostitution of genius.

novelists that the novel might be put to good practical use to teach, quite directly, improved ways of life. Certainly Scott's novels contained no "message" and had been written to give pleasure, not to serve a cause. And they did, of course, cast a glamour over feudal ideas. The charge has persisted too, rather surprisingly perhaps, in our own age, where it takes the form of thinness and superficiality, a kind of light-headed fondness for romantic trappings and picturesque feudalism, without any concern for the realities of life or the good of the people. This charge may be easily combined with the one of commercialism, and Sir Walter may be made to seem a selfish, sentimental worshipper of the past who capitalized and exploited his literary fluency and adroitly made it produce the trivial toys which delighted him.

Against these latter two charges Scott's chief bulwark has been Lockhart's *Life*. The really careful critics of the novels have from the first noticed his fairness in political concerns, the even keel on which he sailed between Whig and Tory, Covenanter and Episcopalian, Jacobite and Hanoverian. *Old Mortality, Waverley, Redgauntlet,* perhaps the novels where his prejudices would be most involved, have seemed to critics always to give each side its just dues. And Lockhart's record of his life, supplemented by the letters and journal, shows how the charges of political bigotry, like those of commercialism, have been exaggerated. After all, the idea that Scott was a narrow and reactionary Tory and a reckless money-grubber to boot must yield to a careful and dispassionate reading of the novels and the biographical material. It must be remembered too that the typical modern biographer, in reaction against hero-worship and sentimental adulation, feels that to do his duty he must provide his idol with feet of clay at least.

The great difficulty with the Waverley novels today, however, is not due to Scott's personal qualities in themselves, but rather to the great change that has come over the novel in the last fifty years. Scott a century or more ago was a tremendous power in France; now the French influence rolls back again and defeats

Sir Walter. The Waverley novels are old-fashioned; if Scott were writing them now, no matter how hasty and careless and fluent he was, he certainly would write them differently, and in many ways, if not in all, would improve them. But the change in moral point of view, the development of realism and naturalism, the highly subjective and minutely psychological nature of the serious novel, and the endless adventures in technic have all outmoded the Waverley novels. Some of the older novels fit much better into the modern scheme of things — notably Fielding's and Jane Austen's. *Tom Jones* has moral freedom and it has form — though latterly form has been eyed askance. We are no longer in the era of Henry James, and plotting and arrangement of life in a pattern is held to distort it. But Jane Austen, who also has form, is an ideal realist in her cool detachment. There is also the modern exaltation of the Brontës, especially Emily, and of Trollope and, above all, of Dickens. The novels of all these writers fit the modern conception better for one reason or another than do the Waverley series. Until the last few years of this period, doubtless Fielding would have been thought by the majority of critics to be our greatest novelist; it seems fairly clear now that for the moment, at any rate, Dickens is ousting him as Scott did once before. The reality and vividness, the intense dramatic quality that Dickens consistently maintains, even in his worser moments, give him an advantage over all the rest, and the idea of caricature and extravagance which the serious Victorian critic could not pass over has been successfully explained away in various subtle and ingenious arguments by Santayana, Chesterton, George Gissing, and even Osbert Sitwell. The qualities the modern critic demands of his own novelists are not to be found conspicuously in Dickens, and in some respects Dickens might be as irritating as Scott — in the matter of morals and love affairs and heroes and heroines, for instance; but Scott seems to have none of the desirable qualities at all, or if he has they are so buried in the mass of his novels that the unsympathetic refuse to believe they are there.

Thus Scott is very badly off with the modern critical public.

And he is just as badly off with the uncritical public, to whom he must seem insuperably dull and heavy when they compare him with the swift, racy, sensational matter provided for them in infinite amounts. Gone are the days when either critic or common reader marveled at the breathless interest and the steady flow of action that "the Author of Waverley" maintained in his novels! It would seem useless to hope that readers brought up on an unrestricted diet of the literary provender so artfully prepared for them out of the startling and sensational, the sentimental, the scandalous, and the pornographic, to hit the exact taste of the moment, could ever read with pleasure what must seem to them endless, ponderous, stilted, antiquated books.

But then one comes back to the fact that most of what has been written about Scott during the last generation or so has been militantly, aggressively friendly, and to the conclusion that scattered throughout the huge mass of the English-reading public all over the world there are many who read his novels. One is told by librarians that he seems to be liked especially by "older men," and it is notable that his defenders are definitely academic and professorial. The "older men" perhaps are willing to read books that are slow and heavy; they are not attracted by the garish bright-lights of commercial fiction and they probably do not care to rise to the difficult levels of the modern serious novel which may seem to them precious, or indecent, or both. As for the friendly critics — the academic and professorial — they are used to the arguments of historical criticism, and are quite willing, even eager, as in an adventure, to meet an author on his own ground in his own century. They do not object to the antique idiom, and having a respect for tradition and historical importance, are willing to investigate. They are readers to whom Scott's importance as an innovator, as a great influence in literature and history, is really an importance. They will persist through the deadly undergrowth that chokes up the approaches to *The Heart of Midlothian,* for instance, and, however conscious of limitations and defects, will be properly disposed to discover things that they can admire. That is, they are willing to read like scholars, making all allowances for the manner of another age, as one must make allowances for virtually all classics if they are to be understood and read with real pleasure.

Their arguments are doubtless effective with readers of their own kind; they have probably encouraged those with a passive or potential, dormant interest to read the novels. But when one gets outside the range of cultivated readers of the right temperament and the special tolerances, how far will their arguments work? Certainly there is no hope, as some of them seem to think, of restoring Scott as a great popular classic, read for pleasure by great masses of people well down through the various levels of the public, as he was until fifty years ago. Are such readers impressed for more than a sentimental moment, perhaps, by the appeal to a sense of gratitude such as the Victorian critic made? Or, for that matter, by a description of the author's personal charm, or by academic arguments of any sort, historical or aesthetic? The novels must seem as easily and naturally interesting as those of Bennett or Conrad or Galsworthy, if one is thinking of the upper levels, or they must meet the strident competition of the "drugstore literature," if one is on the lower levels. And, as everyone knows, the literature of one's own age is inevitably for the average reader the most easily comprehensible and interesting.

Yet the arguments used by the modern critics are well chosen, the best calculated to influence cultivated readers who can be touched by historical or aesthetic argument. For one thing it is the habit of the most understanding critics now as formerly to ignore almost completely the historical romances and to write of the Waverley novels as though they were produced for the most part between 1814 and 1820. That is, it is the romantic realism in Scott that appeals to them, and it is Scott as the romantic historian of Scotch life that they are anxious to present. To do this they sweep aside all the old stock objections, admitting them freely and demanding of the reader an enthusiasm for the fine passages where Scott's genius for portraying the life of his native country shines forth. Thus it is Scott the romantic realist whom they celebrate. They may praise a few of his great figures — Louis XI, James I, Elizabeth; but it is Dandie Dinmont, Meg Merrilies, Bailie Nicol Jarvie, Edie Ochiltree, the Mucklebackits, the old women of *Lammermoor,* and Jeanie Deans that they conjure up to prove Scott's greatness, his deep insight into the core of Scotch life.

Idea and philosophy, a meaning of life, they find shadowed forth in these characters and others — "essential loyalties" to the ideals represented in chivalry and feudalism, and dramatized at great moments in "the swift word and the swift deed," which they would have us take in lieu of the careful exposition and analysis of intricate motives to which we are used. They find in Scott a noble and unaffected love and reverence of the people, a fine democratic spirit which gives the lie to the narrow, reactionary Toryism he is charged with, and which some of them, at least, find deeper and sounder than the democracy of that professed democrat, Charles Dickens.

Even the strong modern reaction against the historical novel as a type is brushed aside as irrelevant by these later defenders. The novels as history, the question of anachronism, of the effect on both the reading and the writing of history, had always been an important concern of the critics, and the argument had for the most part been settled strongly in Scott's favor. His anachronisms were not important; he encouraged the reading of history; he improved the style of the historian. And in our own time it has been easy to defend the Scotch novels, always recognized as his greatest and most representative work, without violating the prevalent dogmas of realism, especially the cardinal one that the novelist must stick to his own time. For it is declared, and quite convincingly, that the Scotland of *The Heart of Midlothian* and even of *Old Mortality* was still in all essentials the Scotland of *The Antiquary,* that Scotch life and character of 1680 and of 1800 were not far apart. Hence, whatever may be said against *Ivanhoe* and *Kenilworth,* the Scotch novels may still be called sound and authentic. They may not only be called great realistic masterpieces by literary critics but may be taken by a distinguished modern historian to prove Scott the greatest of all historians of his native country.

In the matter of style, Sir Walter's modern critics have also developed the best possible line of defense. They refer us to those high points where Scott's inspiration rises freest, when the nobility and grandeur of the common Scotch character is revealing itself in a crisis — the offered sacrifice of Fergus MacIvor's henchman at the trial, the mourning and funeral scenes of the Mucklebackits, Edie Ochiltree in the storm, Jeanie Deans at Effie's trial and before the queen. Scott's national sweep and eloquence in these moments as he expresses himself in the dialect of his people (an eloquence celebrated a century and more ago by Maria Edgeworth, Hazlitt, and numerous others, and today especially by Chesterton) they would have us believe mark him as a great stylist. All the rest they would have us ignore or pass over rapidly and lightly, reading as Scott read — and wrote — in great handfuls.

This of course means going to meet the author halfway or more. Only the sympathetic or the more cultivated readers will be willing to do it. They may be willing to cross the monotonous plains (or even the arid deserts, perhaps) for the sake of the oasis they think is coming. But the great mass of readers must have their attention caught at once, their interest inspired from the beginning, else there is no hope. And with them, at any rate, it must seem that there can be no hope. Unless there is some unforeseen revolution of taste, Scott can never again be the great popular novelist that he was in the nineteenth century. But he has now many devoted and highly convincing spokesmen, whose arguments are suited to stimulate interest in readers of special sorts, readers who find in the Scotch novels the utterance of great genius.

It is sometimes said that a fondness for Scott is merely the result of tradition, of anecdotes about him or the sentimental association with childish or youthful reading, and that a serious rereading of the novels would be bound to dispel all such mists of sentiment. This may be true in some cases; it is not true in all. The modern partisans of Scott seem well stored with specific information and with carefully selected passages for quotation — passages, moreover, which illustrate the maturest and most significant side of Scott — by no means merely those a boy might remember from *Ivanhoe* or *The Talisman*. Their criticism is in most cases careful, responsible, detailed, not couched in terms of tender appreciation.

On the other hand, is it not just as fair to assume that the modern disregard or contempt of Scott which certainly permeates the atmosphere may be the result of modern prejudices and assumptions that might yield to, or at least be qualified by, an unprejudiced, even sympathetic, rereading, if that were possible? Certainly the indifferent or derogatory critic, with his tone of peremptory and sweeping dismissal, is less well fortified with instance and illustration and is more likely to be dogmatic. Possibly a fresh start might reveal to him some of the powers and qualities that have led many notable readers in the past to think Walter Scott a great genius.

Even such a critic might at last grudgingly admit that he had caught a glimpse or two of what Spenser depicts in certain lines in *The Faërie Queene*, lines which Sir Walter quotes in the epistle introductory to *The Fortunes of Nigel*:

    . . . Bestrew'd all with rich array
    Of pearl and precious stones of great assay,
    And all the gravel mix'd with golden ore.

No one today will maintain that the ore of the Waverley novels is unmixed with gravel; yet there are still, and doubtless ever will be, the faithful, the convinced, whose eyes see the gravel all mixed with gold, and even with pearl and precious stones of great assay.

Index

INDEX

Many casual allusions have been omitted from the index, as well as purely biblio-graphical citations, except as they seemed to be needed to clarify *op. cit.* references in the footnotes. Fictitious characters, including historical characters who appear in the Waverley novels, are entered in single quotation marks. The innumerable references to Sir Walter Scott and the Waverley novels are not included; under Sir Walter Scott, aside from a few minor works, will be found only topical entries for which Scott seemed the most convenient heading.

Abbot, The, 26, 34–35, 36n, 37, 45, 69, 75, 78, 79, 110, 111, 114, 150, 167, 210; 'Mary Stuart,' 26, 35, 69, 79, 187, 219, 322, 326

Abbotsford, 5, 174, 215, 223, 226, 261, 313, 336, 338

L'Abeille, 12

Addison, Joseph, 77n, 130, 259

Adolphus, J. L., 29, 80, 107 ff., 163, 240

Aeschylus, 178, 242

'Ailsie,' i.e., Ailsie Gourlay, *see The Bride of Lammermoor*

Ainger, Alfred, 252, 281, 288, 310

Ainsworth, Harrison, 21, 46, 123, 161, 188, 253, 337

Aitken, Miss, 115

'Alasco,' *see Kenilworth*

Alfieri, 274

Alfred, King, 35

Alison, Sir Archibald, 190

Allsop, Thomas, 149, 150

Anastasius, 54, 102, 108, 157

Anne of Geierstein, 28, 93–94, 98, 102, 163, 164, 165, 186

Antigone, 241

Anti-Jacobin Review, 72

Antiquary, The, 24, 25, 42, 48, 49, 72, 113, 116, 118n, 122, 143, 163, 165, 173n, 224, 256n, 267, 269, 312n; 'Dousterswivel,' 16; 'Edie Ochiltree,' 42, 81, 89n, 240, 256n, 304, 305, 307, 344; the 'Mucklebackits,' 240, 256n, 344

'Argyle, Duke of,' *see The Heart of Midlothian*

Ariosto, 97, 189, 274

Arnold, Matthew, 196

Arnold, Thomas, 278

'Ashton, Lucy,' *see The Bride of Lammermoor*

'Ashton, Sir William,' *see The Bride of Lammermoor*

'Athelstane,' *see Ivanhoe*

Athenaeum, 98 ff., 249

Austen, Jane, 7, 48, 116, 119, 176, 177, 185, 187, 189, 267, 290, 335, 340; *Pride and Prejudice*, 189, 310; 'Darcy,' 321

Bagehot, Walter, 133, 168, 182, 217 ff., 222, 225, 244, 276n, 302, 307

Baillie, Joanna, 118n

Baker, E. A., 37n, 240–41, 306–07

'Balderstone, Caleb,' *see The Bride of Lammermoor*

Baldensperger, Fernand, 320

Balfour, A. J., 273

Balfour, Graham, 269

Ballantyne brothers, 5, 32n, 166n, 167, 170, 265, 338; James Ballantyne, 23n, 30n, 31, 35n, 36n, 38, 38n, 50n; John Ballantyne, 21

Balzac, 11, 37n, 232, 233, 264, 269, 275, 299, 300, 304, 327n, 328, 335

Banim brothers, 265

Barrett, Eaton S., *see The Heroine*

Barrie, J. M., 120

Bartholomew Fair, 33

Beach, J. W., 255, 286n

Beacon, 128

Beers, H. A., 322–23

Beggar Girl, The, see Mrs. Bennet

Bennet, Mrs., 151, 253n

Bennett, Arnold, 236, 237, 255, 337, 338, 342

Benson, A. C., 176n

Bentham, Jeremy, 125
Bernbaum, Ernest, 317n
Betrothed, The, 16, 36, 97
Black Dwarf, The, 18, 42, 85, 164
Blackwood's Magazine, 55 ff., 78, 173, 192n
Blanchard, Frederic, 189, 196
Blessington, Lady, 145
'Bois Guilbert,' *see Ivanhoe*
Bonaparte, Lucien, 139
Borrow, George, 212, 278
Boswell, Sir Alexander, 128
Boswell, James, 176n
Bourget, Paul, 233
Braddon, Mrs., 244, 253
'Bradwardine,' *see Waverley*
'Bradwardine, Rose,' *see Waverley*
Brandes, Georg, 258, 259 ff., 270, 323
Bray, Mrs., 123
Bride of Lammermoor, The, 14, 44, 51, 58, 65, 74, 98, 108, 111, 116, 145, 149, 151, 158, 163, 177, 193, 195n, 224, 231n, 240, 265, 292; 'Ailsie,' 44; 'Lucy Ashton,' 58, 286; 'Sir William Ashton,' 44; 'Caleb Balderstone,' 28, 44, 58, 74, 152; 'Ravenswood,' 95n, 101, 116, 209, 222, 305
British Critic, 212n
Brontë, Charlotte, 189, 200, 201; *Jane Eyre,* 196, 227, 244
Brontë, Emily, 340
Brown, Dr. John, 170
Brunton, Mrs., 69
Bryant, W. C., 88, 178n
Buccleuch, Duke of, 19n, 113
Buchan, John, 166, 217, 220, 238, 239, 241, 291, 292 ff., 302 ff., 308, 313
Bulwer Lytton, 46, 87, 159, 174, 190, 191, 192 ff., 233, 243, 306n, 319n
Bunyan, John, 179
Burke, Edmund, 278
'Burley, Balfour of,' *see Old Mortality*
Burney, Fanny, 7
Burns, Robert, 41, 62, 169, 179
Butterfield, Herbert, 317n
Byron, Lord, 9n, 11n, 62, 67, 70, 104, 110n, 113, 126, 133–34, 142, 144–45, 146, 158, 159, 169, 193, 209, 222, 319n, 331, 332

Cadell, publisher, 248n, 249
Campbell, Thomas, 63n, 143
Canning, Thomas, 279n
Carey, Philadelphia publisher, 11n
Carleton, William, 265
Carlyle, Thomas, 3, 13, 99, 103, 169n, 178, 186, 187, 197, 200, 201, 202, 214 ff., 220, 222, 226, 228, 273, 276n,

278, 281, 294 ff., 298, 299, 302, 303, 307, 314, 336
Carswell, Catherine, 238n
Carswell, Donald, 238n, 265–66, 267
Carter, H. H., 210n
Castle Dangerous, 36, 98, 102–03, 110, 164, 272
Catholics, Victorian, 210 ff.; later Catholic criticism, 277 ff.
Cazamian, L. F., 262n, 297
Cecil, Lord David, 231, 238, 293–94, 305–06, 335
'Cedric,' *see Ivanhoe*
Cervantes, 54, 59, 72, 102, 112, 157, 160, 177, 179, 199, 238, 266, 284, 299, 304, 308, 331, 334, 335
Chambers Cyclopedia, 202
Chambers, Robert, 161, 250
Chambers, W., 250
Characters, Scott's creation of, 307 ff.
Charles II, 92, 168n
Chasles, Émile, 263n
Chateaubriand, 162, 259
Chesterton, G. K., 118, 191, 281, 284–85, 314, 340
Chevalley, Abel, 262, 267
Christian Examiner, 198
Christian Observer, 83
Christian Spectator, 95n
Chronicles of the Canongate (first series), 53, 60, 97. *See also Highland Widow, Two Drovers,* and *Surgeon's Daughter*
'Chrystal Croftangry,' 'editor' of *Chronicles of the Canongate,* 53
'Claverhouse,' *see Old Mortality*
'Cleishbotham, Jedediah,' 'editor' of *Tales of My Landlord,* 17n, 19, 36
Clephane, Miss, 18n
'Cleveland,' *see The Pirate*
Clive, Mrs. Archer, 253
Clough, A. H., 196
Cobbett, William, 129, 215
Cockburn, Lord, 5–6, 8, 167
Colburn's, see *New Monthly*
Coleridge, Edward, 148
Coleridge, S. T., 87, 142, 146, 147 ff., 178, 249n, 252, 331
Collins, A. S., 249n
Collins, Wilkie, 253, 283
Colvin, Sidney, 268n, 269n, 270n
Commercialism, charges of, against Scott, 337
'Conachar,' *see The Fair Maid of Perth*
Conrad, Joseph, 286n, 337, 342
Constable, Archibald, 5, 21, 26, 38n, 45n, 111, 166n, 167
Cooper, J. F., 11n, 81, 87, 113, 135, 148,

166, 286; *Heidenmauer*, 166n; *The Pioneers*, 81; *The Spy*, 81; 'Leatherstocking,' 170; 'Long Tom,' 113
Corneille, 274
Cottagers of Glenburnie, 48
Count Robert of Paris, 36, 98, 102–03, 110, 115, 164, 272
Courthope, W. J., 297
Covenanters, Scott's attitude toward, 17 ff.
Crawford, F. Marion, 233
Critical Review, 75 ff., 78n
Croce, Benedetto, 7, 9, 258, 261 ff.
Croker, J. W., 13, 47 ff.
'Cromwell, Oliver,' see *Woodstock*
Cruse, Amy, 175, 211n, 253n
Cunningham, Allan, 161, 171, 242
Curtis, L. P., 114n
Cyril Thornton, 87

'Dalgetty,' see *A Legend of Montrose*
'Dalzell, General,' see *Old Mortality*
Dante, 172, 201, 299, 334
Daudet, Alphonse, 269
Dargan, E. P., 11n, 12n
Dawson, W. J., 312, 314
Day, Thomas, 198
'Deans, David,' see *The Heart of Midlothian*
'Deans, Effie,' see *The Heart of Midlothian*
'Deans, Jeanie,' see *The Heart of Midlothian*
Decker, C. R., 235n
Defoe, Daniel, 18, 22, 169, 179, 232, 264, 327, 328; *Robinson Crusoe*, 333
Demosthenes, 60
Dennie's Port Folio, see *Port Folio*
Dennis, John, 273
De Quincey, Thomas, 67n, 124–25, 178, 331
'Derby, Countess of,' see *Peveril of the Peak*
Devonshire, M. G., 250n, 263n
Dickens, Charles, 46, 109n, 167–200 *passim*, 227, 233, 234, 243–67 *passim*, 276, 292, 296, 298, 315, 332, 333, 337, 340, 343; *Christmas Carol*, 338; *David Copperfield*, 173n; *Dombey and Son*, 247n; *Nicholas Nickleby*, 109n
'Dinmont, Dandie,' see *Guy Mannering*
Disraeli, Benjamin, 136
Dostoevski, 239, 292, 304, 335; *Crime and Punishment*, 269
'Dousterswivel,' see *The Antiquary*
Dublin Review, 167
Dumas, Alexandre, 11, 178n, 268n, 269, 298, 306

Eckenrode, H. J., 318n
Eckermann, J. P., 9n
Edgeworth, Maria, 7, 10, 23, 30n, 48, 72, 76, 77, 81, 82, 87, 88, 90, 117 ff., 253n; *The Absentee*, 48, 118; *Castle Rackrent*, 48, 109n, 118; *Ennui*, 48; *Tales of Fashionable Life*, 48
Edinburgh Review, 7, 8, 40 ff., 93, 157, 161
Eighteenth century, its closeness to Scott, 50n
Elford, Sir William, 112
Eliot, George, 170, 176, 177, 181, 183, 185, 200, 211, 231, 239, 243, 256, 263n, 264, 271, 273, 296, 298, 332, 333, 335, 337
Elizabeth, Queen, 35; see also *Kenilworth*
Elton, Oliver, 238, 282, 290, 291, 293, 296, 299, 322
Emerson, Ralph Waldo, 176, 178 ff., 301
Ernle, Lord, 281
Erskine, John, 301–02
Erskine, William, 17n
Essayists, contemporary, on Scott, 124 ff.
Euripides, 301, 302
Everett, Edward, 87
Examiner, 95 ff.
'Ewart, Nanty,' see *Redgauntlet*

Fair Maid of Perth, The, 52, 98, 102n, 158, 164; 'Conachar,' 37
'Fairservice, Andrew,' see *Rob Roy*
Farinelli, 215
'Fenella,' see *Peveril of the Peak*
Ferrier, Susan, 119, 283
Fielding, Henry, 54, 64, 76, 82, 83n, 87, 109n, 112, 117, 145, 151, 159, 160, 171, 176, 179, 189, 195n, 196, 197, 217, 256, 264, 267, 273, 306, 307, 327, 332, 334, 335, 340; *Tom Jones*, 34, 48, 150, 151, 169, 188, 189, 332, 333, 340; 'Parson Adams,' 113, 151, 160, 194, 333
Firkins, Oscar W., 180n, 290
Fitzgerald, Edward, 176 ff.
Flaubert, Gustave, 13, 232, 263n, 264, 269, 284, 293, 328, 335; *Madame Bovary*, 232n, 311
Flaxman, John, 147
Fletcher, C. R. L., 247, 251n
Ford, Ford M., 235n, 267
Forman, 26
Forster, E. M., 256
Forster, John, 247n, 337
Fortunes of Nigel, The, 26, 35n, 46, 52, 58–59, 64, 65, 75, 96, 128, 163, 177, 209, 270, 323; Preface, 29 ff.; 'George Heriot,' 26; 'King James I,' 26, 46,

52, 59, 65, 207, 320, 322; 'Richard Moniplies,' 46
'Foster, Anthony,' see Kenilworth
Fox, Henry Edward, 110
France, Scott's popularity in, 11–12; French influence on the modern novel, 231 ff.
Fraser's Magazine, 160, 192n
Freeman, E. A., 206
'Front de Boeuf,' see Ivanhoe

Galsworthy, John, 255, 342
Galt, John, 54, 120 ff., 283
Garrick, David, 50n, 136
Gaskell, Mrs., 181
George IV, 138, 139, 223
Gifford, William, 47, 128
Gillies, R. P., 143
Gissing, George, 284, 340
Godwin, 101, 132n, 135, 137, 143
Goethe, 8–9, 21n, 62, 100–01, 146, 187, 274, 331
Goldsmith, Oliver, 179; The Vicar of Wakefield, 333
Gordon, R. H., 11n, 37n, 327n
Gosse, Edmund, 234, 262, 274, 275
Graham, P. A., 298
Graham, Walter, 47n
Granville, Lady, 110, 111
Gray, W. F., 167n
Green, T. H., 182
Greville, Charles, 110
Grierson, H. J. C., 23n, 166, 266n, 295, 304n, 314, 326, 327–28, 338
Grillparzer, 254
Grose, Francis, 70
Gundolf, Friedrich, 9n
'Gurth,' see Ivanhoe
Guy Livingstone, 191n, 225
Guy Mannering, 13, 24, 25, 48, 49, 72, 73, 76, 78, 84, 112, 116, 118n, 119, 143, 151, 163, 210, 224, 240, 269, 318n; 'Dandie Dinmont,' 42, 49, 85, 103, 118n, 318n; 'Dirk Hatteraick,' 42, 85; 'Meg Merrilies,' 27, 42, 59, 73, 76, 78, 85, 113, 118, 131, 142, 143, 293, 307; 'Pleydell,' 42, 49, 89n; 'Dominie Sampson,' 78, 85
Gwynn, Stephen, 295

Hamilton, Elizabeth, see Cottagers of Glenburnie
Hamilton, Thomas, see Cyril Thornton
Hannay, James, 169–70
Hannay, N. C., 176n, 177
Hannigan, D. F., 245, 263 ff., 270
Hardy, Thomas, 231, 276, 282, 292, 293, 296, 299, 301, 311; 'Eustacia Vye,' 38n

Harper, G. M., 276
Harrison, Frederic, 274
'Hatteraick, Dirk,' see Guy Mannering
Hawthorne, Nathaniel, 176, 272, 324
Hazlitt, William, 13, 47, 67, 95, 103, 125–41, 143, 153, 215, 228, 271, 302, 307, 312, 326
'Headrigg, Cuddie,' see Old Mortality
'Headrigg, Mause,' see Old Mortality
Heart of Midlothian, The, 12n, 25, 35n, 44, 51, 56–57, 71, 72, 74, 116, 128, 131, 146, 163, 174, 201, 224, 240, 260, 262, 263n, 290, 293, 310; Address to the Reader, 19; 'Duke of Argyle,' 44, 57; 'David Deans,' 25, 44, 68, 222; 'Effie Deans,' 118, 286, 310; 'Jeanie Deans,' 25, 26, 44, 57, 65, 68, 96, 106, 159, 174, 187, 199, 201, 219, 260, 264, 286, 304, 305, 307, 310, 323, 344; 'George Staunton,' 44; 'Madge Wildfire,' 57, 222
Henderson, T. F., 321
Henley, W. E., 268
Henry, Robert, 70
Herford, C. H., 276n, 327n
Heroine, The, 109n
Hewlett, Maurice, 283
Highland Widow, The, 38n, 53, 60, 272
Historical novel, the Victorian belief in its dignity, 188 ff.
History, Scott's concern with, 20 ff.; his treatment of, 204 ff., 316 ff.
Hobhouse, J. C., 110
Hogg, James, 303
Homer, 11n, 33, 60, 61, 79, 100, 102, 177, 179, 211, 212, 213n, 238, 242, 259, 268, 283, 304, 309, 335
Hook, Theodore, 136
Hope, Thomas, see Anastasius
Howells, W. D., 263n, 285–86
Hudibras, 121, 194
Hudson, W. H., 298
Hughes, H. S., see Lovett, R. M.
Hughes, Mrs., 36n, 147n
Hugo, Victor, 11, 224n, 264, 268, 328
Hume, David, 78, 168n, 194
Hunt, Leigh, 67, 124
Hutton, R. H., 4, 186, 207, 276n

Ibsen, 235n
Idman, Niilo, 122
Imitators, Scott's attitude toward his, 22
Inchbald, Mrs., 131, 132
Irving, Washington, 326
'Isaac of York,' see Ivanhoe
Ivanhoe, 12, 22n, 39n, 43, 44, 51, 53, 58, 69, 70, 74, 78, 80, 110, 114, 121, 122, 130, 138, 149, 151, 163, 172, 174, 193,

209, 223, 243, 245, 249, 262, 320, 322;
Final Preface, 37; 'Athelstane,' 114;
'Bois Guilbert,' 276n; 'Cedric,' 14n;
'Front de Boeuf,' 58, 114; 'Gurth,'
103; 'Isaac of York,' 69; 'Ivanhoe,'
286; 'Rebecca,' 58, 69, 74, 106, 163n,
202, 264, 286, 304n, 307; 'Richard I,'
78, 218; 'Rowena,' 74, 114, 286

Jack, A. A., 289, 291, 309–10
James, G. P. R., 123, 164, 188, 248, 337
James, Henry, 172, 173, 207, 232, 243,
245, 255, 269, 272, 285
'Jarvie, Nicol,' see Rob Roy
Jeaffreson, J. C., 168
Jeffrey, Lord, 6, 7, 8n, 13, 40 ff., 47, 49,
51, 93, 103, 109, 126, 153, 188, 236,
249, 293, 331
Johnson, Dr. Samuel, 50n, 278, 297
Journals, criticism in contemporary,
107 ff.
Joyce, James, 238

Keats, 142–43, 146
Keble, John, 211
Kenilworth, 10, 21, 26, 36n, 45, 51, 58,
59, 69, 74, 78, 96, 110, 146, 163, 177,
270, 318; 'Alasco,' 46; 'Queen Eliza-
beth,' 20n, 26, 28, 46, 58, 69, 96, 187;
'Anthony Foster,' 46, 206n; 'Michael
Lambourne,' 46, 69; 'Leicester,' 46,
59, 206n; 'Sir Walter Raleigh,' 96;
'Amy Robsart,' 46, 96, 110, 205–06;
'Tressilian,' 58; 'Varney,' 46
Kent, W. H., 277
Ker, W. P., 238, 300–01, 302, 313, 319
Kingsley, Charles, 181, 200, 217, 243,
296; 'Amyas Leigh,' 225
Klopstock, 148
Knight, Charles, 253n
Knox, John, 178
Kotzebue, August, 215

Lady of the Lake, The, 249
Laing, David, 32n
Lamb, Charles, 109, 124, 164n
'Lambourne, Michael,' see Kenilworth
La Motte-Fouqué, 25
Landor, W. S., 145–46, 178
Landrum, Grace W., 319n
Lang, Andrew, 47n, 237, 238n, 246, 324
Lanier, Sidney, 183
Lansdowne, Lord, 111
Lawrence, D. H., 238
Lawrence, G. A., see Guy Livingstone
Lay of the Last Minstrel, 147n
Leavis, Q. D., 111n, 238n, 251n, 255,
280n
Le Fanu, Sheridan, 265

Legend of Montrose, A, 14, 44, 58, 74,
145, 164; 'Dalgetty,' 30, 44, 93, 164;
'Annot Lyle,' 116; 'Montrose,' 164,
322
'Leicester, Earl of,' see Kenilworth
Le Sage, 54, 72, 160, 331, 335; Gil
Blas, 34, 48
Letters and journals, criticism in con-
temporary, 107 ff.
Lever, Charles, 265
Lewes, G. H., 189
Loch Katrine, 174
Lockhart, J. G., 4, 5 ff., 23n, 27n, 32n,
33n, 36, 39n, 47, 53, 62, 162 ff., 171,
172, 174, 197, 212, 234, 242, 244, 247,
248, 249, 265, 270, 278n, 336, 337,
339; Reginald Dalton, 91
London Magazine, 67 ff.
London Review, 52
Lope de Vega, 215
'Louis XI,' see Quentin Durward
Lovett, R. M., and H. S. Hughes, 239n,
316n
Lowell, Amy, 142
Lowell, J. R., 182n
Lubbock, Percy, 239
Lumley, Elizabeth, 114n
'Lyle, Annot,' see A Legend of Montrose

Macaulay, Lord, 83n, 167, 168n, 194,
206, 234
McCrie, Thomas, 17
Machen, A. W., 206n
'Macgregor, Helen,' see Rob Roy
'MacIvor, Fergus,' see Waverley
'MacIvor, Flora,' see Waverley
Mackenzie, A. M., 238
Mackenzie, Henry, 7, 77n, 122
McKillop, Alan, 16n, 234n, 290n
'Maclure, Bessie,' see Old Mortality
'Madge Wildfire,' see The Heart of
Midlothian
Maginn, William, 161, 167
"Magnum Opus," Scott's collected edi-
tion of the novels, 15, 71, 248
Maigron, Louis, 11, 262n, 322n
Mallock, W. H., 236, 246
Malthus, 50n
Manzoni, 100, 162
Mark Twain, 283, 300, 318
Marmion, 108, 117, 121, 145, 159, 249
Marryat, Captain, 267
Martineau, Harriet, 104 ff., 176, 216,
220, 291n, 294, 297, 336
Mary, Queen of Scots, 20n, 35, 168n. See
also The Abbot
Masson, David, 221
Matthews, Brander, 317n, 318n

Maturin, Robert, 122–23, 249n
Maupassant, 232, 233
Maurice, F. D., 99
Maynadier, G. H., 320
Meredith, George, 231, 263n, 264n, 269, 276n, 282, 292, 299, 300n, 301, 337; *Richard Feverel*, 233n, 296
'Merrilies, Meg.' *see Guy Mannering*
'Mignon' (Goethe's), 9n
Mill, J. S., 94n
Millar, A. H., 273
Miller, Hugh, 203
Mills, Charles, 28
Milsand, J. A., 297
Milton, 68, 114, 121, 148, 158, 172
Minerva Press, 91, 92, 152, 253
Mitford, Miss, 112
Molière, 314
Monastery, The, 26, 31, 34–35, 38n, 39n, 45, 58, 69, 78, 79, 110, 114, 115, 150, 152, 164, 167; 'Sir Piercie Shafton,' 34, 45, 79; 'White Lady of Avenel,' 34, 45, 58 (also in *The Abbot*)
Montagu, Lady M. W., 113
Monthly Review, 72 ff., 78n, 161
Moore, C. L., 281
Moore, George, 283
Moore, Thomas, 134, 159
More, Paul Elmer, 288, 324, 328, 334
Morgan, Lady, 76, 77
Morris, William, 328
Morritt, J. B. S., 8n, 22n, 23, 26, 31, 36n
'Morton,' *see Old Mortality*
'Mowbray, Clara,' *see St. Ronan's Well*
Moysey, Abel, *see Forman*
'Mucklebackit' family, *see The Antiquary*
Muir, Edwin, 306n
Murray, John, 18n, 109
Murray, Sir John (d. 1928), 250

Napoleon, 194
Needler, G. H., 9n, 21n
Nesbitt, G. L., 95n
Newman, Cardinal, 204, 211, 212n, 277, 278
New Monthly ("Colburn's"), 63 ff., 95n, 159
Nicoll, W. R., 238n
Nietzsche, 254
Noble, J. A., 199
'Norna,' *see The Pirate*
'North, Christopher,' *see Wilson, John*
North American Review, 84 ff., 160, 171 ff., 242 ff.
North British Review, 190
Northcote, James, 138, 139
Novel, its value as a form, 89 ff.;

changes after *1880*, 231 ff.; French influence on, 231 ff.; decline of the classic English novelists, 234 ff.; modern revolution in, 339–41
Novelists, contemporary, on Scott, 116 ff.
Novel-reading, 81 ff.

'Ochiltree, Edie,' *see The Antiquary*
Old Mortality, 18 ff., 25, 43, 53, 76, 85, 95n, 111, 119, 128, 151, 152, 163, 165, 224, 240, 262, 292, 293; 'Burley,' 194; 'Claverhouse,' 19, 93, 168n, 194, 322, 326; 'General Dalzell,' 18; 'Cuddie Headrigg,' 116; 'Mause Headrigg,' 68, 116; 'Bessie Maclure,' 304; 'Morton,' 114
"Old Plays," quotations from, 45n
Oliphant, Mrs., 173n, 200, 203
Omond, T. S., 297
'Osbaldistone, Rashleigh,' *see Rob Roy*

Palgrave, Sir Francis, 28
Palgrave, F. T., 207
Parr, Dr. Samuel, 125
Peabody, W. B. O., 87, 89, 207
Peacock, T. L., 119
'Peebles, Peter,' *see Redgauntlet*
Pepys, 32n
Peveril of the Peak, 10, 31, 35n, 52, 65, 75, 111, 115, 118, 119, 128 ff., 164, 209; Preface, 31–32; 'Countess of Derby,' 115; 'Fenella,' 9n, 75, 118, 164
Philosophy, modern critics on Scott's, 294 ff., 343
Pichler, Mme. Caroline, 100
Pindar, 211, 212
Pirate, The, 10, 11n, 26, 46, 52, 58–59, 64, 75, 78, 83, 96, 111, 127–28, 163, 176; 'Cleveland,' 46, 52; 'Norna,' 27, 59
'Pleydell,' *see Guy Mannering*
Plutarch, 179
Poets, contemporary, on Scott, 142 ff.
Politics, Scott's attitude, 313–15
Poole's Index, 47n
Pope, Alexander, 130
Porter, Jane, 122, 253n
Port Folio (Dennie's), 11n, 77 ff.
Prescott, W. H., 88, 89n, 90, 160
'Pretender,' *see Redgauntlet*
Priestley, J. B., 256, 284n, 311

Quarterly Review, 47 ff., 93, 244
Queenhoo Hall, 37
Quentin Durward, 12, 21, 22n, 26, 35n, 38n, 52, 53, 55, 65, 102, 209, 270, 274, 318n; 'Louis XI,' 36n, 65, 66, 260, 320, 321n, 323

Quotations from "Old Plays," 45n

Racine, 11, 130, 132, 274
Radcliffe, Mrs., 38n, 81, 82, 98, 111, 115, 123, 143, 253n, 327
Radical criticism of the novels, 9 ff.
Rae, W. F., 272
Rait, R. S., 16n, 326
Raleigh, Sir Walter, the critic, 239
'Raleigh, Sir Walter,' see Kenilworth
'Ravenswood,' see The Bride of Lammermoor
Reade, Charles, 208, 217, 243, 253, 291, 296, 300n, 337, 338
Reading public, the range of Scott's contemporary readers, 8 ff.; in the United States, 10–11; Scott's attitude toward his readers, 32–34; novel-reading, 81 ff.; extent of Scott's modern popularity with, 241 ff.; the sale of Scott's novels, 247 ff.; degeneration of, 252 ff.; and the modern novel, 254
'Rebecca,' see Ivanhoe
Redgauntlet, 38n, 53, 55, 65, 70, 78, 80, 114, 134, 165, 209, 241; Wandering Willie's Tale, 92, 134, 241, 303; 'Nanty Ewart,' 118, 134; 'Peter Peebles,' 80, 92, 134, 241; 'Pretender,' 97; 'Redgauntlet,' 37n, 114, 305
Rendall, David A., 11n
Rendall, Vernon, 282
Reynaud, Louis, 9n, 307, 321n
Riccardo, David, 50n
'Richard I,' see Ivanhoe and The Talisman
Richard II, 15
Richardson, Dorothy, 238
Richardson, Samuel, 76, 83, 87, 90, 151, 171, 176, 179, 189, 196, 267, 332; Clarissa Harlowe, 109n, 150, 231n, 332; 'Clarissa,' 69; 'Lovelace,' 151; Sir Charles Grandison, 150
Roberts, R. Ellis, 147n
Robertson, James Burton (?), 28
Robin Hood, 138
Robinson, Crabb, 111, 146, 147
Rob Roy, 37n, 43, 72, 86, 98, 118, 268n, 269, 310; 'Andrew Fairservice,' 43, 240; 'Nicol Jarvie,' 30, 43, 68, 72, 86, 93, 164, 222, 240, 314; 'Helen Macgregor,' 310; 'Rashleigh Osbaldistone,' 310; 'Rob Roy,' 72, 86, 95n, 97, 138; 'Diana Vernon,' 43, 86, 106, 191n, 240, 260, 307, 323
'Robsart, Amy,' see Kenilworth
Rogers, Samuel, 146–47
Romanes, E. M., 275
Rousseau, 8, 82, 298

'Rowena,' see Ivanhoe
Ruskin, John, 176, 182, 204, 208, 278

Sainte-Beuve, 12
St. Ronan's Well, 27, 35–36, 37, 52, 55, 75, 78n, 115, 122, 130, 186, 187, 209; 'Clara Mowbray,' 37n, 38n, 240
Saintsbury, George, 239, 297, 323, 334
Salvator Rosa, 78
'Sampson, Dominie,' see Guy Mannering
Sand, George, 196
Santayana, George, 340
Schiller, 9n, 54, 254, 274; Wallenstein, 54, 55
Schücking, Levin, 254, 255
Scotsman, 95n
Scott, Lady, 6, 110n, 165
Scott, Daniel, 38
Scott, John, 67n
Scott, Thomas, 19
Scott, Sir Walter, his review of Old Mortality, 17 ff., 22n, 24, 50, 160; his review of Hoffmann's novels, 24; his life of Fielding, 24; his "Metrical Romances," 24; his essay on Kemble, 24n; his Lives of the Novelists, 53; his life of Napoleon, 94n, 97, 100, 145, 146; contemporary fame, 1 ff.; effect of his personality, 3 ff.; range of his contemporary readers, 8 ff.; popularity in the United States, 10–11; popularity in France, 11–12; adverse contemporary criticism, 12 ff.; his own criticism of his novels, 15 ff.; attitude toward his own work, 15 ff.; attitude toward the Covenanters, 17 ff.; concern with history, 20 ff.; attitude toward imitators, 22; feeling about technical considerations, 23n; critical detachment, 28–29; defense of himself, 29 ff.; attitude toward the public, 32–34; failures, 34 ff.; desire for novelty in the novels, 37 ff.; influence of the Ballantynes and Constable on him, 38n; quotations at heads of chapters, 45n; closeness to the eighteenth century, 50n; continued popularity among the Victorians, 157 ff.; feeling toward him at the time of his death, 157 ff.; hostile Victorian criticism, 168–69; Victorian reverence for him, 169 ff., 225 ff.; effect of his personality during the Victorian period, 174 ff.; history in his novels, 204 ff., 316 ff.; the modern militant defense of him, 236 ff.; extent of his popularity since 1880, 241

ff.; sale of his novels, 247 ff.; modern depreciation, 258 ff.; continuation of Victorian reverence, 271 ff.; Catholic criticism of his novels, 277 ff.; modern criticism of his style, 288 ff., 344; modern criticism of his philosophy, 294 ff., 343; creation of character, 307 ff.; political attitude, 313–15; height of his fame, 331 ff.; comparison with Shakespeare and others, 334–35; his "commercialism," 337; his Toryism, 338–39; the preference for his Scotch novels, 342–43

Seccombe, Thomas, 47n, 238, 288, 291, 299–300, 334

Sedgwick, C. M., 88

Sedgwick, H. D., 275, 298–99, 334

Senior, Nassau, 38, 47, 50 ff., 55, 162, 164, 172, 243

Seward, Miss, 32

Shadwell, Thomas, 320

'Shafton, Sir Piercie,' see The Monastery

Shakespeare, 12, 17n, 41, 43, 44, 60, 61, 62, 68, 74, 79, 88–103 passim, 130 ff., 140, 151, 158, 159, 161, 170–205 passim, 212, 216, 218, 220, 222, 238, 240, 272, 273, 274, 276, 284, 293, 299, 300, 303, 309, 334–35; in Kenilworth, 69; Hamlet, 121; Macbeth, 44, 45, 131; 'Falstaff,' 19n, 44; 'Pistol,' 44

Sharpe, C. K., 33n, 109n

Shaw, G. B., 235n

Shelley, 67n, 142, 159, 169

Sheppard, A. T., 236, 317n

Shorthouse, J. H., 300

Siddons, Mrs., 136, 140

Sidney, Sir Philip, 69, 96

Sismondi, J. C. L., 100

Sir Walter Scott Quarterly, 237n

Sitwell, Osbert, 340

Smiles, Samuel, 261

Smith, Horace, 21, 22, 54, 55, 123, 124, 164

Smith, M. O., 239

Smith, Sydney, 111

Smollett, Tobias, 76, 83n, 87, 109n, 143, 160, 171, 267, 273, 306n, 327; Humphrey Clinker, 109n, 143; Peregrine Pickle, 48; Roderick Random, 34, 82, 150; 'Lieutenant Bowling,' 151; 'Strap,' 151

Sophocles, 65, 301, 302

Southern Literary Messenger, 174n

Southey, Robert, 145

Spalding, William, 197

Sparks, Jared, 88

Spenser, 121, 345; in Kenilworth, 69

Stalker, Archibald, 265, 275

'Staunton, George,' see The Heart of Midlothian

'Stuart, Mary,' see The Abbot and Mary, Queen of Scots

Stendhal, 11

Stephen, Leslie, 4, 132, 182, 190, 192n, 208, 217, 222 ff., 244, 245, 251n, 268, 276n, 278, 294

Sterne, Laurence, 114, 148, 151, 169, 179, 189

Steuart, J. A., 268n

Stevenson, R. L., 224n, 268 ff., 283, 286n, 288, 304

Stoddard, F. H., 280

Stowe, Harriet Beecher, 196; Uncle Tom's Cabin, 50n

Strutt, Joseph, 70

Stuart, Lady Louisa, 17n, 18n, 19n, 20n, 22n, 36n, 39n, 111n, 113 ff., 177, 327

Style, modern critics on Scott's, 288 ff., 344

Sue, Eugene, 178n

Surgeon's Daughter, The, 53

Swift, Jonathan, 273

Swinburne, Algernon, 235n, 271–72

Swinnerton, Frank, 338n

Synge, J. M., 293

Taine, 258–59, 264, 265, 276n

Tales of a Grandfather, 95, 99

Tales of the Crusaders, 37, 45n, 53, 66, 70, 73, 75, 96n, 209. See also The Betrothed and The Talisman

Talfourd, T. N., 161

Talisman, The, 16, 36, 53, 88, 97, 163; 'Richard I,' 28, 97

Tasso, 274

Teniers, 259

Tennyson, Lord, 177, 208, 210, 234

Terry, Daniel, 26

Thackeray, W. M., 27n, 170–71, 173, 174, 176, 185, 200, 211, 227, 232, 238, 239, 243, 256, 267, 269, 284, 291, 292, 296, 298, 306n, 332, 334, 337, 338; Denis Duval, 173n; Henry Esmond, 196, 264, 276, 309, 333; The Newcomes, 27n, 176n; Novels by Eminent Hands, 170; Pendennis, 176n, 188; Rebecca and Rowena, 170; Vanity Fair, 50n, 231n

Thompson, Denys, 237n

Tolstoi, 239, 263n, 285, 286, 292, 304, 335; War and Peace, 239

Toryism, charges of, made against Scott, 338–39

Train, Joseph, 18n

Tremaine, 71

Trent, W. P., 282, 288, 292
'Tressilian,' see Kenilworth
Trollope, Anthony, 170, 192, 211, 337, 338, 340
Trossachs, 174, 226
Trueba, Telesforo de, 100
Tuckerman, Bayard, 202
Turgeniev, 239, 285, 286
Turnbull, A., 147, 150
Turner, J. M. W., 209
Two Drovers, 56, 60, 71, 97, 272; Preface, 26

United States, Scott's popularity in, 10–11

'Varney,' see Kenilworth
'Vernon, Diana,' see Rob Roy
Verrall, A. W., 289, 291, 292
Victorians, Scott's continued popularity among, 157 ff.; hostile criticism of Scott, 168–69; reverence for Scott, 169 ff., 225 ff.; attitude toward Scott's personality, 174 ff.; emphasis on "message," 181 ff.; increase in critical detachment, 183 ff.; belief in the dignity of the historical novel, 188 ff.; moral point of view, 196 ff.; Victorian medievalists, 208 ff.; Victorian Catholics, 210 ff.
Vizetelly, E. A., 235n
Voltaire, 8, 35, 69, 82

Wallace, Edgar, 237n, 251n
Wallace, M. W., 304n
Walladmor, 16, 67n, 92, 124
Walpole, Horace, 327
Walpole, Hugh, 283, 304n, 310, 316
Walton, H. E., 277
Wandering Willie's Tale, see Redgauntlet
Ward, R. P., see Tremaine

Ward, Wilfrid, 246, 280–81
Watts, Alaric, 148
Watts, H. H., 195n
Waverley, 13, 24, 37, 40, 46, 50n, 53, 55, 58, 71, 72, 73, 76, 111, 112, 116, 117, 119, 143, 145, 158, 159, 171, 174, 177, 186, 196, 224, 270, 290n, 320, 328; Preface, 25; Preface of 1829, 23; 'Bradwardine,' 112, 144; 'Fergus,' 77n, 95n, 144, 305, 344; 'Flora,' 77n, 96, 106, 112, 328; 'Rose,' 30n; 'Waverley,' 13, 49, 111, 328
Wedgwood, Julia, 202
Weekley, Ernest, 289
Wellington, Duke of, 58, 178, 194, 225
Wells, H. G., 337
West, Mrs., 72, 117
Westminster Review, 91 ff., 98, 217
Whipple, E. P., 171n
'White Lady of Avenel,' see The Monastery
Wilson, John ("Christopher North"), 59, 60 ff., 67
Wood, Mrs. Henry, 173, 253
Woodberry, G. E., 246, 288, 308–09, 313, 324, 334
Woodstock, 10, 11n, 52, 71, 92, 93, 123, 124, 164, 165, 209, 248, 323; 'Charles II,' 92; 'Oliver Cromwell,' 92
Woolf, Leonard, 129n
Woolf, Virginia, 236, 239, 247, 256, 282, 288, 311–12, 334
Woollcott, Alexander, 257
Wordsworth, 25, 62, 99, 111n, 134, 143–44, 146, 150n, 178, 263n

Yellow Book, 235n
Young, C. A., 276n

Zeitlin, Jacob, 67n
Zola, Émile, 232, 235n, 274, 296